CLARIFYING
Communication Theories

CLARIFYING
Communication Theories

A Hands-On Approach

Gerald Stone
Michael Singletary
Virginia P. Richmond

Iowa State University Press / Ames

Gerald Stone received his PhD in mass communication from Syracuse University and is presently professor and director of graduate studies in the College of Mass Communication and Media Arts at Southern Illinois University at Carbondale. Formerly dean of the College of Communications and Fine Arts, Dr. Stone also chaired the journalism program at the University of Memphis. His professional experience is in reporting, editing and public relations.

Michael Singletary received his PhD in journalism from Southern Illinois University at Carbondale and is presently professor and associate dean of the Graduate School at the University of Tennessee at Knoxville. Dr. Singletary also has experience as both a newspaper reporter and a television reporter.

Virginia P. Richmond received her PhD in speech communication from the University of Nebraska. Dr. Richmond is presently a professor in the Department of Communication Studies and coordinator of Communication Extended Learning Programs at West Virginia University at Morgantown.

© 1999 Iowa State University Press
All rights reserved

Iowa State University Press
2121 South State Avenue, Ames, Iowa 50014

Orders: 1-800-862-6657
Office: 1-515-292-0140
Fax: 1-515-292-3348
Web site: www.isupress.edu

This text was produced directly from camera-ready copy provided by the authors.

Authorization to photocopy items for internal or personal use, or the internal or personal use of specific clients, is granted by Iowa State University Press, provided that the base fee of $.10 per copy is paid directly to the Copyright Clearance Center, 222 Rosewood Drive, Danvers, MA 01923. For those organizations that have been granted a photocopy license by CCC, a separate system of payments has been arranged. The fee code for users of the Transactional Reporting Service is 0-8138-0292-X/99 $.10.

Printed on acid-free paper in the United States of America

First edition, 1999

Library of Congress Cataloging-in-Publication Data

Stone, Gerald (Gerald C.)
        Clarifying communication theories: a hands-on approach/Gerald Stone,
    Michael Singletary, Virginia P. Richmond
        p. cm.
        Includes index.
        ISBN 0-8138-0292-X
        1. Communication—Philosophy. I. Singletary, Michael W.
          II. Richmond, Virginia P.
P90.S8176   1999
302.2'01—dc21   98-54330

The last digit is the print number: 9   8   7   6   5   4   3   2   1

Contents

PART FOUR — Research Methods

Preface

Dozens of excellent scholarly texts exist on human communication and mass communication theory. These books are used in courses ranging from undergraduate through doctoral study in the several communication disciplines. Yet, while the theories are difficult to decipher and concepts derived from them defy easy interpretation, no textbook is designed specifically to lead students through the maze. Even when taught by the most knowledgeable and congenial professors, communication theory is often a bewildering enigma from the first week of class through the final exam.

Clarifying Communication Theories takes a novel approach. It is a textbook, in that it contains the essential elements of human and mass communication theories. But it is also a "workbook," chockfull of examples and exercises designed to make communication theories user-friendly. Each of the chapters is a relatively short and easy-to-read explanation of a communication theory. Each is *intended* to be the most straightforward explanation ever written on the topic.

The book presents an overview or distillation of each theory, including terms with clear definitions, the time frame during which the theory developed, its chief proponents and critics, its current status, and how the theory can be applied to the study or practice of communication. Chapters begin with a "founding" or early journal article reference and a more recent article reference that can be assigned to increase student understanding of the theory.

This text's real strength is its interactive dimension. Instructors will offer supplemental lecture material from their own continuing study of the field, and will discuss assigned readings from texts and additional outside articles. But *Clarifying Communication Theories* offers dozens of in-class activities and out-of-class projects: assignments that involve students in the topics, drive home the principles, demystify the concepts and make them come alive. Some are games. Some are self-assessing questionnaires. Some are think-pieces. All are fashioned to approximate the research approaches that helped formulate the theories.

Students will discover a bounty of interesting assignments that challenge yet clarify the most perplexing theoretical concepts. Some teachers will rely on this book as their single required text for the course. Others will use the book in conjunction with another theory text or with a series of outside readings. But no other published source of communication theory will offer the compendium of examples, exercises, activities and class projects available in this text. And no other book will involve students in the interplay that serves as a practical, engaging guide through the maze of communication theories.

The authors are particularly pleased to offer a text that combines some basic principles of human communication and mass communication. Adopters in both fields may question the rationale of this combination — whether communication studies and mass communication share significant precepts. But students are likely to enjoy this merger and gain from the alliance. Those interested in mediated communication need to know the fundamental principles of interpersonal communication, and communication studies students are likely to find themselves in careers that involve the mass media. We encourage teachers in both disciplines to give this amalgamation a try.

Great care was taken to ensure the accuracy of citations used in this text through a highly recommended research technique: going back to the original source. The authors are grateful to Jae-Young Kim, a doctoral student at Southern Illinois University's School of Journalism, whose diligent efforts may have reclaimed the original titles, authors and full citations of countless "lost" articles and books that now appear in this work.

Additionally, the authors wish to thank guest authors for their chapter contributions: Charles E. Caudill, Donna Besser, Stephen A. Banning, Lyombe Eko, Carolyn A. Lin and Sandra Bowman Damico. And finally, our thanks to the editors at Iowa State University Press: Laura M. Moran, former acquisitions editor, and Judi Brown, acquisitions project manager, who shepherded the work through rugged terrain to completion.

Part One
Theoretical Foundations

Communication Theory: An Introduction

Textbooks generally are books full of theories, so it is not an exaggeration to claim that most textbooks are "theory books." This textbook presents one or more theories in each chapter. But before you cringe in anticipation of extreme boredom, know that the authors believe theories don't have to be boring, difficult to understand or something you cannot apply in your real world. Actually, you work with theories every day, although you may not recognize you are doing so. **Theories** are simply *explanations of how or why things happen the way they do.*

Just about everyone wants to know how and why things happen. Normal curiosity causes us to try to understand our environment and each other. We want to know why things are like they are, and why people behave the way they do. One of the things people wanted to know even 5,000 years ago was how human communication works and how they could make their own communication more effective.

The oldest essay ever discovered, written in Egypt about 3000 B.C., consists of advice on how to speak effectively.[1] It was inscribed on parchment and addressed to Kagemni, the eldest son of the pharaoh Huni. The oldest book ever discovered was written by Ptah-Hotep in Egypt in about 2675 B.C. This book, entitled *Precepts*, was written for the guidance of the pharaoh's son. It was a treatise on effective communication: what we would now call a "communication theory" book.

People are interested in communication theories for the same reasons they are interested in other theories, whether they be Einstein's theory of relativity or a friend's theory of what attracts the opposite sex. People want to be able to explain, predict and control what goes on in their environment. Theories generally are more accurate when they are based on solid empirical research. **Empiricism** implies knowledge based on experience. It is knowledge based on observation or experiment. Empiricism in its early days was used only to generate communication theories. Today, **quantitative empirical research**, with improved scientific methods, is used both to *generate and to test communication theories.*

---

1. James C. McCroskey (1968). *An introduction to rhetorical communication: The theory and practice of public speaking.* Englewood Cliffs, NJ: Prentice-Hall.

Explanation is the lowest level of theory, but that does not mean it is unimportant. Sometimes the explanation is not fully correct (a weak theory) but is the best available at the time. For example, before the advent of modern weather forecasting, people often explained thunder storms simply as something that is caused by hot weather. While there is much more to thunderstorms, this primitive explanation put people on alert for such storms in hot weather, when most of them actually do occur. While their ability to predict thunder storms was imperfect, they were less likely to be surprised by the storms that did occur. Today, modern scientific methods allow weather forecasters to explain how storms are formed and to **predict** with a fairly high degree of accuracy (the next higher level of theory) when and where those storms will occur. Even today, however, no theories exist that can do much to help **control** (the highest level of theory) the weather.

Communication theories are much like weather theories. Quite good theories have been developed about how and why human communication functions. Modest success has been made in theories that predict how certain communication acts will occur under certain circumstances. Development of theories that will permit control of communication behavior (other than our own), has progressed more slowly.

Early communication theory

Although people were developing very primitive communication theories as long as 5,000 years ago, it was not until about 2,500 years ago that theoretical development gained momentum. The work began in ancient Greece and Rome. In the fifth century B.C., works by Corax and Tisias on rhetorical (persuasive) communication appeared. As democratic regimes formed in Greece, effective public speaking and argumentation skills were needed, and rhetorical works were written to meet those needs. Perhaps leaders in government, commerce, religion — in every field of human endeavor — have always known that effective communication is power.

About a century later, the greatest communication scholar of antiquity, Aristotle, composed the work now known as *The Rhetoric of Aristotle*. Some today still consider this the greatest work on rhetoric ever written. It certainly was the most influential during the next 2,300 years. From that time forward, through the era of the founding of this country and well into the 20th century, the rhetorical approach to communication was the primary source of communication theories for people living in democratic societies. While these theories were empirically rooted, because they were built on observations, the observations were not what would today be called solid science. Hence, communication scholars argued with great enthusiasm in favor of or against theories that were posited with no real basis for determining the correctness of anyone's theoretical positions. Much later, **social scientific methods** began to be employed to determine the **validity** of communication theories, or whether they should be believed.

Recent developments

In discussing the development of theories, *recent* becomes a very relative word. In this instance, it means about the last hundred years. The study of mass communication is among the more recent communication disciplines. It emerged quietly, hardly noticed, as an outgrowth of the evolution of communication technologies, industrial development and public education in the early years of the 20th century, offering explanations for the **effects** of communication.

Mass communication theory earned its place as an increasingly educated electorate longed for knowledge about the power of communication. The blending of rhetorical theory with mass communication theory was a natural event, because both were concerned with sources (individuals or groups) attempting to influence large numbers of receivers. The two areas differed in only one important aspect: whether the communication efforts involved live interaction or some form of print or electronic mediation.

Communication technology (such as the rotary press, the telegraph and then the radio) made possible the mass distribution of information; industrial development brought people into closer contact with one another, built cities and encouraged knowledge as a way of reaching and moving markets; and public education created an increasingly literate and circumspect population. This natural evolution of conditions set the stage for a slow but steady expansion of communication studies.

Mass communication theory got a major boost from the propaganda practices of the protagonists in the First World War. Like Aristotle 2,000 years earlier, governments in 1914-1918 knew there was strength in public opinion, and the propagandists of the time worked diligently at building strength for their political positions. After the war, researchers began to focus attention on the nature of propaganda. At roughly the same time, there was a growing popular concern about the effects of movies and comic books on young people, the precursors of the concerns expressed today about the effects of television. As a result, numerous research studies were undertaken to shed light on the issue of media effects. These studies were empirical and pragmatic in style, and they helped set the direction of future research in the field: It was to be objective and decision-oriented.

The Second World War, which the United States joined in 1941, provided the next great impetus for growth in mass communication theory. Again the approach was **pragmatic**, or designed to be put to use in a real-life situation. The Army wanted to indoctrinate troops with ideas designed to optimize the Allied position (e.g., to promote the will to fight), so it produced what it hoped were persuasive films and training sessions. Studies of the effectiveness of those efforts, which included both mediated and interpersonal communication, were the beginning of the next generation of research in the field.

4   THEORIES

Carl Hovland, a social psychologist and an officer in the Army, along with several colleagues, led the scientific investigations that set the tone for mass communication research, and some of the human communication research, for the next 50 years.[2] He studied the effect of persuasion on U.S. troops in a manner that was meticulous, methodical, systematic and impressive in every respect. His intent was to determine the effects of such variables as source credibility on the persuasiveness of communicative messages. He used careful experimental controls to find effects for variables of interest (attitude toward the enemy) while controlling other elements (education, age, etc.) that might explain the effects observed.

After the war, as former soldiers used G.I. Bill benefits to attend college, interest in communication studies grew steadily. By the 1960s many new departments of "Communication" were formed. In the 1970s and 1980s many established departments changed their focus and name from "Speech" to "Speech Communication" or "Communication Studies." And so, while the field commonly known as "Communication Studies" is only two to three generations old, most of its growth and development has been within the past 40 years.

The development and expansion of communication theory and research has occurred coincidently with a cultural revolution in the U.S. Many of the theories developed in rhetorical studies and during the early era of mass communication remain of value today. But changes in the society have made communication, other than that which fits the traditional "one-to-many" mold of rhetoric and mass media communication, a major concern to a new group of communication scholars. These scholars represent a blend of orientations from the traditional field of *speech* and the fields of *social* and *personality psychology*. This group primarily employs social science research methodologies to theory building and focuses on communication in contexts other than one-to-many. This side of the field of Communication often is called "Human Communication" to distinguish it from "Mass Communication."

To appreciate this approach to communication study, it is important to understand the cultural shift that brought it to prominence. Until the 19th century, the culture in the United States (and most other Western, African and Asian societies) was quite similar in one important way to the culture of ancient Greece. Although both societies described themselves as democratic, the people who were allowed to participate in the society's governing rhetorical communication were a very small percentage of the total population.

---

2. Karl Erik Rosengren (1981). "Mass media and social change: Some current approaches," in Elihu Katz and Tamas Szecsko, eds. *Mass media and social change: The Uppsala papers.* Beverly Hills, CA: Sage Publications, pp. 247-263. See also: Wilbur Schramm (1997). *The beginnings of communication study in America: A personal memoir.* Steven H. Chaffee and Everett M. Rogers, eds. Thousand Oaks, CA: Sage Publications.

Those in the ruling class were virtually all male, non-slaves, who owned considerable property and were relatively well-educated. Many in the population were slaves; half of the non-slaves were nonproperty-owning women, or people who had virtually no rights at all. The theories of rhetoric, then, were designed for the elite educated males who ran the society, because no one else was allowed to participate in the society's governance. In fact, most were heavily restricted even in their participation in the society's economic system.

This same basic pattern survived throughout the world until recently. The United States abolished slavery in the 19th century, but until the 1960s the descendants of those slaves still were not generally allowed to vote or participate fully in most aspects of everyday economic or political life. Although women were finally given the right to vote in the United States in the 1920s, they did not gain the legal status of economic equals until the 1960s. Regrettably, in much of the rest of the world many of these advances still remain to be achieved.

These social changes, along with the coming of age of the "baby boomers," resulted in unprecedented growth in college populations. More students were attending, and they were extremely different in orientation. These were not predominantly the children of the elite members of the society (although theirs were included); they were mostly the first children in their family ever to attend college. They did not typically have aspirations of governing the country. Rather, they were seeking an education so they could enter the economic mainstream of society.

While these students were permitted, and often required, to study the rhetorical communication theories being taught at the time, many of them did not find such information of value. They recognized, before many of their professors, that the kinds of communication they needed to understand were not being discussed in their classes. Of course, the reason their communication needs weren't being discussed was because few people knew anything to discuss. The research had not been done, and the theories had not been developed.

The explosion of research and theory development in the Human Communication side of the field led to extensive development of theories in communication areas such as: organizational, interpersonal, health, nonverbal, intercultural, gender and aging, instruction and development. Most of these communication areas began to be studied only in the late 1960s, but they are rapidly expanding areas of study today. Many of these areas are included in this text's chapters, as well as theories that developed earlier or more recently in rhetorical or mass communication.

Four areas of communication study are: 1) interpersonal, 2) group, 3) organizational, and 4) mass communication. The first portion of *Clarifying Communication Theories* deals with the first two areas, the second portion deals with mass communication, and the organizational communication theme is found in both portions. Of course, this approach[3] is just one of many ways to group communication studies,[4] and the separation *between the four areas is only a convenience.* Throughout the text, examples will overlap. It is not possible today to discuss how two people communicate without including their social groups, the more structured organization of the workplace and social system, or the influences of mass media.

Increasingly, the discipline is gaining definition, defining its territory and contributing to what is known about communication. Still, a certain amount of definition is still lacking. Academicians in the field are sensitive to the fact that, despite years of intense research, relatively few broad and enduring theories have emerged. Perhaps communicators have looked too hard for **principles** and **laws**, like those in the physical sciences, which have not been forthcoming.[5]

Some think that communicators should concentrate on smaller **systems**, subsets of the interpersonal or mass experience rather than grand theories. For example, instead of studying a broad phenomenon such as "Internet use," the topic would be narrowed to "news use on the Internet," focusing only on using the Internet to keep up with news events. Some question whether quantitative measures are useful in a field where precise measurement is usually impossible. They suggest that research through observational techniques (see Qualitative Research chapter) offers a more exciting approach to communication theory.

Communication theory is closely allied with, and sometimes infringed by, other disciplines such as social psychology, sociology and political science, to name just a few. For example, a political scientist might write a book about the role of television advertising during a presidential campaign; a social psychologist might study how people communicate in sports bars; and a sociologist might study an

3. Stephen W. Littlejohn (1989). *Theories of human communication, 3rd ed.* Belmont, CA: Wadsworth, pp. 10-14.

4. Stanley J. Baran and Dennis K. Davis (1995). Mass communication theory: Foundations, ferment and future. Belmont, CA: Wadsworth. See also: Charles R. Berger and Steven H. Chaffee, eds. (1987). *Handbook of communication science.* Beverly Hills, CA: Sage Publications; Hanno Hardt (1992). *Critical communication studies: Communication, history and theory in America.* London and New York: Routledge; Denis McQuail (1994). *Mass communication theory: An introduction, 3rd ed.* Thousand Oaks, CA: Sage Publications; Everett M. Rogers (1994). *A history of communication study: A biographical approach.* New York: The Free Press; Bradley S. Greenberg and Michael B. Salwen (1996). "Mass communication theory and research: Concepts and models," in Michael B. Salwen and Donald W. Stacks, eds. *An integrated approach to communication theory and research.* Mahwah, NJ: Lawrence Erlbaum, pp. 57-72; Stuart Hall (1989). "Ideology and communication theory," in Brenda Dervin, Lawrence Grossberg, Barbara J. O'Keefe and Ellen Wartella, eds. *Rethinking communication, Vol. 1: Paradigm Issues.* Newbury Park, CA: Sage Publications, pp. 40-52.

5. William Paisley (1984). "Communication in the communication sciences," in Brenda Dervin and Melvin J. Voigt, eds. *Progress in Communication Sciences, Vol. V.* Norwood, NJ: Ablex, pp. 1-43.

issue such as how mass communicators entering the profession learn the unwritten rules of an organization. But increasingly, it will be up to the communication disciplines to define their territory and pen the principal contributions to the field.[6] Leaving the work to others not trained in the discipline would risk overlooking nuances that only those experienced and dedicated to the field can see. Luckily, the trend today seems to be in the right direction.[7]

The rise and fall of communication theories

New students of communication theory often are exasperated by the dearth (if not absence) of rock-solid theories in their field, and also by the tendency of communication theories to rise and fall, i.e., to seem plausible at first but then to become mired in conflicting research. It's true there are few rock-solid theories in communication, but there are numerous areas in which researchers test hypotheses about relationships among variables that lead to predictions about behavior.

In regard to the tendency of communication theories to seem plausible in one period but implausible in another, students' incredulity is understandable. How can an idea that seemed so certain yesterday, and on which presumably acceptable decisions were made, be discredited today? The literature of the field reveals several theoretical propositions that were researched enthusiastically but that subsequently died on the vine.

Bullet Theory. The "bullet" or "hypodermic needle" theory was of that type, although it was less than a real theory. It was the presumption made from the very early days until the 1940s that when the mass media spoke, people listened. The media were viewed as a syringe loaded with a dose of message content and aimed at the receiving masses. This implied that the media were very powerful, and that media messages were like bullets that went straight to their intended target, with the intended effect.[8] In the 1940s the power of the media was called into question and, the bullet seemed more like a nerf ball.

---

6. Suzanne Pingree, John M. Wiemann and Robert P. Hawkins (1988). "Toward conceptual synthesis," in Robert P. Hawkins, John M. Wiemann and Suzanne Pingree, eds. *Advancing communication science: Merging mass and interpersonal processes.* Newbury Park, CA: Sage Publications, pp. 7-17. See also: Kathleen K. Reardon and Everett M. Rogers (1988). "Interpersonal versus mass media communication: A false dichotomy," *Human Communication Research* 15(2):284-303.

7. James A. Anderson (1996). *Communication theory: Epistemological foundations.* New York: Guilford Press. See also: Arthur Asa Berger (1995). *Essentials of mass communication theory.* Thousand Oaks, CA: Sage Publications; John Downing (1996). *Internationalizing media theory: Transition, power, culture.* Thousand Oaks, CA: Sage Publications; Michael B. Salwen and Donald W. Stacks (1996). *An integrated approach to communication theory and research; op cit.*; James H. Watt and C. Arthur Vanllear (1996). *Dynamic patterns in communication processes.* Thousand Oaks, CA: Sage Publications.

8. Werner J. Severin with James W. Tankard Jr. (1988). *Communication theories: Origins, methods, uses, 2nd ed.* Longman: New York, p. 116.

Opinion Leadership Theory. The bullet theory withered when Paul Lazarsfeld and his colleagues[9] conducted survey research during the 1940 presidential election. Rather incidentally, they came upon data that indicated individuals get their persuasive information from other individuals, not from mass media. The media seemed not so powerful after all, and individuals using interpersonal communication in social settings seemed more powerful (see Two-Step Flow chapter).

But even the opinion leadership theory faltered when research revealed that nearly everyone was an opinion leader. For example, the auto mechanic was an opinion leader for the banker about automotive issues, and the banker was an opinion leader for the mechanic on economic issues. If someone asked your opinion about what movie to see or which candidate to vote for, you would be an opinion leader. And so, one of the knocks on the theory was that it was too broad to be useful. By the mid-1960s, the opinion leadership theory was no longer viable.[10]

Cognitive Dissonance. Dissonance theory inspired a flood of interesting research in the 1950s and 1960s (see Cognitive Dissonance chapter). Led by the work of Leon Festinger,[11] researchers tried to explain people's response to dissonant information. When people are confronted with something that challenges what they "know," how do they respond? Do they ignore the information, adopt it or find ways to strengthen their own position in the face of the new information?

While cognitive dissonance generated a huge flurry of research, continuing even today, the outcome failed synthesis. It did not lead to a principle that was useful in predicting behavior. Instead, the research became more and more tangled with conflicting outcomes, and by the 1970s it seemed to die. But cognitive dissonance, like opinion leadership, had intuitive appeal; it made sense. Today there is a revival in variations of the dissonance idea, and this example is similar to the ebb and flow in acceptance that has occurred with dozens of other communication theories.

What could explain the "rise and fall" of these and other theories? For one thing, because researchers cannot "get into the head of respondents" (cannot see what they are measuring), they cannot be certain of the accuracy of their measures. Social science measures are vulnerable to error. For example, if people are asked about their "comfort" with the economy, they *might* provide a good estimate and then again they *might not*, depending on the wording, timing, context and so forth.

9. Paul Lazarsfeld, Bernard Berelson and Hazel Gaudet (1944). *The people's choice*. New York: Duell, Sloan & Pearce. See also: Elihu Katz and Paul F. Lazarsfeld (1964). *Personal influence: The part played by people in the flow of mass communications*. New York: The Free Press, pp. 137-148.
10. Verling Troldahl (1966). "A field test of a modified 'two-step flow of communication' model," *Public Opinion Quarterly* 30(4):609-623.
11. Leon Festinger (1957). *A theory of cognitive dissonance*. Stanford: Stanford University Press.

Add to that the fact that not all researchers are equally skilled at measurement, and not all researchers have access to high quality samples of respondents. (Much communication research is unfunded, and researchers must use whatever resources are at their command.) Given these conditions, among others, it really is no wonder that the findings of occasional studies conflict and that concepts are hard to untangle.

Exercise:

Even within the field of communication theory, differences of perspective exist. Review these selected topics in three scholarly journals. First are titles from a recent edition of *Communication Theory*, published by the International Communication Association, Vol. 7, No. 4, (Nov. 1997):

1. "From the 'I' to the 'we': Discourse ethics, identity and the pragmatics of partnership in the West of Scotland," by Darryl Gunson and Chik Collins.

2. "Communication without constellation? Habermas's argumentative turn in (and away from) critical theory," by William Fusfield.

3. "Communication and eschatology: The work of waiting, an ethics of relief, and areligious religiosity," by Ramsey Eric Ramsey.

Following are some additional titles from another journal, the *Journal of Communication* 46(3), 1996, also published by the International Communication Association.

1. "Sexually explicit media, gender differences, and evolutionary theory," by Neil M. Malamuth.

2. "Hardwired for news: Using biological and cultural evolution to explain the surveillance function," by Pamela Shoemaker.

3. "A bio-informational theory of emotion: Motion and image size effects on viewers," by Benjamin H. Detenber and Byron Reeves.

Compare the two sets of titles with articles from a 1997 *Newspaper Research Journal* 18(3-4):

1. "Protecting 1st Amendment? Newspaper coverage of hate speech," by M. Mark Miller and Julie Andsager.

2. "Role of special sections and subsidiary publications in competitive environment," by Mary Alice Shaver and Regina Louise Lewis.

3. "City characteristics and coverage of China's bid to host the Olympics," by John C. Pollock, Beverly Kreuser and Eric Ouano.

Perhaps it would be fair to say the three sets of titles present a continuum from the most abstract to the most specific. That is an indication of the range of theory in communication studies. The topics can involve the broadest precepts in communication or the most pragmatic elements. Whenever the research uses one set of variables to explain another, it is theory. Whenever a researcher tries to explain how a system functions, whether small or grand, it is theory.

Above all, theory is not a four-letter word, not something to be avoided or ridiculed. For purposes of this text, theory suggests practicality; theory explains how things work. What could be more practical? Theory is understanding, and understanding is the goal of education.

Summary

Theories are merely explanations of how or why things happen the way they do. Communication theories can be interesting, easy to understand and applicable to everyday life. The field traces its roots to the oldest essay and book ever found: Both were on effective communication. The chapter describes how communication study developed from Aristotle through the next few thousand years as societies' governing elites used the art of rhetoric to wield power and influence.

The formation of the communication discipline is quite recent. It followed advances in the 19th century such as **technology**, **industrial development** and **public education**. Developing slowly, it picked up strength in the 20th century with the experience of World War I propaganda studies, World War II persuasion studies, and the subsequent growth of communication studies programs in colleges and universities across America.

Several communication scholars offer ways to classify the discipline. Among these divisions are: 1) interpersonal, 2) group, 3) organizational and 4) mass communication. The four divisions are intertwined in communication studies; one cannot be explored without considering the others.

Communication theory's two grand divisions of human communication and mass communication are closely allied with several other disciplines, notably social psychology, sociology and political science. Methods derived from these associated fields have been used by communication researchers only in the last three generations. The methods have brought the communication discipline from an art form to a social science that takes its principles from empirical studies to build theories.

As the discipline matured, many of its original theories and principles fell to the wayside or were rejuvinated with continued research. The short history of the field has witnessed the **rise and fall of communication theories** on many occasions.

While communication researchers are somewhat sensitive about the lack of laws and axioms in the field, they recognize that the discipline is still relatively young and open to the next generation of discovery by inquisitive scholars who will build on the work of their predecessors.

Exercises:

A. Following are several communication journals. Visit your library, select at least three of the journals and review the tables of contents. In a page or so, describe your impression of each journal's contents (from reading the titles and perhaps the *abstracts* at the beginning of each article).

> *Communication Research*
> *Communication Education*
> *Communication Quarterly*
> *Gazette*
> *Human Communication Research*
> *Journalism & Mass Communication Quarterly*
> *Journal of Broadcasting & Electronic Media*
> *Mass Comm Review*
> *Media Studies Journal*
> *Southern Speech Communication Journal*

B. After reviewing the tables of contents, select one article from each of three journals on the list and review it to contrast the focuses of the different journals. In a **two-**page, double-spaced paper that includes a full citation of each article you read (immediately preceding your commentary on that article), say whether you think the article added to theory in the communication discipline.

C. Using any of the references in the chapter, or any other source you choose, write a maximum **one**-page paper that distinguishes communication **theory** from communication **research**.

2

Social Construction:
The Human Element in Theory Building

Edward Caudill
University of Tennessee-Knoxville

> **Journal article**: Christopher Simpson (1996). "Elisabeth Noelle-Neumann's 'spiral of silence' and the historical context of communication theory," *Journal of Communication* 46(3):149-173.

> **News article**: William H. Honan (1997). "U.S. professor's criticism of German scholar's work stirs controversy," *The New York Times*, Education Section, (Aug. 27), A13 (N); B8 (L).

In 1938, as humanity lurched toward the abyss of world war, a young German writer fabricated this piece of propaganda for *Das Reich*, Hitler's Nazi party hate tabloid:

> "To reach into the darkness to find the Jew who is hiding behind the *Chicago Daily News* is like sticking your hand into a wasp's nest...[In the United States], Jews write the newspapers, own them, and have close to a monopoly over the advertising agencies...They control the film industry, own the big radio stations and all the theaters...."[1]

A few hundred miles away and a few years later, after the war started and fascism was at its pinnacle, a Hungarian ex-poet immigrated to the United States. Having witnessed fascism's evil, he enlisted in the Office of Strategic Services (OSS) and began his training as a saboteur. He and his comrades joined Slovenian partisans near the war's end, fighting the Germans as they retreated from Greece. By the end of the war his brigade of 400 was down to 70. He had seen enough violence.[2]

---

1. See Simpson's (1996) introductory "journal article," p. 149, quoting Noelle-Neumann, "We Informiert Americka?" *Das Reich*, (June 8, 1941), pp. 6-7.
2. Scott Stossel (1997). "The man who counts the killings," *Atlantic Monthly* (May), pp. 86-87.

In the wake of war, the German *Das Reich* writer and her husband founded an institute for the study of public opinion whose most important client was Germany's ruling Christian Democratic Party. She had started the ascent to becoming one of the most important figures in the study of public opinion in post-war Germany. Elisabeth Noelle-Neumann went on to develop a theory of the connection between mass media and the development of public opinion.

Her thesis states that public opinion is a "social skin" that holds society together. Individuals use what she calls a **quasi-statistical organ** to divine socially acceptable opinions. Because most people wish to avoid social isolation or, worse, condemnation, they move in the direction of what is perceived to be the majority opinion. The media are critical factors in feeding perceptions of what constitutes majority opinion.[3] Noelle-Neumann called it the "spiral of silence" (see Spiral of Silence chapter). Her critics called the theory an excuse for Nazi sympathizers.

The OSS enlistee returned to the United States, earned his Ph.D. degree from the University of Southern California, and began a life-long career of studying the impact of television violence on viewers. He became the dean of the Annenberg School of Communication at the University of Pennsylvania in 1964. George Gerbner also emerged as a major figure in communication research and theory. He collected data on televised violence and developed the "cultivation hypothesis."

Gerbner argued that television violence feeds the **perception** that we live in a violent culture. Television cultivates the idea of violence by making it seem common or normal. His critics, though tame in comparison to Noelle-Neumann's, claim that his focus on violence seems obsessive at times. And many have snickered at the idea that cartoon anvils flattening cartoon characters can really be deemed "violent." Gerbner states, "The disempowering effects of television lead to neo-fascism. That kind of thing is waiting in the wings. Nazi Germany came on the heels of a basic sense of insecurity and powerlessness like we have here now. I don't want to oversimplify, but that is the direction we might be heading."[4]

Social constructionist view

This pair of vignettes and theories is used to illustrate the idea that scientific theories are shaped not only by empirical observation but also by the culture and experiences of their creators. Where "pure" scientific empiricism ends and culture begins in the development of theory is difficult, if not impossible, to know. A radical social constructionist might argue, for example, that Charles Darwin's theory of

---

3. Noelle-Neumann (1984). *The spiral of silence.* Chicago: The University of Chicago Press, p. 179.
4. Stossel, *op. cit.,* pp. 87, 92.

natural selection is nothing more than a restatement of Victorian England's prevailing values, which included the superiority of the English over other people.

But Darwin's theory applies beyond the shores of England. Evolution's generalizability contradicts a radically social-constructionist view of *On the Origin of Species*. Yet it also is evident that Darwin himself believed some races of human beings were more advanced than others, and so in this small respect feeds the idea that Darwin's culture contributed to the greatest scientific theory of the 19th century.

The response to Darwin shortly after *On the Origin* was published in 1859 also illustrates the social-constructionist view. His critics were aghast that he would exclude God from his theory. The traditional view held that the earth was young, perhaps only about 6,000 years old by the estimates of some theologian-scientists. Natural scientists in the 18th century were preoccupied with taxonomy, or classifying, ordering, and naming plants and animals. It was simply assumed that species of plants and animals existed now as they had always existed, unvarying across time.

When Darwin even asked the question "Why do plants and animals vary?" he was defying social, theologic and scientific convention, which held that life was unchanging across time. Convention held life unchanging because change implied imperfection, and God's creations could not be imperfect. Darwin's theory of natural selection clearly showed that life was "imperfect" because organisms were always changing in order to be better suited to their environments. Thus, Darwin defied conventional thinking of his time and shattered the constraints of the social construction of reality. Prior to Darwin, most scientists simply agreed on the correctness of their Biblically based assumptions about the origins of the varieties of life.

To bring the argument back to the realm of social science and communication, a radical social-constructionist view means such theories as agenda setting or the knowledge gap would be of little or no value beyond the shores of the United States. And such has not been the case.

The spiral of silence

In the spiral of silence theory, Noelle-Neumann argues that the powerful impact the media have on public opinion has been greatly underestimated. Media shape public opinion by helping shape people's views about which ideas and opinions are in the majority; by helping form impressions about what opinions are "permissible" or can be touted without public condemnation; and by contributing to impressions about which opinions and ideas are ascendant.

People's willingness to speak out on an issue is heavily influenced by their perception of the prevailing climate of opinion. Those who perceive their opinion is a minority opinion will remain silent, and so become part of the growing "spiral of silence." In this way, a large number of people — even a majority — could erroneously perceive themselves to be a minority and in danger of social isolation. Because of the media depiction of prevailing opinion and people's fear of ostracization, individuals remain silent on an issue in which they might in reality be a majority. Though she never presented the theory directly as a defense of the German people during the Third Reich, it obviously "fits" the case very well.

In fact, Noelle-Neumann has been accused of developing a theory that served a generation in denial of its complicity in Nazi atrocities. She presented the idea at a time when Western scholars, even policymakers, were amenable to relieving the German people of guilt.

Following WWII, the Marshall plan for reconstructing Europe, including Germany, not only was a way to rebuild, but also was a way to begin the healing process, to leave the war behind. At the same time, the Nuremberg trials handled the problem of punishing the guilty, as Nazis were tried and often imprisoned or hanged. And so German society could be purged of its guilt. The spiral of silence fit nicely because it explained away the complicity of the German people in the holocaust. Her idea was attractive to a world eager to put war and guilt behind it.

Christopher Simpson has shown how Noelle-Neumann prior to 1945 participated in pro-Nazi organizations and propaganda, and how her writing on U.S. media depicted a Jewish-controlled industry bent on furthering an anti-German bias. He called the spiral of silence "a type of excuse...upon which all responsibility for the Holocaust and related crimes could be heaped, and thereby avoided...The German people's silence in the face of Nazi crimes and their conflicted, often contradictory efforts since World War II to come to grips with the Holocaust...are not examined in [*The Spiral of Silence*] text....In this way, her book not only describes a spiral of silence, it enacts it."[5]

Gerbner and cultivation

Gerbner argues, on the basis of several decades of research and data collection, that television is central to American culture, and that heavy viewers of television tend to perceive the world in terms of "TV reality." Cultivation, for Gerbner, means that television teaches a common worldview to its audience. For example, one result of the preponderance of police and crime shows, and other violent fare, is that heavy viewers tend to overestimate the likelihood of being crime victims and have a greater sense of insecurity than light viewers of television. Gerbner calls this view of heightened risk and violence the "mean world" syndrome.

---

5. Simpson, *op. cit.*, p. 160.

His research has shown that in the "TV world" people in lower socio-economic classes are significantly under-represented, that white females are 17 times more likely than white males to be crime victims, and villains are disproportionately Latino or foreign males.

All of the television violence, Gerbner argues, leads people to perceive that violent behavior is normal, which in turn means citizens are more willing than ever to grant the state more police power and to increasingly support the death penalty. With all this violence and public approval of stern countermeasures, fascism is an ever-present threat. And that completes the circle, returning to Gerbner's experiences with fascism in his earlier days. Even in his retirement, Gerbner calls himself a "part-time researcher, full-time agitator."[6]

Theorists or activists?

Even one of Noelle-Neumann's severest critics concedes that she is "one of the most prominent living European analysts of mass communication," and a very sophisticated thinker. But her theory illustrates the ways in which social scientists' experiences can shape their work. Simpson concluded that she has persisted in her beliefs that most people are ignorant and incapable of genuine self-rule.[7]

Gerbner's critics condemn his obsession with violence and his activism for propounding the "mean-world" syndrome. Fascism's intrusion into his life at an early age has obviously shaped Gerbner's research and thinking. But both Gerbner and Noelle-Neumann have collected massive data in support of their theories. And they are insightful intellectuals who have contributed substantially to mass communication research.

Communication research's bigger picture

A broader view of trends in mass communication research also reveals the impact of society on theory building. Prevailing perspectives have evolved from "powerful effects" to "limited effects" to "limited-powerful effects." This is attributable to a number of factors, including the accumulation of knowledge about media effects, increasingly sophisticated measurement devices and more powerful statistical techniques for analyzing data. However, this evolution also follows the contours of social and cultural phenomena.

The powerful effects model emerged in times of profound social stress: war and economic depression. People were insecure, and new media such as film and

---

6. Stossel, *op. cit.*, pp. 91-92, 100.
7. Simpson, *op. cit.*, pp. 150, 166-167.

radio, with their unknown potential, often elevated that insecurity and were viewed as a threat. Fascism was sweeping Europe, and the Nazis had shown themselves masters of using radio and film for propagandizing.

However, after World War II and the return of prosperity and peace, the nature of communication research changed. The crises were over, and new research was showing that the media were not so all-powerful. Instead, "opinion leaders" and interpersonal communication were found to be strongly mitigating factors in the persuasive power of mass communications.[8] As the insecurity of earlier years subsided, so did the reasons to be fearful of the negative consequences of new media. The "limited effects" model prevailed in this climate. In many respects, this view reflects a "re-empowerment" of individuals over great and impersonal forces such as a fascist state. The threat of totalitarianism had diminished, and so had the fear of all-powerful media.

The next several decades, however, saw a resurgence of the powerful effects, along with increased social insecurity. The 1960s combined the previous two perspectives in many ways. It was a decade of grandiose ideals and slogans about the power of the people. Conversely, it was a time of paranoia about the power of the state and the willingness of political leaders to abuse their power. So here was the specter of individuals contending with powerful forces, but being capable of confronting and changing those forces. In this atmosphere, the "powerful-limited" effects perspective emerged. Agenda-setting, for example, showed how the media are quite powerful in telling us what to think about, but very limited in their ability to tell us what to think.

Though tempting, the development of theory cannot be dismissed merely as a reflection of cultural and social evolution. The accumulated data and the increasingly powerful ability of theory to explain the workings of the world still exist. In the cases of Noelle-Neumann and Gerbner, it is unfair to simply dismiss them and their ideas because of the past they bring to their research.

Exercises:

A. In your library, find volumes of *Journalism Quarterly* published from 1950-1955. Scan them for research on minorities and mass media. Then move forward 30 years, using *JQ* for the years 1980-1985, and look for content about minorities and media. Has the content changed in respect to this single topic? What events intervened from 1955-1980 that may have influenced the research scholars were pursuing?

---

8. A classic work on this subject is Paul Lazarsfeld, Bernard Berelson and Hazel Gaudet (1944). *The people's choice: How the voter makes up his mind in a presidential campaign.* New York: Duell, Sloan and Pearce.

B. Recent research in genetics has begun to locate the physical foundation of many hereditary diseases. Does this have longer-range implications for current thinking about the causes of numerous social problems, such as crime, poverty or weak performance in school, that are believed to be heavily influenced by environment? Consider the number of government programs dedicated to alleviating social ills by improving the environment in which individuals live.

Most people dislike the idea that humans are driven by biology. However, most accept the idea that heredity has some role in individual and social makeup. This is a point of general agreement — i.e., it is "social construction" in that almost everyone accepts the dual impact of "nature" and "nurture." What would happen if science were eventually able to prove that one or the other was all powerful, and the other absolutely meaningless?

C. Peruse the program listings for several evenings of prime-time television. Make note of the types of programs being offered, in particular the police-crime dramas. After watching a few of these programs, consider the implications for answers to these questions:

1. Is crime a problem in America?

2. Is violence a "normal" part of human behavior? In other words, is it inevitable?

3. Is there approval or disapproval of violence (by good guys or bad guys)? Is violence seen as a positive act in that it has the power to alter our environment in a positive fashion: getting rid of bad guys?

Consider what your answers to these questions say about the general social agreement on the place of violence in society: That perhaps violence is simply a routine part of living (the Social Construction of reality).

Consider, too, what the answers say about attitudes toward the violent acts themselves, their pervasiveness in society, and the results of violence (Cultivation).

Doing Journal Synopses

3

Resources: These three sources offer guidelines for journal writing, for evaluating journal articles and for using on-line data bases to search for journal articles:

     1. Susan MacDonald (1994). *Professional academic writing in the humanities and social sciences*. Carbondale and Edwardsville, IL: Southern Illinois University Press.

     2. Ellen R. Girden (1996). *Evaluating research articles from start to finish*. Thousand Oaks, CA: Sage Publications.

     3. Jeannette A. Woodward (1997). *Writing research papers: Investigating resources in cyberspace*. Lincolnwood, IL: NTC/ Contemporary Publishing Group.

In thousands of communication theory courses at hundreds of colleges across the world, students are replicating the ritual that their teachers experienced, and the generation of teachers before them. Students are being taught how to read the literature of the field. In many communication graduate classes, the entire theory course may revolve around weekly assignments of journal articles and seminar-type discussions of the finer points found in those journal articles. Several of this text's chapters require reading the original version of a communication or other social science journal article, and many of the chapters begin with a "classic" or "founding" article on the topic followed by a more recent article.

What's the purpose? Is this merely a time-honored tradition, like moving the tassel on a mortarboard from right to left at commencement to signify being graduated, or rubbing the nose on Plato's bronze bust in the library for luck on the next exam? Traditions have their place, but reading journal articles provides more than a sense of connection to the communication field's body of knowledge. These are the original published articles, usually based on primary research, that led to basic principles in the communication discipline. Textbooks and chapters in books of readings cite the original journal articles, often merely as bibliographic references, but these are secondary sources. The journal articles are where it all began, the foundations upon which communication theories are built.

Students who are in advanced classes — far enough along in their studies to be using this text — are likely to have completed term papers and similar extensive projects that required reading and evaluating journal articles. However, even those experiences might fall short of the expectations suggested in this chapter. Here the concept is to actually read the original journal article, make sense of it, critique its merit, add it to your store of information and be prepared to discuss it meaningfully in class.[1] Achieving these goals can be a two- or three-hour exercise. The assignment is even more arduous if it requires limiting the journal synopsis to a single, double-spaced typed page and doing one synopsis per week. Yet that is the expectation in many of those thousands of communication theory classes across the country.

Reiterating the scope of this process, students are expected to: 1) locate journal articles that are relevant to the communication subject being discussed; 2) select one journal article to read and write about; 3) read the article in enough detail to dissect its component parts; 4) evaluate the article's strengths and weaknesses; and, 5) write a synopses of the article on a single, double-spaced typewritten sheet. Because many teachers expect students to do several such synopsis assignments, or even one per week, here are some hints to make the job more manageable.

Locating relevant articles

The communication field, like many other disciplines, has a guide to journals in the field: *The Iowa Guide*.[2] Updated every few years, the guide contains a directory of journals in the field. University libraries also offer lists of communication journals held in bound volumes, and most journals offer periodic (sometimes annual) indexes of the articles, usually by subject headings and by authors, usually alphabetically. However, most searches today will take place on-line using databases in the social sciences or humanities. Keywords, such as "gatekeeping," can lead to a variety of articles on that topic, or it may be necessary to combine keywords such as "gatekeeping" and "communication."

Regardless of how the journal or the individual article is accessed, remember that the article must be relevant to the subject matter. For example, using the keywords "gatekeeping" plus "communication" might detect an article titled

---

1. Thomas R. Black (1993). *Evaluating social science research: An introduction.* London: Sage Publications.

2. Ana C. Garner and Carolyn Stewart Dyer (1989). *The Iowa guide: Scholarly journals in mass communication and related fields, 3rd ed.* Ames, IA: Iowa Center for Communication Study, School of Journalism and Mass Communication, University of Iowa.

"Quality control in cellular phone production: Lessons in gatekeeping communication devices," which is an unlikely candidate for studying gatekeeping theory.

Among available journals with relevant articles for communication theory are: *Canadian Journal of Communication; Communication; Communication Education; Communication Monographs; Communication Quarterly; Communication Research; Communication Research Reports; Communication Theory; Critical Studies in Mass Communication; Discourse: Journal for Theoretical Studies in Media and Culture; ETC: A Review of General Semantics;*

European Journal of Communication; Media Studies Journal; Gazette; The Howard Journal of Communications; Human Communication Research; The Information Society; Journal of Advertising; Journal of Broadcasting & Electronic Media; Journal of Communication; Journal of Communication Inquiry; Journal of Mass Media Ethics; Journal of Media Economics; Journal of Public Relations Research; Journalism & Mass Communication Educator; Journalism & Mass Communication Monographs; Journalism & Mass Communication Quarterly;

Mass Comm Review; Media, Culture and Society; Media History Digest; Newspaper Research Journal; Political Communication and Persuasion; Public Opinion Quarterly; Public Relations Review; Quarterly Journal of Speech; Social Forces; The Southern Communication Journal; Southwestern Mass Communication Journal; Telecommunications Policy; Text: Interdisciplinary Journal for the Study of Discourse; Visible Language; Western Journal of Speech Communication; Women's Studies in Communication; and, Written Communication.

This list is only the tip of an iceberg. Dozens, perhaps hundreds, of journals in related fields such as psychology, sociology, political science, business, history, culture, race and gender issues, new technology and a variety of other disciplines contain articles that qualify as relevant to communication theory. And, in case these suggestions are too unwieldy, try using a basic human communication, mass communication or speech communication textbook. Most basic texts list theoretical concepts in the index, along with page numbers, that lead to a brief discussion of those concepts with related references to the original journal article.

Selecting a journal article

Once a relevant article is identified, selection might seem axiomatic. Don't be fooled. Just as a book can't be judged by its cover, a journal article can't be judged by its title. If the assignment is to do one journal synopsis per week, the harried student might spend five hours in the library searching through titles, then print out or copy a series of articles for later reading. This process is almost the right approach, but not quite.

Communication should be a discipline that values clarity of expression, and researchers in the field would like to believe they have communicated their ideas clearly and succinctly. But because they are social science researchers, their writing must be precise and must contain enough detail to meet the rule of replication: Other researchers should be able to duplicate the procedures. To be accepted for publication, to pass muster by the journal reviewers, the articles are usually written by academicians for their academic peers. Often a student, even a doctoral student, will be stymied by the article's language or statistical procedures.

Think about these points before selecting the article:

a. *length* — An 8-page article may be a better selection than a 40-page article.

b. *background* — Some articles are written with the assumption that the reader is already well versed on the topic. Such articles may make casual references to a long string of previous research unfamiliar to the student. Gaining enough familiarity with the topic to understand the article might require extensive additional reading. Such a time investment is probably beyond the scope of the journal synopsis assignment. Choose another article.

c. *scope* — Some journal articles cover a topic broadly; some delve deeply into only a single aspect of the topic. Either of these alternatives can be a good choice for a synopsis, but students will be better served by an article that takes the middle ground. A wide-ranging article will be difficult to synthesize on one page of text, and an article that focuses too narrowly is likely to fall short of explaining the concept adequately.

d. *depth* — Journal articles can be extremely complex. If the article appears too difficult to understand, even on a second reading, choose one that is more easily understood. A baffling article is likely to result in a poor synopsis.

e. *language* — Clarity of writing should be a prerequisite for every journal article, but often the jargon defies understanding. Choose another article.

f. *statistics* — Unless a student is literate in research methods and statistics, some journal articles will be indecipherable. The essence of most articles (purpose, methods used, outcomes) can be followed without knowing statistics. But if the math gets in the way, choose another article.

Dissect the component parts

Students will be pleased to learn that they can succeed at dissecting most journal articles. The articles usually follow scientific method: 1) statement of the problem, 2) the hypotheses, 3) operational definitions, 4) measurement procedures, 5) data collection, 6) data analysis, 7) report findings, and 8) relate the findings to the wider body of knowledge in the field...tell what the findings mean.[3] Usually, data analysis will be the most difficult of these steps to decipher, but even that step can be understood if the author does a good job in presenting the findings. And if the data analysis section of the article is too complex, skip past it to what should be a summary of important findings at the end.

Evaluate strengths and weaknesses

Yes, even published research articles contain weaknesses. Very often, the authors discuss shortcomings of the research in the article, possibly in three different places: the measurement procedures, data collection and reporting the findings.

An insightful evaluation usually requires noting the shortcomings the authors mention, and then looking for additional weaknesses. Does the study accomplish what the author attempted to do? Was the study's purpose worth investigating? Is the student convinced that the sample was adequate, the procedures well controlled, the findings believable, the conclusions supported by the data? If the article's outcomes conflict with previous research on the topic (often included in the literature review portion of the article), does the author adequately explain or try to reconcile the differences?

Undergraduates, who may be reading journal articles for the first time, can make the mistake of believing everything they see in print. After all, the authors of these journal articles might be senior research professors with distinguished careers and dozens of books to their credit. But undergraduates are also the most severe (and insightful) critics. They can be skeptical of research that pretends to herald new information, and they can be downright uncharitable when they judge an article's content a waste of their reading time.

All students will do well in the evaluation process if they **critique the general worth** of the article. Strengths and weaknesses are less a matter of writing style or clarity of presentation. The evaluation should be an assessment of the contribution the article makes to knowledge in the communication field.

Write a single-page synopsis

Holding the synopsis to a single, double-spaced typewritten page is a problem. Think of this as an exercise in studying for a final exam. Pretend that an

3. Jeffrey Katzer, Kenneth H. Cook and Wayne W. Crouch (1998). *Evaluating information: A guide for users of social science research*, 4th ed. Boston: McGraw Hill.

instructor's lecture on gatekeeping is a final exam topic. Instead of trying to type out and memorize the entire lecture, a far better procedure is to type the important points with enough information about those points so that reviewing these notes before the exam covers the gatekeeping topic adequately. Even in preparing for a term paper, students are advised to write notes on every reading using a three-by-five-inch index card, then arrange the cards in the order they will include that reading in the term paper.

Similarly, graduate students whose degree depends on passing a comprehensive exam would be well advised to prepare a synopsis of each book or journal article they read during all of their classes and to use these as a study guide for the exam. This is how students in dozens of countries still prepare for important qualifying tests. It is a time-honored tradition because it works.

What should the format and content of these journal synopses be? An example is offered of a one-page synopsis for a journal article on gatekeeping. Although the example might not depict the best organization for all journal synopses, it will suffice for most. It begins with a full citation to the article, including author, complete title, the journal in which the article appeared, volume number, edition number, date and pages.

After providing the full citation of the article, the **problem** being investigated is given. Although the problem statement in the article might have been five paragraphs long, it is reduced to its essence in the synopsis.

Then the study' **method** is reviewed. This section also boils what might have been two or three pages in the article to just enough essentials so that a reader, unfamiliar with the study, would understand how the research was done.

Next comes the **findings** section in which the synopsis presents the study's outcomes. Findings might include half a dozen or more outcomes, but the synopsis should be limited to the most important findings the article offers.

Finally, the synopsis provides an **evaluation**, or an assessment of the research's value to the communication discipline. In the example, the synopsis evaluation acknowledges that the research is interesting, but finds fault with the case-study approach (a sample of only one) and notes that the article fails to address broad theoretical issues.

"Gatekeeping"

David Manning White (1950), "The 'gatekeeper': A case study in the selection of news," *Journalism Quarterly* 27(4):383-390.

Problem: A news item travels through communication channels past a series of "gates" presided over by a "gate keeper" who controls what happens to the item. Each gate keeper affects each item's destiny. What influences may be found to effect the gate keeper's choice?

Method: The study analyzed the choices of news items made by a wire editor, the final gate keeper in the news-flow chain. If the final gate keeper rejects a story, all the previous gate keepers' work is negated. This wire editor was at a 30,000-circulation morning paper in a Midwest industrial city of 100,000. He was in his mid-40s with 25 years in journalism.

The gate keeper agreed to store all his rejected wire copy and note on each why the story was not used. The amount of wire copy received was compared with that actually used, and the reasons for rejecting stories were analyzed.

Findings: Only 10% of the wire copy received was used. Reasons for rejecting 90% of the copy were found to be highly subjective. Decisions were based on value judgments filtered through the gate keeper's own set of experiences, attitudes and expectations. The gate keeper himself cited many reports on the same event, the lack of news value in an item and limited space in the newpaper as reasons he rejected, but the researcher found that the gate keeper: 1) used stories that interested him, and 2) his view of his readers was far from the actual composition of people in his readership audience.

Evaluation: The study is interesting, but not well controlled. Would the findings have been the same if many wire editors were studied? The study does not deal with a broad theory of how mass communication works.

4
Communication Models

Early commentary: Karl W. Deutsch (1952). "On communication models in the social sciences," *Public Opinion Quarterly* 16(3):356-380.

Recent use: Glen M. Broom, Shawna Casey and James Ritchey (1997). "Toward a concept and theory of organization-public relationships," *Journal of Public Relations Research* 9(2):83-98.

Models are drawings, charts, diagrams, pictograms, schematics — possibly even cartoons — used to **reduce complex ideas to a graphic representation**. Communication study didn't invent models. They were borrowed from the physical sciences or engineering fields where they accomplish basically the same goals of representing relationships, flows, structures or interactions. Rather than imply that a model is some mysterious, cryptic puzzle, here's one that began as a verbal communication model (in this case a list of statements)[1] and was later framed as a chart to depict the flow of signals in electronic communication devices.[2]

Who
Says What
In Which Channel
To Whom
With What Effects?

Figure 1. Lasswell's verbal model of communication

---

1. Harold D. Lasswell (1948). "The structure and function of communication in society," in Lyman Bryson, ed. *The Communication of Ideas*. New York: Harper & Brothers, pp. 37-51.
2. Claude E. Shannon and Warren Weaver (1949). *The mathematical theory of communication*. Urbana: University of Illinois Press.

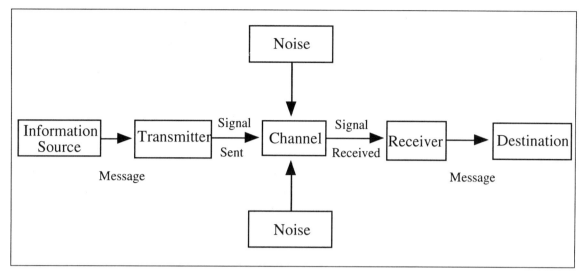

Figure 2. Shannon and Weaver communication transmission model

Harold Lasswell used the list of statements in 1948 to describe human communication (see Figure 1); Claude Shannon and Warren Weaver, scientists at the Bell Laboratory, presented the diagram in 1949 (see Figure 2). Other than being among the first models in the discipline and remaining as staple examples of communication theory model building today, the two depictions are nearly unique in being so similar in concept and yet totally separate approaches to describing how communication works.

Lasswell, a social scientist, was describing human communication, probably a speaker delivering a persuasive message to an audience. "Who" is the speaker or message sender, "says what" is the message itself, "in which channel" might refer to the difference between a speaker at a podium in a conference hall versus President Franklin Roosevelt delivering a "Fireside Chat" using radio; "to whom" is the receiver; and "with what effect" is the outcome or receiver's reaction to the message. Lasswell was not the first to envision human communication this way because most of the same ideas were expressed by Walter Lippmann in 1922,[3] except the "channel," which was Lasswell's innovation.

Other innovators were approaching the transmission of information from an entirely different perspective. The Shannon and Weaver model was related to work by Norbert Wiener.[4] All three were physical scientists and mathematicians who were trying to explain how transmitters send **information**, in this case defined as

---

3. Walter Lippmann (1922). *Public opinion.* New York: Macmillan.

4. Norbert Wiener (1948). *Cybernetics: Or control and communication in the animal and the machine.* New York: John Wiley & Sons.

signals rather than messages, through electronic circuits or airwaves to receiving devices. Their concern was telephone, radio and television communication but chiefly the transmission and reception rather than the meaning or effects of messages.

The Shannon and Weaver model is a linear model that describes what happens in the electronic flow of signals. "Transmitter" is the switching and amplification device that breaks the message into coded signals (bits), sends the signals through a wire (or over airwaves) to a "receiver," a decoding device such as a television set, which translates the signal back into the original message that a receiver or "destination" can understand. The novel aspect of this model is the introduction of "noise," or anything that might reduce the fidelity, clarity or integrity of the signal on its path between transmitter and receiver. One other aspect of this model deserves notice: the arrows. Communication models usually do include arrows to denote direction or flow of messages.

Additional classic models

Charles Osgood brought models to human communication in the mid-1950s with his recognition that both senders and receivers play a role in message transmission.[5] Osgood (top model in Figure 3) accounts for communication stimulus producing communication response, which in turn produces additional stimulus.

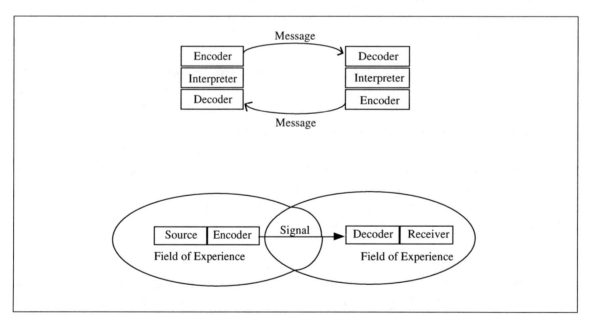

Figure 3. Osgood-Schramm interpersonal communication model

---

5. Wilbur Schramm (1954). "How communication works," in Wilbur Schramm, ed. *The process and effects of mass communication*. Urbana: University of Illinois Press. The model was a co-authored concept that is usually attributed to Charles E. Osgood.

Wilbur Schramm, an early and continuing influence in the mass communication field, offered several models that dealt with both human and mass communication.[6] One is presented as the lower model in Figure 3 that includes the concept of **shared experience**, suggesting that successful message encoding and decoding depends on the source and receiver having sufficient commonalties, such as similar language and cultural backgrounds. Another of Schramm's models (not shown) included the first depiction of **feedback** or information the receiver sends back to the source, which might be used by the source to clarify or otherwise alter the future message. Feedback is usually an element depicted in communication models since Schramm first included the concept.

Another model offered in the mid-1950s was Theodore Newcomb's Symmetry Model, an interpersonal communication model depicting how two individuals might communicate about an object, an idea or even another person.[7] The model, depicted in Figure 4, suggests cognitive consistency, balance or agreement (see Coorientation chapter). In the years since their inception, symmetry models have been widely used to show interactions between an organization, such as a cigarette manufacturer; public interest groups, such as those that oppose tobacco use or an employee union; and an objective, such as outlawing sales of cigarettes or a wage increase.

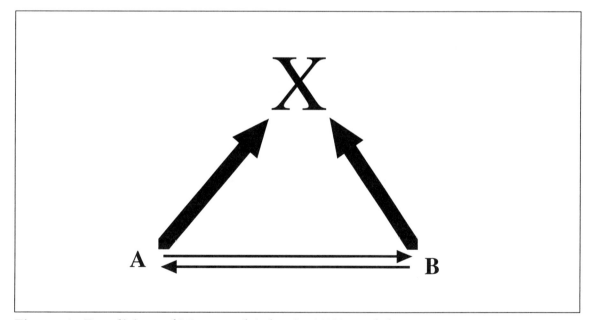

Figure 4. Rendition of Newcomb's basic ABX model

6. *Ibid.*, pp. 3-26.
7. Theodore M. Newcomb (1953). "An approach to the study of communicative acts," *Psychological Review* 60(6):393-404.

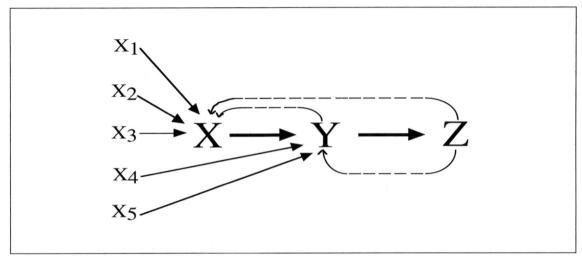

Figure 5. Adaptation of Westley-MacLean model

A classic model (see Figure 5) in the mass communication field is the Westley-MacLean Model offered in the late-1950s to depict the flow of news from a source (big X) or the entire range of possible news events (numbered x's), through the communicator (medium or news outlet, Y) to the receiver or the audience of news (Z).[8] The model includes implications for decisions that depend on shared experiences (a person's sensory field) and feedback loops.

A classic model for human communication is David K. Berlo's 1960 **SMCR** model of communication where the acronym stands for source, message, channel and receiver.[9] The model emphasizes elements of each part of this process:

Source	Message	Channel	Receiver
communication skills	content	seeing	communication skills
attitudes	elements	hearing	attitudes
knowledge	treatment	touching	knowledge
social system	structure	smelling	social system
culture	code	tasting	culture

---

8. Bruce H. Westley and Malcolm S. MacLean (1957). "A conceptual model for communications research," *Journalism Quarterly* 34(1):31-38. See also: Bruce H. Westley (1976). "MacLean and I and 'the model,'" in Luigi D. Manca, ed. *Essays in honor of Malcolm S. MacLean, Jr.* Iowa City, IA: Center for Communication Study, pp. 26-34.

9. David K. Berlo (1960). *The process of communication*. New York: Holt, Rinehart & Winston, p. 72.

Notice that the source and receiver columns contain the *same* five elements; message includes five components of communication; and channel includes the five senses. In its original depiction, the model presents the message component as a huge, wide "M" with the five components winding their way inside the letter as if progressing on a game board. Feedback is not depicted, but is assumed. Although Berlo's model still qualifies as an early conceptualization, it and the Shannon-Weaver model form the basis for many later attempts to explain communication concepts in models.[10]

Just to avoid any implication that communication models were a passing fancy of the 1950s, a more recent model is offered in Figure 6. This one, presented by Edelstein, Ito and Kepplinger in 1989 is an amalgamation of ideas proposed by a wide variety of communication scholars with a pattern borrowed from Alex Bavelas' research on communication within task-oriented groups.[11]

In Figure 6, news has five dimensions. Clockwise from the top of the star are: 1) structural, in which economic pressures drive social forces to maintain elites'

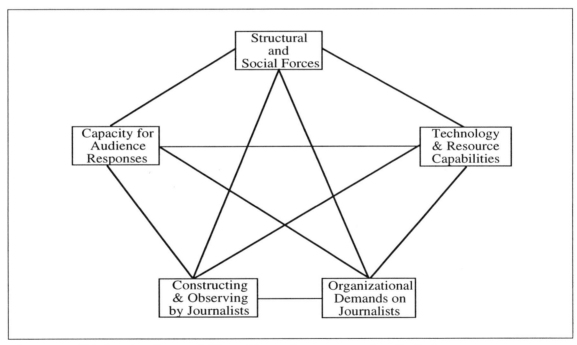

Figure 6. Edelstein, Ito and Kepplinger's contexts for defining news

---

10. James C. McCroskey (1993). *An introduction to rhetorical communication, 6th ed.* Englewood Cliffs, NJ: Prentice-Hall, p. 26.

11. Alex S. Edelstein, Youichi Ito and Hans Mathias Kepplinger (1989). *Communication and culture: A comparative approach.* New York: Longman, p. 101. See also: Alex Bavelas (1951). "Communication patterns in task-oriented groups," in Daniel Lerner and Harold D. Lasswell, eds. *The policy sciences: Recent developments in scope and method.* Stanford, CA: Stanford University Press, pp. 193-202.

power; 2) technological advances that empower the media to define reality; 3) organizational constraints journalists face; 4) observational, or the way journalists cover and define events; and, 5) the audience's capacity to respond to media messages. The depiction resembles the Chrysler logo. Four lines emanate from each point, which is a way of depicting that each of the five units interacts with all of the other four units.

Many additional models are found in the communication literature of the past 50 years, including more visually oriented depictions that incorporate funnels, umbrellas, mushrooms, Christmas trees, tornadoes and so forth.

Purpose of models

Models are useful for their graphic representation, and simplification, of complex ideas. In fact, the value of a model depends on how well it accomplishes the goal of reducing complex ideas to easily and quickly grasped concepts. Further, a model should be easily understood by anyone with a background in the discipline. It should not be so technical that it defies interpretation by experts, otherwise the model is no better than a four-page, jargon-laden explanation of the relationship or process being described.

If goals of a model were enumerated, they would be to: 1) describe the main points of the process or relationship; 2) do it simply and clearly; and 3) do it with as little textual explanation as possible. If these are the ideal purposes, then how does the Westley-MacLean Model (see Figure 5) rate? It is fair to say that this model approaches the outer boundaries of what a model should do because considerable explanation is required before the ideas presented can be interpreted. Actually, Figure 5's depiction is the last in a series of four progressivley complex diagrams: three graphics with explanations for each of the component parts preceded the final representation. Even so, the Westley-Maclean Model was, and still is, a powerful tool to explain the mass communication process.

Models do not have to encompass the entire communication process or the entire scope of any discipline's interests. For example, it is possible to present a model of the entire Democratic process, and it is possible to offer a model of voter decision making in local elections. Many such models have been proposed, and improvements in the models are made as research evidence accumulates and theory building crystalizes.

However, models do not require waiting until enough research evidence accumulates to point to a theory. The more usual route is that a model will be proposed so that its relationships can be tested. In this way, models are very much like hypotheses. They state a relationship and propose the component parts or directions of influence, and they do so in a manner that can be tested.[12] Even if a model is derived from extensive previous research evidence, the model's component parts are still available, still "out there," to be examined and tested.[13]

Model building example

Many communication researchers would argue that a new idea in the discipline is *not worth discussing* or exploring unless the idea can be represented in a model. Those who take this position are emphasizing that a theoretical discussion among colleagues, say over drinks after a long day at a conference, is nothing more than idle talk until the theory being discussed can be represented in a model. If this viewpoint is accepted, then every person in the discipline including beginners should be able to depict an idea in the form of a model. Is this expecting too much? Actually, models are not that difficult to form.

Look at this book's chapter on "Selectivity and the Communication Process." Five types of selectivity processes are discussed: selective exposure, selective attention, selective perception, selective retention and selective recall. To be effective, a message must get past each of these barriers. Although these ideas required decades of research to achieve, the concepts are relatively easy to present in a model. Figure 7 offers such a model, worthy of critique.

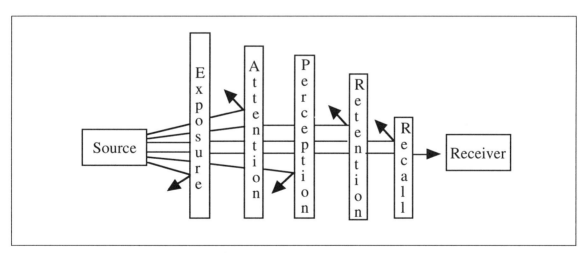

Figure 7. A model of the communication selectivity process

12. Denis McQuail and Sven Windahl (1993). *Communication models for the study of mass communication, 2nd ed.* New York: Longman. See also: Bradley S. Greenberg and Michael B. Salwen (1996). "Mass communication theory and research: Concepts and models," in Michael B. Salwen and Don Stacks, eds. *An integrated approach to communication theory and research.* Mahwah, NJ: Lawrence Erlbaum Associates, pp. 62-69.

13. Greg Leichty and Jeff Springston (1993). "Reconsidering public relations models," *Public Relations Review 19*(4):327-339.

First, because communication selectivity is a process, the Figure 7 model calls for arrows or directional indicators. A source sends countless messages, all of which must pass through the barriers of the receiver's communication selectivity or screening mechanisms. In the model, each barrier is represented by a wall, and the walls are aligned in a progressive order beginning with exposure and ending with recall. Some of the source's messages bounce off each of the barriers and never reach the receiver, but some messages penetrate the barriers and are received.

The graphic presentation could be enhanced by depicting the source as a person's head, mouth open, sending messages. The receiver could be another person's head, ear turned toward the source. Each of the barriers could be pictured as stone walls. Using a single arrow line to depict many messages might be an error, because the idea that each line represents many messages bouncing off each wall could require additional explanation. Perhaps the model needs feedback loops: a suggestion that the receiver signals the source about what messages are getting through the barriers. However, the more complicated the depiction becomes, the more difficult it is to grasp the underlying concepts. Too little detail can result in misunderstanding; too much detail is cumbersome and self-defeating.

But Figure 7 has a more significant problem. However graphically pleasing the model may be, it is inaccurate. The communication selectivity barriers are not independent of source and receiver. Selectivity is usually determined by the receiver. The model should incorporate this essential aspect of the process, even if the outcome is less graphically pleasing. Figure 8, therefore, is a better representation of the communication selectivity process because it correctly depicts that the barriers are associated with the receiver.

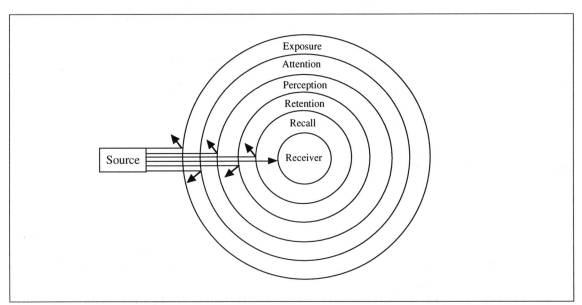

Figure 8. A better model of the communication selectivity process

Summary

Models may be drawings, charts, diagrams, pictograms or schematics used to **reduce complex ideas to a graphic representation**. The communication field didn't invent them but borrowed the concept from physical science disciplines.

Many communication models were first offered in the 1950s, but those are still studied today. The early models provided concepts such as **noise**, or interference with the transmission of a message, and **feedback**, or ways in which receivers let senders know that the message is getting through as intended. Models presented are those by Lasswell, Shannon and Weaver, Osgood, Schramm, Newcomb, Westley and MacLean, and Berlo. However, models are still developed today, as seen from the Edelstein, Ito and Kepplinger model of the five dimensions of news.

Models are very much like hypotheses in that they state a relationship in a manner that can be tested. Models can be the outcome of extensive research findings, or they can be an expression of an idea yet to be tested.

A model should reduce complex ideas to quickly grasped concepts. It should: 1) describe the main points of the process or relationship; 2) do it simply and clearly; and, 3) do it with as little textual explanation as possible. With these goals in mind, the five types of selectivity in the communication process are modeled, and the models are critiqued.

Exercises:

A. Select one of the communication theories offered as chapters in this text — one that does not include a graphic representation of the concept — and create a model that includes the basic elements of the theory. If your model requires labeling, provide a one-paragraph explanation. Be prepared to discuss and defend your model in class.

B. Select a communication journal article other than those used as references in this chapter, that includes a model (many do). Copy the entire article and write a **one-page critique of the model** using the principles for models addressed in this chapter. Attach the article to your one-page critique and submit at the next class period for a grade.

C. Create a model of the communication process that occurs **in this class** during a normal class session. If your model requires labeling, provide a one-paragraph explanation. Be prepared to discuss and defend your model in class.

5
A Media-Use Inventory

Media use study: Elihu Katz, Michael Gurevitch and Hadassah Haas (1973). "On the use of the mass media for important things," *American Sociological Review 38*(2):164-181.

Survey question bias: Floyd Jackson Fowler Jr. (1992). "How unclear terms affect survey data," *Public Opinion Quarterly 56*(2): 218-231.

This chapter's questionnaire has four purposes: 1) improve awareness of individuals' mass media and interpersonal communication use, 2) improve awareness of questionnaire construction, 3) provide media-use data for analysis in class and 4) address several theoretical issues. As an *inventory*, this questionnaire is designed to cover the range and depth of your use of mass media and general communication habits.

Media

Give your best estimate of the number of days in a typical week and your best estimate of the average length of time in a typical day you use each of these media:

	Days in a typical week:	*Hours in a typical day:*
newspaper (*days only*):	/ / / / / / / / 0 1 2 3 4 5 6 7	
television news (ABC, CBS, etc., *days only*):	/ / / / / / / / 0 1 2 3 4 5 6 7	
television for entertainment:	/ / / / / / / / 0 1 2 3 4 5 6 7	/ / / / / / / / 1 2 3 4 5 6 7+
commercial radio:	/ / / / / / / / 0 1 2 3 4 5 6 7	/ / / / / / / / 1 2 3 4 5 6 7+

	Days in a typical week:	*Hours in a typical day:*
Internet, www	/ / / / / / / / 0 1 2 3 4 5 6 7	/ / / / / / / / 1 2 3 4 5 6 7+
magazines (news & specialty)	/ / / / / / / / 0 1 2 3 4 5 6 7	/ / / / / / / / 1 2 3 4 5 6 7+
movies (in-home or theater, *days only*):	/ / / / / / / / 0 1 2 3 4 5 6 7	
public television (PBS):	/ / / / / / / / 0 1 2 3 4 5 6 7	/ / / / / / / / 1 2 3 4 5 6 7+
public radio (non-commercial):	/ / / / / / / / 0 1 2 3 4 5 6 7	/ / / / / / / / 1 2 3 4 5 6 7+

1. If you read a **daily** newspaper **yesterday**, about how much time did you spend reading it?

     _____ did not read
     _____ 10 minutes or fewer
     _____ 11-20 minutes
     _____ 21-30 minutes
     _____ more than 30 minutes

2. If you watched a national network television **newscast** yesterday **evening**, was your choice: (*select only one; leave blank if answer is none*)

     _____ ABC   _____ CBS   _____ CNN   _____ NBC   _____ PBS
     _____ other: which one _____

3. If you watched a national network television newscast yesterday **evening**, did you watch (*leave blank if none*):

     _____ all or nearly all of it
     _____ half or more, but not all
     _____ less than half of it
     _____ very little of it

4. Did you listen to one or more **radio** newscasts yesterday?

     _____ yes
     _____ no

     (IF NO, SKIP TO Question 6)

5. If yes, was it:

_____ local

_____ network

_____ one or more local AND network

_____ If network, which? _____

6. In general, where do you think you get **most** of your information about what's going on in the world today? (*If more than one, rank those you wish to mark according to their importance to you: "1," "2," etc.*)

_____ commercial radio	_____ public television
_____ public radio	_____ magazines
_____ newspapers	_____ interpersonal sources
_____ commercial television	_____ the Internet
(cable or broadcast)	

7. In general, how **informed** do you think you are about the affairs of government today? (*circle one number for each*)

National government:

7	6	5	4	3	2	1
very informed			undecided			not very informed

State government:

7	6	5	4	3	2	1
very informed			undecided			not very informed

Local government:

7	6	5	4	3	2	1
very informed			undecided			not very informed

8. In general, do you think the mass media have a significant impact on **your** life? Stated differently, do the media influence **your thinking**:

7	6	5	4	3	2	1
a lot			undecided			a little

9. What about the lives of **other people**? Do you think the media influence <u>their</u> **thinking**:

7   6   5   4   3   2   1

a lot   undecided   a little

10. How much influence do you feel that you have to affect change in state or federal government? Some people feel influential and some do not. What about yourself? Select the number that represents the influence you feel in being able to affect change in government.

7   6   5   4   3   2   1

very   undecided   not very

influential   influential

Interpersonal communication

11. When you watch the news on television or read a newspaper, how likely are you to subsequently discuss some aspect of the news with a friend or relative?

7   6   5   4   3   2   1

very   undecided   not very

likely   likely

12. Are you more likely to **initiate** a discussion of the news, or more likely to be a **receiver** of news from others?

_____ initiator

_____ receiver

_____ undecided

13. What level of confidence do you have, personally, for the news you see on commercial television and in newspapers?

television:

7   6   5   4   3   2   1

a great deal   undecided   none

newspapers:

7   6   5   4   3   2   1

a great deal   undecided   none

Demographics

Now, just a few questions to help sort the responses:

14. gender:
    _____ male
    _____ female

15. academic standing:
    _____ freshman
    _____ sophomore
    _____ junior
    _____ senior
    _____ graduate student

16. academic major:
    _____ speech communication
    _____ communication studies
    _____ journalism
    _____ broadcasting
    _____ public relations
    _____ advertising
    _____ other: which? _____

*   *   *

Item review and critique

The response options: First, look at the items that asked you to estimate the hours and days in a typical week that you use the mass media. As you responded to each item, did you sometimes have trouble deciding on an appropriate answer? Were you able to recall how many hours you watched television last week? Accuracy is an issue, and a researcher should always be alert for estimates that appear unrealistic. Did the response options always fit your needs? Did you need an option such as "a half hour," but you found no such option?

Here is another question for consideration: Did the media use inventory include all appropriate media? Should it have included billboards? Bulletin boards? CD's? Wire services? Newsletters? Word-of-mouth? Fax machines? Email?

Why study media use: Researchers measure media use because media are central to the modern life experience, and many researchers (and very many others) think there is a strong relationship between media use and people's behavior. Media use also is important for advertisers. The greater the audience, the more valuable it is to advertisers. Advertising is a big business (estimated a $140 billion in the United States alone),[1] and media are in the business of *delivering an audience* to advertisers.

Newspapers' future in the technological age: With the development of technologies, more is being heard about the supposed death of newspapers. Some evidence does show that readership is declining, along with the number of newspapers. But more evidence suggests that the death of newspapers is exaggerated. Readership has declined a little, but the audience remains very strong, and the surviving newspapers are generally financially sound. Furthermore, newspaper researchers argue that when survey questions are phrased properly, the readership decline is smaller.[2] Aware that researchers report most people get most of their news from television, Stempel phrased the question without a television bias and found that newspapers and television come out even: About 59% of Americans use each medium as a source for news.[3]

Therese Baker wrote, "The ability to create questions to tap ideas that may be on the surface undesirable to answer or be lacking in interest requires an artistic touch."[4] However, the artistic aspect yields to experience — learning from mistakes — and to recognizing potential pitfalls in advance.[5] Earl Babbie, along with dozens of social science researchers, offers guidelines to improve the phrasing of questions or just to avoid making blunders.[6] In fact, the "art" of asking survey questions may approach a "science" as researchers provide more suggestions about care in asking questions.[7] The media use survey has a few pitfalls that deserve further inspection.

---

1. Robert J. Cohen (1994). "Ad gain of 5.2% in 93 marks downturn's end," *Advertising Age*, (May 2), p. 4.

2. John Mennenga (1992). "Decline in newpaper readership should not be overestimated (Shop Talk at Thirty), *Editor & Publisher*, (Feb. 15), 125(7):52-53.

3. Guido H. Stempel III and Thomas Hargrove (1996). "Mass media audience in a changing media environment," *Journalism & Mass Communication Quarterly* 73(3):549-558, see p. 552.

4. Therese L. Baker (1988). *Doing social research*. New York: McGraw-Hill, p. 161.

5. Anne E. Polivka and Jennifer M. Rothgeb (1993). "Redesigning the CPS questionnaire. (Overhauling the current population survey)," *Monthly Labor Review* 116(9):10-28.

6. Earl Babbie (1994). *The practice of social research, 7th ed*. Belmont, CA: Wadsworth, pp. 141-147.

7. Improving questionnaires receives considerable attention in research methods sources such as: Arlene Fink (1995). *How to ask survey questions (The Survey Kit, Vol. 2)*. Thousand Oaks, CA: Sage; Judith M. Tanur (1992). *Questions about questions: Inquiries into the cognitive bases of surveys*. New York: Russell Sage; Norbert Schwarz (1997). "Questionnaire design: The rocky road from concepts to answers," in Lars Lyberb et al., eds. *Surevy measurement and process quality*. New York: Johy Wiley & Sons, pp. 31-34; Michael W. Traugott and Paul J. Lavrakas (1996). *The voter's guide to election polls*. Chatham, NJ: Chatham House, pp. 96-119; Floyd J. Fowler Jr. (1989). *Improving survey questions: Design and evaluation*. Thousand Oaks, CA: Sage; Jean M. Converse and Stanley Presser (1986). *Survey questions: Handcrafting the standardized questionnaire*. Beverly Hills, CA: Sage Publications, Paper No. 63, 80 pp.; Robert C. Adams (1989). *Social survey methods for mass media research*. Hillsdale, NJ: Lawrence Erlbaum; Kenneth D. Bailey (1994). *Methods of social research, 4th ed*. New York: The Free Press, pp. 109-140.

Reviewing individual questionnaire items

Question 1. This question reflects four key issues: 1) Why were you asked whether you read a <u>daily</u> newspaper, 2) Why was <u>yesterday</u> specified? 3) What is meant by "reading"? and 4) Is the time measure accurate? Each issue is addressed.

a) As you probably know, not all newspapers are produced <u>daily</u>. Some are weekly, bi-weekly, tri-weekly, 4-day, 5-day, 6-day. They can be free-circulation (such as "shoppers") or specialty newspapers (such as entertainment guides). When <u>daily</u> newspapers were specified, the respondents' options were narrowed a bit to improve the precision of the reply.

b) The emphasis on the word <u>yesterday</u> is interesting. Newspaper researchers have found that when the question is: "About how often do you read a newspaper?" the frequency of reading tends to be less than when the question is phrased as: "Did you read a newspaper <u>yesterday</u>?" As always, the answer received depends on the question asked.[8]

c) What is meant by the word "read," as in: "If you <u>read</u> a daily newspaper..." Can spending 30 seconds with the paper be called "reading"? How much time should constitute "reading"? And should the 30-second reader be called a reader, the same as the person who spends 30 minutes? Even if a reader spends 30 minutes reading, the usefulness of the response is unclear: The reader might have spent lots of time in one section, such as sports, but missed all the others.

d) The questionnaire asked, "If you read a daily newspaper yesterday, about how much time did you spend reading it?" Could you answer such a question accurately? Suppose the same question was asked about TV viewing? How many minutes did you spend watching the network news yesterday? Last week? Might accuracy suffer from questions that demand too much of the respondent's memory?

Question 2. This question specified (a) <u>national</u> network tv news and (b) yesterday <u>evening</u> to narrow the response options and clarify the response. Still, there are many different daily newscasts and many times of presentation, usually including at least two "evening newscasts." They are not equal in content, coverage or influence. Equating them is not useful.

Question 3. The problem in this question is directly comparable to the "reading" problem in the newspaper readership question. What is meant by "watching"? If you are in a room with a tv on, are you watching? If you see the broadcast only as you go and come, or while talking with another person, are you watching? This is an important issue, and not easily resolved.

---

8. Mennenga, *op. cit.*

Questions 4 and 5 are self-explanatory.

Question 6. This is the question that most gratifies broadcasters and vexes newspaper publishers. For 30 years, pollsters have reported that most Americans say they usually get most of their news about what's going on in the world from television.[9] But is it so? If a person does not read a newspaper or listen to the radio, but watches television, then there's no argument. But if the person does read a newspaper, the issue is less clear. Which has more information, the newspaper or the television news show? It's said that the full script of an evening newscast includes fewer words than the front page of a newspaper. Can a person make an accurate judgment about how much information is received from each source?

Question 7. If people get most of their information from television, how much do they know?[10] Question 7 asks about the person's informedness about national, state and local government. Do you see a problem with the question? If a person self-reports as being very informed, does that mean that it is so? Self-perception of informedness might actually be a measure of satisfaction with the news, or even self-confidence. Nevertheless, as a classroom activity, it will be interesting to compare the answers to question 7 with the check-list that preceded Question 1.

Questions 8 and 9. These questions tap an interesting line of mass media research, the observation that individuals tend to think the media influence them little, but influence others a lot. This is called the "third person effect" (see Third-Person Effect chapter).

Question 10. This question measures what is called political "efficacy" or effectiveness. Some people feel that their vote is important while others say it is not. What explains this difference in perception? Is the measure of efficacy explained by individuals' use of mass media? As a class exercise, should the instructor think it appropriate, this can be tested in the form of a correlation coefficient representing the relationship between efficacy and one or more of the media-use items.

Questions 11 through 13. These questions deal with issues of interpersonal communication, particularly who is likely to be involved in a discussion of the news, and whether a person is more likely to initiate or receive such discussion. Finally, respondents are asked about confidence in what they see and read. These questions deal with news "diffusion" (see Information Diffusion chapter) and news media "credibility," both of which are important in understanding the role of mass media in society today.

---

9. Stempel and Thomas Hargrove, *op. cit.*

10. M. Mark Miller, Michael W. Singletary and Shu-ling Chen (1988). "The Roper question and television vs. newspapers as sources of news," *Journalism Quarterly* 65(1):12-19.

Question 14 through 16. These items provide "demographics" that are useful for sorting (grouping) questionnaire responses. Demographics are defined as the study of population statistics, but in practical research terms **demographics** are people's characteristics such as age, gender, race and religion. These are used to group subjects for more refined data analysis. For example, the gender demographic could be used to compute the third-person effect and the efficacy effect for males only, or females only; the academic standing demographic could compare freshmen with seniors, and so on. Demographic variables help to refine the analysis and explain the results.

Summary

In this chapter, you have responded to a questionnaire, critiqued some of its questions, and analyzed some of its findings. You have seen the difficulty of writing good questions, and especially the vagueness of some terms that seemed so familiar, such as "reading" and "watching."

The questionnaire demonstrates that questions may not measure exactly what they were supposed to measure. For example, a measure of "informedness" might really have been a measure of personal satisfaction or confidence.

Questionnaire self-reports are not always reliable. Watching the news on PBS might be vastly different from watching the news on a commercial network or cable. So a response to a questionnaire depends entirely on the question that was asked, and writing questions must be done with great care. Still, if such problems are accounted for, the questionnaire can be a powerful instrument in the professional communicator's arsenal.

Exercise:

Review the questionnaire. Write a one-page critique of the items, the response options and the questionnaire's scope. Did the questionnaire try to do too much? Too little? On a second page, make a note of any difficulty you experienced, and any reservations you had about your ability to answer items. Comment on the usefulness of the information, and suggest ways to improve the instrument.

Part Two
Human Communication

6

The Human Communication Process

Early article: C. David Mortensen and Paul H. Arntson (1974). "The effect of predispositions toward verbal behavior on interaction patterns in dyads," *Quarterly Journal of Speech* 60(4):421-430.

Contemporary article: Janet Beavin Bavelas and Linda Coates (1992). "How do we account for the mindfulness of face-to-face dialogue?" *Communication Monographs* 59(3):301-305.

On a daily basis the average person spends the majority of time communicating with another individual or groups of individuals. With the expansion of technology, human communication can cross oceans. McCroskey and Richmond suggest, "There are now three things that are certain in life: death, taxes, and communication."[1] Human communication is certainly the most appealing of the three.

Exercise 1:

Consider your own communication with other people, and make a list of the reasons why you communicate with others. For example, do you communicate with another person to get class notes, a date or tickets to a concert? Bring your list of reasons for communicating with others to the next class. Your list may be compared with a classmate's to see if significant reasons to communicate aren't on the lists.

This chapter provides a definition of human communication, reviews the types of communication that can occur, discusses a model of human communication

1. James C. McCroskey and Virginia P. Richmond (1996). *Fundamentals of human communication: An interpersonal perspective.* Prospect Heights, IL: Waveland. See also: Gustav W. Friedrich (1996). "The future of theory and research in communication: Human communication," in Michael B. Salwen and Don W. Stacks, eds. *An integrated approach to communication theory and research.* Mahwah, NJ: Lawrence Erlbaum Associates, pp. 547-550.

and reviews the elements involved in the human communication process. Consider first, the most common, practical, applied definition of human communication.

Definition of human communication

While communication can have many different meanings to different people, human communication is defined here as a **two-way process by which one person stimulates meaning in the mind(s) of another person (or persons) through verbal and/or nonverbal messages**. This definition acknowledges that human communication is an ongoing, dynamic process and not simply a one-way transmission.

Also, this definition notes that individuals stimulate meaning through either verbal or nonverbal messages, or both. Lastly, this definition acknowledges that different meanings can be stimulated in the minds of the receivers. In other words, this definition emphasizes meaning, not simply the exchange of messages.[2]

Three types of communication

The three primary types of human communication are expressive, accidental and rhetorical communication. **Expressive communication** involves a message that indicates a person's emotional state, feelings about something or someone, or well being at a given time. For example, if a friend borrows your car and returns it with a large dent in the door, you might voice words that cannot be printed here. You might even use gestures that match your words. This is expressive communication.

Intention or forethought may or may not be a component of expressive communication. For example, if you want to express "liking" for another person, you might intentionally, purposefully hug that person. On the other hand, expressive communication can be unintentional and spontaneous. It often occurs when people are caught by surprise. Some believe that expressive communication reveals people's true feelings about their relationship with the other person.[3]

Accidental communication involves a message that unintentionally stimulates some meaning in the mind of other people, sometimes a meaning the sender does not want them to have. Accidental communication occurs when individuals are not consciously and with forethought controlling their verbal and nonverbal behaviors. Hence, those who observe the behavior will attribute meaning to it even

---

2. David K. Berlo (1960). "The fidelity of communication," in *The process of communication: An introduction to theory and practice*. New York: Holt, Rinehart & Winston, pp. 40-72. See also: Charles R. Berger (1991). "Communication theories and other curios," *Communication Monographs* 58(1):101-113.

3. Paul Watzlawick, Janet Helmick Beavin and Don D. Jackson (1967). *Pragmatics of human communication: A study of interactional patterns, pathologies, and paradoxes*. New York: Norton.

when the sender had no intention of stimulating a meaning. For example, in communicating with people from other cultures, Americans may send messages that they do not mean to send. In some cultures the normal American head nod of approval or yes, means no. The culture sees Americans as impolite, unapproving and rude.

As vice president, Richard Nixon visited South America. When he stepped from the plane, someone shouted up to him, "How was the trip?" Mr. Nixon could not shout over the crowd, so he gave the awaiting crowd the American hand signal of "OK." Nixon meant the signal to say he was glad to be in South America and appreciated the friendly welcome. However, the "OK" signal in parts of South America is equivalent to raising a hand with the middle finger extended. Mr. Nixon accidentally insulted the South Americans by using a common gesture from this culture without any knowledge of the content behind the signal in the host culture.

Accidental communication occurs more frequently than the sender would like. The ways people talk, walk, wear clothing, move, gesture, sit, how much they talk, to whom they talk, and the words they use often communicate meanings that they do not even realize are being stimulated. People should be more conscious and attentive to what they might be communicating (accidentally) to others.

Rhetorical communication is intentional, purposeful and goal-directed. It is concerned with stimulating a *certain* meaning in the mind of another, persuading or influencing another to do something. As with expressive and accidental communication, rhetorical communication occurs frequently in the U.S. culture. For example, when sales people are attempting to make a sale, they are using rhetorical communication. They are goal-directed. Their goal is to sell the product.

Many public speakers, television personalities and advertisers are rhetorical communicators because of the nature of their work. The more effective rhetorical communicators (persuaders) usually sell more, achieve more and get what they want from others. The rhetorical sender (or the source) of a message has a specific purpose in mind when communicating. Thus, those speaking rhetorically may investigate or analyze how to stimulate meaning (intentionally) in the mind of the receiver.

Exercise 2:
At this juncture, generate a list of three examples each of expressive, accidental and rhetorical communication. Your lists might be shared with the class, so keep the examples clear and easy to understand.

*   *   *

Model of communication

The model of communication (see Communication Models chapter) presented here has been in use for more than 30 years. It is McCroskey's Rhetorical Model of Communication.[4] (See Figure 1).

- This model allows for thought prior to communication, source encoding of information, messages being sent through various channels, receivers decoding the messages, feedback and noise.

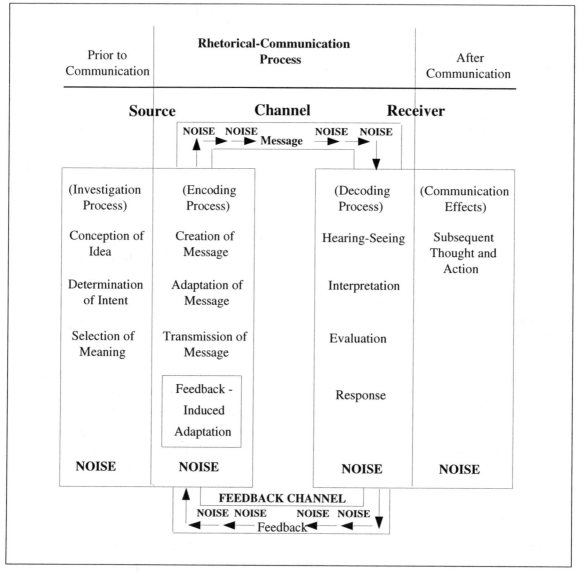

Figure 1. McCroskey's Rhetorical Model of Communication

4. James C. McCroskey (1996). *An introduction to rhetorical communication, 7th ed.* Boston: Allyn and Bacon.

- The model depicts communication as an ongoing, non-static, dynamic process of a person or persons attempting to stimulate meaning in the mind of another person or persons.

- It allows for the participants in the process to act as either source or receiver.

- It acknowledges the fact that noise can interfere with effective communication.

- It shows that through the use of feedback receivers can be active participants.

- Lastly, this model allows both the source and receiver the opportunity to adapt and rethink messages.

In all, the Rhetorical Model of Communication considers many elements of the human communication process and examines what happens prior to, during and after communication. The model demonstrates that if a source communicates effectively with and adapts to the receiver, a certain response should be expected.

Elements in the process

Fundamental knowledge of the seven elements or components of human communication is critical for understanding the process. These elements will be reviewed: source, message, channel, receiver, feedback, noise and context.

Source. The source in the human communication process is the person or persons who originates, constructs, creates or formulates the message that is to be sent to the receiver. Some texts distinguish between the source and sender of the message. Here the source and sender will be the same concept. A source can be a friend persuading another friend to try mushrooms on a pizza. A source can be the Rev. Billy Graham communicating a message to thousands of followers, Donald Trump speaking to his employees or Tina Turner singing to a sold-out stadium. A source can be a mother speaking with her son about his school classes. A source can be one individual, two people, a group of individuals or an organization.

In the human communication process the source is a critical component who often determines how the receiver will react. The source usually has three functions: 1) decide what should be communicated to the receiver; 2) encode the message (put it in terms the receiver will understand); and 3) transmit the message to the receiver. If the source fails in any of these steps, the message the receiver acquires may be distorted, confusing or simply uninterpretable. This happens often in the process.

Message. The message is any verbal or nonverbal catalyst (or trigger) that evokes or produces meaning in the mind of the receiver. Either verbal or nonverbal triggers can stimulate meaning. Verbal messages tend to be composed of words. Nonverbal messages include any gesture, movement or behavior (other than words) that stimulates meaning in the mind of the receiver. The underlying assumption is that the source and receiver both have a shared understanding of the verbal and nonverbal messages being encoded and hopefully decoded correctly.

If the source does not identify with the receiver or vice versa, the communication will be faulty. If the meaning of nonverbal behaviors are misinterpreted by the receiver, the communication will be faulty. For example, if a sales person uses concepts or terminology that customers do not understand or identify with, then communication will be faulty and sales will drop. Therefore, a source must think carefully about what the message will be prior to sending it. If a source can apply **triggers** (words that stimulate the meaning), then communication has a higher likelihood of being successful.

Channel. The channel is the means by which the source conveys or transmits the message to the receiver. Channels come in many forms, such as touch, sight, sound, hearing, smell, interpersonal talk, billboards, faxes, computers, books, television and many others. Often a source will need to use two or three channels to assure that the message is conveyed the way in which it was intended and received by the receiver. For example, teachers might say what they expect from a class, then give a handout and then ask for feedback from the class. By vocalizing the assignment, providing a handout and encouraging feedback about the assignment, the teacher improves the likelihood that successful communication will take place.

Receiver. The receiver is the person or persons who receives the message, or the person for whom the message is designed. The receiver's role is as critical as the source's role in the communication process. Receivers have three functions: 1) receive the message, 2) decode or interpret it, and 3) respond or give feedback. If the receiver doesn't receive the message, communication doesn't occur. If the receiver misinterprets the message, communication will be flawed. If the receiver doesn't give a verbal or nonverbal response, future communication might be flawed.

Feedback. Feedback is the receiver's observable verbal or nonverbal responses to the source's message. A receiver's response to the message is critical because this feedback helps the source know how to react, construct new messages and adapt to the receiver. If feedback is reduced or absent, the communication process will often be flawed. Not having effective feedback or being unable to interpret feedback can lead to communication misunderstandings, distortions and inaccuracies.

Noise. Noise in the communication process is any physical or psychological stimulus that distracts participants from focusing on the communication process. Quite simply, noise is any interference or disturbance during the communication process. People have difficulty concentrating on messages being sent because of external noise, the time of day, hunger, change in seasons or a host of other distractions that prevent them giving their full attention. A psychological stimulus can also be noise. For example, a person who is worried about a sick relative cannot concentrate on the messages being sent. Still, people should learn to block out most physical or psychological noise if they wish to improve communication with others.

Context. Context refers to the circumstances or situations in which the communication takes place. Context must be an important concern in human communication because individuals communicate differently with different people in the same context or situation or with the same person in different contexts or situations. As contexts change so does the communication, even if the person is communicating with someone considered to be a very close friend.[5]

Roles and rules are two important constructs influenced by the context. **Roles** are the characters or parts people are expected to play in each context. **Rules** are the guidelines or codes that regulate interactions according to the role a person is to play. For example, in the context of school, students interact or play many roles that have rules. A student may interact as the helpful classmate or the class clown. Students also interact with others in the role of a male or female friend. As contexts change, so do the roles and rules. School is only one of the many contexts in which students interact. They also interact in family, work, social and religious contexts. People's communication will often change or adapt to the context and the role they are expected to play and the rules they must follow.

The human communication process is a dynamic, ongoing, change-oriented process. By having a better understanding of this process and its elements, individuals can learn to become more effective communicators across contexts.

Summary

Human communication is *a two-way ongoing process by which a person or persons stimulates meaning in the mind of another person (or persons) through verbal and/ or nonverbal messages*. It is not simply a one-way transmission, but the exchange of ideas via verbal and/or nonverbal messages that stimulates meaning in the other person's mind.

The three primary types of human communication are expressive, accidental and rhetorical. **Expressive** involves a message that indicates an individual's

---

5. Charles R. Berger (1992). "Curiouser and curiouser curios," *Communication Monographs* 59(1):101-107. See also: John A. Daly, Anita L. Vangelisti and Suzanne M. Daughton (1987). "The nature and correlates of conversational sensitivity," *Human Communication Research* 14(2):167-202.

emotional state or feelings about another person or situation at a given time. **Accidental** involves messages that *unintentionally stimulate* meaning in the mind of another person, a meaning the source does not want the other person to have. **Rhetorical** communication is forced, focused and goal-directed; it is *persuasion*.

The chapter presents the **Rhetorical Model of Communication** that examines what happens prior to, during and after communication. The model demonstrates that if a source communicates effectively with and adapts to the receiver, then a certain response should be forthcoming from the receiver.

Seven fundamental elements or components of the human communication process are: 1) source, 2) message, 3) channel, 4) receiver, 5) feedback, 6) noise and 7) context. **Source** is the person or persons who originates the message. A **message** is any verbal or nonverbal catalyst that produces meaning in the receiver's mind. The **channel** is the means by which the source conveys or transmits the message to the receiver. **Receivers** are those who receive the message sent by the source.

Feedback is the receiver's observable verbal or nonverbal response to the source's message. **Noise** is any physical or psychological stimulus that distracts participants in the human communication process from focusing on the communication.

Context is the circumstances or situations in which the communication takes place. Context determines the *roles* people are expected to play and the *rules* that regulate their interaction.

Having a better understanding of the human communication process and its elements helps individuals become more competent communicators.

Exercises:

A. Make a list of the many **contexts** in which you communicate on a regular basis. Then list the **roles** and **rules** that apply in each of the contexts. Take some time to prepare the list of contexts and roles because they are likely to be shared with others in class.

B. Based on the chapter's content, give five rules for improving your communication with others. Your list of five rules will be part of a class exercise.

Misconceptions about Human Communication

Early article: Mark Snyder (1974). "Self-monitoring of expressive behavior," *Journal of Personality and Social Psychology 30*(4):526-537.

Contemporary article: Michael Toolan (1991). "Perspectives on literal meaning," *Language & Communication 11*(4):333-351.

Because many people in other academic disciplines assume that communication is "an easy thing to master," it is no surprise that the way people communicate is often not effective. Why do businesses usually identify the No. 1 problem in the work place as the lack of effective communication? Why do students and teachers alike complain that the other group doesn't communicate well? Have you ever felt that you had your communication under control only to have it go all wrong?

Lots of people think they know how communication is supposed to work, only to discover that communication is not the "easy thing to master" they thought it was, or they simply blame the other person for the ineffective communication that occurred.

Exercise 1:

Before going further, please complete the short true/false Communication Background Test presented in Figure 1 (this is not a graded assignment).

Your instructor will discuss how to score the test.

A look at each of the following misconceptions, and consideration of some alternative ideas, should be useful in achieving more effective communication.

Communication Background Test

This is a brief test of the background knowledge you have about communication. Please respond by circling the "T" for true or the "F" for false before each statement to indicate whether your background and experience with communication supports the idea that the statement is true or false. No maybes are permitted! There are only ten statements, so this test should only take you a few moments to complete.

1.	T	F	Words have meaning.
2.	T	F	Communication is a verbal process.
3.	T	F	Telling is communicating.
4.	T	F	Communication will solve all our problems.
5.	T	F	Communication is a good thing.
6.	T	F	The more communication, the better.
7.	T	F	Communication can break down.
8.	T	F	Communication is a natural ability.
9.	T	F	Interpersonal communication is personal communication.
10.	T	F	Communication competence equals communication effectiveness.

Figure 1. Communication background test

Misconception 1: Meanings are in words.

Effective communication has been prevented repeatedly in relationships because many people still operate believing that "meanings are in words." In fact, many words have multiple meanings. "What a particular word means to us may not be what it means to someone else. The word stimulates a meaning in our mind that is different from the meaning it stimulates in the mind of our receiver."[1]

Words are simply codes or symbols people use to try to convey their meaning to another person or group. Words don't carry meaning apart from the individual using the words. If the source and the source's intent behind the words aren't

---

1. James C. McCroskey and Virginia P. Richmond (1996). *Fundamentals of human communication: An interpersonal perspective*. Prospect Heights, IL: Waveland, p. 26. See also: James C. McCroskey and Lawrence R. Wheeless (1976). "Human communication and change," in *Introduction to human communication*. Boston: Allyn and Bacon, pp. 1-11.

known, no decision can be made about what the source means. Still, the words themselves often have more influence than the person using the words. This misconception is the most difficult because mastering it requires considering the source and the context of the information more than the actual words.[2]

Only when the other person is known extremely well (almost intimately) may the same meaning for a word be shared. However, no two people share precisely the same meaning for all words because no two people have the same background, knowledge, experience, thoughts, feelings, education or even language usage. Not even identical twins or couples who have been married for 50 years will share precisely the same meaning for all words. The obvious conclusion is that *meanings are in people, not in words.* For more accurate communication to occur, the misconception that meanings are in words must be avoided.[3]

Exercise 2:

Following is a list of words or group of words. Read each and then record what the words stimulated in your mind. After you have completed the process, be prepared to compare your answers with a classmate. You may find that you are very dissimilar in some meanings, even though you and the other person share much in common. This exercise is also used as a way of learning about others in the class.

Word List:

Ugly creatures	Great Songs
Good movies	Disgusting foods
Naughty people	Bad words
Superstars	Fun things to do
Love	Boring things to do

Misconception 2: Communication is a verbal process.

Most people in this culture place a high value on the verbal process. This is emphasized early in formal education. However, the lessons learned from informal education may be that *the process of communication is **both verbal and nonverbal**.*

---

2. Michael T. Motley (1986). "Consciousness and intentionality in communication: A preliminary model and methodological approaches," *Western Journal of Speech Communication* 50(1):3-23.

3. Michael Toolan (1991). "Perspectives on literal meaning," *Language & Communication* 11(4):333-351.

As people develop and mature, they begin to understand that the nonverbal component of communication may be equally important to the verbal component. Often it is *not what is said but **how it is said*** that stimulates most of the meaning. For example, your steady date swears devotion to you, but then you see your date out with someone else. The nonverbal (the behavior) overrides the verbal communication.

Research suggests that nonverbal communication may be more important than verbal communication in stimulating meaning in the mind of another. When people are in conflict about what to believe, they will often go with communication's nonverbal component. They look at the other person's nonverbal behaviors, actions, movements, mannerisms and conduct to decide what that person is truly saying.[4]

Misconception 3: Telling is communicating.

This is the misconception that people use to blame others for their own communication inadequacies. Many people assume that saying something is communicating it. This misconception leads to faulty communication.

Telling is only half of the communication process. The other half is listening and providing feedback. Receivers must be active participants in the communication process. Only by encoding a message, sending it, and then requesting and listening to feedback is the communication process complete.

People love to blame the receiver for faulty communication. The scenario goes like this. Teacher to a student: "I told you Chapter 8 would be on the test." Student: "I didn't hear you." Teacher: "Typical, you never listen." Student: "I guess so." If only one student didn't know Chapter 8 would be on the test, the student is at fault. If several students didn't know about Chapter 8, the teacher is at fault. The teacher simply "told" the class and assumed all understood. But telling is only half of the communication process. Providing and listening to feedback is the other half.

Misconception 4: Communication will solve all our problems.

Most people tend to believe that *whether* communication occurs is more important than *what* is communicated. Many people in a variety of professions (politicians, consultants, counselors) believe that communication will solve all problems. *Communication not only can help solve problems but also **can create them.*** Communication is often the catalyst that causes problems to escalate.

---

4. Edward T. Hall (1966). *The hidden dimension.* Garden City, NY: Doubleday. See also: Charles R. Berger and Robert A. Bell (1988). "Plans and the initiation of social relationships," *Human Communication Research* 15(2):217-235; Virginia P. Richmond and James C. McCroskey (1995). *Nonverbal behavior in interpersonal relations, 3rd ed.* Boston: Allyn and Bacon.

Communication is a needed tool in solving problems, but communication can also fuel conflict. For example, you decide to tell your significant other to work out and lose some weight. Your motive might have been good: improved appearance and health. However, that suggestion could easily become the source of great interpersonal conflict causing the relationship to deteriorate. While communication *did* occur in this instance, and the intention *was* positive, what was communicated could be perceived as "a cheap shot" about the other person's appearance.

If the weight issue is a sensitive topic in the relationship, then communicating *more* about it will not change the weight, it will only create animosity, lower self-esteem and risk losing the other person. Effective communication can help solve problems, but *ineffective communication often creates more problems than it solves.*

Exercise 3:

Think of two or three topics that seem to cause problems in your relationship with a close friend. List these topics and then consider other topics (more pleasant topics) that could be discussed in place of the unpleasant topics. During the next week, each time you think about communicating the less pleasant topic, try to communicate the more positive topics in their place. Record what happens when more pleasant topics are substituted for the less pleasant topics.

If assigned as a grade, this week-long experiment in improving communication effectiveness may become the subject of a two-page essay on strategies and outcomes.

Misconception 5: Communication is a good thing.

Again, people have a misconception that simply focuses on communication being present, not necessarily on the topic of communication. This misconception is an extension of No. 4. *Communication is neither good nor bad.* Instead, it is a **tool**. Like any tool, communication can be used for positive or negative purposes.

For example, repeatedly remarking (in public and private settings) that a close friend has a big nose is not making the best use of the communication tool unless alienation is the objective. If the goal is to keep the friendship, then nose size must become less of an issue. If the goal is to end the friendship, then continuing to use the communication tool to stress nose size will effectively destroy the friendship.

Misconception 6: The more communication, the better.

Combine this misconception with Nos. 4 and 5, and the outcome is a recipe for total communication failure. More communication about some things may not be positive. More communication might be better, however, if it is on a topic about which both participants agree. Communication quality matters, not how much people communicate. In communication *quality is more important than quantity.*

Analogies in this quality vs. quantity issue can be found by thinking about work. Often it isn't how much a person works but the quality of the work that counts. The motto, "Work smart, not hard" comes to mind here. So is the case with communication: "Communicate smart, not hard."

Misconception 7: Human communication can break down.

This misconception has been part of modern culture for many years. People hear the phrases "communication breakdown" or "communication misunderstandings" used in dozens of contexts. Human communication does not stop, break down or end, but it might be unsuccessful. Saying that there is a communication breakdown is a source's way to ignore real issues that require attention. The source is blaming the process, not taking blame, for unsuccessful communication.

Often as a way to cease communication, people stop talking. Ceasing talk does not stop communication or cause a human communication breakdown. Because communication has a nonverbal component, human communication breakdowns do not occur. In a very real sense, *we cannot not communicate.* The double negative illustrates a significant idea about human communication. The absence of talk does not end communication. Silence only signifies that verbal communication has ended. Nonverbal aspects persist, and the receiver is still interpreting and giving meaning to each nonverbal cue. Technology can break down. Human communication does not break down because it involves both verbal and nonverbal messages that make communication an ongoing, ever changing, dynamic process.

Misconception 8: Human communication is a natural ability.

Communication, unlike many sports, is *not* a natural ability but is a learned ability. Certainly people are born with the capability to communicate, and some may be born with a higher willingness and less fear about communication. From their first year of life, infants learn what is appropriate and inappropriate communication. As with sports, people learn the rules and subtleties of communicating in restaurants, college dorms, jobs, dating relationships and so on.

Communication is a life-long skill. As people age, mature, acquire job skills, leave jobs, marry, divorce, have children, they have opportunities to constantly expand their communication experiences. Poor communicators usually only have a few, limited communication styles, possibly because they chose not to learn more about communication. Good communicators usually have many communication styles, possibly because they chose to learn more about human communication.

Misconception 9: Interpersonal communication is equal to intimate communication.

Many people still assume that when they have interpersonal communication, they must communicate in an intimate way. This is not true. Interpersonal communication can be intimate, but most is not. Most interactions in this culture are *not intimate, only interpersonal.* Talking with a clerk or a server is not usually intimate. Talking with a priest, spouse or a close friend might involve intimate communication.

Most people's lifetimes will only include a few other people with whom they communicate intimate details, thoughts and feelings. In an intimate relationship there is a high level of trust and self-disclosure, usually about very personal, intimate feelings or thoughts. As a culture, Americans have been taught to keep intimate secrets and feelings to themselves or to share them only with close friends and family. Disclosing too much intimacy may hurt people in the classroom, on the job and in interpersonal relationships. Most in this culture are guarded about their intimate communication. Everyone has been in or heard about situations where a communicator said: "Keep your personal life personal. There is no room for it here."

Misconception 10: Communication competence is equal to communication effectiveness.

How often have you encountered a communicator who was competent (had the knowledge) but was ineffective in delivering the content? A professor might know physics but be unable to deliver the content so students can understand it. Conversely, how often have you encountered a communicator who was effective in delivery (good speaker) but was not competent (not knowledgeable about topic)? Even a salesperson who knows little about a product might still be able to make sales.

These examples suggest that communication *competence and effectiveness are two distinct concepts.* Competence has to do with knowing content or information about a topic. Effectiveness has to do with delivering the content successfully. The truly capable, *expert communicator* is the person who *is competent and effective across contexts.* This is the person who is well-versed and knowledgeable about the subject matter and effective at delivering the content.

Summary

Individuals' misconceptions about communication are commonly believed in Western cultures, although they are at odds with clear thinking about communication. Often the ten misconceptions lead to poor or ineffective communication between individuals. To avoid confusion attributed to faulty concepts, it is useful to remember the following corrections for each misconception:

1. **Meanings** are not in words, they *are in the mind of the receiver* of the words.

2. Communication is not just a **verbal** process; it is also a *nonverbal* process.

3. **Telling** is only half of the communication process. The other half is *listening* and *providing feedback*.

4. Communication cannot **solve all our problems**. It solves or *creates them*.

5. Communication is neither a **good** nor a **bad** thing. It is a *tool*. Like any tool, communication can be used for positive or negative purposes.

6. **More** communication is not always better. *Quality* counts over quantity.

7. Human communication does not stop or **break down**. It is simply ineffective when the source or receiver or both are *ineffective communicators*.

8. Communication isn't a **natural ability** but a life-long *skill that can be learned*.

9. Interpersonal communication does not equal **intimate** communication; most interactions in this culture are not intimate.

10. Communication **competence** and **effectiveness** are two distinct concepts. Competence is knowing content; effectiveness means delivering it successfully. An expert communicator is competent and effective across contexts.

Exercises:

A. List communicators (from various backgrounds, ethnic groups, etc.) you think are competent and effective. Then, in groups, discuss the lists of competent and effective communicators. Your instructor will provide some questions for discussion.

B. Select **five** of the ten human communication misconceptions and write a brief paragraph on each telling when you observed others following the misconception, along with resulting outcomes. Or, select five of the ten and write a brief paragraph on each telling when **you** acted as if it were true, along with resulting outcomes.

C. Watch a popular television show of your choice where at least one (or more) of the communication misconceptions are being followed. Then write a paper of less than two pages about the show, the misconception and the resulting outcomes. Your teacher may have more instructions about this exercise.

8

Communication Quietness and Anxiety

Founding synthesis: Theodore Clevenger Jr. (1959). "A synthesis of experimental research in stage fright," *Quarterly Journal of Speech* 45(2):134-145.

Later synthesis: Michael J. Beatty, Jean A. Dobos, Gary L. Balfantz and Alison Y. Kuwabara (1991). "Communication apprehension, state anxiety, and behavioral disruption: A causal analysis," *Communication Quarterly* 39(1):48-57.

Before reading the material in this chapter, complete the following survey:

1. In a social context, do you usually attempt to become a wallflower or go to the recesses of the room so you don't have to talk with many people? Yes   No

2. Do you date less frequently than your friends? Yes   No

3. When you date, is it difficult for you to "break the ice" and begin talking? Yes No

4. If someone breaks up with you, do you feel devastated and find it extremely difficult to go out and begin dating again?   Yes   No

5. On a date, do you avoid telling your date how you feel about something? Yes No

6. Do you have a small group of friends rather than a large group?   Yes   No

7. In a social context, do you often sit and listen rather than talk?   Yes   No

8. In the classroom, do you rarely speak up and contribute in class?   Yes   No

9. In the classroom, if given a choice, would you sit in the back of the room? Yes No

(continued)

10. If given the option, would you rather take the large
lecture type of class than the small, somewhat intimate class?   Yes   No

11. In small-group discussion settings, do you avoid talking if you can?   Yes   No

12. In small-group discussion settings, do you try
to do the tasks for the group that require little talking?   Yes   No

13. In general, do you feel that when you talk you are not very effective?   Yes   No

14. In general, do you avoid talking whenever possible?   Yes   No

15. In general, do you desire to talk less than many people you know?   Yes   No

16. In general, do you consider yourself to be a quiet person?   Yes   No

If you answered Yes to five or more of these questions, then you may consider yourself to be a "quiet" person. Based on such questions, at least 25% to as much as 40% of people perceive themselves to be "quiet persons." So, if there are 25 people in your class, possibly ten of them think of themselves as "quiet persons."

Researchers suggest that: "In general, as a person's habitual level of talk increases, the person is perceived more positively," and a person is perceived less positively as talking level decreases.[1] In the U.S. culture, then, quietness is not a virtue. Most quiet people recognize this and consider their quietness an impediment, maybe even a liability.

Being quiet, scared speechless or having a fear of communication has been studied for decades under names such as stage fright, shyness, communication apprehension, reticence and willingness to communicate.[2] These distinctions are important in conducting research on shyness,[3] however, for this overview, people who have this communication problem will be termed "quiet." The unit reviews the behaviors of quiet people, some possible causes, and some resulting outcomes in a variety of contexts in the general culture of the United States.

---

1. Virginia P. Richmond and James C. McCroskey (1997). *Communication: Apprehension, avoidance, and effectiveness, 5th ed.* Boston: Allyn and Bacon, p. 29.

2. Gerald M. Phillips (1968). "Reticence: Pathology of the normal speaker," *Speech Monographs* 35(1):39-49. See also: Virginia P. Richmond and K. David Roach (1992). "Willingness to communicate and employee success in U.S. organizations," *Journal of Applied Communication Research* 20(1):95-115.

3. Philip G. Zimbardo (1977). "Understanding shyness," in *Shyness: What it is, what to do about it.* Reading, MA: Addison-Wesley, pp. 9-21.

Causes of quietness

Trait-like Causes. There are several "trait-like" or inborn reasons why a person might be shy or quiet, and the reasons vary from person to person. Heredity and expectancy learning seem to be the primary reasons.

Heredity. One look at your parents or grandparents is evidence of where you inherited traits such as height, eye color, hair color, tendencies to gain or lose weight and so on. Heredity or the "genetic" component of quietness was not thought to be important in early research. Recently, researchers have established that certain social traits can be measured in very young infants. For example, "sociability" or the tendency to be more outgoing, can be measured in infants within the first few weeks of birth. Social babies tend to smile more, look more, engage more in eye contact, move more and respond to others more readily. In other words, they seem more outgoing. These infants might become gregarious, talkative children.

While the research is fairly recent, the idea that heredity can have a major impact on one's willingness to talk verses one's tendency to be quiet simply cannot be disregarded. Predispositions to talk or be quiet can certainly preprogram a child toward a certain level of communication. However, while heredity probably plays an important role in willingness to communicate, it is only one explanation.

Expectancy Learning. This concept posits that people seek to learn what consequences are likely to occur as a function of their behaviors (what to expect) and then try to adapt their behaviors so they can increase positive outcomes and avoid negative outcomes. In other words, behavior choices are made on the basis of the expectations of others in the environment.

For example, if people learn that the more they talk in class, the more the teacher rewards them, then the more likely they are to increase their talking behavior. In fact, some teachers give a portion of the class grade on "class participation." Talkative students know the expectations, so they talk. Quiet students know the expectations but often cannot meet them so they attempt to excel in other ways.

Exercise 1:

List the expectations that your teacher has for you in terms of speaking up. Then list how you can meet these expectations. If you are not quiet, listing ideas on how to meet your teacher's expectations is easy, but not so if you are quiet.

Therefore, regardless of your usual talkativeness, list **other** ways (**besides speaking**) that you might be able to meet the expectations. Use this chart to help you organize your ideas:

Expectancy Learning

<u>What my teacher expects</u>   <u>How I can meet these expectations</u>

1.

2.

3.

4.

Related to expectancy learning is a phenomenon called **learned helplessness**. In many areas of life people learn solid expectations that are continually reinforced, but not in all areas. When people cannot determine the expectations and the corresponding reinforcement, they simply become *helpless* and *do nothing*. Some people encounter communication situations with no clear expectations and no clear reinforcement. No matter how they communicate, they cannot learn to predict other's expectations, so they become quiet because this is the only safe reaction.

Much of this learned helplessness is created by inconsistent reinforcement. For example, one day a child is encouraged to talk during dinner, scolded the next two days, praised the fourth. Erratic reinforcement patterns for communication can make children avoid communicating. Lacking a consistent pattern of reinforcement for communicating, children will frequently become quiet as a means of *not doing*.

People are often unable to identify the situational differences that produce different response from others even though their own communication behaviors are the same. They become *helpless*, and the only solution for them is to withdraw from communication and become quiet. Withdrawal is characteristic of highly quiet people, who often report feeling helpless in communication situations.

Situational Causes. The several causes of situational quietness can vary from one person to another or from one situation to another. It is the situation, not the trait-like factor, that produces quietness. Here only the primary causes of situational quietness are reviewed, using the major causes of shyness or apprehension: **novelty, formality, subordinate status, conspicuousness, unfamiliarity, dissimilarity, degree of attention from others, degree of evaluation and prior history.**[4]

• **Novel** situations cause most people to be somewhat quiet because they don't know how to communicate. For example, attending a banquet and dance with your date and your date's parents might contribute to your quietness. The novelty, unpredictability and uncertainty of the situation caused the quietness.

• **Formal** situations increase quietness because there is a narrow range of expected deviation from the norm. For example, attending a dinner at the White House has a very formal, even strict, protocol. Most people would remain quiet and observe the appropriate communication behaviors before speaking.

• **Subordinate status** occurs when one person has "higher status" than another person. This higher status can take many forms such as title, rank, age, competence and so on. For example, last-semester seniors in college tend to have higher status than any other group of students. So a sophomore who is spending time with graduating seniors may be quieter than normal.

• Feeling **conspicuous** can cause a person to become quiet. For example, if a student is invited to an instructor's home for a gathering, and spills red wine all over the new cream-colored carpet, the student would feel conspicuous. Almost nothing makes people become quiet more than being the most prominent, observable person in a room full of people.

• When people are **unfamiliar** with the norms, rules or procedures in a system, they tend to become quiet. Often in unfamiliar surroundings people will wait to communicate until they have more familiarity and knowledge about how things work. This is often the case on a new job. Many people in their first six months find the new work environment completely unfamiliar (almost foreign), so they will do a lot of watching, listening, learning, and little talking.

• **Dissimilarity** is an extension of unfamiliarity. The more dissimilar a person is to others or with a situation, the more difficulty that person will have communicating. Often the person simply becomes quiet.

_____

4. Arnold Buss (1980). *Self-consciousness and social anxiety.* San Francisco: W.H. Freeman. See also: John A. Daly and Joy Lynn Hailey (1984). "Putting the situation into writing research: State and disposition as parameters of writing apprehension," in Richard Beach and Lillian S. Bridwell, eds. *New directions in composition research.* New York: Guilford Press, pp. 259-273.

- **Excessive attention** is when a person becomes the center or focus of attention. This situation usually makes the person very uncomfortable and causes the person to become very quiet and withdrawn. Most people like a moderate but not an excessive amount of attention. How would you feel if asked to give an impromptu speech in front of a class of 100 students? Excessive attention differs from conspicuousness in that excessive attention is being put in the "hot seat" or given an unusual amount of attention. Excessive attention can contribute to feelings of conspicuousness, but excessive attention is not the same as feeling conspicuous.

- The degree to which people feel they are **being evaluated** by others can cause them to become anxious and quiet. For example, when you are giving that impromptu speech and the instructor is sitting in your line of vision completing the evaluation form, you are likely to try to finish quickly, sit down and be very quiet.

- If people have a **prior history** of failure when communicating with a certain person, group or in a certain situation, the quietness and even anxiety may increase when confronting that person, group or situation. If there is a family member with whom you have rarely had a positive conversation, then when that person is present, based on prior history, you might remain quiet.

Exercise 2:

Think of two communication situations that interfered with your normal behavior. Write a brief paragraph about each and discuss your behaviors during the two situations. How might you have reduced your fear in each of these situations?

Quiet people's behaviors and outcomes

School environment. The school is a major communication environment in which the behavior of quiet students differs distinctly from the not-so-quiet. Here is a summary of findings about the differences between quiet and not-so-quiet students in school environments:

- When given a choice about which classes to take, quiet students tend to avoid small-enrollment classes in favor of larger, lecture-type classes where students simply listen and take notes. Highly verbal students prefer small-enrollment classes where there is opportunity for students to interact with each other and the teacher.

- Quiet students avoid classes that require oral reports, speeches and have class participation as part of the grade. Talkative students seek out these classes.

- Once enrolled in a class, the student is assumed to simply accept the communication requirements of the teacher. This is not the case for quiet students.

If possible, they will drop a class that requires high communication (taking it only for graduation), be absent on days they are scheduled for presentations, or find another way not to talk in front of the class. Even in primary grades with "show and tell" or book reports, quiet children find ways to avoid these activities. Generally, high talkers thoroughly enjoy most of the opportunities to talk in the classroom.

• Where a person chooses to sit in a classroom also reflects the person's level of quietness. In a traditional classroom setup, quiet students tend to sit along the sides and rear of the room (the areas best suited to hiding), whereas talkative students tend to sit in the front and center of the first few rows.

• Quiet students may be less likely to complete the standard four-to-five-year college program and be a greater drop-out risk than more talkative students.

• Type and amount of participation in the class and group discussions are both affected by level of quietness. Quiet students almost never volunteer to participate, or speak up, even if part of the grade depends on this type of communication. When called upon, they may willingly give a wrong answer, ignore the teacher or classmate talking to them, or say "I don't know" because these responses will decrease their chances of being called upon at a later date.

• When a quiet student is told to expect to **relay content** (talk about course content) to another student, the quiet student focuses on the impending communication act, not the content. Their fear of communication prevents quiet students from recalling major portions of the content.

• In small-group discussions in the classroom, quiet students typically avoid participating at all or sit rather quietly in the group, if they must be present. Talkative students enjoy such experiences, participate fully or even dominate the group. They often are group leaders, whereas quiet students try to avoid this role.

• When students are required to work with their peers and asked to evaluate other students, the talkative students fare well. Quiet students often get lower ratings in terms of social and task attractiveness, competence, character, leadership potential, and are generally perceived as less appealing people with whom to work.

• Quiet students are less likely to be **assertive** (speak up for themselves) and **responsive** (approachable) in the classroom. Talkative students are more likely to be assertive, perhaps even aggressive, and responsive in the classroom.

In the school environment, then, students who are quiet have very different behaviors from those who are talkative. Such behaviors have a direct effect on how quiet students are viewed. Based on the above depictions, there are very few positive outcomes in the classroom setting for the quiet student in contrast to the talkative student. While there may be some positive qualities (quiet students are less likely to get into trouble with the teacher), most of the effects are negative.

Quiet students receive less help and attention from teachers, ask fewer questions, talk less to clarify things they don't understand, have fewer opportunities to speak to the teacher, have fewer friends and fewer opportunities for learning compared to more talkative students. Given these obstacles, quiet students are perceived as nice, but perhaps a little slow or lazy. Teachers also perceive them as having lower self-confidence, being less interested in content, less competent, less approachable, less friendly, less attractive and less likely to perform well in school.[5]

Social environment. The social environment is another major communication setting in which quiet people's behavior differs distinctly from the not-so-quiet. Following is a summary of the findings about the differences between quiet and not-so-quiet people in the social environment:

• In general, quiet people are less involved in social functions and activities, and they tend to have far fewer people they refer to as friends.

• While the quiet and talkative person may have an equal desire for social relationships, the talkative person has more than twice as many dates in a given time than the quiet person. Talkative people date more than one person; quiet people tend to be exclusive-relationship oriented.

• Quiet persons are less venturesome than talkative persons. They are less likely to frequent singles bars or attend after-game parties. Quiet people are less likely to approach others in a social context, while talkative people "work the room."

• Quiet persons are more likely to marry sooner than talkative persons.

Obviously, quiet people will fare less well in social environments. Quiet persons have difficulty establishing and maintaining social relationships. They may be perceived by other people as less approachable (somewhat cold even) and less attractive in social contexts. Quiet persons often report being unhappy or dissatisfied with their social relationships but do not know how to change the relationship. However, quiet people may find it easier to maintain a social relationship that is not completely acceptable to them. More verbal people "want out now!"

---

5. Michael J. Beatty and Ralph R. Behnke (1980). "An assimilation theory perspective of communication apprehension," *Human Communication Research* 6(4):319-325. See also: James C. McCroskey (1977). "Oral communication apprehension: A summary of recent theory and research," *Human Communication Research* 4(1):78-96.

Work environment. The work environment is probably the last well-studied communication environment in which behavior of quiet people differs distinctly from the not-so-quiet individuals. Following is a summary of work-place findings:

• Quiet people tend to choose occupations with low communication demands, while talkative people choose occupations that require communication.

• Quiet people are less likely to be offered a job interview than are talkative people. To be referred to as "a nice, quiet individual" may be the kiss of death in terms of job interviews, unless the job is designed specifically for a quiet person.

• During an interview, quiet people may not interview well. They talk less, give less information about themselves and initiate less in the interview process, often making their interviewer uncomfortable. Interviewers get the impression that they know too little about the quiet person. Talkative people are much more likely to make positive impressions in the interview situation, however, talkative people may substantially over-talk, or disclose negative information about themselves.

• Quiet people do obtain employment, but the positions they obtain typically provide lower status and pay than positions obtained by more talkative people.

• Quiet people are less likely to be assertive and stand up for themselves on the job than talkative people. They are less likely to be perceived as **task attractive**, or a person others would want to work with in a group. Quiet people report lower satisfaction with their jobs than do talkative people.

• Quiet people are less likely to be promoted. If promoted to a higher-status position that demands more talking, quiet persons are usually dissatisfied. If quiet persons become supervisors, they may be unhappy as may be their employees. Quiet people may hide in their offices, avoiding work-place interaction.

• When employers must "down-size, " they would rather fire the quiet person than the talkative person. The quiet person will usually go quietly; the talkative person won't. In fact, the talkative person may even initiate a lawsuit.

Obviously, effective communication is required to obtain and retain a job. Quiet people often are "last to be hired, first to be fired." Talkative people find it easier to obtain quality employment, tend to be successful in their work, are likely to be promoted and retained, and tend to be more satisfied with their work.[6]

---

6. Joe Ayres and Steve Crosby (1995). "Two studies concerning the predictive validity of the personal report of communication apprehension in employment interviews," *Communication Research Reports* 12(2):145-151.

From the effects outlined about school, social and work environments, it is possible to offer a profile of the talkative person and the quiet person.[7] Talkative people are more likely to be successful in school, to establish good social relationships and to be successful in the work world. Quiet people are less likely to be successful in school, have difficulty establishing and maintaining social relationships, and have difficulty obtaining and retaining employment.

Summary

Several generalizations about the behaviors of quiet vs. nonquiet persons in school, social and work environments are reviewed in this chapter.

In school, quiet persons tend to **avoid** classes that require high interaction and small-group discussion. When quiet people do communicate in either situation, their comments may be irrelevant. They sit where interaction demands are low.

In occupations and social life, quieter persons may select jobs that require little communication with others, date less often than others and marry early. Quiet people are often perceived by others as less interpersonally competent, less communicatively assertive and responsive, possessing fewer communication skills, less likely to be a leader, more anxious, and less socially and task attractive than talkative persons.

Overall, the **talkative** person is *more likely to be successful* in the school environment; to establish good social, task and interpersonal relationships; and to be more successful in the work world. The **quiet** person is *less likely to be successful* in school, have difficulty establishing and keeping good interpersonal relationships, and have difficulty obtaining and retaining solid employment in the work world.

Exercises:

A. Write a job recommendation for yourself that you would like your teacher, friend or supervisor (if you are employed) to write about you. Emphasize your positive "people" skills, communication competencies and communication qualifications. Remember that obtaining an interview and subsequently a good job depends on being able to sell yourself as an effective communicator.

---

7. John A. Daly and Laura Stafford (1984). "Correlates and consequences of social-communicative anxiety," in John A. Daly and James C. McCroskey, eds. *Avoiding communication: Shyness, reticence, and communication apprehension*. Beverly Hills, CA: Sage, pp. 125-143. See also: Virginia P. Richmond (1997). "Quietness in contemporary society: Conclusions and generalizations of the research," in John A. Daly, James C. McCroskey, Joe Ayres, Tim Hopf and Debbie M. Ayres, eds. *Avoiding communication: Shyness, reticence, and communication apprehension, 2nd ed.* Cresskill, NJ: Hampton Press, pp. 257-268.

B. Complete the following measure. Your teacher will give you more information about the kind of scale scores people receive and the meaning behind the score.

Shyness Scale

Directions: The following 14 statements refer to talking with other people. If the statement describes you very well, circle "YES." If it somewhat describes you, circle "yes." If you are not sure whether or not it describes you, or if you do not understand the statement, circle "?." If it somewhat does not describe you, circle "no." If the statement is a very poor description of you, circle "NO." There are no right or wrong answers. **Record your first impression.**

1. I am a shy person.	YES	yes	?	no	NO
2. Other people think I talk a lot.	YES	yes	?	no	NO
3. I am a very talkative person.	YES	yes	?	no	NO
4. Other people think I am shy.	YES	yes	?	no	NO
5. I talk a lot.	YES	yes	?	no	NO
6. I tend to be very quiet in class.	YES	yes	?	no	NO
7. I don't talk much.	YES	yes	?	no	NO
8. I talk more than most people	YES	yes	?	no	NO
9. I am a quiet person.	YES	yes	?	no	NO
10. I talk more in a small group (3-6) than others do.	YES	yes	?	no	NO
11. Most people talk more than I do.	YES	yes	?	no	NO
12. Other people think I am very quiet.	YES	yes	?	no	NO
13. I talk more in class than most people do.	YES	yes	?	no	NO
14. Most people are more shy than I am.	YES	yes	?	no	NO

Scoring: YES = 1, yes = 2, ? = 3, no = 4, NO = 5.

Please score your responses as follows:
Step 1. Add the scores for items 1, 4, 6, 7, 9, 11 and 12: _____
Step 2. Add the scores for items 2, 3, 5, 8, 10, 13 and 14: _____
Step 3. Complete the following formula:
        Shyness = (42 + Total of Step 2) – (Total of Step 1): _____

Figure 1. Shyness Scale[8]

8. Virginia P. Richmond and James C. McCroskey (1997). *op. cit.*

9
Communication Competence

Early article: John M. Wiemann (1977). "Explication and test of a model of communicative competence," *Human Communication Research* 3(3):195-213.

Contemporary article: Kathy Kellermann (1992). "Communication: Inherently strategic and primarily automatic," *Communication Monographs* 59(3):288-300.

Defining communication competence may be as difficult as defining pornography. We know pornography when we see it, and we know an incompetent communicator when we hear one. But there isn't one specific way to be a competent communicator.

Many researchers have tried to define communication competence.[1] This chapter aims at a definition at the basic level: Communicatively competent persons have "adequate ability to make ideas known to others by talking or writing."[2] If others understand what a person is saying or writing, then that person is competent. This means that many effective communication styles exist for different people.

Communication competence depends on three components: 1) understanding the communication process, 2) the capacity to produce necessary verbal and/or nonverbal communication behaviors, and 3) a positive affective orientation toward communication. Thus, competent communicators must: 1) understand what needs to be done, 2) develop behaviors necessary to produce a message (write, articulate), and 3 have concern and caring toward communication.

---

1. Some of the attempts at defining communication competence are offered by: David W. Merrill and Roger H. Reid (1981). *Personal styles and effective performance: Make your style work for you.* Radnor, PA: Chilton Book; James C. McCroskey (1982). "Communication competence and performance: A research and pedagogical perspective," *Communication Education* 31(1):1-7; Robert Norton (1983). *Communicator style: Theory, applications, and measures.* Beverly Hills, CA: Sage Publications; James C. McCroskey (1984). "Communication competence: The elusive construct," in Robert N. Bostrom, ed. *Competence in communication: A multidisciplinary approach.* Beverly Hills, CA: Sage Publications, pp. 259-268; Virginia P. Richmond and James C. McCroskey (1990). "Reliability and separation of factors on the assertiveness-responsiveness measure," *Psychological Reports* 67(2):449-450.

2. James C. McCroskey (1984), *op. cit.*, p. 263.

If any of the three conditions is not met, communication may not be effective. However, the *affective orientation* of the source is critical to the process. A source can **understand** what needs to be done and have or learn the **skills** needed to communicate a message, but the source must be positively predisposed toward communication if it is to be effective. Some corporate executives understand the communication process, have the skills to write or speak, but simply do not care about the process. Their communication is less than effective for their employees and the public.

A real case was a teacher who understood and had communication skills, but lacked feelings about communication. Walking into class, rarely looking at the class, the teacher read lecture notes to students for exactly 50 minutes and walked out. If a student interrupted to ask a question, the teacher would simply say, "Read the text and you'll know." Students didn't do well in the class. They knew the teacher didn't care about communicating effectively with them. They thought the teacher should care: This was a class in interpersonal communication competence.

Those reading this text are likely to have developed sufficient skills to communicate effectively. They have a positive attitude toward communication. Thus, their greatest need when beginning this chapter was a better understanding of the communication process.[3] Three critical elements that lead to being a more competent communicator are: assertiveness, responsiveness and versatility.

Exercise 1:

Before continuing, complete the Socio-Communicative Orientation (SCO) measure in Figure 1. Compute your scores as shown at the bottom of the figure. Your teacher will help interpret your scores.

Communication and assertiveness

Assertiveness is the capability to firmly and in a self-assured manner state beliefs and attitudes, take a stand, actively disagree, present arguments in a confident manner, express positive or negative feelings, stand up for oneself without attacking another person, and initiate, maintain and disengage from communication.

---

3. Arthur P. Bochner and Clifford W. Kelly (1974). "Interpersonal competence: Rationale, philosophy, and implementation of a conceptual framework," *Speech Teacher* 23(4):279-301. See also: Robert L. Duran (1992). "Communicative adaptability: A review of conceptualization and measurement," *Communication Quarterly* 40(3):253-268; Robert W. Norton (1978). "Foundation of a communicator style construct," *Human Communication Research* 4(2):99-112; Brian H. Spitzberg and Michael L. Hecht (1984). "A component model of relational competence," *Human Communication Research* 10(4):575-599; Charles R. Berger (1975). "Proactive and retroactive attribution processes in interpersonal communications," *Human Communication Research* 2(1):33-50.

Socio-Communicative Orientation

Directions: This questionnaire lists 20 personality characteristics. Please indicate the degree to which you believe each of these characteristics applies to **YOU**, as you normally communicate with others, by marking whether you (5) strongly agree that it applies, (4) agree that it applies, (3) are undecided, (2) disagree that it applies or (1) strongly disagree that it applies. There are no right or wrong answers. Work quickly; **record your first impression**.

	Strongly agree				Strongly disagree
1. helpful	5	4	3	2	1
2. defend own beliefs	5	4	3	2	1
3. independent	5	4	3	2	1
4. responsive to others	5	4	3	2	1
5. forceful	5	4	3	2	1
6. has strong personality	5	4	3	2	1
7. sympathetic	5	4	3	2	1
8. compassionate	5	4	3	2	1
9. assertive	5	4	3	2	1
10. sensitive to needs of others	5	4	3	2	1
11. dominant	5	4	3	2	1
12. sincere	5	4	3	2	1
13. gentle	5	4	3	2	1
14. willing to take a stand	5	4	3	2	1
15. warm	5	4	3	2	1
16. tender	5	4	3	2	1
17. friendly	5	4	3	2	1
18. act as a leader	5	4	3	2	1
19. aggressive	5	4	3	2	1
20. competitive	5	4	3	2	1

Items 2, 3, 5, 6, 9, 11, 14, 19 and 20 measure assertiveness. Add the scores on these items to get your assetiveness score. Items 1, 4, 7, 8, 10, 12, 13, 15, 16 and 17 measure responsiveness. Add the scores on these items to get your responsiveness score.

Figure 1. Socio-Communicative Orientation scale

In Bem's 1974 research,[4] these assertiveness communication aspects are termed **masculinity**. Although not only males exhibit assertive behaviors, in many societies the stereotype of appropriate male communication is masculinity. Terms used to describe a person who engages in assertive communication behaviors include: defends own beliefs, independent, forceful, strong personality, dominant, willing to take a stand, a leader and competitive. These terms often denote the stereotypical American male image, but more importantly they describe a person who is in control both of self and the communication process.

The terms **assertiveness** and **aggressiveness** must be differentiated. These two terms are not the same concept. Aggressiveness is assertiveness-plus or *beyond assertiveness*. Aggressiveness refers to people who not only stand up for their beliefs, but also attack, assault and demand that others yield to them and their ideas. Other terms to describe aggressive people are: quarrelsome, demanding, outspoken, threatening, overbearing, outspoken, hostile, contentious, domineering, belligerent and pushy.

Assertive people make *requests*; aggressive people make *demands*. Assertive individuals insist that others respect their rights. Aggressive individuals demand that others submit to them and their views, often attempting to take away or ignore the rights of others. Clearly, either assertiveness or aggressiveness helps people get their way. In communicating, however, assertive people maintain positive relationships while aggressive people often destroy relationships and alienate others. Thus, a communication-competent person must be assertive but not aggressive.

Communication and responsiveness

Responsiveness is the capability to be sensitive and understanding of others, to be a good listener, to make others comfortable, and recognize their needs and desires. Bem terms this communication aspect **femininity**.[5] Again, not only females exhibit responsive behaviors, but many societies' stereotype of appropriate female communication is femininity. Terms that commonly describe a person who engages in responsive communication behaviors include: helpful, sympathetic, compassionate, sensitive to other's needs, sincere, gentle, warm, tender and friendly. These terms describe stereotypical female images in American society, but they also describe a person who is open and empathic to the communication of others.

Often people assume that **responsiveness** and **submissiveness** are the same concept. They are not the same.

---

4. Sandra L. Bem (1974). "The measurement of psychological androgyny," *Journal of Consulting and Clinical Psychology* 42(2):155-162.
    5. *Ibid.*

Responsive people are amiable, agreeable, amenable, attentive, mindful, open and understanding of other's feelings. Submissiveness is responsiveness-plus or *beyond responsiveness*. Submissiveness refers to a person who is compliant and docile, acquiescent, meek, obsequious, malleable, pliable and yielding. Responsive persons *recognize* and *understand* the feelings of the other person. Submissive persons understand the feelings of others but yield to the others' requests even if those requests contradict their own needs and feelings.

Either responsiveness or submissiveness will evoke liking from another person and thereby improve communication. However, the responsive person is likely to maintain the respect and consideration of others. Submissive people may not be respected, and they regularly agree to ideas at the cost of their own well-being. Thus, a communication-competent person must be responsive but not submissive.

Communication competence and androgyny

As noted in Section 1 of Figure 2, persons considered the most competent communicators have high assertiveness and responsiveness. They are called **androgynous**,[6] meaning they exhibit both masculine (assertive) and feminine (responsive) behaviors. Section 4 includes those persons considered least likely to be competent, referred to as **undifferentiated**. Rarely exhibiting either assertive or responsive behaviors, they are often very quiet and submissive.

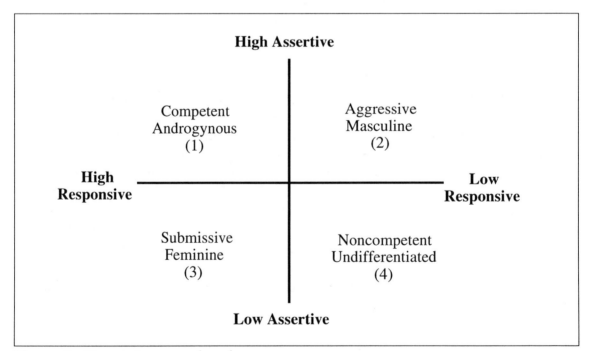

Figure 2. Competence and androgyny

---

6. Bem, *op. cit.*

Sections 2 and 3 include people who characteristically are either assertive or responsive, but not both. People classified into these two sections are **partially competent**. Section 2 has Bem's aggressive/masculine people who are highly assertive but lack responsiveness. They stand up for themselves but lack concern for others. Section 3 has submissive/feminine people who are highly responsive but lack assertiveness. They respond to other's needs and desires but are unable to stand up for themselves.

While much of communication has a genetic component, the contextual component cannot be forgotten. In general, people who are assertive, responsive, undifferentiated or androgynous will usually communicate with their primary Socio-Communicative Orientation. However, the competent communicator can do more than just be assertive or responsive.

Sometimes being assertive might cost a person a job. Sometimes being responsive might attract the wrong type of people. While the androgynous person has the best chance to be competent, there is no guarantee that this type of person will be competent in all communication contexts. And, the undifferentiated person might occasionally behave in an appropriate manner in some contexts.

Communication and versatility

The critical element in communication competence is **versatility** or the capacity to be *appropriately* assertive and *appropriately* responsive depending on the context.[7] Terms that describe the versatile communicator are: adaptable, accommodating, changeable, flexible, multifaceted and open-minded. Terms for those who lack the ability to be versatile communicators are: inflexible, rigid, unaccommodating, obstinate, bullheaded, headstrong, uncompromising, stubborn and unyielding.

Versatile, competent communicators are those persons who are constantly attempting to adapt their communication to the person and the context. Adapting is much easier for people with less rigid personality orientations. Versatile communicators work at communication, study communication (both on a formal and informal basis), and learn from their communication errors. Also these persons are concerned about their communication with others, so they make attempts to be adaptable and flexible.[8]

7. James C. McCroskey and Virginia P. Richmond (1996). *Fundamentals of human communication: An interpersonal perspective*. Prospect Heights, IL: Waveland.

8. John M. Wiemann and Philip Backlund (1980). "Current theory and research in communicative competence," *Review of Educational Research* 50(1):185-199. See also: Candice Thomas, Virginia P. Richmond and James C. McCroskey (1994). "The association between immediacy and socio-communicative style," *Communication Research Reports* 11:107-114.

Socio-Communicative Style Questionnaire

Directions: This questionnaire lists 20 personality characteristics. Please indicate the degree to which you believe each of these characteristics applies to **THE PERSON WHO HANDED YOU THIS QUESTIONNAIRE**, as that person normally communicates with others, by marking whether you (5) strongly agree that it applies, (4) agree that it applies, (3) are undecided, (2) disagree that it applies or (1) strongly disagree that it applies. Work quickly; **try to give an honest assessment of your impression of this person's communication characteristics.**

	Strongly agree				Strongly disagree
1. is helpful	5	4	3	2	1
2. defend own beliefs	5	4	3	2	1
3. acts independent	5	4	3	2	1
4. is responsive to others	5	4	3	2	1
5. is forceful	5	4	3	2	1
6. has strong personality	5	4	3	2	1
7. acts sympathetic	5	4	3	2	1
8. is compassionate	5	4	3	2	1
9. acts assertive	5	4	3	2	1
10. sensitive to needs of others	5	4	3	2	1
11. acts dominant	5	4	3	2	1
12. is sincere	5	4	3	2	1
13. is gentle	5	4	3	2	1
14. is willing to take a stand	5	4	3	2	1
15. is warm	5	4	3	2	1
16. is tender	5	4	3	2	1
17. acts friendly	5	4	3	2	1
18. acts as a leader	5	4	3	2	1
19. is aggressive	5	4	3	2	1
20. is competitive	5	4	3	2	1

Figure 3. Socio-Communicative Style questionnaire

Exercise 2:

Now, take a look at Figure 3. You should duplicate and give this measure to a half dozen people you know well, other than your best friends or family. Notice that this measure is very similar to Figure 1. Rather than representing your perception of yourself, this is a measure of other people's perception of you. Score each returned form using Figure 1's scoring method. Total the scores for all questionnaires, then divide by the number of returned questionnaires to average the scores.

This measure is the Socio-Communicative Style (SCS). SCO was the way you see yourself; SCS is the way others see you. If your SCO and others' SCS of you are very similar, then communication is probably fairly easy between you and people you know well. However, if there are great differences between your SCO and others' SCS of you, there is probably some friction in the communication process. You may want to talk to the people who completed the SCS of you and gain insight into why they see you the way they reported. If you want to become a more competent communicator, read on to learn how to make improvements.

Becoming a competent, versatile communicator

Communicating effectively with different people on different topics and at different times requires versatility and flexible communication behaviors. These suggestions assume that a person wants to change and is capable of change.

• **Observe versatile communicators**: Study the context or situation, determine what style of communication to use and adapt accordingly. Listen carefully to what others are saying. When it is your turn to talk, begin with what was said last.

• **Keep using your best communication qualities**: Assertive people believe that if they stop being assertive they will become responsive. They will only become less assertive and nonresponsive, which puts them in the undifferentiated category. Undifferentiated group people will find it easier to work toward responsiveness.

• **Nonverbal cues**: Use positive, attentive nonverbal cues when communicating. Positive head nods, smiling and so forth makes communication easier. Look at people when speaking to them. Nonverbal behaviors should reinforce verbal communication to avoid sending conflicting cues. Try to seem comfortable with yourself while talking. Eliminate any *nervous mannerisms* you have when speaking.

• **Communicate in an articulate manner**: Pronounce words correctly or substitute others. Words must be spoken clearly. Avoid using disclaimers such as, "I am not sure but...." Become a fluent communicator whose speech flows smoothly. Repetitions of sounds or vocalized pauses such as, "you know," "er," "ahhh," "like," "well ahhh," interrupt the flow of speech.

• **Voice control**: Use a voice that has some vocal variety. Nothing is more ineffective than a tone that sounds dull, uninterested or listless. Monotony bores; variety keeps people interested. Maintain a conversational quality. Voice volume should be neither too loud nor too soft.

• **Word choice**: Use words that encourage others to communicate. The words "we" or "us" implies joint ownership; "I" and "you" means only one. Verbal messages that encourage openness or that designate friendship increase the perception of your communication competence. Always use the other person's name to indicate that you care about the person or that you remembered the name. Use terms that your receiver will understand. Use positive words that evoke positive orientations.

Finally, practice. This does not mean standing in front of a group and giving a formal presentation. Most people only make public presentations on a few occasions, but they communicate daily with many people in many contexts. Select a context in which you'd like to be perceived as more competent, and practice.

Summary

Effective communicators exhibit three important elements in their communication: assertiveness, responsiveness and versatility. **Assertiveness** is the capacity to make requests, actively disagree, express feelings, initiate, maintain or disengage from communication. It is the ability to *stand up for oneself without attacking another*. **Responsiveness** is the capacity to be *sensitive to the communication of others*. It is being a good listener, recognizing and responding to others' needs and desires.

Versatility is the final important characteristic of the effective communicator. It is the capacity to be *appropriately assertive and appropriately responsive, depending on the situation*. People who are versatile in their communication behaviors can be described as accommodating, adaptable and willing to adjust. People not exhibiting communication versatility are often described as rigid, inflexible and unyielding.

Exercises:

A. The competent communicator must learn to be versatile. In a one-page essay, 1) describe a communication situation in which you know you were incompetent and 2) describe how you should have communicated.

B. In groups, list ten people you consider competent communicators. What are their common characteristics? How do these characteristics relate to issues presented in this chapter?

10

Perceptions of the Source

Early article: Kenneth Andersen and Theodore Clevenger Jr. (1963). "A summary of experimental research in ethos," *Speech Monographs 30*(3):59-78.

Recent Article: Mark Douglas West (1994). "Validating a scale for the measurement of credibility: A covariance structure modeling approach," *Journalism Quarterly 71*(1):159-168.

Perceptions of the source are fundamental concepts in the human communication process. If a receiver's perceptions of the source are positive, the receiver is more likely to listen and retain information given by the source. If the receiver's perceptions are negative, the source's information will be ignored.

Quite simply, a receiver's judgment of the content of communication depends on the receiver's view of the source. This principle holds true for all messages. For example, radio talk show hosts, television personalities, newspaper columnists, motivational speakers, candidates, parents, teachers, supervisors, enemies and best friends are only a few of the sources who send messages. The person who delivers the message affects how receivers perceive or create meaning from message content.

This chapter focuses on the image, perception or attitude toward the source and how source perception influences communication. Three categories of perceptions that human communication scholars have been using for more than 60 years are reviewed. These are source credibility, interpersonal attraction and homophily.[1]

---

1. James C. McCroskey and Thomas J. Young (1981). "Ethos and credibility: The construct and its measurement after three decades," *Central States Speech Journal 32*(1):24-34. See also: Charles C. Self (1996). "Credibility," in Michael B. Salwen and Don W. Stacks, eds. *An integrated approach to communication theory and research*. Mahwah, NJ: Lawrence Erlbaum Associates, pp. 421-441; Keith Stamm and Ric Dube (1994). "The relationship of attitudinal components to trust in media," *Communication Research 21*(1):105-123.

Ethos or source credibility

Great philosophers, writers and rhetoricians such as Aristotle, Cicero, Plato and Quintillion were aware that the image or **ethos** of a source had a major influence on a message's impact. According to McCroskey, "ethos is the attitude toward a source of communication held at a given time by a receiver."[2] Berlo, Lemert and Mertz offered three ethos dimensions: competence, trust-worthiness and dynamism.[3] Other researchers identified two ethos dimensions: competence and character.[4]

The **competence** dimension of source credibility is the degree to which receivers perceive a source to be knowledgeable about content or an expert in a content area. A source can be perceived from completely incompetent to completely competent. If a receiver thinks a source is competent, then the receiver is more likely to listen, learn and be persuaded; if perceived as incompetent, listening, learning and persuasion will not occur. Receivers simply avoid exposure to a source who is viewed as incompetent.

The **character** dimension of source credibility refers to the degree to which receivers perceive a source to be trustworthy or honest about what the source knows. A source can be perceived as completely untrustworthy to completely trustworthy. If a source is perceived as honest and trustworthy, the receiver is more likely to listen, learn and be persuaded.

To be perceived as credible and believable, a source must establish high credibility with receivers through competence and character. Credibility perceptions are one set of source perceptions that influence a receiver's attitudes about a source.[5] Another fundamental set of perceptions relates to the source's attractiveness.

Interpersonal attraction

Like credibility, interpersonal attraction is a multidimensional construct. McCroskey and McCain posited three dimensions of interpersonal attraction as physical, social and task attraction.[6]

---

2. James C. McCroskey (1996). "Ethos: A dominant factor in rhetorical communication," in *An introduction to rhetorical communication, 7th ed*. Boston: Allyn and Bacon, p. 87.

3. David K. Berlo, James B. Lemert and Robert J. Mertz (1969-1970). "Dimensions for evaluating the acceptability of message sources," *Public Opinion Quarterly* 33(4):563-576.

4. James C. McCroskey and Robert E. Dunham (1966). "Ethos: A confounding element in communication research," *Speech Monographs* 33(4):456-463. See also: James C. McCroskey (1966). "Scales for the measurement of ethos," *Speech Monographs* 33(1):65-72.

5. David K. Berlo and James B. Lemert (1961). "A factor analytic study of the dimensions of source credibility." Paper presented at the Speech Communication Association of America Convention, New York.

6. James C. McCroskey and Thomas A. McCain (1974). "The measurement of interpersonal attraction," *Speech Monographs* 41(3):261-266.

A source's physical appearance can influence how the source is perceived by the receiver. **Physical attractiveness** is a perception that can vary from person to person or from one culture to another. Although some generalizable norms exist across cultures, each has norms for what is attractive and what is not. For example, in this culture persons with poor dental hygiene (e.g., yellow teeth) are perceived as less physically attractive, whereas this physical attribute may not be an issue in other cultures. Physical appearance and attractiveness do not guarantee that receivers will listen and learn from a source, but negative physical attractiveness almost guarantees that receivers will not be influenced.

Social attractiveness refers to the degree to which a receiver perceives a source to be someone with whom the receiver would like to spend time and socialize. Social attractiveness is not based on physical attractiveness, although physical attractiveness might initially attract one person to another. Social attractiveness is based primarily on how friendly, outgoing and personable the source is perceived to be by the receiver. This is the likeability factor of the interpersonal attraction. When receivers **like** or find a source to be socially attractive, then the receiver is more likely to listen and learn from the source.

Task attractiveness refers to how much a receiver perceives a source to be someone with whom the receiver would like to establish a working relationship. A sources who is task attractive is confident, easy to work with, properly prepared and gets things accomplished. Initially, receivers may assume that if a source is physically attractive or socially attractive, then the source is task attractive. However, some physically and socially attractive people are not task-oriented and thus not viewed as task attractive by receivers.

Typically, no matter how physically or socially attractive a source is perceived to be, if the source is lazy or not task-oriented, then the receiver will lose task attractiveness for the source. For example, a "great looking person" could have physical attraction but be boring or dull. Or this "great looking person" could have social attraction but be disorganized and lazy.

Receivers, then, can be attracted to a source based on one, two or all three dimensions of interpersonal attraction. The three dimensions are **independent of one another**. A source could be perceived to have high social attractiveness but low task attraction, or to have high physical attractiveness but low social or task attractiveness. However, if a source is physically pleasant, socially skilled and task oriented, then generally a receiver will listen, learn and be persuaded by that source.

John F. Kennedy was perceived by many as physically, socially and task attractive. Mel Gibson, Brooke Shields and Denzel Washington are contemporary public figures who may be perceived in the same manner as JFK.

Exercise:
Make three lists of entertainers, politicians or public figures who are *primarily*: 1) physically attractive, 2) socially attractive or 3) task attractive. You may be asked to share lists with other class members to look for differences and similarities.

Names of Attractive People by Type

Physically Attractive	Socially Attractive	Task Attractive
1.		
2.		
3.		

Now list entertainers, politicians or public figures who have either two or all three dimensions of interpersonal attractiveness. Note their careers. Often these people will be at the top or close to the top of their fields.

Two Dimensions	Three Dimensions
1.	
2.	
3.	

* * *

Simply put, a source is attractive only to the extent that receivers find the source attractive: a matter of perception. With more attractive sources, receivers are more likely to listen, learn and be persuaded. But attractiveness is not the only credibility dimension. Another set of perceptions that influence receiver perception of the source is homophily or perceived similarity.

Homophily or similarity

Homophily is the perceived similarity between a source and receiver. The **principle of homophily** suggests that the more similar a source and receiver are: 1) the more likely they are to communicate with one another, 2) the more likely the communication will be successful and 3) the more similar the source and receiver *will become*. Also, the more similar a source appears to a receiver, the more likely that a receiver will listen, learn and be persuaded by that source. Three dimensions of homophily that affect a receiver's perception of a source are demographic, background and attitude homophily.[7]

Demographics are the physical, educational, social or economic characteristics of a source that a receiver can objectively identify (See Media Use chapter). These are specifics such as: age, sex, height, religion, ethnicity and socio-economic status. These traits are identifiable, quantifiable, observable characteristics. For many receivers, the more a source *looks* similar to the receiver, the more likely the receiver is to respond favorably to the source and the source's message.

Attitudes are the positions or viewpoints that a source communicates to a receiver. **Attitudinal homophily** refers to the degree to which a receiver perceives the source's viewpoints, positions or attitudes as being similar to the receiver's. As attitudinal homophily increases, so does the source's ability to get the receiver to listen, learn and be persuaded. For example, if a source's view of gun control or the need to recycle waste is very different from the receiver's, then the receiver may "tune out" the source. To be effective, a source must establish attitudinal homophily.

Background similarity is the degree to which a receiver perceives the source to be from a similar background, social, regional or ethnic group as the receiver. Often some background homophily is needed for individuals to consider communicating beyond the initial stage. College students may perceive they have similar backgrounds with other students, but because they are from different regions and countries, many college students may have little background homophily. Still, the perception that other college students are similar allows for communication. As the communication increases so might the attitude homophily. However, if the communication reveals little or no background homophily, then the students will see themselves as less similar.

Greater perceived background homophily increases the likelihood of interaction. A source who can establish background homophily with the receiver is likely to have a receiver who will listen, learn and perhaps be persuaded by the source.

---

7. James C. McCroskey, Virginia P. Richmond and John A. Daly (1975). "The development of a measure of perceived homophily in interpersonal communication," *Human Communication Research* 1(4):323-332.

Summary

This chapter illustrates the impact of source credibility, attractiveness and homophily on receivers' communication. If a receiver's perceptions of the source are positive, then the receiver is more likely to listen and retain information given by the source. In fact, judgment of the content of communication depends on the receiver's view of the source. This principle holds true for all messages.

Among dimensions of source credibility are **competence** or source expertise, and **character** or source trustworthiness. Additionally, interpersonal attraction influences source credibility. These dimensions are **physical**, **social** and **task attraction**. When sources are more attractive, receivers are more likely to listen, learn and be persuaded.

One other aspect of credibility is homophily or similarity. The **principle of homophily** suggests that the more similar a source and receiver are, the more likely: 1) they are to communicate with one another, 2) the communication will be successful and 3) the source and receiver *will become* similar. The more similar a source appears to a receiver, the more likely it is that a receiver will listen, learn and be persuaded by that source. Among aspects of homophily are: demographics, attitudinal similarity and background similarity.

These, then, are the qualities a source should know about and strive for if the source expects to be an effective communicator.

Exercises:

A. List the five most credible public figures you know. Next list the five least credible. After making your lists, your teacher will give further instructions.

Five highly credible people   Five least credible people

1.

2.

3.

4.

5.

B. Following are measures of perceived credibility, attraction and homophily. Complete each set and score. Be prepared for class discussion about responses.

Measure of source credibility

Using the scales, please indicate your feelings about a source such Oprah, Barbara Walters, Peter Jennings, Colin Powell or any other source you may choose. Circle the number between the adjectives that best represents your feelings about the source here. Numbers "1" and "7" indicate a very strong feeling. Numbers "2" and "6" indicate a strong feeling. Numbers "3" and "5" indicate a fairly weak feeling. Number "4" indicates that you are undecided or you think these adjectives do not apply to your source. There are no right or wrong answers.

SOURCE: _____

Competence

Reliable	7	6	5	4	3	2	1	Unreliable
Uninformed	1	2	3	4	5	6	7	Informed
Intelligent	7	6	5	4	3	2	1	Unintelligent
Unqualified	1	2	3	4	5	6	7	Qualified
Valuable	7	6	5	4	3	2	1	Worthless
Inexpert	1	2	3	4	5	6	7	Expert

Character

Virtuous	7	6	5	4	3	2	1	Sinful
Nasty	1	2	3	4	5	6	7	Nice
Honest	7	6	5	4	3	2	1	Dishonest
Unfriendly	1	2	3	4	5	6	7	Friendly
Pleasant	7	6	5	4	3	2	1	Unpleasant
Selfish	1	2	3	4	5	6	7	Unselfish

To compute scores for competence and character, add the numbers circled for each measure separately. To measure the credibility of a different source, simply replace the source each time.

Competence Total = _____   Character Total = _____

The score for each credibility dimension should be between 6 and 42. Higher scores indicate higher perception of competence and character. If competence is high but character low, then the source is not trustworthy. If character is high but competence low, then the source is not competent. To be completely credible, sources must be perceived as moderate to high in both competence and character.

Measure of interpersonal attraction

These scales are designed to indicate how attractive you find another person. Indicate your perceptions of a chosen source's attractiveness by circling the number that best measures your feeling on each of these scales. "1" and "7" indicate very strong feeling; "2" and "6" indicate strong feeling; "3" and "5" indicate a fairly weak feeling; "4" indicates you are undecided. There are no right or wrong answers.

SOURCE:_____

Physical attraction
I think this person is very handsome/pretty:

Strongly Disagree   1   2   3   4   5   6   7   Strongly Agree

This person is very sexy looking:

Strongly Disagree   1   2   3   4   5   6   7   Strongly Agree

I find this person very attractive physically:

Strongly Disagree   1   2   3   4   5   6   7   Strongly Agree

I don't like the way this person looks:

Strongly Disagree   1   2   3   4   5   6   7   Strongly Agree

Social attraction
I think this person could be a friend of mine:

Strongly Disagree   1   2   3   4   5   6   7   Strongly Agree

It would be difficult to meet and talk with this person:

Strongly Disagree   1   2   3   4   5   6   7   Strongly Agree

This person would not fit into my circle of friends:

Strongly Disagree   1   2   3   4   5   6   7   Strongly Agree

I could never establish a personal friendship with this person:

Strongly Disagree   1   2   3   4   5   6   7   Strongly Agree

Task attraction

This person would be a typical goof-off when assigned a job to do:

Strongly Disagree   1   2   3   4   5   6   7   Strongly Agree

I have confidence in this person's ability to get the job done:

Strongly Disagree   1   2   3   4   5   6   7   Strongly Agree

If I wanted to get things done, I could probably depend on this person:

Strongly Disagree   1   2   3   4   5   6   7   Strongly Agree

I could not get anything accomplished with this person:

Strongly Disagree   1   2   3   4   5   6   7   Strongly Agree

To compute your scores for the three dimensions of attraction, add the numbers circled for each measure separately. To measure the attractiveness of a different source, simply put the other source's name in place of the original source.

Physical Total = _____   Social Total = _____   Task Total = _____

The scores for each dimension can range from 4 to 28. The higher the scores, the higher the physical, social or task attraction.

Measure of perceived homophily

Indicate your feelings about a chosen source by circling the number that best describes your feeling on each of these scales. "1" and "7" indicate very strong feeling; "2" and "6" indicate strong feeling; "3" and "5" indicate a fairly weak feeling; "4" indicates you are undecided. There are no right or wrong answers. Because demographic homophily is based on actual characteristics, only attitudinal and background homophily, which are based on perceptions, are measured.

SOURCE: _____

Attitudinal homophily

The person named above is:

Like me	7	6	5	4	3	2	1	Unlike me
Different from me		1	2	3	4	5	6	7	Similar to me
Thinks like me	7	6	5	4	3	2	1	Doesn't think like me
Doesn't behave like me		1	2	3	4	5	6	7	Behaves like me

Background homophily
The person named is/has:

| Status like mine | 7 6 5 4 3 2 1 | Status different from mine |

Status like mine   7   6   5   4   3   2   1   Status different from mine

     Culturally   Culturally
     different   1   2   3   4   5   6   7   similar

Economic situation   Economic situation
like mine   7   6   5   4   3   2   1   different from mine

From social class   From social class
different from mine   1   2   3   4   5   6   7   similar to mine

      To compute scores for the two dimensions of homophily, add the numbers you circled for each measure separately. To measure the perceived homophily of a different person, simply put the other source's name in place of the source named above.

      Attitudinal Total = _____   Background Total =_____

      Scores for each dimension should be between 4 and 28. The higher the score, the higher the perceived attitudinal or background homophily.

11

Selectivity and the Communication Process

Early article: Lawrence R. Wheeless (1974). "The effects of attitude, credibility, and homophily on selective exposure to information," *Speech Monographs* 41(4):329-338.

Contemporary article: Brant R. Burleson and Wendy Samter (1990). "Effects of cognitive complexity on the perceived importance of communication skills in friends," *Communication Research* 17(2):165-182.

Human communication is an ongoing, ever changing, non-static process. Often during this process a person decides to listen or not listen to the source. A receiver's ability to select when to attend to information can be overlooked as a significant part of the communication process. Being more aware of the tendency to selectively listen or not listen can make the communication process more effective.

People who actively listen to other's messages are generally perceived as more responsive, competent communicators. Those who do attend to messages from others are often perceived as cold, aloof, rude and uncaring communicators. By electing *not to listen*, individuals also have less information to use when making decisions, responding to others, and establishing and maintaining relationships.

Getting people to listen, comprehend and understand a message is challenging under the most favorable of conditions. Even when a person is motivated to listen, circumstances and internal or external noise can interfere with the communication process.[1]

---

1. Marian Friestad and Esther Thorson (1993). "Remembering ads: The effects of encoding strategies, retrieval cues, and emotional response," *Journal of Consumer Psychology* 2(2):1-23. See also: Herbert E. Krugman (1977). "Memory without recall, exposure without perception," *Journal of Advertising Research* 17(4):7-12; Chris Janiszewski (1993). "Preattentive mere exposure effects," *Journal of Consumer Research* 20(3):376-392.

This chapter reviews the five selectivity processes that can directly interfere with reception and comprehension of messages. These five selectivity processes are: selective exposure, selective attention, selective perception, selective retention and selective recall.[2] Communicators must recognize how each selectivity process can be an obstacle to effective information and communication processing.

Selective exposure

Selective exposure refers to a person's conscious or unconscious *choice to receive messages from a specific source.* Most people engage in this type of behavior on a daily basis. People, consciously or unconsciously, make decisions about which television shows to watch, with whom to communicate, to whom to listen and whom to "tune out."[3] Often these decisions are based on preference for the subject or person. Receivers can make predictions about the nature of the message by knowing the message source. Students who have negative affect for an instructor do not listen, so they do less well in the class. Following are the five factors to overcome selective exposure, the first obstacle to communication effectiveness.[4]

• **Utility**. Content that seems useful or interesting is more likely to be selected for exposure than content that seems less useful. People who want to learn more about home improvement might select to listen to Bob Vila. People who want to know the top ten music videos of the week often "tune into" VH1 or MTV.

• **Enlightened self-interest**. People generally pay more attention to beneficial or advantageous information. For example, the infomercial related to "making more money" receives considerable public attention because most people can see immediate benefits. Any communicator who wants audience members to attend to the information being presented must first be able to answer the question, "What will this do for my listener?" If this question cannot be answered, then many in the audience simply will not expose themselves to the communicator's message.

2. Melvin L. DeFleur, Patricia Kearney and Timothy G. Plax (1993). "Listening as communication," in *Mastering communication in contemporary America: Theory, research, and practice.* Mountain View, CA: Mayfield Publishing Co., pp. 19-123. See also: James C. McCroskey and Virginia P. Richmond (1996). "Selectivity and attribution: Why our messages don't get through," in *Fundamentals of human communication: An interpersonal perspective.* Prospect Heights, IL: Waveland Press, pp. 141-156; Dolf Zillmann and Jennings Bryant (1985). *Selective exposure to communication.* Hillsdale, NJ: Lawrence Erlbaum Associates.

3. Brenda K. Helregel and James B. Weaver (1989). "Mood-management during pregnancy through selective exposure to television," *Journal of Broadcasting & Electronic Media* 33(1):15-33.

4. Elihu Katz (1968). "On reopening the question of selectivity in exposure to mass communications," in Robert P. Abelson, Elliot Aronson, William J. McGuire, Theodore M. Newcomb, Milton J. Rosenberg and Percy H. Tannenbaum, eds. *Theories of cognitive consistency: A sourcebook.* Chicago IL: Rand McNally and Co., pp. 783-796.

• **Proximity**. Information that is immediately available or *close* to a person is most likely to be elected for exposure. If a source wants to persuade a receiver, then the source must be available for communication when the receiver is likely to want to communicate. Marketing experts recognize *when* to offer certain ads and *how* to make the ad seem **proximate** to the audience. For example, many fast-food chains air their commercials during the viewing period preceding the evening meal. These commercials appear in the home and create a feeling of nearness to the restaurant. Consequently, the now-hungry person is more likely to get in a car and go directly to the restaurant advertised or call for delivery.

Teachers who want students to ask questions need to ask, "Am I available to students?" Teachers who seek to avoid students put space in the way. Those who want to help try to reduce the physical and psychological distance a student feels by being available. This is true of company executives interacting with their employees.

• **Involvement**. The more important a topic is to a person, the more exposure the person will seek. For example, avid football fans never miss the Super Bowl. These fans seek more information, become more involved with the sport, videotape the game and shun anything negative about the sport. Sports fans love to talk about sports. Often people ask, "Why should I listen to this?" or "How does this topic relate to me?" Therefore, unless the question, "How will people become involved in this topic?" can be answered, those to whom the topic is directed might not listen.

• **Consistent and reinforcing**. People allow exposure to information that is consistent with and reinforces their views. They "tune out" sources or information that is inconsistent or not reinforcing with their attitudes, beliefs and values.

Selective attention

Selective attention occurs when a receiver cannot control messages to which the receiver is exposed. Because receivers cannot avoid exposure, they simply select not to pay attention to the message but to pay attention to something else. Members of a church congregation cannot avoid exposure to the sermon, but they may select not to pay attention to it. Instead they might whisper, doze or gaze out a window.

This type of selective attention behavior occurs in many facets of life such as business meetings, teacher/student or teacher/parent conferences, lectures and so on. As with selective exposure, many factors contribute to determining which messages will receive attention at any given time.[5] The following five factors influence selective attention.

---

5. Anne M. Treisman (1969). "Strategies and models of selective attention," *Psychological Review 76*(3):282-299.

• **Attention span**. No matter what people choose to pay attention to, that attention can "only last so long." Children have shorter attention spans than adults. For example, many children can only pay attention to a source for about one-to-three minutes or what is known as "commercial time." Adults can usually pay attention to a source for about 15-20 minutes before their attention span wanes.

Television programmers are very aware of the attention span factor. This explains why "Sesame Street," "Barney" and "Blues Clues" are such hits with children. These shows use brief, attention-getting messages adapted for children. Shows such as "60 Minutes," "Dateline" and "20/20" use 15-20 minute segments aimed at adults. If a source wants a receiver to stay attentive, the message should be designed to be compatible with the receiver's attention span. A source should always ask, "Should I condense this message? Who is its intended receiver?"

• **Novelty**. Sources, messages and things that are unusual, different or distinctive hold a person's attention longer than the ordinary, usual or commonplace. When traveling, Texans may pay little attention to cows while New Yorkers might gawk at cows. VH1 has been very successful with the "Pop Up Video" format. It is distinctive and novel. People are attracted to the idiosyncratic, fascinating formatting of this particular segment of VH1. Additionally, Pop Up Video segments are *short* enough so a person's attention span does not deteriorate. Sources should ask, "Is this message novel or different? Will it catch a receiver's attention?"

• **Concreteness**. Messages that are simple, concrete, easy to understand, straightforward and tangible are easier to pay attention to than messages that are abstract, intangible, confusing or obscure. Most people do not like to search for meaning behind a message or from a source. Consequently, sources need to transmit messages that are real, easy to understand and clear. In addition, messages should relate to what the receiver understands or has experienced. The rule is KISS or "keep it short and sweet" or "keep it simple, stupid." Sources who send messages that are too complex or abstract will not hold the attention of receivers for very long.

• **SIZE**. In general, bigger things tend to draw more attention than smaller things. If a source really wants a receiver to hear or read a message, then the message should be set apart, enlarged or emphasized. Billboards along highways are often very simple yet functional ways of catching attention. They are large and attract attention because of their SIZE and novelty.

• **Length**. Attention is directed toward messages that are moderate in length (written) or duration. Very brief messages may be ignored or missed. Lengthy messages may be ignored because they are too long, confusing, or they may be misinterpreted because too many ideas are included. If a source must communicate a large amount of information, it is desirable to do so with messages that contain smaller chunks of information. Therefore, sources should organize and group information before delivery. A good assumption to follow is "if the message can be communicated in more concise terms, then do so." But a source must be cautious not to fragment the message so much that it has little or no meaning to the receiver.

Selective perception

Messages do not carry meanings. The meanings behind the messages are in the minds of the receivers. **Selective perception** is the process of attributing meaning to messages. The meaning that is stimulated by a source depends on both the message and the receiver. Several factors can be considered that may cause a receiver to select perceptions different from those the source intended.

• **Puzzling messages**. Messages are often ambiguous, uncertain, imprecise and open to misinterpretation. Words that a source uses in different ways can lead a receiver, even one who is trying diligently to get the intended meaning, to choose one the source did not intend. Confusion can be avoided by encouraging people to ask clarifying questions, not using too many complex words, and not using abstract terms or language above the receiver's level of knowledge.

• **Absence of message redundancy**. Redundancy enables receivers to have a second or third opportunity to comprehend the intended meaning of a source's message. Single messages are far more likely to be misunderstood than multiple messages aimed to stimulate the equivalent meaning. The rule is to say it once, say it twice, say it thrice and the receiver should get the intended meaning.

• **Absence of receiver schema**. Receivers learn by assigning information into categories known as **schema**. A source must help the receiver create schema for new ideas. This means a source must keep using a variety of words and language until the "light bulb goes on in the receiver's mind."

• **Early experiences**. Sources and receivers know the world through their past or early experiences. A person growing up in the '80s has had a breadth of different experiences from a person growing up in the '90s. Therefore, both sources and receivers should try to understand and relate to the backgrounds of the other. This means constantly learning and relearning concepts, language and meaning.

• **Assumptions and biases**. An **assumption** is a guess, conjecture or hypothesis about how another person will react or communicate. A **bias** is a preconception, opinion or evaluation about another person. All people have assumptions and biases about other people. A source's message may be perceived in a way that is consistent with the receiver's assumption or bias, not in the way the source intended. Unfortunately, this is more the norm than the exception.

People tend to perceive what they expect to see or hear and are likely to interpret messages in ways that conform to their assumptions and biases. Selective perception always occurs to some extent, but communication effectiveness increases as sources and receivers seek feedback to improve selective perception accuracy.

Selective retention

Selective retention is the decision to save or not to save information in **long-term memory**. Short-term retention is "in one ear and out the other." Therefore, sources and receivers must work to store information in long-term memory so it can be recalled when needed. This is like word processing programs. When exiting a document, the screen flashes, "Do you want to save?" Usually, the answer is "yes," and the document is stored to be recalled or retrieved later. Several factors influence selective retention.

• **Absence of highlighting**. Lack of highlighting can result in the information being lost. Often students do not know what teachers expect, so students attempt to store too much information or simply forget it all. Educators can be very good at highlighting relevant information. This is done by handing out learning objectives, speaking articulately, writing on the board, giving significant facts and terms to know, and by reemphasizing significant content points for each unit.

• **Absence of redundancy**. Again, lack of redundancy lowers the opportunity for a variety of ways to learn and retain material.[6] Redundancy assumes that the more a person hears or sees information, the more likely the person is to recall it. Redundancy must be used for children, but it is not always needed for adults. However, if in doubt about whether a person understands a message the way it was intended, say it again, use different terms, different examples. In other words, review the ideas in a variety of ways until the receiver understands the concept.

• **Absence of schema**. The lack of a schema often explains why people do not save or store information. Without a mental filing system for storing, they often filter out the information. Therefore, sources need to help construct a schema or filing system so receivers can save and retrieve new information.

• **Absence of tangible application**. For people to store and then recall information, it must have real, concrete applications. If a physics teacher says, "This model will be used later in life," students may not store the nebulous idea. Receivers need **handles** or "clear practical application" before saving information for retrieval. The physics teacher should say, "This model is the system in automobile engines."

---

6. Charles R. Berger and Patrick DiBattista (1993). "Communication failure and plan adaptation: If at first you don't succeed, say it louder and slower," *Communication Monographs* 60(3):220-238.

• **Primacy and recency principles**. Generally information given first in a message (primacy principle) and information given last (recency principle) are the most recalled items of information.[7]   Therefore, when presenting information, remember that ideas presented near the beginning or the conclusion of the message will be easier for receivers to retrieve. Additionally, this information may be more effective or more persuasive than information given in the middle of a presentation because of the primacy/recency principles. Speakers, business persons and teachers who use primacy/recency principles usually have receivers who perform better in recalling information.

Selective recall

Selective recall is the successful retrieval of information.   Sources must attempt to assure that through effective communication and overcoming the obstacles associated with selectivity, receivers can recall the messages they are sent. If a receiver never had selective exposure to information, then the information cannot be recalled. If a receiver paid little attention to the information, then the information may not be recalled or may be recalled incorrectly. If the receiver had a different perception about the information than the source intended, selective perception may distort the message. If a receiver does not have or cannot create a schema for incoming information, then the information may be lost. If a receiver had little or no retention of information, then recall of the information is almost impossible.[8]

For example, from the first to 12th grade, students get a break from school in the summer. During the break, students often don't retain much of the information from the school year. In the fall when the new school year begins, many teachers spend the first few weeks exposing students to content they had in the past but have lost during the summer. When there is a significant time span between selective exposure, attention, perception and retention, selective recall is limited.

With all of the possible barriers implicit in the five selectivity processes, effective human communication requires effort. The degree to which a receiver chooses to be exposed to, attend to, perceive, store and recall a message from a source is associated with effective communication and comprehension.[9] If communication participants strive to eliminate the significant selectivity barriers, then human communication can be more successful.

---

7. Carl I. Hovland, Irving L. Janis and Harold H. Kelley (1953). *Communication and persuasion: Psychological studies of opinion change*. New Haven, CT: Yale University Press.

8. Michael D. Miller and Timothy R. Levine (1996). "Persuasion," in Michael B. Salwen and Don W. Stacks, eds. *An integrated approach to communication theory and research*. Mahwah, NJ: Lawrence Erlbaum Associates, pp. 261-276.

9. Lewis Donohew and Philip Palmgreen (1971). "A reappraisal of dissonance and the selective exposure hypothesis," *Journalism Quarterly* 48(3):412-420, 437.

Summary:

A receiver's ability to select when to attend to information is an important part of the communication process. This chapter reviews five selectivity processes that can interfere with reception and comprehension of messages. These five types of selectivity processes, with their attendant factors to overcome, are:

Selective **exposure**, or the *choice to receive messages from a specific source*, can be improved with attention to message qualities such as: utility, enlightened self-interest, proximity, involvement, and consistent and reinforcing.

Selective **attention**, which occurs when receivers cannot avoid exposure but simply select not to pay attention to the message. Here factors include concern for receivers' attention span and message novelty, concreteness, size and length.

Selective **perception**, or the process of attributing meaning to messages. This depends on puzzling messages, absence of message redundancy, absence of receiver schema, early experiences, and assumptions and biases.

Selective **retention** is the decision to save or not to save information in long-term memory. Its factors are absence of: highlighting, redundancy, schema and tangible application; and primacy and recency principles.

Selective **recall** is the successful retrieval of information, and it depends on whether the source has been able to overcome all of the previous selection barriers.

Exercises:

A. In groups, students should discuss teacher or class variables that may cause students to give more attention during class (e.g., the teacher tells a joke, the teacher is dramatic, the student gets enough sleep the night before). List at least 15 variables of this sort.

B. The teacher will read information to students from *USA Today*. Students should listen, but not take notes during the reading. After the teacher completes the recitation, students will have five minutes in which to write all the information they can recall.

Establishing
Interpersonal Relationships

12

Early study: Mary Anne Fitzpatrick and Patricia Best (1979). "Dyadic adjustment in relational types: Consensus, cohesion, affectional expression, and satisfaction in enduring relationships," *Communication Monographs* 46(3):167-178.

Contemporary study: Barbara M. Montgomery (1993). "Relationship maintenance versus relationship change: A dialectical dilemma," *Journal of Social and Personal Relationships* 10(2):205-223.

To date no researcher, scholar, teacher or Dr. Ruth has been able to definitively answer these three questions: 1) How do people get a relationship started? 2) How do people maintain successful relationships? 3) Why do relationships fall apart?

Exercise 1:

To prepare for class discussion, list your own responses to the three questions above. You might be able to list 10 reasons for each question, but instead write your **five best** reasons for each. You may be asked to hand in your work for a class grade.

This chapter will not attempt to give definitive answers to the three questions. As is often the case, there are no guarantees in life, or relationships. Instead, the chapter reviews characteristics of relationships, stages of relationship development, and the impact of affinity-seeking in interpersonal relationships.

Characteristics of interpersonal relationships

Most interpersonal relationships are characterized by a variety of factors. These factors can be present across many types of interpersonal relationships, such as close friends, student and teacher, supervisor and subordinate, parent and child and so on. Eight interpersonal relationship factors are variability, duration, frequency, revelation, meshing, support, anxiety reduction and proximity.

Variability is the characteristic of interpersonal relationships that indicates partners in the relationship engage in many *different types* of interactions. For example, friends at work may interact in a job-oriented manner at work, in a social way after work and in a more reserved manner at church.

Duration is the interpersonal relationship factor that is present when a relationship lasts over some period of time.[1] For example, many people have friends who have been their friends since grade school, middle school or college.

Frequency is closely linked with duration. This factor indicates that people involved in an interpersonal relationship engage in interactions with each other regularly and frequently. Both duration and frequency are important to interpersonal relationships because the more a person interacts with another individual, the better a person knows the other individual. Contrast, for example, someone who has been your friend for more than five years with a friend of only one year's acquaintance.

Revelation occurs as a relationship grows and develops. Individuals in the relationship share basic and more personal attitudes, beliefs and values with one another. Revelation is the revealing of thoughts, ideas, feelings and opinions to another person. The amount of revelation is often determined by the duration and frequency factors mentioned above. High levels of *self-disclosure* usually do not occur early in relationships, but self-disclosure becomes high during revelation.

Meshing refers to how the behavior of two people in a relationship is organized and interpreted with respect to each other. Most relationships are either complementary or symmetrical. In **complementary** relationships, one person's behavior balances the another's. If one person is unusually talkative and the other person is quieter, this is a complementary relationship. In **symmetrical** relationships, one person's behavior is very similar to the other's. If both persons in the relationship are very talkative, this is a symmetrical relationship.

Support occurs in a relationship when the actions of each partner are helpful to the well-being of the other person. Two brothers may fight constantly. Yet when an intruder presents some threat to one, the other brother is quick to come to his sibling's aid. Support can be in the form of physical, emotional, intellectual or psychological support.

---

1. Robert A. Bell and Jonathan G. Healey (1992). "Idomatic communication and interpersonal solidarity in friends' relational cultures," *Human Communication Research* 18(3):307-335.

Anxiety reduction is a type of emotional support. Anxiety reduction in a relationship is when one person attempts to reduce the other person's fears and anxieties. When a person attempts to make another person's world more comfortable or less stressful, anxiety reduction is taking place. Often in the work force, one co-worker will try to make another's job less stressful and easier to perform.

Proximity is the final characteristic of interpersonal relationships. This refers to the physical distance between individuals in a relationship. Most interpersonal relationships are characterized by the spatial closeness of its partners. Proximity may be the most important of all the factors presented. Proximity is the *greatest predictor of initial interaction* between two people. A person is more likely to communicate and establish a relationship with another person who is physically close than with a person who is physically more distant.

Granted that in today's world of computers and high-level technology, relationships can *seem physically close* even when the physical distance is 3,000 miles apart. Even in cyber relationships, the people usually decide to *get together* and *physically meet*. Ongoing, well-established relationships typically are characterized by close proximity between the partners.

The eight interpersonal relationship factors depicted are interdependent. For any given relationship, a change in one characteristic is likely to lead to changes in several other factors. For example, if one person relocates, the move changes many other aspects in the relationship besides proximity. It is no wonder that people strive to keep these factors under control so relationships have the opportunity to grow.

Stages of relationship development

Knapp has created a ten-stage model of relationship development including five stages of *coming together* and five stages of *coming apart*.[2] In coming together, the stages are initiating, experimenting, intensifying, integrating and bonding. In falling apart, the stages are differentiating, circumscribing, stagnating, avoiding and terminating. Each of these stages is discussed.

Coming together

Initiating is the conventional stage in coming together. This stage usually lasts only a few seconds or minutes. The primary decision made in this stage is whether to initiate verbal communication with the other person. This stage involves

---

2. Mark L. Knapp (1978). *Social intercourse: From greeting to good-bye*. Boston: Allyn and Bacon. See also: Mark L. Knapp and Anita L. Vangelisti (1992). *Interpersonal communication and human relationships, 2nd ed.* Boston: Allyn and Bacon.

a lot of *scanning* of the other person. When a person looks and sees that the other person is attractive and appealing, then verbal communication is initiated.

Initiating is the stage where brief verbal exchanges such as "Hi. I'm Jerry," "How you doing?" or other such brief one-liners are used. At this stage, if the scanning reveals a person who is perceived to be unattractive and unappealing to the scanner, then the verbal interaction may never take place. Some acquaintances never get past the "pre-initiation" or scanning stage.[3]

Exercise 2:

List the various "verbal exchanges" or "lines" you have heard others use, or that you have used when trying to get to know another person. List five lines others have used and five lines you have used. Bring these to class and be prepared to either discuss them or to turn your work in for a grade.

The **experimenting** stage is when one person tries to discover the similarities that he or she has in common with the other person, and vice versa. This is the phase where people are attempting to find homophily or similarity so that communication is easier and more relaxed. Interests, similar backgrounds, attitudes and experiences must be discovered or the relationship will not progress. If too many dissimilarities are found, the relationship ends before it really begins. Often people talk about music, food, movies, classes, hobbies and so on to determine if there is sufficient similarity to warrant moving to the next stage.

Intensifying is the stage where people feel comfortable referring to the other person as a close friend, significant other or partner. Interaction at this stage involves much deeper and broader self-disclosure or revelation.[4] Each person reveals confidential, secret feelings, information and attitudes to the other person.

At this stage the verbal interaction often employs the first person plural (we). There may even be nicknames, terms of endearment and caring being used at this stage. Nonverbal communication is very important at this stage. The pair are now sharing things like music, clothing, property and so on.

---

3. Charles R. Berger and Richard J. Calabrese (1975). "Some exploration in initial interaction and beyond: Toward a developmental theory of interpersonal communication," *Human Communication Research* 1(2):99-112. See also: Charles R. Berger (1975). "Proactive and retroactive attribution processes in interpersonal communications," *Human Communication Research* 2(1):33-50.

4. Charles R. Berger, Royce R. Gardner, Glen W. Clatterbuck and Linda S. Schulman (1976). "Perceptions of information sequencing in relationship development," *Human Communication Research* 3(1):29-46.

Integrating is when a mature relationship has developed. At this stage there is a fusion of the two partners at both a psychological and social level. Not only do the persons think of themselves as one, but they also want others to recognize them as one, or a unit. In this stage, the partners do almost everything together and go almost everywhere together. The relationship is now special, unique and unlike any other relationship either person has. Most people have experienced this stage. It is a delightful stage where all is perfect and *oneness* is emphasized.

Bonding is the final stage in coming together. Bonding is different from integrating in that bonding is formal and public. Bonding is often recognized by society and is institutionalized in the form of prenuptial agreements, marriages, moving in and other such contracts. It is a lasting commitment to a future together.

Coming apart

Differentiating is the opposite of the integrating stage of coming together. In the differentiating stage of coming apart, the individuals focus on their differences and disagreements.[5] Verbally, the partners move away from using the terms "we" and "ours." Terms such as "I," "you," "me" and "mine" are used often. This is the first sign that a relationship is moving from a highly immediate or intimate status to a nonimmediate status.

The **circumscribing** stage is when both the quantity and the quality of communication decreases. Topics of discussion between the individuals are restricted to safe areas. Touchy subjects are avoided. Interaction frequency and duration begin to decrease.

The **stagnating** stage is when a relationship has ceased to be functional, productive, active or alive. Much of the communication at this stage is nonverbal and negative. The participants feel that saying anything or talking with the other person is a waste of time because they *know* what will be said. Many interactions are now similar to those engaged in with strangers. The communication is rigid, difficult, narrow, awkward, artificial and constrained. Just as a stagnating pond loses its means to support organic life, a stagnating relationship loses its means to support communicative life.

Avoiding is the fourth stage of coming apart. Avoiding involves an attempt to increase physical distance and space. Both the verbal and nonverbal communication are very limited. Both are aimed so the other person understands there is a direct

---

5. Michael J. Cody (1982). "A typology of disengagement strategies and an examination of the role intimacy, reactions to inequity and relational problems play in strategy selection," *Communication Monographs* 49(3):148-170.

avoidance of interaction. One person avoids being where another person is. One person avoids speaking to the other person. For example, one person may leave the answering machine on 24 hours a day to avoid talking with the other person.

Terminating is the last stage of coming apart. This stage can occur any time for any reason. Two people may recognize "they have grown apart." One person may move away or take an extended trip. One person may decide the relationship is over even though the other person does not think so. Knapp contends that communication during termination is generally characterized by messages of distance and disassociation.

Relationships are similar to the life cycle. They begin, mature and sometimes fall apart or die. How then do people maintain a healthy, active relationship? The next section on affinity-seeking reviews ways to increase liking and thus maintain a solid, healthy relationship.

Affinity-seeking: Being liked by others

It is clear that relationship formation and maintenance are not easy processes. Relationship adjustment, trust, satisfaction and disengagement are significant areas of research in the human communication field.[6] The process of affinity-seeking is important to most interpersonal relationships. Often, people use affinity-seeking strategies to develop and maintain positive relationships with supervisors, teachers, ministers, friends and family. **Affinity-seeking** is the degree to which people attempt to get other people to like, appreciate and want to spend time with them. Bell and Daly completed much of the research that led to understanding relationship development and maintenance.[7] They produced a typology of 25 affinity-seeking behaviors that people can use to gain liking, acceptance and respect from others.

The most commonly used affinity-seeking strategies tend to be Conversational Rule-Keeping, Self-Concept Confirmation, Elicit Other's Disclosures, Nonverbal Immediacy, Self-Inclusion, Listening, Facilitate Enjoyment, Similarity, Supportiveness, Comfortable Self, Altruism, Optimism, Trustworthiness, Physical Attractiveness and Sensitivity. The Figure 1 typology presents the 25 affinity-seeking strategies people can learn to use. Each person has to select strategies with which he or she is comfortable that might work to increase liking with others. As liking increases, communication increases, and relationships tend to thrive, not die.

---

6. William R. Cupach and Sandra Metts (1986). "Accounts of relational dissolution: A comparison of marital and non-marital relationships," *Communication Monographs* 53(4):311-334.

7. Robert A. Bell and John A. Daly (1984). "The affinity-seeking function of communication," *Communication Monographs* 51(2):91-115.

Typology of Affinity-Seeking Strategies

Strategy	Definition	Example
Altruism	try to be of help	hold door; run errands
Assume Control	present self as leader	lead dialogue, activities
Assume Equality	present self as equal	avoid showing off
Comfortable Self	act relaxed, at ease	"nothing bothers me"
Concede Control	let others control	other gets to set agenda
Conversational Rule-Keeping	follow cultural rules	cooperation; politeness
Dynamism	act enthusiastic	be very lively; outgoing
Elicit Other's Disclosure	encourage other's talk	ask questions; show interest
Facilitate Enjoyment	have fun together	tell jokes, interesting stories
Inclusive of Other	make part of the group	include in social activities
Influence Perceptions of Closeness	increase friendly feeling	use nicknames; use "we"
Listening	pay close attention	respond to other's ideas
Nonverbal Immediacy	signal nonverbal cues	eye contact; stand close
Openness	disclose information	make other feel trusted
Optimism	appear cheerful, positive	avoid being a "drag"
Personal Autonomy	free-thinking; confident	show independence
Physically Attractive	appear clean, attractive	wear fashionable clothes
Present Interesting Self	demonstrate intelligence	highlight accomplishments
Reward Association	be worth being with	"like me, and you'll gain"
Self-Concept Confirmation	bring other self-respect	compliment, boost ego
Self-Inclusion	set frequent encounters	be available to other
Sensitivity	act warm, empathetic	"I care about you"
Similarity	share attitudes, values	stress similarities; agree
Supportiveness	encourage; reinforce	side with the other person
Trustworthiness	be reliabile, sincere	act natural, be consistent

Figure 1. Typology of affinity-seeking strategies

Summary

Establishing and maintaining interpersonal relationships is a fundamental goal of the human communication process. This goal is central to both social and personal survival. Most social scientists will agree that just as human survival depends on the fulfillment of certain physiological and psychological needs, so too does it center on satisfying relational needs.

The process of **establishing, building** and **maintaining** relationships is based on effective communication. To build relationships, people must be liked, therefore, they must get others to like them. Winning other people's favor has its greatest impact in the early stages of relationship development. Building good interpersonal relationships requires practicing the affinity-seeking strategies.

The most useful **affinity-seeking strategies** at the beginning of a relationship are: conversational rule-keeping; self-concept confirmation; eliciting other's disclosures; nonverbal immediacy; self-inclusion; listening; and, facilitating enjoyment, altruism, similarity, trustworthiness and supportiveness.

Exercises:

A. Select among the 25 affinity-seeking strategies the **10** strategies that you think work best when attempting to develop a good relationship with another person. Discuss how you have used (or how you have seen others use) each of the 10 and the outcomes from their use.

B. Using each stage of coming together and coming apart as an outline or guide, write an essay on a successful relationship and a second essay on an unsuccessful relationship that has happened to you. Each essay should be **no more than three pages**. Describe what happened at each stage of coming together and falling apart.

13

Power and Interpersonal Influence

Early article: Bertram H. Raven and John R.P. French Jr. (1958). "Legitimate power, coercive power, and observability in social influence," *Sociometry* 21(1):83-97.

Contemporary article: K. David Roach (1990). "A reliability assessment of the Kearney, Plax, Richmond, and McCroskey (1984) BATs and BAMs model," *Communication Research Reports* 7(1):67-74.

Exercise 1:

List tactics or strategies you have used to get a friend to *do something, perform a task or go along with something* that the friend didn't necessarily want to do. Your instructor may ask you to compare strategies with those of a classmate. Pairs or groups in the class may also be asked to list strategies that can be used to get others to do something. The tactics can be simple (promise a reward, such as a candy bar); more challenging (withhold a favor, such as refusing to go to a movie); or ethically questionable (such as agreeing to do the friend's math homework for a week).

Other than being liked, included and having a sense of belonging, there may be no greater motivation for communication than the ability to exert power and achieve influence over another person. This chapter defines power, reviews the five types of power proposed by French and Raven,[1] and examines the level of influence that can be achieved. In addition, this unit expands on the knowledge surrounding the types of power and influence.

---

1. John R.P. French Jr. and Bertram H. Raven (1968). "The bases of social power," in Dorwin Cartwright and Alvin Zander, eds. *Group dynamics: Research and theory, 3rd ed.* New York: Harper & Row, pp. 259-269.

Power

Barraclough and Stewart defined **power** as "the potential or capacity to influence the behavior of some other person or persons."[2] Based on the works of communication researchers who have studied power during a 40-year period,[3] several assumptions about power can be presented as have been strongly supported:

• A certain amount of power exists in almost every relationship (e.g., supervisor-subordinate; teacher-student; physician-patient; parent-child; siblings and so on).

• Power and communication are inextricably related. It is through verbal and nonverbal communication that most power is delivered and influence achieved. Power can be viewed as a positive, negative or legitimate influence.

• Power can be established at any time during a relationship. It can shift from one person to the next person in a relationship at any given time. Many times one person in a relationship is perceived as more powerful than the other person.

• Power is granted to a person by another person. In other words, people *allow others to control or influence them.* Communicating different types of power leads to different levels of influence in a relationship. Situations influence the type of power a person chooses to use. People can learn to use positive power strategies that result in identification and internalization influence, not simply compliance.

The bases of power

Many typologies and categorizations of power exist. This chapter reviews the five common bases of power that are found across a wide range of relationships and explores the level of influence achieved by each type of power.

Coercive Power. This type of power is based on an individual's expectations that punishments or threats will be carried out for failure to conform to the other person's coercive power. For example, in the classroom, students often feel that

---

2. Robert A. Barraclough and Robert A. Stewart (1992). "Power and control: Social science perspectives," in Virginia P. Richmond and James C. McCroskey, eds. *Power in the classroom: Communication, control, and concern.* Hillsdale, NJ: Lawrence Erlbaum Associates, pp. 1-18 (see pg. 4).

3. Barraclough and Stewart, *Ibid.* See also: Bertram H. Raven and John R.P. French Jr., (1958). "Group support, legitimate power, and social influence," *Journal of Personality* 26(3):400-409; Herbert C. Kelman (1958). "Compliance, identification, and internalization: Three processes of attitude change," *Journal of Conflict Resolution* 2(1):51-60; Timothy G. Plax and Patricia Kearney (1992). "Teacher power in the classroom: Defining and advancing a program of research," in Virginia P. Richmond and James C. McCroskey, eds. *Power in the classroom: Communication, control, and concern.* op. cit., pp. 67-84.

teachers have the capacity to use coercive power. They can give low grades, revoke privileges, make and carry out threats, and generally make a student's life unpleasant. Conversely, teachers may feel that students can make threats, carry out some threats and make the teacher's life unpleasant. However, in most cases the *person with higher status has more opportunity to use coercive power*. Therefore, in the classroom setting, teachers are often in a "one up position." They are perceived as having more opportunity to communicate coercive power than students.

For coercive power to have an impact, certain assumptions must be in place. The person who is on the receiving end of coercive power must believe that: 1) the source of power is *credible and believable*, 2) the source of power has the *capacity to carry out* a threat or punishment, and 3) the threat is *reasonable and could be carried out*. For example, if a coach tells the team to stay quiet or, "I'll rip your arm off and stuff it down your throat," most team members would perceive this as an unrealistic threat and ignore it or snicker.

Finally, the source of the coercive power *must know what punishes another person* for the coercion to have any impact. For example, school systems still send misbehaving students home as a punishment. In fact, most misbehaving students view being sent home as a reward! However, if being sent home affects grades and possibly graduation, then misbehaving students might view the action as punishment.

Reward Power. This type of power is based on an individual's expectations that rewards, payoffs, privileges or bonuses will be given if the individual conforms to the other person's requests. For example, on an assembly line, workers often feel that the line supervisor has the capacity to use reward power. The supervisor can give good evaluations, recommend workers for raises and award bonuses.

On the other hand, line supervisors know that their workers can have power to give rewards such as cooperation, respect, good evaluations and higher productivity. As with coercive power, manufacturing plant supervisors are often in a "one up position." They are perceived as having more opportunity to communicate reward power than the assembly line workers.

For reward power to have impact, the same assumptions must be in place as those for coercive power. The person on the receiving end of reward power must believe: 1) the source is *credible and believable*, 2) has the *capacity to carry out promises and rewards*, and 3) the reward is *reasonable and could be carried out*. For example, if the supervisor tells workers, "Beat yesterday's output, and I'll buy you a new car," workers would perceive this as unrealistic and ignore or laugh at the reward.

Lastly, to have any impact, the source of the reward power must know what rewards another person. For example, manufacturing firms offer cash prizes for the "best cost-saving suggestion" and so on. The worker chosen for this award is usually thrilled until the worker realizes that the prize requires giving a speech about the suggestion to the entire plant's employees. Even well intended rewards may not be seen as such by the recipients. Many people view public speaking as a punishment.

Legitimate Power. This type of power is granted to or assigned to an individual. It is often referred to as **assigned** or **positional** power. Legitimate power is power that gives a person the "right" to evaluate, direct, demand, reward, punish, oversee and report on others within certain, usually well defined limits. Bosses, physicians, teachers, ministers, politicians, parents, older siblings and so on all have some amount of legitimate power that comes with an official or unofficial job title. In many work relationships, the legitimate power is carefully spelled out so that both supervisor and subordinate know what is "a reasonable request" and what is not.

As with coercive and reward power, legitimate power exists only if persons who are on the receiving end of legitimate power acknowledge and comply with the person communicating legitimate power. For example, supervisors expect employees to be on time for work. No reward or coercion is attached to this expectation, legitimized by the supervisor's title or assigned position in the organization. If the employee is late, the supervisor can drop back to coercion or reward to enforce the rule. Supervisors can take this stance because of their legitimate power base.

Exercise 2:
Detail a list of punishments and rewards that previous teachers have used to get you or your classmates to conform to their demands. Your instructor may ask you to share your lists with other students or the entire class. Class discussion will focus on which punishments and rewards worked and which did not work.

Punishments	Rewards

1.

2.

3.

Referent Power. This type of power has its basis in the receiver identifying with or having respect for the source. Referent power is earned rather than granted, so it may be more complex and difficult to obtain than legitimate, coercive or reward power. Many people who have legitimate, coercive and reward power never earn referent power. It is achieved by hard work, being diligent, cooperative, respectful of others and responsive to their needs. Referent power is usually *earned over long periods of time*. For example, new police academy recruits who work with, learn from and support the trainer are likely to earn some referent power from the trainer. Trainers will respect and like the recruits who do their best in the program.

Expert Power. This type of power is based upon the receiver believing the source is knowledgeable, competent and experienced. If a receiver believes a source to have expert power, then the receiver will attend and listen to the source's messages. Often interns new to the job believe that their mentors have expert power, so interns allow mentors to influence their attitudes and beliefs. Expert power is also called **informational** or **knowledge** power. People who communicate with expert power are often viewed as leaders, persons to whom others want to listen and whose advice they want to follow. A person earns expert power by doing the job, being diligent and dedicated, and by being the most knowledgeable person.

Expert power can be a very powerful communication tool. People listen to experts in variety of areas and then make decisions about issues. For example, Colin Powell would be perceived by most persons in this country as an expert on military intervention. Therefore, when Colin Powell speaks, others listen. Even less high-profile people gain expert power. During national political campaigns beginning in 1994, network television featured Kathleen Hall Jamieson as a commentator. Dean Jamieson is a professor whose specialty is political communication. She's not a celebrity, but her expertise is likely to be called upon in future national elections.

A person can have and employ all five types of power. However, the *most effective types of power are the types that are earned: referent and expert*. With referent and expert power, people do things, say things, perform duties without being pushed or bribed. Referent and expert power are personal powers. They denote friendship, respect, liking, commitment and knowledge. Coercive, reward and legitimate only offer control, not long-term influence or commitment. Communicating referent and expert power can lead to long-term commitment and motivation by the receiver.

It is clear from the research that *coercive power should only be used as the last resort*. If people learn to perform only when a reward is offered, the rewards will be used up very quickly. Additionally, if people expect rewards that don't materialize, their absence feels like punishment. Legitimate power is only good to use for basic types of policies and procedures. Over-communication of legitimate, coercive or reward power leads to dislike, little motivation and resentment.

Obviously, the bases of power offer many options for influencing people. The question is, "Which types of power will motivate or influence people?" It is clear that some types of power are more preferred and lead to better outcomes than others. The next section reviews the power strategies and how each relates to influence. The three levels of influence are: *compliance, identification* and *internalization*.

Compliance occurs when an individual accepts another person's request. Compliance does not mean commitment; it means *obedience* and *conformity*. For compliance to have an impact, three things must be present: control, concern and scrutiny. The source must be able to *control the situation, show concern,* and most importantly *watch* to see that the receiver does what the source wants. If companies want people to be at work on time, often the companies scrutinize by having a time clock. Compliance only gets people to **conform**, not to internalize a specific request.

Identification occurs when a receiver wants to understand and establish a decent relationship with the source. In other words, the receiver at least identifies with the request or idea. A child many not like doing homework or housework but will identify with the parent's request. People who identify with ideas and persons are motivated to do well. For example, many students know they can probably get away with peeking at another student's test sheet, yet the student also identifies with the teacher's beginning-of-class reminder that "cheating is not ethical or professional."

Internalization occurs when the receiver has become intrinsically motivated. The receiver believes that performing is the right or good thing to do. These persons are motivated to do tasks and other assignments without being pushed, coerced, bribed, threatened or watched. For example, many people who drink alcohol have internalized the idea of the "designated driver"; they don't drink and drive. A judge may have "coerced" them into internalizing the designated driver idea, or they may have internalized the message through mass media ads or through interpersonal communication with friends and family. The point is, they have "bought into" the concept and made it part of their habits: drinking and driving don't mix.

Compliance leads to movement, not motivation. Identification leads to motivation. Internalization is motivation. How do the five bases of power relate to the three levels of influence? The type of power employed by a source affects the level of influence over a receiver (see Figure 1). All types of power lead to compliance, which is acquiescence. Only referent and expert power lead to identification and internalization. Identification brings understanding and motivation. Internalization brings understanding, commitment, dedication and motivation to do tasks without being asked. Sources who want only compliance may use coercive, reward or legitimate power. But if commitment and motivation are desired, a source must learn to use referent and expert power. Your best friend, for whom you would do almost anything, has established referent or expert power with you.

Five Bases	Levels of Influence		
of Power	*Compliance*	*Identification*	*Internalization*
Legitimate	X		
Coercive	X		
Reward	X		
Referent	X	X	X
Expert	X	X	X

Figure 1. Bases of power and impact on levels of influence

Summary

Power can be influential **only when a person allows** or is willing to acknowledge that another person in the relationship has any power. In organizations, managers are granted the first three types of power: **coercive, reward** and **legitimate**. These have no lasting commitment. **Referent** and **expert** power is earned when the receiver respects the source's abilities or knowledge and wants to perform tasks to please the source. This power is lasting.

Some types of power lead to better outcomes than others. Coercive, reward and legitimate power result in **compliance** or mere obedience. **Identification** occurs when the receiver identifies with the person making the request. **Internalization** occurs when the receiver becomes intrinsically motivated. If commitment and motivation are desired, a source must learn to use referent and expert power.

Exercises:

A. In a **one**-page essay, discuss a situation in which you have had to use coercive power and the resulting outcomes. Review the communication that ensued. Be prepared to discuss your experience in class.

B. In a **one**-page essay, discuss a situation in which you have had to use reward power and the resulting outcomes. Review the communication that ensued and be prepared to share your experience in class.

C. How can a stronger power and influence base be built through referent and expert power? Review the communication strategies that you could use to build referent and expert power. (See Establishing Interpersonal Relationships chapter for ideas.)

14
Disagreement and Conflict

Early article: Jack R. Gibb (1961). "Defensive communication," *Journal of Communication 11*(3):141-148.

Recent article: Timothy R. Levine and Eugenia E. Badger (1993). "Argumentativeness and resistance to persuasion," *Communication Reports 6*(2):71-78.

Prior to beginning the unit, your instructor may assign this X/Y simulation game for group participation in class. Follow the rules and observe the behaviors and communication of other students.

Instructions: You and your group must select an X or Y during 10 trials of decision-making. Depending on your group's selection, as well as the selection of the other groups, you will be rewarded or punished as a function of the pay-off matrix shown. THE OBJECT IS TO WIN AS MUCH AS YOU CAN.

Pay-off matrix:
1. 1 X and 3 Y's = X wins 3 points, Y's lose 1 point
2. 2 X's and 2 Y's = X's win 2 points, Y's lose 2 points
3. 3 X's and 1 Y = X's win 1 point, Y loses 3 points
4. 4 X's = X's lose 1 point
5. 4 Y's = Y's win 1 point

Points are converted to dollars. For every point won, your group just won $1,000.

Round Number	Group One	Group Two	Group Three	Group Four
1.				
2.				

(continued)

Round Number	Group One	Group Two	Group Three	Group Four
3.				
4.				
*5. x 3				
6.				
7.				
*8. x 5				
9.				
*10. x 10				

* During rounds 5, 8 and 10, your winnings or losses will be multiplied by 3, 5 and 10 respectively.

Perhaps nothing is more distressing than a person feeling as if he or she is in conflict with another person. There are those rare individuals who thrive on conflict but, for the most part, people prefer harmony. People spend nearly equal amounts of time in their lives developing positive relationships and tearing down relationships. Communication is present in both situations. This chapter looks at communication differences between disagreement and conflict. Additionally, issues such as tolerance for disagreement, and causes, prevention and management of conflict are reviewed.

Disagreement and conflict

Before understanding the nature of conflict, it is necessary to distinguish between disagreement and conflict. All too often in this culture, the two terms are used synonymously, but they are very different and have very distinct meanings.

Disagreement is simply a difference of opinion. Disagreement allows the relationship to remain stable and productive. People can disagree on facts, on what the facts imply, or on what each of them might want to do with the facts. Disagreement does not necessarily lead to conflict, but it can be a precursor to conflict. People can disagree loudly, strongly and for long periods of time. But they can also disagree quietly, softly and for brief periods. Disagreement can occur on a daily basis without conflict arising, or disagreement can lead to conflict. Conflict occurs primarily when the level of affinity between the communicators is low.

Conflict is characterized by hostility, dislike, belligerence, distrust, suspicion, antagonism and combative communication. In other words, it is *very clear when people are in conflict*. The verbal and nonverbal cues generally demonstrate to the world that conflict is present. **Conflict** can be defined as disagreement plus negative affect (or dislike) for the other person.

As noted, disagreement is a critical component in conflict. However, the way a person habitually deals with disagreement has more to do with whether disagreement will lead to conflict than with the simple presence or absence of disagreement. People differ in the extent to which they can tolerate disagreement.

Tolerance for disagreement

Some people become hostile almost instantaneously when another person disagrees with anything they say. Some people never seem to become hostile, always remain unemotional, even when others strongly disagree with them. These characteristic variations in disagreement are referred to as the person's tolerance for disagreement. **Tolerance for disagreement** (TFD) is defined as the amount of disagreement in which a person can engage *before being thrust into conflict with another person*. Every individual has a different level of tolerance for disagreement. If a person's TFD can be determined, then other people know when to stop disagreeing so the relationship does not move into conflict.

The first box in Figure 1 illustrates the tolerance for disagreement construct and the distinction between disagreement and conflict. This box generally represents a moderate TFD before a person feels pushed into conflict with another. The figure shows that, other things being equal, the lower the degree of difference of opinion or the higher the degree of positive affect or liking, the less likely people's communication will enter into conflict. So, if a moderate level of disagreement is expressed and the relationship remains positive, the likelihood of conflict is greatly reduced.

The second box presents the type of situation in which people in an interaction have a **low tolerance for disagreement**. As indicated by the placement of the diagonal line, even an average level of difference of opinion can lead to conflict, as

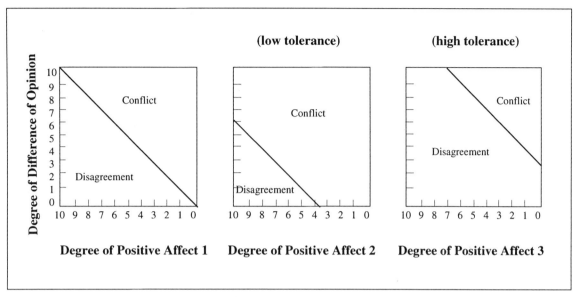

Figure 1. Disagreement vs. conflict; diagonal is "tolerance for disagreement"

can even an average reduction in positive affect or liking. People with this type of personality orientation will be in conflict much of the time. These persons might be dogmatic or authoritarian by nature. When communicating with a person who is highly dogmatic and authoritarian with low TFD, avoiding conflict requires work.

People with low TFDs are often those who have the "short fuses." Often there are so many topics and persons who ignite the fuse, that other people start avoiding the short-fuse person. These are the people who often explode, go into a rage, or simply walk away in a manner that indicates their level of hostility. Unfortunately, it is the other person who must adapt his or her communication to the person with low TFD. Low TFD persons are not very versatile or flexible. Their lack of adaptability leads to their perceiving conflict even when the other person perceives no conflict. Much of what the low TFD perceives as conflict is only disagreement.

Many people spend a lot of valuable time adapting their communication to the low TFD to avoid unpleasant feelings and confrontation. Is it worth it, or is the time investment wasted? That depends on the answers to the following questions: How strong is the desire to keep the low TFD as a friend, a coworker, etc.? Will conflict improve the situation? The answer to the latter question is usually a resounding NO. How will alienating the low TFD impact future interactions?

The third box represents the opposite of the low TFD person: a high TFD person. For conflict to occur, a major degree of difference of opinion must be communicated, or substantial reductions in positive affect or liking must be present. People with the higher TFD are likely to experience very little conflict in their everyday communication.

In all, then, there are three types of persons. Those with low TFDs can tolerate less disagreement before moving into conflict. Persons with high TFDs can tolerate much more disagreement before moving into conflict. People with moderate TFDs assess each communication situation before being moved into conflict. The next section will review some causes of conflict.

Causes of conflict

There are numerous causes for conflict, but only the major causes will be reviewed here. Following is a listing of the primary causes of conflict:

• The *primary cause of conflict is communication*. How people communicate with each other often determines whether a situation will be supportive or combative.

• The next most common cause of conflict is *low self-esteem*. People with low self-esteem have difficulty dealing with disagreement because these persons *perceive it as recognition of their inadequacies*.

• Conflict can be exacerbated by one person constantly pointing out the *other person's faults and failures*.

• Conflict can occur when two people have *extremely low affect or liking for each other*.

• Conflict can occur when two very *dissimilar personality orientations* attempt to communicate.

• Conflict can occur when two very *dissimilar cultures collide*. Extreme cultural differences often lead to conflict. Initially, if affect is low, then the extreme differences in culture and communication often lead to cross-cultural conflicts.

• Conflict can occur if a person is *highly aggressive and overbearing* when communicating with others.[1]

• Conflict can occur when a person communicates with *negative power tactics* rather than using more positive power tactics.

• Conflict can occur when *negative stereotyping* takes place between communicators. For example, New Englanders making fun of Texans or vice versa.

---

1. Dominic A. Infante and Andrew S. Rancer (1982). "A conceptualization and measure of argumentativeness," *Journal of Personality Assessment* 46(1):72-80.

• Conflict can occur when *demeaning or patronizing language* is used.

• Conflict can occur when *negative nonverbal messages* are sent and received, (e.g., student rolling eyes while the teacher is talking).

• Conflict can occur when disagreement is allowed to *continue for extremely long periods* of time without any resolution.

• Conflict can occur when *volatile people* are expected to communicate with *other volatile people.*

• Conflict can occur when people believe that their contributions at school, work, relationships, etc. are *devalued by significant others.*

• Conflict can occur when *obscene, disgusting or politically incorrect language* is used on a long-term basis.

• Conflict can occur when a *defensive atmosphere is created.* Variables leading to defensiveness are: superior-acting persons, people who respond to issues apathetically, feeling threatened, intimated, evaluated, helpless, manipulated or controlled.

Although many factors can lead to conflict, most of these factors can be monitored, controlled or changed if people select to do so.[2]

Conflict prevention and management

Disagreement can be positive for relationships. Conflict is destructive for relationships and should be avoided or prevented. However, it may not always be easy to prevent conflict. If conflict cannot be prevented, then the conflict will have to be managed. This section reviews ways to prevent or avoid conflict.

• People need to learn to *manage their mouth.* This is often difficult because each individual has very patterned (almost scripted) ways to communicate with others. The idea here is to think before opening mouth and inserting foot. If people were more conscious of human communication skills, conflict might be avoided.

• When communicating with another person, attempt to *find common ground or similar attitudes and beliefs.* This is also referred to as "huntin' homophily." Recall

---

2. Stephen P. Robbins (1978). "'Conflict management' and 'conflict resolution' are not synonymous terms," *California Management Review* 21(2):67-75. See also: Richard Wendell Fogg (1985). "Dealing with conflict: A repertoire of creative, peaceful approaches," *Journal of Conflict Resolution* 29(2):330-358.

from a previous chapter (see Perceptions of the Source) that homophily is the perceived similarity between a source and receiver. The more a person feels similar to another, the better the communication and the lower likelihood of conflict.

• People should attempt to develop mutual liking, respect and trust for others. If these are present, then conflict is not likely to occur.

• If possible, build affect through *affinity-seeking strategies*. These strategies, used to build and maintain relationships, are discussed in the chapter on Establishing Interpersonal Relationships.

• Often people have to learn to *avoid situations and persons in which conflict is likely to occur*. This is not always easy, however, many times people can request to work with a person or to not work with another person.

• People who have a low TFD should *attempt to increase their TFD*. Often this is difficult to do because TFD is difficult to change. It can be done with effort and more effective communication skills.

• If a combative confrontation is likely, *try to stay objective; keep an open mind*.

• Lastly, people need to select very carefully the issues or topics on which to argue. Remember good warriors know when to approach and when to avoid. Good warriors also know when they can win or lose. Here, losing is not just losing an argument. It is losing a friend or colleague.

Management of conflict is very difficult.[3] At the point of full-blown conflict, people are probably attempting to hurt, sabotage, undercut or avoid others. This is why prevention is the better alternative. When management is required, it usually means the conflict is now present, ongoing and starting to divide people into camps. If people become involved in serious conflict, it is probably not likely to be resolved.

Generally the only things that might resolve conflict tend to be time and distance. This is often why couples who divorce want to put as much time and distance between themselves as possible. For example, Woody Allen and Mia Farrow may never be able to communicate amicably again because of the seriousness of their conflict. The same is true for the United States and Iran. Because of the seriousness of the conflict, at this point all the United States can do is to attempt to manage conflict. The following are ways in which conflict might be managed:

---

3. Virginia E. Schein (1985). "Organizational realities: The politics of change," *Training and Development Journal* 39(2):37-41. See also: "You can't change the boss, so change yourself," (1995). *Executive Strategies* (October), pp. 1-2.

• People who do not like each other should not be expected to work together on projects. If they are forced to work together, the conflict often escalates.

• Communication between feuding parties should be kept to a minimum.

• Third-party intervention may be required. The third party should be a person who is completely objective.

• Negotiation and compromise need to be tried to manage conflict.[4] Contracts can be written that specify what each person is to do or not to do. Unions and management often use this method.

• If people in conflict must communicate, they must focus on common goals.

• If people in conflict must communicate, keep the communication reinforcing and positive. People should not be allowed to unleash their stockpiled irritations and resentments.

• If people in a conflict attempt to restore trust through affinity-seeking strategies, the conflict may lessen, however, one negative word can cause the conflict to escalate.

Disagreement, then, can be a positive growth experience where people share and learn from challenging, non-threatening communication. Conflict is destructive and dysfunctional. Often conflict cannot be resolved, only managed. As a student once said, "Conflict is a very bad, bad thing. It ruins good feelings about others." The student was absolutely correct. Conflict invades, corrodes and destroys relationships. It is similar to a plague. It often cannot be cured.

Summary

The nature of disagreement and conflict, and the impact of communication on disagreement and conflict are explained. There is a strong relationship between the **possibility that conflicts will occur** and the **level of hostility between individuals**. There is also a strong relationship between the lowered possibility that conflicts will occur and the high level of affinity between people. If people **build affinity**, communicate **objectively** and **positively**, conflict is less likely to occur.

It is **impossible to be conflict free**. Therefore, when conflict arises it must be managed. Conflict can be managed by **reducing contact** between perceived

4. M. Afzalur Rahim (1985). "A strategy for managing conflict in complex organizations," *Human Relations* 38(1):81-89.

combatants, **negotiation** and **compromise, reduction in communication**, and **restoration of trust**. It is important to develop effective human communication skills so people do not find themselves in **irreconcilable** communication situations. Conflict destroys relationships.

Exercises:

A. Virtually all people have been in conflict at one time or another. Write a maximum two-page essay about a time when conflict was present in your life. Describe the situation, the communication and feelings about the situation. If you could go back and rewrite the situation, how would you? Why would you?

B. List two ways to prevent or avoid conflict and two ways to manage conflicts that were **not** given in the chapter. The lists may be shared with the entire class.

Additional methods to avoid conflict:

1.

2.

Additional methods to manage conflict:

1.

2.

15

Communication in the Organizational Setting

Early article: Charles A. O'Reilly III and Karlene H. Roberts (1978). "Organizations as communication structures: An empirical approach," *Human Communication Research* 4(4):282-293.

Middle article: Allan D. Frank (1985). "Trends in communication: Who talks to whom?" *Personnel* 62(12):41-47.

Recent article: Ronald F. Wendt (1994). "Learning to 'walk the talk': A critical tale of the micropolitcs at a total quality university," *Management Communication Quarterly* 8(1):5-45.

Organizations are such an omnipresent facet of people's lives today that many corporations are establishing on-site counselors, wellness programs, programs for total body fitness, diet centers, food distribution centers, relaxation centers, reading rooms, movie viewing rooms and even bars. Organizations have become to the current adult in the United States what churches in smaller communities have been for years: a gathering place to learn about the world and to socialize with others.

In this culture, people spend most of their adult lives working within and for some type of organization (profit, non profit, not-for-profit). Given this fact, it is important that people learn the basics about effective and successful communication in the organizational environment.[1]

---

1. Ronald J. Burke (1984). "Mentors in organizations," *Group and Organization Studies* 9(3):353-372. See also: Sue DeWine (1994). *The consultant's craft: Improving organizational communication.* New York: St. Martin's Press; Brenda J. Allen, Philip K. Tompkins and Stephen Busemeyer (1996). "Organizational communication," in Michael B. Salwen and Don W. Stacks, eds. *An integrated approach to communication theory and research.* Mahwah, NJ: Lawrence Erlbaum Associates, pp. 383-395.

Communication is the tool by which people succeed or fail in organizations. It takes effective communication to make job experiences work. This chapter reviews concepts and information that employees need to know about communication to survive and thrive in the organizational environment. It provides information that should help people survive organizations on a daily basis and not "look like idiots."

As Scott Adams, creator of *Dilbert* suggests, in the work force, "Everyone is an idiot, not just the people with low SAT scores. The only difference among us is that we're idiots about different things at different times. No matter how smart you are, you spend much of your day being an idiot." The communication ideas presented in this unit should help "idiot proof" employees in organizations.[2]

Idea 1: "It's not what you know but who you know." Sad, but true in too many cases. Whether a person works in a school, prison, business, health care, education, military, public service or an insurance system, unless the person is extremely multi-talented and incredibly brilliant the person needs to know the informal networking in the organization. Formal networking is usually rather straightforward. It follows the "chain of command" and is based on organizational charts.

Informal networking can be complex. The informal network is often described as the grapevine that grows throughout the organization. It is also referred to as the unseen communication connections that usually have little or nothing to do with the formal network. Every employee needs to know the formal network, but equally important is the informal network (who is really talking with whom).

Employees who fail to become socialized and do not learn the informal networking system in their organization are likely to make many communication mistakes. Employees need to know who is talking to whom, who is spending time with whom, who eats lunch together, who plays golf together, who lives where, and who was last promoted and why. Through socialization, employees can learn the unspoken and unwritten norms of the organization.[3] Employees learn what to wear, how to talk, what to say and what not to say. Again, brilliant employees may not need to be aware of the socialization process and informal networking, however, less-than-brilliant employees will find this information essential. Often decisions are made on the basis of whom a person knows, not what the person knows.

---

2. Scott Adams (1996). *The Dilbert Principle: A cubicle's-eye view of bosses, meetings, management fads and other workplace afflictions.* New York: HarperBusiness, p. 2.

3. Fredric M. Jablin and Kathleen J. Krone (1987). "Organizational assimilation," in Charles R. Berger and Steven H. Chaffee, eds. *Handbook of communication science.* Newbury Park, CA: Sage Publications, pp. 711-746.

Exercise:

Each student should interview a professional in some organization about how that professional obtained her or his job and how important communication is to job success. Questions to be asked include:

Who, in school, helped you obtain this job?

What advice did people give you for obtaining a job?

What, if any, were their connections to the organization for which you work?

How many other people in the organization are from your area of study?

How many other people in the organization are from your school or region of the country?

How important is communication in your job?

Do you attend social functions sponsored by the organization? Why or why not?

Who helped you get integrated or socialized into the organization? Was their mentoring useful? Please explain.

How do you get news about what is happening in the organization, other than from formal means, such as newsletters, office memos and so on?

Write a maximum three-page essay, or use the questions as headings for a maximum three-page Q&A paper. Be prepared to discuss your findings in class and to submit your work for a grade.

Idea 2: When in doubt, listen more, talk less. This is a very difficult idea for most people in this culture to absorb. In the organizational setting, there are many people who have input on decision-making. Often employees are expected to give input on decisions about which they have little knowledge. However, most of the organizational writers suggest that if a person is in doubt about her or his contribution, it is probably best to listen more and speak less. In this society speaking receives much more attention, listening less. However, if employees participate in discussions they know little about, they are only revealing their ignorance, not their brilliance. New employees need to listen, learn and position themselves where the action is in the organization.

Idea 3: People in organizations should establish themselves first, then argue about issues. Employees should be less disagreeable and argumentative and more supportive in the initial stages of assimilation into an organization. To become an accepted, liked and a respected colleague, new people will have to "pay dues" and prove that they are good colleagues and subordinates. In organizations, regardless of a person's skill, education or experience, people are expected to demonstrate that they can assimilate into the organizational culture before others will listen to their ideas about change or other company concerns.[4]

Most new employees have wonderfully innovative ideas for improvement, but the organization was there long before the new employee, and most likely will be there long after the new employee has moved on. The people who have been in the organization for a substantial period of time are committed to the organization the way it is. Organizational culture says their way is best. Therefore, only after a person has been acculturated into the organization should the person begin to disagree or argue about important issues.

In general, organizations do not reward the argumentative new person. Organizations often listen or simply tolerate the argumentative veteran employee, but with new employees the overall reaction to disagreement is negative.

Idea 4: Employees need to dodge conflicts with others. There may be nothing more damaging to a person's potential for success in an organization than getting into a conflict situation with another person in the organization. If new people find themselves in conflict situations, then the communication will be mostly negative. Additionally, new employees may not know sufficient persons to give them support or guidance. The new employee who becomes involved in a conflict situation in an organization is likely to fail.

Perhaps the best way to remember this idea is to keep in mind that risk-taking is very risky for new employees. If well-established employees make mistakes, get into conflict or have other issues occur, these veteran people have a history of good efforts to fall back on. Newer employees do not. If the conflict escalates, it is likely that the supervisor will support the veteran employee, not the newer employee.

Idea 5: New employees need to talk the talk and walk the walk. This idea reinforces the importance of the "homophily principle." People like to talk with and work with others who are similar in attitudes, beliefs, language, background, dress, education, work ethic and so on. In organizations, opposites do not attract. Generally, any employee who seems too independent or autonomous is usually

---

4. Allan O. Frank and Judi L. Brownell (1989).*Organizational communication and behavior: Communicating to improve performance, 2+2=5*. New York: Holt, Rinehart and Winston.

perceived by other employees as being very different and perhaps out-of-line. The problem with being too different is that the new person will not be integrated and socialized into the informal network.[5] Hence, the new person is missing much of the valuable interpersonal communication the organization has to offer.

Idea 6: Stop the whining and do the job. Almost everyone is hired on a trial basis in any organization. Many employees do not survive the trial phase (this is often the first six months) before others have made negative evaluations that will adversely affect the new employee's career.[6] Whiny employees usually whine openly and loudly about their boss and co-workers behind their backs, perhaps at social gatherings or functions outside the immediate work unit. Whiners usually think this will help them obtain higher status, when in fact all whining does is keep the new employee from being considered for other types of work or positions.

Often the new employee who whines is isolated by the work group. No employee wants to be seen talking with the whiner because it could negatively influence that employee's advancement. Lastly, if a supervisor has substantial evidence that a new employee is whining about the work or the supervisor, the supervisor will make sure that the whiny employee does not want to stay with the organization.

Idea 7: When in doubt about how to get something done, follow the proper communication channels in the organization. Often new employees will be perceived as if they are not following the proper communication channels because they fail to go to their immediate supervisor for assistance.[7] New employees' fear being perceived as stupid. Therefore, they will often ask someone other than their immediate supervisor about an issue or task. This is a mistake.

When new employees do not follow the chain of command, their immediate supervisor will perceive them as "bypassing" or going over their head. Almost any supervisor (even an amiable one) will become upset with an employee who seems to ignore the chain of command and bypasses the immediate supervisor.

Idea 8: Keep the nose clean and out of other people's business. Very few people in organizations will tolerate the employee who is always "poking their nose" into everyone else's work or business. These are the people who think they are "in the know" when in fact they are not in the know but in the idiot's mode. Such

---

5. Mark Hickson III and Don W. Stacks with Marilyn Padgett-Greely (1998). *Organizational communication in the personal context: From interview to retirement*. Boston: Allyn and Bacon.

6. Fredric M. Jablin (1985). "An exploratory study of vocational organizational communication socialization," *Southern Speech Communication Journal* 50(3):261-282.

7. Fredric M. Jablin (1979). "Superior-subordinate communication: The state of the art," *Psychological Bulletin* 86(6):1201-1222.

employees try to gain access to the rumor mill by telling others what they learn from snooping. After awhile, people stop communicating significant issues with these employees for fear anything said will be misinterpreted or used against them.

New employees should view their position in the organization this way:[8]

1. They were hired by or placed under the domain of their immediate supervisor who will be perceived as a more capable manager if the new employee succeeds (accomplishes assigned tasks and is accepted by the people in the task force).

2. Failure by a new employee reflects poorly on the managerial skills of the supervisor.

3. One aspect of success is the level of rapport between employee and supervisor, measured in part by close and positive communication between the two.

4. If a work colleague is always saying negative things about co-workers and bosses to you, what might that colleague be saying to others about you?

Lastly, always CYA (cover your behind). Never talk or write yourself into a corner. Terms and statements such as "never, always, there is only one way, it's impossible," should be avoided. CYA is not lying, cheating and blaming colleagues; it is simply using common sense and good communication skills. People must be flexible and versatile in communication if they expect to be perceived as competent communicators. Persons who do not CYA often are not competent communicators.

Summary

Why do some people do well in their jobs and others do not? Some of the answers to this question are reviewed in the chapter. Often people receive good education and training for the workplace, however, these same people sometimes seem to forget the information as soon as they get their first job.

Getting a job is often easier than keeping a job. Therefore, new employees should implement the guidelines, the **eight ideas** the chapter provides. When entering a new organization for the first time do the following: talk with people who can help, listen to others who have been in the organization for some period of time, don't whine, focus on your work not other people's work, be agreeable, dodge conflicts, build homophily and follow the proper communication channels.

---

8. George Fuller (1996). *The workplace survival guide: Tools, tips and techniques for succeeding on the job*. Englewood Cliffs, NJ: Prentice Hall.

Exercise:

A. Develop ideas to add to the eight already reviewed in the chapter. Try to add **three** ideas that are not subsumed by the eight ideas given. Prepare the three ideas in three separate paragraphs below. Your ideas might be discussed in class and submitted for a grade.

New idea 1:

New idea 2:

New idea 3:

16
Communication, People and Change

Early article: Everett M. Rogers and A. Eugene Havens (1962). "Predicting innovativeness," *Sociological Inquiry 32*(1):34-42.

Contemporary article: Virginia E. Schein (1985). "Organizational realities: The politics of change," *Training and Development Journal 39*(2):37-41.

In organizations, regardless of how bad things are now, many persons resist change. Most often the reasons for resisting are centered on status, money and job complications. In today's organizational climate, change is inevitable. People should understand what is taking place and be prepared to deal effectively with change.

For decades, scholars and practitioners have studied why people adopt certain innovations (or make change) and reject others. Change and innovation is a key topic in the organizational communication process. Most major firms have change agents, consultants or trainers on site to assist with the change process. Because of advances in technology and human relations, change is an ongoing process in most organizations. However, the majority of changes fail.

Rogers suggests that changes fail primarily because organizations and change agents do not target the people in communication networks who determine if change will adopted and continued. Rogers suggests that "an individual's network links are important determinants of his or her adoption of innovations."[1] This chapter reviews the network roles of people in organizations, the influence each role has on change and the conditions needed for successful change.

---

1. Everett M. Rogers (1995). *Diffusion of innovations, 4th ed*. New York: Free Press, p. 310. See also: Terrance L. Albrecht and Bradford 'J' Hall (1991). "Facilitating talk about new ideas: The role of personal relationships in organizational innovation," *Communication Monographs 58*(3):273-288.

Change and communication network roles

The roles discussed here are primarily representations of roles some employees play in an organization's informal communication network. Each role affects the diffusion of a new idea. Most personnel realize that to produce change they need the support of upper management (the formal network). However, people in the informal network (those not listed on the organization's hierarchical chart, but who may be highly influential) also are integral to any successful change process. Six critical roles and their influence on change are reviewed.

The first role is called a **bridge**. This is a person who connects two or more groups in a system because of the person's position as a member of one of the groups. Figure 1 illustrates a bridge. Bridges are important in the change process because they have a close and influential relationship with the other members of their primary group, and they establish strong communication links with other groups.

Change agents should target the bridge to assist with introducing an organizational change. If a bridge accepts the change, then that person might persuade the primary group and possibly influence other groups about the change. Because the bridge exchanges information between that person's primary group and members of other groups, the person influences at least two groups in the organization.

A **liaison** is a person who links two or more groups in a system without being a member of any specific group. This individual does not have a primary group connection (like a bridge) but serves as a link between or among groups (see Figure 2). This person is often referred to as a *linker* or *linking pin* within organizations.

Rogers and Agarwala Rogers note that "liaisons are positioned at the crossroads of information flows in an organization. Liaisons have been called the cement

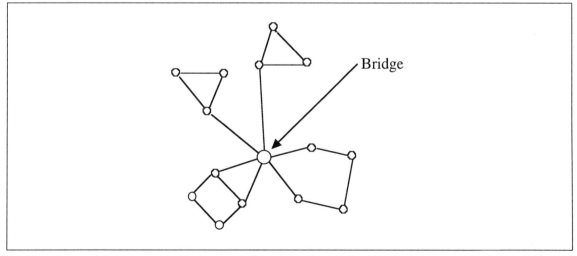

Figure 1. Bridge connecting organizational groups as a group member

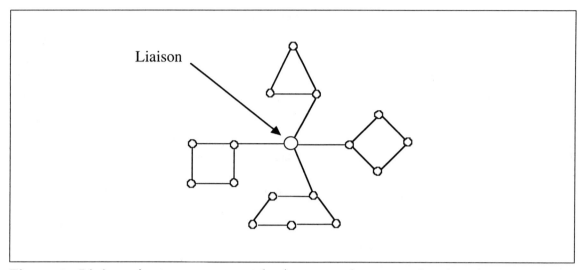

Figure 2. Liaison (not a group member) connecting organizational groups

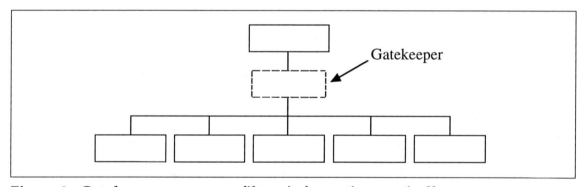

Figure 3. Gatekeeper screens or filters information vertically

that holds the structural brick of an organization together; when the liaisons are removed, the system tends to fall into isolated cliques."[2] Being at the crossroads of information systems, with access to both information and people, liaisons can influence individuals and groups to accept or reject a change.

A **gatekeeper** is an individual who is located in a position in the communication structure with the ability to control the flow, progression and movement of messages throughout the organization (see Gatekeeping chapter). These are people who, by virtue of their positioning in the formal network, have access to much of the information that flows upward or downward in the system (see Figure 3). The gatekeeper can screen or filter information. Gatekeepers can be very influential in the change process because they control access to information, ideas and concerns that members of an organization might want or need to have.

---

2. Everett M. Rogers and Rekha Agarwala Rogers (1976). *Communication in organizations.* New York: Free Press, p. 135.

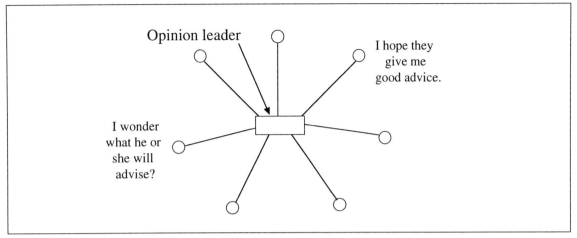

Figure 4. Opinion leader acts as informal leader in the change process

Another critical informal role in the change diffusion process is the **opinion leader**. Others in the system view this person as an informal leader who can provide valuable information or advice about the change or innovation. Opinion leadership is an individual's ability to influence other people's attitudes or behaviors in a desired way. These informal leaders are not born or appointed; their influence is not a function of their formal position or status in the system. Opinion leadership is earned, maintained and perpetuated by competence, accessibility, homophily, willingness to communicate, and referent and expert power with others (followers). Opinion leaders can be highly influential because other persons in the organization allow opinion leaders to influence their attitudes and behaviors.

A **cosmopolite** is an individual in a primary organization who has a high degree of communication with the external society that may affect the organization. These people are similar to gatekeepers in that "they control the communication flow by which new ideas enter the system."[3] Cosmopolites are usually well-versed, well-traveled and highly educated persons who have affiliations with national and international organizations. They are often in professional occupations with high migration rates, such as regional sales manager or public relations (see Figure 5). Cosmopolites are great resources to most systems and can be very influential in terms of change. Their education, travel and expansive contacts outside their own organization give openness to the system and can assist with needed change.

Last but not least is an established group of persons that can be highly influential in the organizational change process. These are the "old boys and old girls."[4] There is no illustration for these persons...just picture an 800-pound gorilla.

---

3. Everett M. Rogers and Rekha Agarwala Rogers, *Ibid.*, p. 140.
4. Virginia P. Richmond and James C. McCroskey (1992). *Organizational communication for survival*. Englewood Cliffs, NJ: Prentice Hall.

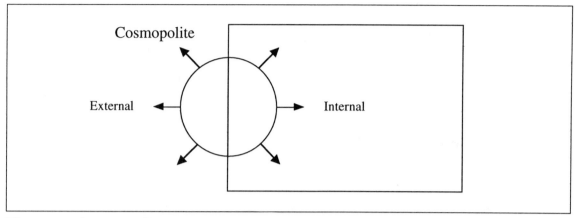

Figure 5. Cosmopolite communicates to organization's external environment

These persons have been in the organization longer, have communication connections throughout the system and know "who is really talking to whom and about what." They know where all the skeletons are buried. In fact, they probably buried a few! Their influence comes from knowing the system's informal communication network better than most of the formal leaders. This is not to suggest that they are all "chronologically old," although some might be. In technology industries, for example, many are very young, but they have been in the organization longer.

The old boys and girls can influence change in either a positive or negative way. If this group supports the change, it has a higher likelihood of being implemented; if not, the change may have little chance of success. People who want the change need to work with the old boy/girl network, regardless of the difficulty. It may only take one old boy or one old girl to stop a change that could benefit all. Making these people part of the process helps the change move through the system.

Necessary conditions for change

The organization must **have or create the needed resources**. The resources most organizations need for change are: personnel, time, finances, space, equipment and so on. If these "slack" (not currently being used) resources are not available or cannot be allocated, then change is not likely to occur. The informal network can often help others secure needed resources. While every group has members with good ideas, many organizations lack the resources to make the good ideas realities.

As suggested earlier, for change to be considered, the new idea must be **supported by both the formal and informal communication networks**. If either of these leaders say "NO," then the change is not likely to be adopted. True, the formal leaders can introduce a change and force members of the organization to use the new idea. However, this type of coercive change usually results in a low adoption rate and poor use of the change. Simply put, forced change usually fails.[5] So for a new idea to have a possibility of success, it usually must have the support of both groups of leaders gained only through effective communication with each group.

People who are expected to implement the change should be **involved from the initial stages of the change process**. This means that *critical personnel* such as opinion leaders, liaisons, managers and the others should be involved if the change is to succeed.[6] When critical personnel who might support and diffuse the innovation are excluded from the change process, the change may fail miserably.

Every change must be **customized to each specific organization**. All too often, people forget this principle. A person cannot assume that what worked at IBM will work at Ford or vice versa. Often a change that works in one organization will be incompatible with another organization. Each organization has specific rules, regulations, norms, culture and personnel that make it different from any other organization.[7] Thus, an innovation must be adapted to each specific organization. People in many of the informal network roles can assist with this adaptation. Opinion leaders, old boys/girls and others can identify problem areas in the proposed change and suggest corrective action. If complications occur during adoption, time must be taken to iron them out or the innovation is almost certain to fail.

Every change must show **obvious, positive results soon** or the change may be discontinued. This is a common practice in American culture. For example, many health and beauty products suggest when and how customers should look for positive results. If a customer buys an expensive, whitening toothpaste that boasts results in seven days or less, the buyer will begin looking for positive results within a week. Unless the change is obvious, the buyer will revert to the previous toothpaste. Organizations need to inform people what the results will be, when to look for the outcomes, and they must assist employees in observing the positive results.

Lastly, change that is **gradual, carefully organized and orderly** is more likely to be accepted than change that is **forced, massive, unpredictable, disorganized or disorderly**. Often during quick changes things seem unpredictable and disorganized.

---

5. J. Scott Armstrong (1982). "Strategies for implementing change: An experimental approach," *Group and Organization Studies* 7(4):457-475. See also: Nancy J. Howes and Robert E. Quinn (1978). "Implementing change: From research to a prescriptive framework," *Group and Organization Studies* 3(1):71-79.
6. Hussein M. Shatshat and Bong-Gon P. Shin (1981). "Organizational communication: A key to successful strategic planning," *Managerial Planning* 30(2):37-40. See also: Noel M. Tichy (1982). "Managing change strategically: The technical, political, and cultural keys," *Organizational Dynamics* 11(2):59-80.
7. Terrance L. Albrecht and Vickie A. Ropp (1984). "Communicating about innovation in networks of three U.S. organizations," *Journal of Communication* 34(3):78- 91.

Even if the change is working as anticipated, quick, massive changes give the impression of chaos. Effective use of communication channels and designated personnel gives sources information from receivers about making the needed changes and how to go about achieving the desired changes.[8]

This is the right way to pursue change, and it also involves the people who will be implementing the change. Once information is accrued concerning the change and the necessary people become committed, the process can be implemented gradually and carefully so that everyone will have an opportunity to incorporate the change and make it work.[9]

Summary

The necessary conditions for change must be met or the change may fail. Part of the change process encompasses working with the people playing several key communication roles. These roles all have some major impact on the change process in organizations.

Bridges help link groups and individuals. **Liaisons** link many groups. **Gatekeepers** screen, filter and highlight information as it flows up and down the organization. **Opinion leaders** are influential because others in the organization listen to them for advice or information. **Cosmopolites** are influential because this role has access to external information and knowledge that can help a change move through a system. **Good old boys** and **good old girls** have access to all the data and communication that has occurred in the organization in the past. They facilitate or impede change by using the information they have by virtue of being in the system longer than most other persons.

Necessary conditions for organizational change include having or creating the **needed resources**. Change must also be supported by both the **formal** and **informal** communication networks. Those who are expected to implement the change should be **involved from the initial stages** of the change process. Change must be **customized** to each specific organization, must show **obvious, positive results** <u>soon</u>, and must be **gradual, carefully organized and orderly**.

---

8. Noel M. Tichy (1983). "Managing organizational transformations," *Human Resource Management* 22(1-2):45-60.

9. Anne Donnellon, Barbara Gray and Michel G. Bougon (1986). "Communication, meaning, and organized action," *Administrative Science Quarterly* 31(1):43-55.

Exercise:

For the following topics, name a student in your class who might be an opinion leader for you. If you don't know the name, indicate who you mean (tall guy on the back row). More than one person may be listed for each of the topics:

Movies _____   Technology _____

Clothing _____   Dating _____

Good food _____   Good books _____

Automobiles _____   Children _____

Politics _____   Music _____

Sports _____   Travel _____

Money
management _____   Healthy
                                   lifestyles _____

Now, tally the number of times the same person's name appeared on your list. For example, how many times did "Student A, Jones" appear?

	Name/Designation	Times Appeared
Student A:	_____	_____
Student B:	_____	_____
Student C:	_____	_____
Student D:	_____	_____
Student E:	_____	_____
Student F:	_____	_____

17
Coorientation: The Other Matters

Donna Besser, APR
Ohio University, Ph.D.

Early article: Richard F. Carter (1965). "Communication and affective relations," *Journalism Quarterly* 42(2):203-212.

Contemporary article: H. Leslie Steeves (1984). "Developing coorientation measures for small groups," *Communication Monographs* 51(2):185-192.

More recent article: Robert W. Jones (1993). "Coorientation of a news staff and its audience," *Communication Reports* 6(1):41-46.

It's all about you — or is it? Ever wonder how someone got elected scrapbook keeper, much less an officer in an important student-run group, or why the student sitting on the left always earns a letter-grade higher than everyone else? And how about that invitation that always seems to be getting "lost in the mail?" Solving these painful but too common mysteries requires a little bit of thought about somebody else. More precisely, "Of course it's all about you, but always in relation to others!"

Exercise 1:
Wait until you are in class to do this exercise on coorientation and its implications. Circle the number that most closely describes **your opinion** about **rap music**:

like	7	6	5	4	3	2	1	dislike
annoying	1	2	3	4	5	6	7	pleasant
uplifting	7	6	5	4	3	2	1	degrading
indecent	1	2	3	4	5	6	7	decent
interesting	7	6	5	4	3	2	1	dull
pointless	1	2	3	4	5	6	7	insightful

Use the same scale, but this time give the opinion you think the **other gender** of students in this class will have about rap music. That is, circle the number that you think most closely describes (men's or women's) opinion about **rap music**:

like	7	6	5	4	3	2	1	dislike
annoying	1	2	3	4	5	6	7	pleasant
uplifting	7	6	5	4	3	2	1	degrading
indecent	1	2	3	4	5	6	7	decent
interesting	7	6	5	4	3	2	1	dull
pointless	1	2	3	4	5	6	7	insightful

Your teacher will have further instructions for discussing these scales in class.

*   *   *

A glance back to scholarly work in the early 1950s, provides answers about "The Other Matters." Social psychologist Theodore Newcomb identified **human interaction** as communicative acts that enable two or more people to *simultaneously orient, or share attitudes and opinions*. Good, bad or indifferent, the opinions are born from emotions and factual knowledge about some object. Such opinions, or simultaneous orientation about a topic, are referred to as coorientation.[1]

Coorientation explains the link between two people and the object of their conversation. This interdependence of communicators and object constitutes a system including three important variables: Accuracy, Agreement and Congruency. Newcomb's model (see Models chapter) shows A communicating with B about X:

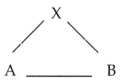

The primary elements in the A-B-X system may be explained as:
1) what A thinks/feels about B
2) what A thinks/feels about X
3) what B thinks/feels about A
4) what B thinks/feels about X

---

1. Theodore M. Newcomb (1953). "An approach to the study of communicative acts," *Psychological Review* 60(6):393-404.

These definitions further clarify the three related coorientational values: 1) **accuracy** is the degree to which A correctly perceives the regard B holds about X; 2) **agreement** is the similarity of opinions held by A and B about X; and, 3) **congruency** is the perceived agreement between A's opinion about X and what A believes is the opinion of B about X.

Yes, it gets tricky right away. John loves Mary, Mary loves John…and there's a Harley Davidson motorcycle involved. Think of accuracy as how *correctly* Mary perceives John's love for his Hog. Think of agreement as how *similarly* John and Mary perceive the Hog (Mary loves that bad bike, too). Think of congruency as this relationship: John loves his Hog, but he thinks Mary doesn't like it (low congruency); John loves his Hog, and he believes that Mary likes it too (high congruency) because they've had some good times on that bike. The analogy ends now because the X in ABX does not mean X-rated.

Although A and B coorient about X, quite possibly they agree to dislike X! Also, their views may differ in degree, being more or less shared. Shared views suggest a symmetrical relationship. The more people talk, the more each gravitates toward the opinion of the other. Scholars label the effect **strain for symmetry**. Certainly, people do not always agree, nor will they reach full agreement regardless of how long they talk. Still, the very human tendency to communicate and solve problems is present even if the two people merely agree to disagree. The real benefit of symmetry is being able to *rapidly predict another person's behavior.*

As simple as the ABX concept may be, Newcomb recognized that this coorientation model offered promise because of its adaptability across a multitude of approaches. First, there is a contextual element, or regard for the environment. Whether the two people are on a tropical island with or without a boat or in downtown Manhattan with or without a taxi is unimportant. What does matter is including the **environment** of their mutual understanding. To maintain coorientation, each person must discover the shared interests in their common environment.

Equally important is **social reality**, or the recognition of the other's orientation to objects in the environment. Social reality is nested, consciously and unconsciously, in everyday language and *expressed as opinions or judgments about other people or objects*. Thinking individuals may derive their own conclusions, but they inherently rely on the opinions of others for verification. A parent warns, "Don't touch the stove! You'll get burned." The headstrong child unhappily learns about hot stoves. For a reality check, a safer test is social confirmation from someone else.

In the late 1950s, when American media use was flourishing, Bruce Westley and Malcolm MacLean expanded on Newcomb's work to create their A-C-B model, purposefully directing researchers to *mass communication* coorientation studies.

Newcomb envisioned A and B as people talking about something. Westley and MacLean included a person, a primary group or a social system as being either or both A and B.[2] This new general model of the total communication process took studies to several new levels and types of messages.

Interpersonal coorientation

Chaffee and McLeod, sufficiently armed to build on earlier theory, introduced their model for interpersonal communication in 1968. They tested whether symmetry is maximized when "two people living together (roommates or spouses) are exposed repeatedly to similar information."[3] The assumptions are that: a) individuals know what they think, b) they have a good grasp of what their partner thinks, and c) as a couple, the two will discuss information they have in common.

Chaffee and McLeod tested the symmetry notion using a sophisticated experiment that controls intervening variables. Each set of "couples," either spouses, roommates or non-cohabitants, was interviewed about their feelings toward the U.S. Selective Service policy: the draft. At that time, the Vietnam conflict was a national dilemma with emotions running hot for those on the left and right sides of the political continuum. The topic was suited for sensitization, or having the couples talk about the topic between survey administrations in a panel design.

First, the groups were given a pre-test survey and some couples were told there would be a follow-up survey. The groups were expected to discuss the topic naturally, without "intervention" by the researcher, and were given ample opportunity to do so between the first and second questionnaire. The idea was to find out what and how the couples talked with each other about the questionnaire, and to make a thorough examination of each couple's answers. The researchers were more interested in the coorientational values of accuracy, agreement and congruency than the actual opinions each person held about the war or the draft.

Couples who live together were expected to communicate more frequently and to more easily achieve understanding of each other's perceptions than the non-cohabitant pairs. Such understanding facilitates agreement, a value that has proven useful in predicting behavior. By definition, the three constructs are intrinsically linked, so a change in any of the variables causes changes in others. As Chaffee and McLeod explained: 1) if agreement is held constant and high, accuracy increases will increase congruency; and 2) if agreement is held constant and low, accuracy

———

2. Bruce H. Westley and Malcolm S. MacLean Jr. (1957). "A conceptual model for communications research," *Journalism Quarterly* 34(1):31-38.

3. Steven H. Chaffee and Jack M. McLeod (1968). "Sensitization in panel design: A coorientational experiment," *Journalism Quarterly* 45(4):661-669.

increases will decrease congruency. The researchers found that communication can increase accuracy, leading to agreement, but communication may not create total agreement. Still, the heart of this study was to determine if strain for symmetry intensifies, especially when each of the two people knows the other has gained additional information on the topic in common.[4]

Couples completed a current events survey during each of the two separate testings. Each test included items asking the participants their opinions about the opinions of their partner. All respondents were asked about their communication activities during the week. Finally, response comparisons were made between those of each couple and all communication activities.

Science confirmed it: People will talk! When each of the two members of a couple realized they and their partner were pre-tested then warned about the next test, each focused on the other's opinions. In this case, each person achieved greater accuracy about the other's opinion. However, couples who were pre-tested but not warned, sought communications outside the home. In those cases, there was higher understanding but lower accuracy reached between members of a couple.

This interpersonal communication experiment revealed the private patterns of communication behaviors, but the study also offered implications for mass communication.

Mass communication coorientation

A free marketplace of ideas requires a diversity of information. Media messages can increase accuracy without the social pressure, or strain for symmetry, that can reduce ideas or opinions by forcing a state of agreement. Indeed, scholars were inspired to build on those concepts to examine wider communication situations:

• A 1973 generation gap study of the perceptions of University of North Dakota students vs. those of Grand Forks "townsfolk" toward the local police.[5]

• Two 1975 studies: Culbertson's commentary on coorientation by mass media gatekeepers in trying to understand their audiences, and Mark Popovich's analysis of the news preferences of reporters, editors and publishers.[6]

---

4. *Ibid.*

5. Keith R. Stamm, John E. Bowes and Barbara J. Bowes (1973). "Generation gap a communication problem? A coorientational analysis," *Journalism Quarterly* 50(4):629-637.

6. Hugh M. Culbertson (1975). "Gatekeeper coorientation: A viewpoint for analysis of popular culture and specialized journalism," *Mass Comm Review* 3(1):3-7; Mark Popovich (1975/1976). *Coorientation in the newsroom: An analysis of the news preferences of reporters, editors, and publishers.* Unpublished dissertation at Southern Illinois University at Carbondale.

• A 1976 study of rural vs. urban Wisconsin state senators' attitude related to constituent opinion by Michael Hesse.[7]

• A 1979 study by Elden Rawlings of what constitutes a good newspaper as perceived by the newspaper editor vs. young adult audience members.[8]

• William Tillinghast's 1983 study of sources' views about the accuracy of newspaper accounts in which sources tended to judge published information from their perspective of what should have been rather than what was.[9]

• A 1984 field study comparing subordinates' communication satisfaction with managers, and supervisors' evaluations of worker performance.[10]

• Two 1986 studies: one of public relations practitioners' vs. journalists' views on one another's roles in providing and processing education news, and another of public relations practitioners' views about corporate social responsibility.[11]

• A 1987 study by Judith Buddenbaum finding that religion reporters' selection of news from a denominational news service depends on the reporter's own religious preference, but even more on the reporter's assessment of the religious composition in the newspaper's circulation area.[12]

• A 1990 Q-sort study of how retailers and advertising representatives viewed customers' perceptions. Here Ann Marie Major reported that coorientation was a "useful and robust theory."[13]

• A 1991 factor analysis study of journalists and public relations practitioners' perceptions toward their own and each other's roles. Daradirek Ekachai found low

7. Michael B. Hesse (1976). "A coorientation study of Wisconsin state senators and their constituencies," *Journalism Quarterly* 53(4):626-633, 660.

8. Elden Rawlings (1979). "What editors and young people think of newspapers: Testing a method for measuring reader expectations," *Newspaper Research Journal*, Prototype:23-29.

9. William A. Tillinghast (1983). "Source control and evaluation of newspaper inaccuracies," *Newspaper Research Journal* 5(1):13-24.

10. Eric M. Eisenberg, Peter R. Monge and Richard V. Farace (1984). "Coorientation on communication rules in managerial dyads," *Human Communication Research* 11(2):261-271.

11. Sandra Kruger Stegall and Keith P. Sanders (1986). "Coorientation of pr practitioners and news personnel in education news," *Journalism Quarterly* 63(2):341-347,393; Michael Ryan (1986). "Public relations practitioners' views of corporate social responsibility," *Journalism Quarterly* 63(4): 740-747, 762.

12. Judith M. Buddenbaum (1987). "Predicting religion reporters' use of a denominational news service," *Newspaper Research Journal* 8(3):59-70.

13. Ann Marie Major (1990). "Attributional bias in predictions of retail advertising content preferences," *Journalism Quarterly* 67(4):826-837.

agreement and congruency, but high accuracy between the two. They were able to estimate each other's views, despite their different opinions about the other's role.[14]

Ohio University scholar Hugh Culbertson applied coorientation to discussion of responsibility and press criticism in a 1981 study.[15] He found that editors operate under one of three schools of thought: 1) **traditional** (neutral), stressing fact accuracy and speed, adherence to conventions about news writing, news judgment and layout; 2) **interpretative**, incorporating social science and historical research to study every aspect of events and their meaning; and, 3) **activist** or proactive reporting with a list of prescriptions to correct the ills of society.

Culbertson compared five groups of newspaper reporters' and editors' perception of the audience and to the three schools of thought. Generally, editors and reporters disagree, but problems focus on organizational operations, not with the concept or practice of journalism. However, disagreement can be viewed as healthy, particularly in observing and revealing human behavior. Coorientation research predicts that increased communication facilitates accuracy and agreement, whether inside or outside an organization.

Three years later, Culbertson revisited those three belief clusters by studying journalists, and how and why the press functions.[16] He found that journalists are usually reporters before they are editors. Reporters tend to coorient with the source, rather than the audience. Then, some of those hard-working reporters become editors. At these more advanced stages in both age and position, more thought is given to gaining and keeping readers. Editors begin thinking about what the audience may be thinking. The longer editors live in a community and feel an integral part of it, the more their views are congruent with media consumers.

Clearly, this model provides direction to define approaches in editorial work. Culbertson also raised the question of **causal direction**. That is, does a person's job determine beliefs, or do those beliefs determine an individual's job choice? Such broad issues certainly pertain to all other organizations and careers.

Using this coorientation perspective, one group of researchers assessed the affects of televised sports in long-standing relationships. The main thrust centered on the "football widow," a partner relationship and behavior transformations due

---

14. Daradirek Ekachai (1991). *Perceptions of journalists and public relations practitioners toward their own and each other's roles: Coorientation and factor analyses.* Unpublished dissertation at Southern Illinois University at Carbondale.

15. Hugh M. Culbertson (1981). "Reporters and editors: Some differences in perspective," *Newspaper Research Journal* 2(2):17-27.

16. Hugh M. Culbertson (1983). "Three perspectives on American Journalism," *Journalism Monographs No. 83.*

to television use among 92 couples in two major U.S. cities.[17] Accuracy, agreement and congruency value responses were compared according to each partner, not according to males vs. females. Results indicate that partners agree, although there were some differences between partners about viewing their favorite sports. In the final analysis, the "football widow" is in a league of her own, and a very small league it is. Actually, the "football widow" is a myth.

Initially, coorientation began with two people having a conversation about a topic. Researchers expanded the idea to several couples dealing with the same topic, then broadened further to members of an organization trying to relate to one another. In another knowledge construction, studies encompassed executives and employees of mass media attempting to understand one another and their outside audiences. Finally coorientation was invoked to look at couples being influenced by a mass medium. Still, the simple model itself is functional in broader contexts.

Societal coorientation

One broader context was examining grassroots efforts to affect social change by altering philanthropic development attitudes at Grameen Bank of Bangladesh.[18] Scholars used coorientation to study communication networks linking those seeking funding with bank loaning operations. Before participating, people who were to benefit from new policies (new bank customers) had to accurately understand and agree with the bank's structure, process and guidelines. Field workers and top bank administrators had to develop plans consistent with the needs of the poor.

Bank executives came to understand that poor people needed environmentally sound but small, profitable projects. The bank supported micro-enterprises fostering self-employment and community economic reforms. In a stunning accomplishment, the bank backed large numbers of Bangladesh's poor people in creating jobs, generating income and vastly improving socio-economic conditions.

Coorientation also was one aspect of a study by Shinobu Suzuki that explored networks, including cultural transmission within international organizations.[19] This project involved surveying 118 Japanese and U.S. employees at a Japanese-

---

17. Walter Gantz, Lawrence A. Wenner, Christina Carrico and Matt Knorr (1995). "Assessing the football widow hypothesis: A coorientation study of the role of televised sports in long-standing relationships," *Journal of Sport & Social Issues* 19(4):352-376.

18. Michael J. Papa, Mohammad A. Auwal and Arvind Singhal (1995). "Dialectic of control and emancipation in organizing for social change: A multitheoretic study of the Grameen Bank in Bangladesh," *Communication Theory* 5(3):189-223.

19. Shinobu Suzuki (1997). "Cultural transmission in international organizations: Impact of interpersonal communication patterns in intergroup contexts," *Human Communication Research* 24(1):147-180.

owned corporation operating in the Chicago area. Results show that members within a network exert social influence (derived from the three coriental values) both with-in and across networking groups. The magnitude of influence depends on several variables including the environment and diversity of cultures and networks.

Prospects for future study are topics dealing with diversity in interpersonal, mass communication and group networking as they affect attitudes. According to Suzuki's study, perception is more susceptible to change than accuracy or agreement. To complete the circularity of the coorientation concept, he recalls Chaffee's and McLeod's reflection, "The tendency to look within the individual for explanations of human behavior is an unmistakable characteristic of American culture."

In maintaining that the true coorientational state is intrapersonal, those early scholars may have had the final word. Perhaps talking to oneself is the first and the last step in forming attitudes about and in relation to others. How those attitudes are affected by others depends on an individual's involvement as a member of a couple, a class, an organization, a network or sometimes as a world citizen.

Summary
Adding to the building blocks of knowledge and expanding human communication research, social psychologist Theodore Newcomb used values of **accuracy**, **agreement** and **congruency** to explain how people's talking about an object is based on the **environment** and **social reality**.

Other researchers moved forward to examine larger groups. First Chaffee and McLeod studied the frequency that couples talk about and evaluate information they have in common. A host of important studies followed. Culbertson added to those blocks of knowledge by studying media representatives' perceptions toward one another inside the organization and their views about their audiences. Recent scholars investigated coorientation effecting a larger social change and international corporate employees' cross-cultural communications.

What scholars have learned is the inextricable connection between and among people, regardless of group size, who innately gravitate to others with an urge to communicate. The more frequently people communicate, the greater the discovery of common issues and universal attitudes. Usually, total agreement is not reached. However, because of that natural **strain for symmetry**, or recognition that others matter, the results often are agreement, even if that is to disagree.

Exercises:

A. One of the more recent areas of coorientation study is in the corporate setting. Imagine that you are a very well paid consultant for a major oil company. Oil prices depend on many variables the company cannot control: the weather; the availability of Middle East oil, which often varies with international incidents; U.S. foreign and domestic policies; taxes levied by states and municipalities; and a host of other unkowns.

Because the company's profits have not kept pace with other industries, such as high tech and pharmaceuticals, stockholders are upset. This year at the corporation's annual meeting, stockholders almost voted in a new board of directors. The company anticipates trouble next year, and asks you to design a strategy to help convince stockholders that the company's lag in profits is beyond the board of directors' control. Using coorientation principles, write a maximum two-page plan of action — not the communication campaign, but the **research strategy** — that the company might use to increase stockholders' understanding of the situation.

B. Coorientation begins as cognitions because it is based on impressions each individual has toward an object, toward another person and toward the other person's view of the object. These impressions can be measured. However, coorientation also involves interpersonal communication because people's views of other's impressions are usually based on conversations with those other people.

In a maximum one-page essay, discuss the third phase of coorientation: those aspects of the theory that relate to mass communication. Obviously, in a one-page essay, it will be necessary to get to the point quickly, to select examples judiciously and to write succinctly.

Part Three
Mass Communication

Two-step Flow

18

First generation: Leo Bogart (1950). "The spread of news on a local event: A case history," *Public Opinion Quarterly* 14(4):769-772.

Second generation: Irving L. Allen (1969). "Social relations and the two-step flow: A defense of the tradition," *Journalism Quarterly* 46(3):492-498

Third generation: Gabriel Weimann and Hans-Bernd Brosius (1994). "Is there a two-step flow of agenda-setting?" *International Journal of Public Opinion Research* 6(4):323-341.

Just as a mood setter — before reading this chapter — complete the following list of statements by noting who among your peers is considered the most knowledgeable about each topic. If *you* are the person in the network of people with whom you communicate who is most knowledgeable about a topic listed, check the box before the statement. If another person in the network is most knowledgeable about the topic, write the person's name or nickname in the blank after the statement. If nobody among your peers is knowledgeable about the topic, leave both sides blank:

Me		*Somebody Else*
☐	1. know about electronic equipment like cell phones, computers, TVs, satellite dishes, etc.	_____
☐	2. familiar with the latest fashions, trends in clothing, new styles; what's hot, what's not	_____
☐	3. follow sports such as football, basketball and baseball; keep up with players, scores, etc.	_____

(continued)

Me   *Somebody Else*

☐   4. know about this academic program, policies,
        faculty, staff; developments at the university _____

☐   5. keep up with new movies, popular music,
        TV shows, the entertainment scene   _____

☐   6. know about politics, public affairs, important
        policy issues, which candidates to vote for   _____

☐   7. adept at shopping, know about bargains, best
        buys, product quality, store sales, etc.   _____

☐   8. general source of information about dates,
        names, places, history and other facts   _____

☐   9. know about local night life, clubs, pubs,
        dancing spots, eating places, meeting places   _____

☐ 10. news hound; keep up with current events;
        latest developments and details of news   _____

Now, for those items checked as being ones *you* are most knowledgeable about, indicate when you had your most recent conversation on that topic, and whether you initiated the conversation or someone else did:

Past 3 days	Past Week	Longer		Topic	Me	Other(s)	
/	/	/	/	1. electronics	/	/	/
/	/	/	/	2. fashions	/	/	/
/	/	/	/	3. sports	/	/	/
/	/	/	/	4. academics	/	/	/
/	/	/	/	5. movies/music	/	/	/
/	/	/	/	6. politics	/	/	/
/	/	/	/	7. bargains	/	/	/
/	/	/	/	8. facts/trivia	/	/	/
/	/	/	/	9. night life	/	/	/
/	/	/	/	10. news events	/	/	/

Now return to the list of events, and mark the issues you said your peers are more knowledgeable about. Mark when you had the most recent conversation on *that* topic, and whether you or another person initiated that conversation.

*   *   *

Possibly the first truly elucidated mass communication theory was offered by researchers studying people's voting decisions in the 1940 presidential election.[1] This landmark study (often called the Erie County study) reported outcomes about interpersonal and mass communication that are still valid today:

1) Socio-economic status (SES) predicts **who a person talks to** about an election and what **media messages a person attends to**, or tends to avoid. Truck drivers would not be expected to socialize with college professors (although some might) or to eagerly await the next edition of *The New England Journal of Medicine*.

2) SES, being older and being male predicts level of interest in politics, and **interest predicts participation** in politics. Other than the gender division, the 1940 predictors of interest and participation are assumed to apply today. More broadly, people have interests in certain topics. Those interests generally relate to a person's social status and suggest the kinds of activities in which they engage.

For example, less-than-college-educated people dominate the ranks of country music fans. Country music fans should know about cowboy boots, frequent places where country music is played and know how to line dance (or watch it on television). Of course, this depiction of country music fans is an excessive generalization because many post-graduates enjoy country music, wear cowboy boots and line dance. The point is that SES suggests a range of interests, and people's interests stimulate their behaviors.

3) People's **interests influence their mass communication use**. This idea was expanded upon in later research (see Uses and Gratifications chapter), but the fundamental finding still persists that people seek out media messages that interest them. For example, people who are interested in science are likely to subscribe to science magazines, watch the Discovery channel, read non-fiction books, belong to science-oriented chat groups on the Internet, etc. Because SES predicts interests, it would not be difficult to draw a profile of the kind of person who is more likely to be interested in science.

---

1. Paul F. Lazarsfeld, Bernard R. Berelson and Hazel Gaudet (1948). *The people's choice: How the voter makes up his mind in a presidential campaign, 2nd ed*. New York: Columbia University press. For an excellent synopsis of *The people's choice* and findings related to mass communication see: Shearon A. Lowery and Melvin L. DeFleur (1995). *Milestones in mass communication research: Media effects, 3rd ed*. White Plains, NY: Longman, pp. 69-92.

Exercise:

Complete these "profiles" of people's socio-economic status based on the topics of interests given. Your answers will be part of a class discussion of SES and interests. Here you are trying to estimate the "typical" kind of person, the average individual you might find if you did a national survey, who likes classical music, wrestling, etc. Fill in all the blanks; if unsure, take your best guess:

Classical music:
1. Education: ___college grad ___some college ___no college
2. Gender: ___male ___female
3. Profession: ___owner/exec. ___white collar ___blue collar
4. Income: ___$60,000-plus ___$30,000-$59,999 ___below $30,000
5. Age: ___50-plus ___30 to 49 ___less than 30

Wrestling:
1. Education: ___college grad ___some college ___no college
2. Gender: ___male ___female
3. Profession: ___owner/exec. ___white collar ___blue collar
4. Income: ___$60,000-plus ___$30,000-$59,999 ___below $30,000
5. Age: ___50-plus ___30 to 49 ___less than 30

Sports cars:
1. Education: ___college grad ___some college ___no college
2. Gender: ___male ___female
3. Profession: ___owner/exec. ___white collar ___blue collar
4. Income: ___$60,000-plus ___$30,000-$59,999 ___below $30,000
5. Age: ___50-plus ___30 to 49 ___less than 30

Gardening:
1. Education: ___college grad ___some college ___no college
2. Gender: ___male ___female
3. Profession: ___owner/exec. ___white collar ___blue collar
4. Income: ___$60,000-plus ___$30,000-$59,999 ___below $30,000
5. Age: ___50-plus ___30 to 49 ___less than 30

The stock market:
1. Education: ___college grad ___some college ___no college
2. Gender: ___male ___female
3. Profession: ___owner/exec. ___white collar ___blue collar
4. Income: ___$60,000-plus ___$30,000-$59,999 ___below $30,000
5. Age: ___50-plus ___30 to 49 ___less than 30

* * *

Returning to the 1940 study, the effects of mass media on voters' decisions was a secondary but fruitful avenue of investigation. Prior to this study, people assumed that mass communication had powerful and equal effects on everyone: the "hypodermic needle" or "bullet" theory. This theory can be viewed as the **one-step flow** of communication, from the media directly to individual audience receivers. The Erie County study showed that even in the heat of a presidential campaign, people used the mass media selectively and that persuasive effects were minimal. It is also fair to say that Erie County was the most far-reaching investigation of media and interpersonal communication of its time, but not the only study.[2]

4) The **mass media's persuasive messages are largely ignored**. Only a select few attend to issues that interest them, and this segment becomes heavily exposed to its preferred medium. For both information and being influenced, people decide which media to use, when and how much. People also have media preferences: high-SES rely more on print, and low-SES individuals rely more on non-print.

5) Even during a presidential campaign, people **rely more on friends and relatives than on mass media** for both **information** and **decision making**. If this is true, then interpersonal communication may be more influential than the mass media at all other times. People turn to those they think have more knowledge about the topic: opinion leaders. Opinion leaders' knowledge comes from the mass media.

Opinion leaders

Before describing the opinion leaders' role, it should be noted that the **two-step flow** of communication is defined as information flowing from the mass media directly to those people in the audience who have interest in the topic (step one), then through interpersonal communication to the rest of the populace (step two).

Two-step flow assumes that individuals interact in groups or networks. Group membership is akin to family membership in that the satisfactions received by belonging also require some relinquishing of self: A group member conforms to group norms in exchange for group support. For example, family members must allow others to participate in conversations and must avoid confrontations that might hurt the others feelings. Likewise, group membership requires conformity in essential attitudes, opinions and actions. Without shared values, the group can't

---

2. Paul F. Lazarsfeld (1942). "The effects of radio on public opinion," in Douglas Waples, ed. *Print, radio, and film in a democracy.* Chicago: University of Chicago Press, pp. 66-78; Herbert Blumer (1946). "The mass, the public, and public opinion," in Alfred McClung Lee, ed. *New outline of the principles of sociology.* New York: Barnes and Noble; William S. Robinson (1941). "Radio comes to the farmer," in Paul F. Lazarsfeld and Frank N. Stanton, eds. *Radio research, 1941.* New York: Duell, Sloan and Pearce; W. Lloyd Warner and Paul S. Lunt (1941). *The social life of a modern community, Vol. 1.* New Haven, CT: Yale University Press.

maintain cohesion.[3] But groups are not static entities; they do change, although they evolve rather than transform. In this milieu, the mass media have little dramatic impact either on the group as a whole or on any individual attached to the group.[4]

Enter the opinion leader whose role was first investigated in the Decatur study.[5] This survey of more than 1,500 women in a midsize Illinois town included nearly 700 self-identified opinion leaders and tracked their characteristics over four interest areas: marketing, or new products; fashion; public affairs; and movie selection. The findings about opinion leadership are still considered valid nearly 50 years later. Opinion leadership depends on: 1) a person's position in the community, or SES; 2) life cycle, or the person's perceived knowledge based on being single, married, a parent or a grandparent; and, 3) the extent of a person's social contacts.

But the likelihood of **being an opinion leader seemed to depend most on the topic**. Young, unmarried women were believed to know most about fashion; older, married women were thought most knowledgeable about public affairs. The most gregarious women (with more social contacts) were considered marketing and fashion leaders. Gregariousness and high social status were related to public affairs knowledge; and youth and gregariousness determined movie selection leadership.

At this point, return to the chapter's opening "mood setter" in which you decided whether you or someone else is more knowledgeable about the 10 topics, when you last discussed the topics and who initiated the discussion. Does the Decatur study describe interactions between opinion leaders and followers when you thought about that process in the "mood setter"?

As a true communication investigation, the Decatur study also tracked the influence of mass media (at that time radio, newspapers, magazines and books) and compared media against interpersonal communication. Personal advice was more influential for new products than media advertising, although radio ads were more important than print ads. In selecting motion pictures, almost everyone consulted newspapers, but personal advice was far more influential. Personal contact was far more important than any medium for fashion, although magazines had some sway. Concrete findings for mass media use in the public affairs area were not reported, although public affairs opinion leaders were thought to use mass media more than non-opinion leaders.

---

3. Harold H. Kelley and Edmund H. Volkart (1952). "The resistance to change of group-anchored attitudes," *American Sociological Review* 17(4):453-465.

4. John W. Riley and Matilda W. Riley (1959). "Mass communication and the social system" in Robert K. Merton, Leonard Broom and Leonard S. Cottrell Jr., eds. *Sociology today: Problems and prospects*. New York: Basic Books, pp. 537-578.

5. Elihu Katz and Paul F. Lazarsfeld (1955). *Personal influence: The part played by people in the flow of mass communications*. Glencoe, IL: The Free Press.

The general impression about opinion leaders is that they are **leaders for specific topic areas**; their leadership **depends on their personal characteristics** such as SES, life cycle, and social contacts; and they **use the mass media** more to follow the topics on which they are opinion leaders. However, the picture is fuzzy rather than clear.[6] Apparently, *nearly everyone is an opinion leader* for certain topics, and the flow of communication is *not in direct steps* from mass media to opinion leaders to followers. Instead, there is an ebb and flow of information among group members.

Given the homogeneous nature of social groups described earlier, opinion leaders should be expected to be **similar to others in the group**, and this is certainly true. Additionally, networks of social groups exist in every social environment providing "unending circuits of leadership relationships running through the community, like a nerve system through the body."[7]

Multi-step flow

Through the late 1940s and 1950s, dozens of studies were undertaken on opinion leaders both in the communication field and in sociology.[8] One **field** study looked at how medical doctors began prescribing a new drug and charted their adoption of this innovation through pharmacy prescriptions.[9] Follow-up interviews were done with the doctors to learn how they found out about the drug and which other doctors they talked to about it. A similar outcome was found for this opinion

---

6. Actually, in a reanalysis of the Decatur study's data, a stronger opinion leadership property was found by Alan S. Marcus and Raymond A. Bauer (1964). "Yes: There are generalized opinion leaders," *Public Opinion Quarterly* 28(4):628-632.

7. This was a finding from the Elmira, NY, study of the 1948 presidential election by Bernard R. Berelson, Paul F. Lazarsfeld and William N. McPhee (1954). *Voting: A study of opinion formation in a presidential campaign.* Chicago: University of Chicago Press, p. 110.

8. Eunice Cooper and Marie Jahoda (1947). "The evasion of propaganda: How prejudiced people respond to anti-prejudice propaganda," *Journal of Psychology* 23:15-25; Wilbur Schramm, ed. *Mass communications.* Urbana: University of Illinois Press; Robert K. Merton (1949). "Patterns of influence: A study of interpersonal influence and of communications behavior in a local community," in Paul F. Lazarsfeld and Frank N. Stanton, eds. *Communications research 1948-49.* New York: Harper & Brothers, pp. 180-219; Frank A. Stewart (1947). "A sociometric study of influence in Southtown," *Sociometry* 10(1):11-31; Frank A. Stewart (1947). "A sociometric study of influence in Southtown: II," *Sociometry* 10(3):273-286; Frederick A. Bushee (1945). "Social organizations in a small city," *American Journal of Sociology* 51:217-226; Elihu Katz (1957). "The two-step flow of communication: An up-to-date report on an hypothesis," *Public Opinion Quarterly* 21(1):61-78; Melvin L. DeFleur and Otto N. Larsen (1958). *The flow of information: An experiment in mass communication.* New York: Harper & Row; Paul F. Lazarsfeld and Herbert Menzel (1963). "Mass media and personal influence," in Wilbur Schramm, ed. *The science of human communication: New directions and new findings in communication research.* New York: Basic Books, pp. 94-115.

9. Herbert Menzel and Elihu Katz (1955). "Social relations and innovation in the medical profession: The epidemiology of a new drug," *Public Opinion Quarterly* 19(4):337-352. See also: James Coleman, Elihu Katz and Herbert Menzel (1957). "The diffusion of an innovation among physicians," *Sociometry* 20(4):253-270.

leadership as in the Decatur study. Influential doctors were: 1) likely to be younger and to have read about the drug in a medical journal; 2) more **cosmopolitan**, attended medical conferences and had more non-local physician colleagues; and, 3) those in the same social **cliques** adopted the new drug at the same time. Interpersonal communication about the new drug was two-way between influential and follower doctors: leaders influenced followers, and followers influenced leaders.

A "lawn care" field test using the *Middlesex Bulletin* with articles advising how low to cut the grass, led to further outcomes. Instead of initiating conversations, opinion leaders were often sought out by followers. After receiving the opinion leader's advice, followers often made their own decisions.[10]

What had been offered as a rather straightforward hypothesis, two-step flow became multi-step flow, and then studies in the early 1970s left the issue in even more confusion.[11] Some found that media information flow bypassed the opinion

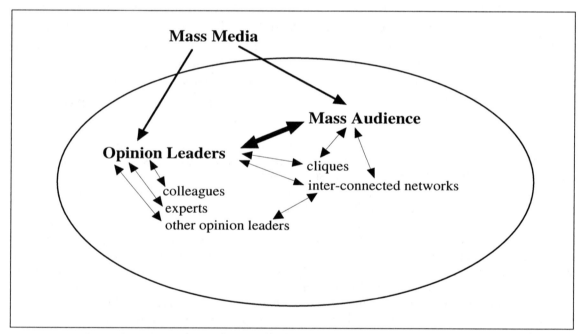

Figure 1. Multi-step flow conceptualization

10. Verling C. Troldahl (1966). "A field test of a modified 'two-step flow of communication' model," *Public Opinion Quarterly* 30(4):609-623.

11. Johan Arndt (1968). "A test of the two-step flow in diffusion of a new product," *Journalism Quarterly* 45(3):457-465; Lloyd R. Bostian (1970). "The two-step flow theory: Cross-cultural implications," *Journalism Quarterly* 47(1):109-117; Nan Lin (1971). "Information flow, influence flow and the decision-making process," *Journalism Quarterly* 48(1):33-40, 61; Florangel Z. Rosario (1971). "The leader in family planning and the two-step flow model," *Journalism Quarterly* 48(2):288-297, 303; A.W. Van Den Ban (1964). "A revision of the two-step flow of communications hypothesis," *Gazette* 10(3):237-249.

leader and went directly to audience members. The picture was even more muddied as: 1) opinion leaders have their own opinion leaders, 2) followers can initiate communication, 3) some people never seek opinion input, 4) followers listen to the advice of other followers, and 5) opinion leaders can be influenced by followers.

Chaffee wrote in 1972 that two-step flow was more of a conceptualization not to be overlooked, but less of a theoretical model to be tested.[12] He said: 1) most people receive information directly from the mass media, 2) opinion leaders rely on the mass media more than do others, 3) information "flow" is really information "seeking" by receivers, and 4) interpersonal is more powerful than media persuasion.[13] Similar restrictions of two-step flow led to suggesting a **limited one-step flow** (media to audience with limited effects),[14] or a **multi-step flow**, which means something important occurs in interpersonal communication of media information, but what it is depends on circumstances. Some called the process the **N-step flow** to describe its unknown properties.[15] In all, the research shows that the communication process is very complex, as the most recent two-step flow summary indicates.[16]

Again, return to the chapter's opening "mood setter" about who is more knowledgeable on the 10 topics, when they were last discussed and who initiated the discussion. Does the multi-step flow idea do a better job of describing interactions between opinion leaders and followers than the two-step flow?

Studies continue

Given two-step flow's mixed reviews, why isn't this theory on the scrap heap of the "tested and rejected"? The answer is nearly as perplexing as the theory itself. Sometimes information flow is exactly as two-step predicts. Almost always, **when researchers look for the two-step flow**, they find a direct flow of information from the media to individuals who manifest the properties that identify opinion leaders. Looking deeper into the **interpersonal communication network**, researchers note that communication waxes and wanes between opinion leaders and followers; the flow of influence is dynamic rather than stable, inconsistent rather than predictable.

12. Steven H. Chaffee (1972). "The interpersonal context of mass communication," in F. Gerald Kline and Phillip J. Tichenor, eds. *Current perspectives in mass communication research*. Beverly Hills, CA: Sage, pp. 95-120.

13. Dorothy F. Douglas, Bruce H. Westley and Steven H. Chaffee (1970). "An information campaign that changed community attitudes," *Journalism Quarterly* 47(3):479-487, 492.

14. Everett M. Rogers (1973). "Mass media and interpersonal communication," in Ithiel de Sola Pool, Wilbur Schramm, Frederick W. Frey, Nathan Maccoby and Edwin B. Parker, eds. *Handbook of communication*. Chicago: Rand McNally, pp. 290-310.

15. Mary B. Cassata and Molefi K. Asante (1979). *Mass communication: Principles and practices*. New York: Macmillan, pp. 83-84.

16. Naoyuki Okada (1986). "The process of mass communication: A review of studies on the two-step flow of communication hypothesis," *Studies of Broadcasting* 22:57-78.

One problem is that few studies are designed to clarify these inconsistencies. Unless a researcher sets out to specifically study two-step flow, the chances of adding to the literature are slim. Often researchers add one or two interpersonal communication measures and then are surprised to find how important these are in voting decisions or learning about news events: They **rediscover** two-step flow.

Another problem is that researchers don't always find this pattern. For many of the topics studied, the media do seem to be influential channels of knowledge. But two-step flow literature also suggests that the nature of the topic itself, the time it occurred, how important it seems — all of these will alter the effect of media vs. interpersonal communication.

Even with the complexities noted, two-step flow research continues, although in a haphazard rather than programmatic manner. Political science studies continue to find the same interpersonal communication effects in most voter studies, such as that reported by Eric Uslaner where policy makers influence opinion leaders who influence voters.[17] Another area of recent study is the flow of information process in emerging nations. These studies sometimes take the form of comparison to what is known about information flow in the United States and, perhaps because of differences in culture, find limited support for two-step flow or multi-step flow.[18]

Just when serious two-step flow investigations began to disintegrate, the field turned to a related issue: the diffusion of innovations.[19] Many of the original two-step flow signs appeared in this emerging literature: the mass media, interpersonal communication, opinion leaders (innovators), influence (attitude change), and the conditions under which new products or ideas are adopted.

Is there a two-step flow in communication? The answer is a qualified yes. Those who understand communications' basic principles know: 1) really important events follow a two-step flow, from media to opinion leaders to the public; 2) for an information campaign to succeed, it must first convince opinion leaders; and, 3) regardless of the media's assumed power, the successful transmission of information (and persuasion in particular) depends on interpersonal channels.

---

17. Eric M. Uslaner (1989). "Looking forward and looking backward: Prospective and retrospective voting in the 1980 federal elections in Canada," *British Journal of Political Science* 19(4):495-513.

18. Xinshu Zhao, Jian-Hua Zhu, Hairong Li and Glen L. Bleske (1994). "Media effects under a monopoly: The case of Beijing in economic reform," *International Journal of Public Opinion Research* 6(2):95-117. See also: Karl Erik Rosengren (1987). "Introduction to a special issue on news diffusion," *European Journal of Communication* 2(2):135-142; Karl Erik Rosengren (1987). "Conclusion: The comparative study of news diffusion," *European Journal of Communication* 2(2):227-255.

19. Everett M. Rogers and F. Floyd Shoemaker (1971). *Communication of innovations: A cross-cultural approach, 2nd ed.* New York: Free Press.

Summary

Two step flow was the first real mass communication theory, reported from a mid-1940s election study. Many of the Erie County study's principles are still relevant to mass and interpersonal communication. People's **social status** generally predicts their interest in topics, their activities and their mass media use.

Prior to two-step flow, mass communication was thought to have powerful and equal effects on everyone. This was the "hypodermic needle" theory or **one-step flow** of communication, from the media directly to individual audience receivers. The Erie County study showed that people attend to the mass media selectively, and that persuasive effects are minimal. People rely on interpersonal communication more than the mass media, and they rely on people in their social groups who have more knowledge about the topic: **opinion leaders**. Opinion leaders have: 1) higher SES, 2) perceived knowledge about a topic, 3) high levels of social contact, 4) similarity to others in the group, and 5) high mass media use.

In **two-step flow**, information goes from the mass media directly to opinion leaders (step one), then from opinion leaders through interpersonal communication to the rest of the public (step two). The theory seemed substantial until later studies in the 1950s and 1960s identified a host of conflicting findings that suggested a **multi-step flow** of communication taking place in interlocking webs of social groups.

Despite the conflicting outcomes of later studies, basic precepts of the two-step flow theory are still found in communication studies and in studies undertaken by a variety of social science disciplines. The principle became part of diffusion of innovations. Classic two-step flow findings still occur, but the conditions under which this happens remain a mystery.

Exercises:

A. What do people talk about? The next time you can be with your circle of friends at a usual meeting place, take a notepad and pen. You should plan to do this exercise at a place where note-taking will be unobtrusive: a research procedure called *participant observation* (see Qualitative Research chapter). As you listen to the conversation, take enough notes to complete about **half a dozen brief scenarios** of exchanges such as:

1) one female asks another about weekend plans; reply, has paper due Monday; male, asks which class; reply, names class and teacher; female, gives advice about that teacher's expectations; more talk about the assignment.

To write this scenario at your keypad, the only note you might have written during the conversation was: "weekend plans; paper due; English class."

However, each scenario should include **three** items: 1) *topic* of conversation, 2) how that conversation *began* and 3) any *media use* mentioned. Most of the scenarios should be about three sentences long and may take the form in the example. Obviously, you will not initiate any of the conversations for the scenarios you describe, and you should avoid even being a participant in those conversations. Bring your paper to class and be prepared to discuss examples. Your instructor might use these papers as a graded assignment.

B. Complete the following set of questions and be prepared to discuss your results in class:

1. In the course of a usual day, about how many people do you have conversations with:

   a. fewer than 5
   b. 5 to 9
   c. 10 to 14
   d. 15 or more

2. Circle the number that comes closest to describing your usual communication activity:

I start conversations	3	2	1	Others start conversations
I am sought out for advice	3	2	1	I seek advice from others
I belong to many groups	3	2	1	I belong to few groups
I am a leader in groups	3	2	1	I am not a group leader
I express opinions freely	3	2	1	I keep opinions to myself

   Score yourself using the following calculations:
In Question 1, (a) = 1, (b) = 2, (c) = 3, (d) = 4.
In Question 2, points are given for the following you circled: starting conversations (3) = 1; being sought out for advice (3) = 3; belonging to many groups (3) = 3, (2) = 1; being a group leader (3) = 3, (2) = 2; expressing opinions freely (3) = 2.

   Your total score: _____

19

Information Diffusion

Traditional article: Rebecca Quarles, Leo W. Jeffres, Carlos Sanchez-Ilundain and Kurt Neuwirth (1983). "News diffusion of assassination attempts on President Reagan and Pope John Paul II," *Journal of Broadcasting* 27(4):387-394.

Recent trends: Andy Grove (1997). "Only the productive survive," *Forbes* (Dec. 1), *160*(12):S22-24.

"Information is power." This axiom has been recognized since humans formed social groups. Information about the movement of herds, aggressive neighboring tribes, planting and harvesting, caravans crossing the desert, ships crossing the sea, impending storms, warring nations...all of this information determined survival. And while humans recognized early that information is power, the study of information flow or diffusion did not begin until the 1950s.

Exercise:

Think of a really major news event: a startling and dramatic event that people talked about for months or even years after. For example, people over age 50 can remember where they were and how they first heard about the assassination of President John F. Kennedy in 1963. Some events that might qualify, depending on your age, are: the Challenger explosion, the Oklahoma bombing, O.J. Simpson's arrest or the death of Princess Diana. Perhaps another event is more memorable to you than these, but focus on one such event.

Write a maximum one-page essay about: 1) how you first found out about the event, 2) what you did when you first found out, 3) what you did in relation to the event during the next several hours, and 4) what you did in relation to the event during the next several days. Be prepared to discuss your scenario in class and to submit your essay for a grade.

* * *

Diffusion was a natural outcome of two-step flow theory. If the mass media were not all-powerful, if they were unable to reach the masses directly with the same effect, then the intervening steps in the process were the logical next area to study. Diffusion fits neatly between two-step flow and gatekeeping. Gatekeeping deals with information flow from the source to the point of dissemination by the mass media. **Information diffusion** deals with news flow from the point of mass media dissemination to the point at which almost all in the population learn about the event. Most classic diffusion studies began with a major news event and traced *how people found out* about the event and whether they *passed the information on to others*.

Diffusion's first generation: the flow

Information diffusion and the **diffusion of innovations** are related concepts because the flow of communication is an integral component of both theories. This being the case, several early innovation studies may be considered precursors of information diffusion including a 1920s city council study,[1] the classic 1943 Iowa hybrid seed corn study,[2] and a 1947 study on the psychology of rumors.[3]

Studying rumors resulted in identifying an **embedding pattern**, like avoiding outcomes in the child's game "telephone" where a message whispered from one person to the next sounds nothing like the original message when the last person says it aloud. Embedding elements are: 1) **leveling**, or shortening the message; 2) **sharpening**, or emphasizing key details; and 3) **assimilation**, or distorting messages to fit preexisting stereotypes, attitudes or expectations. In all, the results suggested that interpersonal communication is a poor channel for information transmission.

The first real information diffusion study charted the flow of news of President Franklin D. Roosevelt's death.[4] Tracking news of the event revealed that an active group informed others within 10 minutes, and that more than 90% surveyed knew of Roosevelt's death within half an hour, primarily through word-of-mouth. However, those who heard the news by radio informed an average of seven other people; those who heard through word-of-mouth informed only one other person. The most common reaction was disbelief. *The New York Times* received nearly 5,000 calls in three hours from people trying to confirm the news. Today such people might turn to television for this **verification** aspect of interpersonal news diffusion.

---

1. F. Stuart Chapin (1928). *Cultural change*. New York: Century Co.

2. Bryce Ryan and Neal C. Gross (1943). "The diffusion of hybrid seed corn in two Iowa communities," *Rural Sociology* 8(1):15-24.

3. Gordon W. Allport and Leo Postman (1947). *The psychology of rumor*. New York: Henry Holt and Co. See also Melvin L. DeFleur (1962). "Mass communication and the study of rumor," *Sociological Inquiry* 32(1):51-70.

4. Delbert C. Miller (1945). "A research note on mass communication: How our community heard about the death of President Roosevelt," *American Sociological Review* 10(5):691-694.

An unique kind of information diffusion study was Operation Revere,[5] the Air Force attempt to assess the effects of dropping leaflets on a civilian population. The military used leaflets extensively in World War II and Korea[6] to warn civilians to evacuate targeted areas, and to confuse, frighten and urge enemy troops to desert. Leaflets had little effect, and the Air Force wanted to know why.[7] In the early 1950s, U.S. towns were bombarded with new coffee slogans and Civil Defense messages.

Among the extensive findings from Operation Revere (named after Paul Revere who rode to warn the Minutemen), was that **first-hand contact** with the message itself is critical. The more removed a person is from first-hand knowledge — hearing it from a friend who might have heard from another friend — the more the message will be distorted. The **intensity** (message redundancy or repetition) determines how faithfully it will be received and remembered. The research also identified a social pattern for the flow of messages dropped from airplanes. Children are most likely to pick up the leaflets and tell their parents, who tell other family members, until the word spreads from adults to friends and neighbors.[8]

Although the leaflet study underscored message fidelity, the mass media got more attention as an information diffusion agent. A 1956 study tracked news of President Eisenhower's decision to run for a second term. All of those surveyed looked to the mass media for further information.[9] At that time, newspapers were the preferred source of 86%, television was second at 54% and radio was third at 46%. Obviously, many people used multiple media sources to supplement information.

Diffusion of a false news story occurred when a Seattle paper published a report of car windshield pitting, which news was followed by similar reports and 3,000 windshield damage complaints to police.[10] The small pit marks were variously attributed to radioactive fallout and sandflea eggs, but no case was ever substantiated. Researchers found that 93% of those suveyed knew about the pitting, but 75% of

5. Stuart Carter Dodd (1953). "Operation Revere," *Newsweek* 40 (Sept. 15), pp. 91-92.

6. Shearon A. Lowery and Melvin L. DeFleur (1995). *Milestones in mass communication research: Media effects, 3rd ed.* White Plains, NY: Longman, pp. 213-237.

7. Martin F. Herz (1949). "Some psychological lessons from leaflet propaganda in World War II," *Public Opinion Quarterly* 13(3):471-486.

8. Melvin L. DeFleur (1962). "Mass communication and the study of rumor," *Sociological Inquiry* 32(1):51-70. See also: Lowery and DeFleur, *op. cit.*

9. Wayne A. Danielson (1956). "Eisenhower's February decision: A study of news impact," *Journalism Quarterly* 33(4):433-441.

10. Nahum Z. Medalia and Otto N. Larsen (1958). "Diffusion and belief in a collective delusion: The Seattle windshield pitting epidemic," *American Sociological Review* 23(2):180-186. For additional early studies of false rumors see: Donald M. Johnson, "The 'phantom anesthetist' of Mattoon: A field study of mass hysteria," pp. 208-219, and Hadley Cantril, "The invasion from Mars," pp. 198-207, in Guy E. Swanson, Theodore M. Newcomb and Eugene L. Hartley, eds. *Readings in Social Psychology, revised ed.* New York: Henry Holt Co., (1952); Edward J. Ruppelt (1956). *The report on unidentified flying objects.* Garden City, NY: Doubleday.

those said they first heard of the epidemic through mass media channels and only 19% heard by interpersonal channels. Such unusual information ought to be a topic of conversation, but apparently discussion of news is restricted to bigger events.

Deutschmann and Danielson studied diffusion of more important news by phone surveys within 24 hours of: 1) Sputnik, 1957; 2) Eisenhower's stroke, 1957; 3) Explorer I, 1958; and, 4) Alaska statehood, 1958.[11] The rate of diffusion for these events was *rapid*, but not instant, taking one to two days to diffuse across the nation. Television and radio were *primary* sources; newspapers and interpersonal communication were secondary. News flowed from the media directly to individuals, and then among people through interpersonal contacts. **Opinion leaders** relayed *supplementary* information during conversations.

The two researchers said that the diffusion process is "far more regular than we suspected."[12] Their **regularity hypothesis** stated that regardless of the news event: 1) diffusion rates follow a basic pattern; 2) television is the first source of news followed by radio, newspapers and interpersonal communication; 3) neither time of day nor story topic affect first exposure; 4) the uninformed differ from the informed in education and occupation; and, 5) most people hear first in their homes.

But the regularity hypothesis was quickly dashed by the assassination of President Kennedy. Hill and Bonjean interviewed 212 Dallas residents the week after Kennedy's death[13] and reported that for momentous news events: 1) *interpersonal communication* is most important; 2) diffusion is *rapid*; 3) people's usual *media routine* is altered; and, 4) media use differences among social classes are *diminished*.

As the late 1960s approached, attention turned from dramatic to more normal news flow. Concerns were the increasing role of television, newspapers' limited role as first contact, the minor role of word-of-mouth in initial contact and the importance of social categories.[14] In 1966, Nikita Khrushchev's resignation (greater news) was compared with news of lesser value.[15] The findings mirrored those in Dallas and added that *higher educated* people are more likely to learn of an event early.

---

11. Paul J. Deutschmann and Wayne A. Danielson (1960). "Diffusion of knowledge of the major news story," *Journalism Quarterly* 37(3):345-355.

12. *Ibid.*, p. 355.

13. Richard J. Hill and Charles M. Bonjean (1964). "News diffusion: A test of the regularity hypothesis," *Journalism Quarterly* 41(3):336-342. See also: Bradley S. Greenberg (1964). "Diffusion of news of the Kennedy assassination," *Public Opinion Quarterly* 28(2):225-232; Stephan P. Spitzer (1964-65). "Mass media vs. personal sources of information about the presidential assassination: A comparison of six investigations," *Journal of Broadcasting* 9(1):45-50.

14. Melvin L. DeFleur and Otto N. Larsen (1987). *The flow of information: An experiment in mass communications.* New Brunswick, NJ: Transaction Inc., p. xxxi.

15. Richard W. Budd, Malcolm S. MacLean Jr. and Arthur M. Barnes (1966). "Regularities in the diffusion of two major news events," *Journalism Quarterly* 43(2):221-230.

Diffusion's second generation: media vs. interpersonal

Funkhouser and McCombs reviewed diffusion studies and described **negative diffusion** where people forget information in a very short time. The researchers were studying the elapse of time between a news event and asking people how they learned about the event. They found that people can be positively diffused if exposed to the information again, and if they have interest in the message.[16]

Rosengren wrote a diffusion research summary in 1973 and offered these findings about news flow of important events: Diffusion occurs quickly and widely through interpersonal channels. Television, newspapers and radio are secondary sources.[17] Still, Rosengren warned against over-generalizing from the early studies.

Diffusion of the 1973 assassination attempt on Alabama Gov. George Wallace was studied in Michigan and elsewhere.[18] Researchers expected this to be a minor news event for which media would be the initial source, but most people heard first from others. The majority of New Yorkers heard about the event within two hours, and they learned equally from interpersonal sources and the mass media. Another study reiterated that word-of-mouth is important only in national calamities.[19]

Most of the news diffusion studies were on "bad news" topics. What about the diffusion of good news? Haroldsen and Harvey found that more than half of their Utah respondents learned about a Mormon Church good news announcement over the weekend from interpersonal contacts, although 91% also sought media coverage after hearing.[20] Researchers concluded that shock and importance contribute to interpersonal communication, but that interpersonal sources lack the credibility of mass media sources to which people turn for verification.

One study asked why people pass on news to others. Gantz and Trenholm[21] tracked reasons given for telling others about the assassination attempt on George Wallace, the resignation of Vice President Spiro T. Agnew, the death of President

---

16. G. Ray Funkhouser and Maxwell E. McCombs (1971). "The rise and fall of news diffusion," *Public Opinion Quarterly* 35(1):107-113.

17. Karl Erik Rosengren (1973). "News diffusion: An overview," *Journalism Quarterly* 50(1):83-91.

18. Thomas M. Steinfatt, Walter Gantz, David R. Seibold and Larry D. Miller (1973). "News diffusion of the George Wallace shooting: The apparent lack of interpersonal communication as an artifact of delayed measurement," *Quarterly Journal of Speech* 59(4):401-412. See also: David A. Schwartz, (1973-74). "How fast does news travel?" *Public Opinion Quarterly* 37(4):625-627.

19. Gary Alan Fine (1975). "Recall of information about diffusion of major news event," *Journalism Quarterly* 52(4):751-755.

20. Edwin O. Haroldsen and Kenneth Harvey (1979). "The diffusion of 'shocking' good news," *Journalism Quarterly* 56(4):771-775.

21. Walter Gantz and Sarah Trenholm (1979). "Why people pass on news: Motivations for diffusion," *Journalism Quarterly* 56(2):365-370.

Eisenhower and the death of a U.S. athlete. In the case of Wallace, people passed on the information to reduce their own anxiety. When Agnew resigned, people told others to "gloat." In the last two cases, people said they were helping "interested others," an altruistic explanation supported by further questioning.

In the 1980s, a group of researchers studied the assassination attempts on President Reagan and Pope John Paul II in 1981.[22] These events, like the Kennedy assassination, had rapid diffusion. Although they should have been diffused by word-of-mouth, interpersonal and media tied as initial information sources.

One other study dealt with an arson death after a rowdy fraternity house party early on a Sunday morning in 1986. The event's timing delayed media coverage, and Gantz, et al.[23] determined that 80% of the sampled students learned of the incident from another person. But when media coverage became available in this college town, people turned to the media for more information and for verification.

Delbert Miller	1945 death of President Roosevelt
Allport and Postman	1947 study on the psychology of rumors
Stuart Dodd	1953 dropping leaflets, Operation Revere
Medalia and Larsen	1958 false news, car windshield pitting
Deutschmann and Danielson	1960 four news events; regularity hypothesis
Hill and Bonjean	1964 Kennedy assassination; refutes regularity
Budd, MacLean and Barnes	1966 large vs. lesser event; supports four qualifiers
Funkhouser and McCombs	1971 "negative diffusion" concept: people forget
Karl Rosengren	1973 overview of diffusion about important news
Steinfatt, et al.	1973 Wallace shooting is "important" news
Gary Fine	1975 interpersonal works best only in calamities
Haroldsen and Harvey	1979 good and bad news diffuse similarly
Gantz and Trenholm	1979 why people pass on information: altruism
Weaver-Lariscy, et al.	1984 Reagan and Pope assassination attempts
Gantz, et al.	1986 seek media confirmation in proximate news

Figure 1. Some key studies of information diffusion

22. Ruth Ann Weaver-Lariscy, Barbara Sweeney and Thomas Steinfatt (1984). "Communication during assassination attempts: Diffusion of information in attacks on President Reagan and the Pope," *Southern Speech Communication Journal* 49(3):258-276. See also: Walter Gantz (1983). "The diffusion of news about the attempted Reagan assassination," *Journal of Communication* 33(1):56-66.

23. Walter Gantz, Kathy A. Krendl and Susan R. Robertson (1986). "Diffusion of a proximate news event," *Journalism Quarterly* 63(2):282-287.

Information diffusion studies reviewed here (see Figure 1) built a compendium of corroborative evidence about how news events diffuse through the population: 1) **routine news** reaches the public through media channels with individual and social categories affecting diffusion; 2) **important news** is diffused rapidly and broadly by interpersonal communication first, although the word-of-mouth is "multi-stage," then by television, radio and newspapers, probably in that order; and, 3) at **all news value levels**, people seek out the mass media for verification and additional information, daily routines and time of the news influence first exposure, and individual and social categories affect diffusion. When results reiterate previous findings, researchers tend to move on to more fertile fields of inquiry. It seemed that information diffusion was a dead issue until the advent of the Internet.

The next generation

Where 1950s research showed that newspapers were the most important news diffusion medium, television became the primary source for verification by the mid-1960s. Even as early as 1963, most Americans used television to keep up with the Kennedy assassination, and by 1991, they were glued to the tube for CNN's live reports of the Gulf War attack. What might be expected for the Internet?

Communication scholars and commentators recognize that the Internet is becoming a player in information diffusion, but the medium was not pervasive enough (in 1998) to be an initial information source for a sizable group of Americans. Still, Internet users probably were opinion leaders for widely discussed topics such as Princess Diana's death and President Bill Clinton's alleged affair with an intern.

The research does suggest that instant, worldwide electronic communication will affect information diffusion. Among topics being discussed are:

• People in post-Communist societies are learning how far behind the Western European countries their standard of living has fallen.[24]

• What are the implications of a new era in political communication with direct communication between politicians, interest groups and voters?[25]

• As the information superhighway's lanes grow wider and faster, governments increasingly want to serve as traffic cops.[26]

---

24. Richard Rose (1997). "How patient are people in post-Communist societies?" *World Affairs* 159(3):130-144.

25. Hal Berghel (1996). "Digital politics: Online political propaganda," *Communications of the AMC* 39(10):19-25.

26. Sigmund Stromme (1996). "An eternal battlefield: New censors," *Index on Censorship* 25(2):110-114. See also: Christina Barron (1997). "Internet: Rights and wrongs," *Europe* 363:10-11; Dwayne Winseck (1997). "Contradictions in the democratization of international communication," *Media, Culture & Society* 19(2):219-246; William M. Arkin (1997). "Blame the Internet," *Bulletin of the Atomic Scientists* 53(3):65.

Summary

Information diffusion is news flow from the point of mass media dissemination to the point at which almost all in the population learn about the event.

The theory is traced to research on the spread of rumors in the late-1940s through an extensive body of literature as investigators tried to determine what role interpersonal communication plays vs. the role played by the mass media. The studies provide a systematic testing during the first generation of research of **verification, first-hand contact** with the information, message **intensity**, the role of **opinion leaders**, the **regularity hypothesis** and importance of the news event itself. The second generation included such ideas as **negative diffusion**, the **rapidity** of diffusion for differing levels of news importance, and **why** people pass on information.

As research moves into the next generation, the Internet is seen as a likely initial and continuing news source that will affect the information diffusion process.

Exercises

A. Go to an eatery, on-campus or off, upscale or fast-food, and eavesdrop on a conversation. Sit at a table close to your target: a group of at least three adults, and keep a log of their conversation. Say how many people were at your target table and their approximate age. Your log might look like this:

Wednesday lunch; Hardees, college students in 20s, two males and a female.
1. 12:05 — talked about getting order wrong
2. 12:10 — impending test
3. 12:15 — male says former member of "Fleetwood Mac" died,
    just heard it on radio; group discusses particulars
4. 12:18 — male says student paper has ad on concert he wants to attend, etc.

Your log should be 20 minutes. Include any **news** item anyone in the group mentions, recording who in the group brought up the topic. Record the news "source" if one is given: television, campus paper, etc. Bring your log to the next class for discussion. Be prepared to turn the log in for a grade.

B. On a sheet other than the log itself, write a **one-page** essay about the ethics of this exercise and how you felt while you were doing it. Be prepared to discuss the ethics of this assignment in class and to turn in your essay for a grade.

C. Provide a journal article synopsis (see Doing Journal Synopses chapter) on an empirical study about the Internet and information diffusion. The article must appear in a communication journal more recently than 1997.

20

Gatekeeping

Early Study: Paul B. Snider (1967). "'Mr. Gates' revisited: A 1966 version of the 1949 case study," *Journalism Quarterly 44(3)*:419-427.

More Recent Study: Dan Berkowitz (1990). "Refining the gatekeeping metaphor for local television news," *Journal of Broadcasting & Electronic Media 34(1)*:55-68.

As you prepare to read this chapter, consider the following questions:

1. Can you imagine an information society without "gatekeepers," the people who help decide what information goes forward and what does not?

2. Are news media editors the only gatekeepers? Who are some others?

3. What are the checks and balances, so to speak, that help offset any non-standard choices a news gatekeeper might make?

"Gatekeeping" is an important concept in communication theory and research as well as in the practice of journalism. Kurt Lewin, a psychologist, coined the term in 1947 to describe the process by which family members made food selections for the dinner table.[1] The term was borrowed by David Manning White in a 1950 study of one editor's news choices.[2]

The gatekeeper decides which information will go forward, and which will not. Gatekeepers exist in many jobs, and their choices hold the potential to color the mental "pictures" that are subsequently created in people's understanding of what is happening in the world around them.

---

1. Kurt Lewin (1947). "Channels of group life," *Human Relations* 1:143-154.
2. David Manning White (1950). "The 'gate keeper': A case study in the selection of news," *Journalism Quarterly* 27(4):383-390.

The gatekeeper concept is now about 50 years old, but it is dynamic and useful. It has slipped firmly into the language of many disciplines. A computer search of the social sciences and humanities databases in 1997 alone identified 18 articles that used "gatekeeping" in their title or text. In communications, a gatekeeper is a person who can open or close the information "gates"; a person with enough influence or authority to affect information flow in a way that might reflect **personal bias**. An example is the wire service editor who alone decides what news audiences will receive from another continent. The idea is that if the gatekeeper's selections are biased, the readers' understanding will therefore be a little biased.

But the implication of gatekeeping is not predominantly negative. Gatekeeping is desirable and useful, as well as inevitable. Without gatekeepers, a reader or viewer would be overwhelmed with detail, some of it trivial and conflicting information. Gatekeepers help sort it out. Gatekeeper bias probably is not much of a problem except in the absence of certain checks and balances.

Some checks and balances that help mitigate the effect of gatekeeping were identified by Shoemaker and Reese.[3] One is "news values." For example, a news story that is compelling for its prominence, human interest, conflict, timeliness or proximity (some of the conventional news values) could get into the newspaper or be aired despite an editor's preferences. After all, editors don't want to miss a compelling story, even if they are opposed to some aspect of it.[4]

Another factor has to do with the principle of **objectivity** that most journalists try to follow. Objectivity is learned early and deeply. Shoemaker and Reese pointed out that one of the functions of objectivity is to protect a reporter, editor or publisher from criticism. In effect, objectivity mitigates gatekeeping bias.

Gatekeeping might also be mitigated by feedback from the audience, whose members express their like or dislike of what they see on the page or screen. Quirky editors who become noticeably cross-wise to their audience probably will not last long in the job.

As Shoemaker and Reese noted, there is also the matter of the newsroom **organizational structure** in which the gatekeeper is found. Gatekeepers do not generally work alone, but are part of a team, an organization that routinely monitors its product. Gatekeeping bias would be quickly noticed, and there would be pressure to objectify the information selections.

---

3. Pamela J. Shoemaker and Stephen D. Reese (1996). *Mediating the message: Theories of influences on mass media content, 2nd ed.* White Plains, NY: Longman.
    4. Doris A. Graber (1997). *Mass media and American politics, 5th ed.* Washington, DC: Congressional Quarterly Inc., pp. 106-108.

Finally, there is the matter of "what the other media are doing." The competitive urges of media drive them to aspire to at least the level of their competitors, so each watches the other. If one gets out of line, it is noticed, and pressure builds toward correction.

Given the importance of White's 1950 study, Paul Snider (see chapter's opening reading) some 17 years later repeated the study and concluded that Mr. Gates (pseudonym for a news wire editor) still chose stories to his liking, stories that he believed would appeal to his newspaper's readership or news he believed his audience should know. The problem with Mr. Gates' selections was that they were heavily influenced by what the Associated Press deemed most newsworthy and by his personal judgment of local readers' interests.

In the 1970s, Maxwell McCombs and Donald Shaw pointed out that the gatekeeping concept is related to the newer concept, agenda-setting.[5] Mr. Gates had the capacity for agenda-setting because his news selections set the agenda for what people would talk about (see Agenda-Setting chapter). McCombs and Shaw said that Mr. Gates' choices were explained not entirely by his intuition and personal bias, but also by the kind and **proportion** of copy available to him on the press wires. In other words, if 20% of the wire news stories involved national political affairs, Mr. Gates tended to use roughly that proportion of political affairs stories in his paper.

The tendency for editors to choose proportionately from the copy available to them was further supported in research by Whitney and Becker.[6] They asked a small sample of editors to select items from a *routine cycle* (actual proportion) of wire news and later from a *non-routine cycle* put together with equal numbers of stories in several categories. Whitney and Becker found that the editors' choices were strongly influenced by the proportion of stories offered in a given category rather than just the story topic. For example, if choosing from an equal number of stories provided about government, economy, environment and health, editors selected proportionately from those categories.

Most of the gatekeeping research debunks the view that editors' personal bias accounts for news selection. For example, Harmon applied gatekeeping to local television news and found that the main reasons for selecting stories to air were based on standard news values of consequence, conflict, proximity, prominence and novelty, although audience interest had more sway than audience need to know.[7]

---

5. Maxwell E. McCombs and Donald L. Shaw (1976). "Structuring the 'unseen environment,'" *Journal of Communication* 26(2):18-22.

6. Charles D. Whitney and Lee B. Becker (1982). "Keeping the gates for gatekeepers: The effects of wire news," *Journalism Quarterly* 59(1):60-65.

7. Mark D. Harmon (1989). "Mr. Gates goes electronic: The what and why questions in local TV news," *Journalism Quarterly* 66(4):857-863.

The gatekeeping concept accounts for the similarity in content across media, such as the national television network newscasts airing such similar stories. Researchers examined the news content of three major networks and found strikingly high correlations with respect to topics, geographic locations represented and story length. The finding was explained by similar sources, common values and backgrounds of the reporters and editors.[8]

And so, gatekeeping is an important concept, but it is not usually singular in the way it operates on communicators' choices. Rather, the gatekeeper's choices are a complex web of influences, preferences, motives, common values and the like.

It was said that gatekeeping has slipped firmly into the language of many disciplines. Indeed, articles appear on residential segregation, the Internet, managed care, court judges, education, criminal justice and medical economics, to name just a few.[9] And because the selection of mass media information is crucial to the public relations field, scholars have even developed specialties in analyzing how press releases are used (or not used) by media gatekeepers.[10]

The mainstream media gatekeepers also face an ethical dilemma as sensational news and gossip continue to capture public curiosity and large audiences. In the past, the major networks and newspapers ignored such sensational news as being beneath their standards of dignity. Today, if a tabloid or television talk show carries a juicy tidbit on Britain's Royals, the U.S. president or a sport celebrity, the mainstream media are obliged to follow suit, relinquishing gatekeepers' control.[11]

---

8. Daniel Riffe, Brenda Ellis, Momo K. Rogers, Roger L. Van Ommeren and Kieran A. Woodman (1986). "Gatekeeping and the network news mix," *Journalism Quarterly* 63(2):315-321.

9. See in order: Judith N. DeSena (1994). "Local gatekeeping practices and residential segregation," *Sociological Inquiry* 64(3):307-321; Thomas J. DeLoughry (1994). "Gatekeeping on the Internet," *The Chronicle of Higher Education* 41(13):A21-22; Douglas G. Cave and Susan Anderson (1997). "Today's managed care market: Examining the effectiveness of the 'gatekeeper' mechanism," *Compensation and Benefits Management* 13 (1):51-57; Sheila L. Birnbaum and J. Russell Jackson (1995). "District court judges, exploring their role as 'gatekeepers' of scientific testimony, discover there are no simple formulas," *The National Law Journal* 17(39):B5; Hanna Ayalon (1995). "Math as a gatekeeper: Ethnic and gender inequality in course taking of the sciences in Israel," *American Journal of Education* 104(1):34-56; Jeff Smith (1997). "Students' goals, gatekeeping, and some questions of ethics," *College English* 59(3):299-320; Ray Surette and Alfredo Richard (1995). "Public information officers: A descriptive study of crime news gatekeepers," *Journal of Criminal Justice* 23(4):325-336; E. James Anderson (1996). "Can a gatekeeper do what's right for the patients?" *Medical Economics* 73(21):209-210, 215.

10. Linda P. Morton (1995). "Gatekeepers as target publics," *Public Relations Quarterly* 40(2):21-25. See also: David Griffiths (1996). "Teaching journalism skills courses to new public relations majors," *Journalism & Mass Communication Educator* 51(1):82-86.

11. George Garneau (1996). "Scandalous dilemma: How a supermarket tabloid offered its paid-for political sex story to mainstream papers and how they reacted," *Editor & Publisher* 129 (37):14-19. See also: David Shaw (1994). "Surrender of the gatekeepers," *Nieman Reports* 48(1):3-6.

Conversely, most of the recent research still views gatekeeping as a powerful media force able to determine what topics are presented to the public. As social interest groups proliferate, research attention has turned to studying mass media content to see if a topic is represented, and if so to what extent and with what kind of slant. Among many such studies are those about negative political ads, HIV/AIDS coverage, reportage of cosmetic surgery and reporting on the environment.[12]

Finally, the gatekeeping literature is vast because this is the single mass media theory that focuses on what happens in the organizational structure of news rooms. Media management is a relatively new field of study dating back about 25 years. Gatekeeping addresses the day-to-day work of reporters, writers, editors and news room managers. It assesses the logistical struggles and professional decisions these people make under deadline pressures, and it provides a theoretical basis for how news organizations process the information that has become society's lifeblood.

To illustrate the concept of gatekeeping, the end-of-chapter exercise offers headlines from *The New York Times*, chosen because of its respect as a national leader in the field.[13] Evidence of this is seen in a story that appeared in a book by Timothy Crouse illustrating how one *NYT* reporter really did determine the day's news:[14]

R.W. (Johnny) Apple Jr., a political reporter for *The New York Times*, sat in the press room ready to write his lead from the outcome of the 1972 Iowa Democratic caucuses. Gathered behind him were the two wire service correspondents, and behind them correspondents from the three major television networks plus the *Baltimore Sun*.

Around this group stood the other reporters, all of whom were waiting to see what Apple would write. Apple called the election "a surprisingly strong showing for George McGovern." This became the thrust of national news coverage the next day, helping McGovern become the Democratic candidate for president. (McGovern lost to Republican Richard Nixon.)

---

12. See in order: Lori Melton McKinnon, Lynda Lee Kaid, Janet Murphy and Cynthia K. Acree (1996). "Policing political ads: An analysis of five leading newspapers' responses to 1992 political advertisements," *Journalism & Mass Communication Quarterly* 73(1):66-77; Michael A. Hallett and David Cannella (1997). "Gatekeeping through media format: Strategies of voice for the HIV-positive via human interest news formats and organizations," *Journal of Homosexuality* 32(3-4):17-36; Camille Galvin and Mark Pearson (1994). "Cosmetic surgery: Newspaper reportage of the Medical Journal of Australia," *Australian Journal of Communication* 21(2):109-121; Colin Lacey and David Longman (1997). "The press and public access to the environment and development debate," *Sociological Review* 41(2):207-243.

13. Robert Karl Manoff and Michael Schudson (1986). *Reading the news*. New York: Pantheon Books.

14. Timothy Crouse (1973). *The boys on the bus*. New York: Random House, p. 79.

Summary

The gatekeeper concept, from a 1950 study of one editor's news choices, is now in the language of many disciplines. Gatekeepers decide which information will go forward, and which will not. They exist in many jobs, and their choices hold the potential to color the mental "pictures" that are subsequently created in people's understanding of what is happening in the world around them.

In communications, gatekeepers open or close the information "gates." These people have the authority to affect information flow in a way that might reflect **personal bias**. If the gatekeeper's selections are biased, the audience's understanding will be biased. But gatekeeping is also desirable, useful and inevitable. Gatekeepers help to sort out the overwhelming detail, some of it trivial and conflicting.

Checks and balances that mitigate gatekeeping's effects are: *news values*, *objectivity*, audience *feedback*, *organizational structure* and *competition*. But gatekeeping still determines information flow. Researchers liken it to **agenda-setting**, and they note that the national media are still powerful gatekeepers accounting for the similarity in media content.

The gatekeeping literature is vast because this is the single mass media theory that focuses on the organizational structure of newsrooms.

Exercise:

Each of the headlines appeared in *The New York Times*, some on Page 1 and others elsewhere. They were not all printed on the same day. Read the list of headlines, and draw an asterisk by each that you think either was or should have been on Page 1. The task requires you to play the role of an editor of the *Times*.

Your teacher has the correct answers, the actual story placement. The list of headlines is about evenly divided between stories taken from Page 1 and elsewhere.

Recognizing that Page 1 is a kind of "showcase" for the newspaper and by implication an index of the importance of selected stories, be prepared to discuss your choices and the extent to which you agree with the *Times* editors. What insights, if any, can you gain from seeing the difference between your own judgments and those of the editors?

(Note: Your instructor realizes that you could make better judgments about the newsworthiness and placement of these headlines if you could also review the news story that accompanied each.)

Selection of Headlines from Editions of *The New York Times*

1. Concern is voiced over the quality of economic data

2. Russian Mars craft falls short and crashes back to earth

3. In Manila, Asians pore over Washington's inner truths

4. Food summit ends with usual earnest vows

5. In Lithuania, legendary Jewish books languish

6. Backers of ousted Serb general defiantly seize a tv tower

7. US trade deficit worsens, and gap with China grows

8. Argentina battles outbreak of rodent-borne disease

9. US gets 'average' grades in math and science studies

10. Jail inmates riot, but then talk to sheriff

11. CIA's latest security breach puts many careers in jeopardy

12. Romania's communist legacy: 'abortion culture'

13. Airlines in accord on disaster plans

14. Zambia's chief re-elected, but vote is questioned

15. Profits rise with taste for comfort

16. In Colombia, smuggling is an old, old custom

17. Files suggest British knew early of Nazi atrocities against Jews

18. Two are charged with kidnapping industrialist

19. Balancing Nature by putting wolves almost at the door

20. World is less crowded than expected, the UN reports

1. Discuss your rationale for deciding which stories probably would have been published on Page 1. What qualities did you look for?

(continued)

2. Does placement of a story on Page 1 give it "extra meaning"? In other words, if you read story 8 on Page 1, and another person reads it on Page 13, would your evaluations of the importance of the story be the same?

3. Examine your own list of Page 1 stories for any patterns. For example, did you select mostly national/international news? What values did you apply? What motives did you have: 1) desire to sell newspapers, 2) desire to inform people of world events or 3) other?

4. Were you, in effect, a gatekeeper? Were your judgments based solely on news values and what the audience might like, or did personal values slip quietly into some of your decisions?

21

Cognitive Dissonance

Doomsday prophecy field study: Leon Festinger, Henry Riecken and Stanley Schachter (1956). *When prophecy fails*. Minneapolis: University of Minnesota Press. Excerpted in Stanley Schachter and Michael Gazzaniga (1989). *Extending psychological frontiers: Selected works of Leon Festinger.* New York: Russell Sage Foundation, pp. 258-269.

Recent synopsis: Elliot Aronson (1997). "A theory of cognitive dissonance (book reviews)," *American Journal of Psychology 110*(1): 127-137.

Influences from people's early lives, such as the way parents and siblings treated them from childhood through their adolescent years, can affect personality and self-esteem. Consider your own upbringing. Would you say that you generally received positive reinforcement about your looks, your behavior and your intelligence? Or did you get negative reinforcement: received few compliments; frequently corrected; often embarrassed about your appearance; told you needed to change your attitude?

Most people probably remember a preponderance of either positive or negative reinforcement when they were young. In which group would you place yourself? *(circle one)*:

Positive   Balanced   Negative

Of course, those early impressions from a doting parent or mischievous older sibling do not determine the self-image people maintain for the rest of their lives. Most people establish a more balanced self-esteem as they mature and discover they are neither the most brilliant student nor the perpetual class dunce; neither the most popular nor the school geek. But people's early impressions of how others relate to them may effect their adolescent and teen years. Answer the questions on the next page by rating each from "0" to "7" with "7" being a statement that closely describes your experiences through high school and "0" a statement that never applied to you.

"7"= closely describes your experiences; "0"= never applied to you

_____ 1. In team sports, I was always captain or picked first or second.

_____ 2. My grades were always better than my friends' grades.

_____ 3. When the phone rang at home, it was usually one of my friends.

_____ 4. I won prizes in school activities such as science and spelling.

_____ 5. In high school I had a date most weekends.

_____ 6. I always expected high scores on standardized achievement tests.

_____ 7. If I joined a school club, I expected to be elected an officer.

_____ 8. I always did my homework and was prepared for class.

_____ 9. My friends were always willing to do the things I wanted to do.

_____ 10. I was expected to attend college, maybe on scholarship.

If this exercise is discussed in class, your answers will be anonymous.

* * *

Cognitive dissonance is a communication theory adopted from social psychology. It had a clear beginning, enjoyed widespread support from the social sciences, fell into disfavor, and then revived as an explanation for how people deal with conflicting information. The title gives the concept: **cognitive** is thinking or the mind; and **dissonance** is inconsistency or conflict. Cognitive dissonance is the psychological conflict that results from holding two or more incompatible beliefs simultaneously.

Everyone can relate to the concept, because you are sure to have had this experience. You introduce your best friend to another of your closest friends, but the two don't get along. How can you have so much in common with each of them, when they act as if they have nothing in common with each other? Something has to be amiss. Obviously, the three of you can never be together without friction, and now you have to reevaluate your relationships. You are experiencing cognitive dissonance.

A peson who opposes capital punishment may become engrossed in a television documentary. Halfway into stories about the families of murder victims, the person realizes that this show favors capital punishment, and that the information just heard about repeat offenders and criminals' lack of remorse — is a shocking revelation. Now there's a small chink in that person's protective armor against capital punishment. The person is experiencing cognitive dissonance.

After World War II, social psychologists' views of persuasion merged with the education field's learning theories and concepts the fledgling communication field was discovering. Termed **reinforcement theory**, experiments showed that people can be persuaded (if not fully convinced) by message repetition, punishment, reward, motivation, intensity and source attributes. The same tactics are used to teach rats to navigate a maze and to sell consumer products through advertising.

Founding the theory

In 1951, Leon Festinger synthesized a set of studies to distill a theory about communication's social influences. His team noticed a communication oddity after a major earthquake in India. The people, frightened and anxious after the earthquake, spread rumors of an even worse forthcoming disaster. The researchers wondered why such alarming rumors, seen as anxiety provoking, would be so widespread and accepted. They concluded that the rumors were anxiety justifying.[1] The people, already distraught, were engaging in communication that fit their state of mind. They were experiencing dissonance and were seeking **dissonance reduction**.

Fleshed out, cognitive dissonance theory suggests that: 1) dissonance is psychologically uncomfortable enough to motivate people to achieve consonance, and 2) in a state of dissonance, people will avoid information and situations that might increase the dissonance. How dissonance arises is easy to imagine: It may be unavoidable in an information-rich society. How people deal with it is more difficult.

Consider a motorist who refuses to use a seat belt despite knowing that the law requires using it, and it saves lives. Then a news report or a friend's car accident stuns the scofflaw into facing reality. Dissonance may be reduced by: 1) altering behavior...start using a seat belt so the behavior is consonant with knowing that doing so is smart; or 2) seeking information that is consonant with the behavior...air bags are safer than seat belts. If the driver never faces a situation that threatens the decision not to use seat belts, then no dissonance-reducing action is likely because the impetus to reduce dissonance depends on the magnitude of the dissonance held.

Among a series of studies done through the 1950s and 1960s was one that emphasized the power and peculiarity of dissonance reduction.[2] Researchers assigned a dull and repetitive task to a subject, then paid the person who just finished the boring task to tell the next subject that the task was interesting. In some cases the "confederate" subject was offered $1 to lie while in other cases the confederate was offered $20. All who agreed to motivate the next subject were later asked to evaluate

---

1. Leon Festinger (1957). *A theory of cognitive dissonance.* Stanford, CA: Stanford University Press.

2. Leon Festinger and James M. Carlsmith (1959). "Cognitive consequences of forced compliance," *Journal of Abnormal and Social Psychology* 58(2):203-210.

the dull task they had just lied about. Those who got $1 to lie rated the task more enjoyable and were better at persuading the next subject than those who got $20. Researchers concluded that the $20 confederates suffered little dissonance because they had "external justification": They had been well paid to exaggerate. However, the $1 confederates experienced great dissonance, and had reduced it by convincing themselves that the task was more interesting than they originally thought.

This lab experiment may seem too contrived to be of any real value, but similar cognitive dissonance findings have been demonstrated in studies about views toward smoking marijuana[3] and initiation rituals in joining groups. Why do ex-Marines greet one another with "Semper Fi"[4] even 30 years after being discharged? Cognitive dissonance suggests that the severity of their training creates an allegiance to the Corps by negating any negative impressions. A harsh initiation ceremony increases loyalty to a fraternity.[5] Ethical social scientists decry such tactics, but the finding helps explain why people value the goals they achieve through adversity.

Dissonance and self esteem

The theory deals with people's thought processes as inferred from their behaviors. It applies equally to interpersonal communication and mass media use. The theory is valid only when dissonance is important to the person, so it is very likely to occur when a person's self-image is shaken. People's self-esteem is generally pretty high, and they try to maintain its balance. Researchers list these as esteem beliefs that people hold dear: 1) I know myself and how I will behave in a variety of circumstances; 2) I am a capable person; and, 3) My decisions are moral.[6]

When essential self-perceptions are challenged, people engage in dissonance-reducing strategies. The decision to purchase a new vehicle provides an example because in this society, the car a person drives is considered an extension of self. Buying a car is an important decision reached only after researching many options. Let's say that as a "moral" person, you support environmental protection, so you know your new car should be fuel efficient. However, you also see yourself as an adventurous, carefree spirit: You want a Mustang convertible. Your decision is likely to prompt dissonance reduction through one or more of these methods:

---

3. Elizabeth Nel, Robert Helmreich and Elliot Aronson (1969). "Opinion change in the advocate as a function of the persuasibility of his audience: A clarification of the meaning of dissonance," *Journal of Personality and Social Psychology* 12(2):117-124.

4. "Always faithful;" motto of the U.S. Marine Corps.

5. Elliot Aronson and Judson Mills (1959). "The effect of severity of initiation on liking for a group," *Journal of Abnormal and Social Psychology* 59(2):177-181.

6. Elliot Aronson, T. Chase, Robert Helmreich and R. Ruhnke (1974). "A two-factor theory of dissonance reduction: The effect of feeling stupid or feeling awful on opinion change," *International Journal for Research and Communication* 3:59-74.

1. Changing one or more of the cognitive elements by adjusting your view of the Mustang's fuel efficiency: After all, it isn't a gas-guzzling sports utility vehicle.

2. Adding new elements to one side of the equation: Many sports cars have far less fuel efficiency than the Mustang, and those others cost a lot more.

3. Reducing the importance of your previous view of fuel efficiency: Most American cars today meet federal fuel efficiency standards, so automobiles aren't affecting the environment as much as they used to.

4. Seeking consonant information: You read ads and consumer articles praising the Mustang's fuel-efficiency and ask Mustang owners about their gas mileage.

5. Distorting the information: Consumer tests list sports cars by fuel efficiency with the Mustang halfway down the list, but you focus on the cars that get worse gas mileage. Or you remember the Mustang's open-road mpg, ignoring its in-city mpg.

Research suggests that people experience greater dissonance depending on: 1) how important the decision is to them; 2) how attractive the chosen alternative is; 3) how attractive the unchosen alternative was; and, 4) how dissimilar the two alternatives were...a Mustang versus a Hyundai might not cause dissonance. Obviously, the more reinforcement one receives from social peers — "Hey, that's a great looking car!" — the more easily the Mustang fits the adjusted self-concept.

Dissonance research continues

Cognitive dissonance enjoyed great popularity from the late 1950s through the mid-1970s. But in the 1980s, a variety of "self" theories supplanted it including: self-verification theory, action identification, self-affirmation, self-evaluation maintenance, self-regulation, self-discrepancy theory and others.[7] Although posited as unique approaches to understanding psychological states, each of these could also be considered a subset of cognitive dissonance.

---

7. In order of listing see: Robert A. Wicklund and Peter M. Gollwitzer (1982). *Symbolic self-completion*. Hillside, NJ: Lawrence Erlbaum; William B. Swann Jr. (1984). "Quest for accuracy in person perception: A matter of pragmatics," *Psychological Review 91*(4):457-477; Claude M. Steele (1988). "The psychology of self-affirmation: Sustaining the integrity of the self," in Leonard Berkowitz, ed. *Advances in experimental social psychology Vol. 21*. San Diego: Academic Press, pp. 261-302; Robin R. Vallacher and Daniel M. Wegner (1985). *A theory of action identification*. Hillside, NJ: Lawrence Erlbaum; Abraham Tesser (1988). "Toward a self-evaluation maintenance model of social behavior," in Berkowitz, ed., *op. cit.*, pp. 181-227; Michael F. Scheier and Charles S. Carver (1988). "A model of behavioral self-regulation: Translating intention into action," in Berkowitz, ed., *Ibid.*, pp. 303-346; Edward Tory Higgins (1989). "Self-discrepancy theory: What patterns of self-beliefs cause people to suffer?" in Berkowitz, ed., *Ibid.*, pp. 93-136; Ziva Kunda (1990). "The case for motivated reasoning," *Psychological Bulletin 108*(3):480-498.

Because many of the responses to dissonance involve exposure to or avoidance of media messages, the communication field incorporated the theory to study people's selective exposure to messages (See Selectivity chapter). For example, "avoiding unsettling messages" in the theory explains why Republicans read conservative columnists, watch Rush Limbaugh and listen to Paul Harvey; and why they avoid liberal columnists, *The New Republic* and Dennis Miller. Dozens of studies during a 30-year period focused on conditions in which people sought or avoided exposure to dissonance-reducing information.[8] Much was learned, but the outcomes were either inconclusive, contradictory or too specific to help build theory.

Reviewing the theory through the late 1980s, Littlejohn identified problems with cognitive dissonance.[9] First is the appropriateness problem: The dissonance construct is too simple to capture complexities of human information processing. Next is the problem of proof: Studies that report attitude change attribute the cause to dissonance; if attitudes don't change, researchers conclude that dissonance did not occur. The theory becomes irrefutable because dissonance is such a general concept, and because dissonance levels are not actually measured but inferred from behavior. The last problem is that cognitive dissonance was supposed to explain a wide range of behaviors but seems to be limited to only a few behaviors.

Despite these drawbacks, communication theoreticians today laud cognitive dissonance for its influence on nearly two generations of researchers and note the massive amount of findings the theory derived. As the studies continue, they seem to be more practical applications designed to investigate ways to help solve significant social concerns. Consider this brief list of studies and their implications:

• High electricity consuming households in Perth, Western Australia, reduced energy use when the inconsistency between these families' attitude toward conservation and their actual electrical use was pointed out.[10]

• AIDS fear tactics failed to motivate students to change their condom use habits, but those who made public statements favoring condom use saw the mismatch between their behavior and the message. They changed their behavior.[11]

---

8. John L. Cotton (1985). "Cognitive dissonance in selective exposure," in Dolf Zillmann and Jennings Bryant, eds. *Selective exposure to communication.* Hillsdale, NJ: Lawrence Erlbaum, pp. 11-33.

9. Stephen W. Littlejohn (1989). *Theories of human communication, 3rd ed.* Belmont, CA: Wadsworth, pp. 88-93. See also Sarah Trenholm (1986). *Human communication theory.* Englewood Cliffs, NJ: Prentice-Hall, pp. 130-136.

10. Steven J. Kantola, Geoffrey J. Syme and Neil A. Campbell (1984). "Cognitive dissonance and energy conservation," *Journal of Applied Psychology* 69(3):416-421.

11. Jeff Stone, Elliot Aronson, A. Lauren Crain, Matthew P. Windslow and Carrie B. Fried (1994). "Inducing hypocrisy as a means of encouraging young adults to use condoms," *Personality and Social Psychology Bulletin* 20(1):116-128.

• How do evangelical Christian lesbians cope with dissonance? The choices are altering one's religious beliefs, living with the dissonance or leaving the church. Leaving the church was the least favored alternative.[12]

• Smokers who participated in cessation clinics because of the health risk but then relapsed reduced their dissonance by lowering their perception of risk. However, the decline was only significant for high self-esteem relapsers. Those high in self-esteem also had greater declines in commitment to quitting.[13]

• Students who owned or voluntarily used a computer scored significantly lower in computer anxiety and higher in computer confidence and liking at the beginning of a computer class. Having made a personal commitment to new technology also adjusts one's attitudes toward it.[14]

• Europe's first carpool priority lane ended when solo drivers who used the lanes engaged in behavior self-justification. Their importance rating for solo travel's flexibility increased, and their rating for carpooling's low travel costs decreased. People drove alone in the carpool lane, and some placed mannequins in their cars.[15]

• Students at a California campus recreation facility were made to feel guily about wasting water by taking long showers. Having them urge other students to take shorter showers, and thus feel hypocritical, the subjects actually did take significantly shorter showers. The researchers said cognitive dissonance might help change behavior in situations where people already support the desired goal, but their behavior is inconsistent with their beliefs.[16]

Summary

Cognitive dissonance is a relatively straightforward social psychology theory that has enjoyed wide acceptance in a variety of disciplines including communication. The theory replaces previous conditioning or reinforcement theories by viewing

12. Kimberly A. Mahaffy (1996). "Cognitive dissonance and its resolution: A study of lesbian Christians," *Journal for the Scientific Study of Religion* 35(4):392-402.

13. Frederick X. Gibbons, Tami J. Eggleston and Alida C. Benthin (1977). "Cognitive reactions to smoking relapse: The reciprocal relation between dissonance and self-esteem," *Journal of Personality and Social Psychology* 72(1):184-195.

14. Thomas S. Parish and James R. Necessary (1996). "An examination of cognitive dissonance and computer attitudes," *Education* 116(4):565-567.

15. Mark Van Vugt, Paul A.M. Van Lange, Ree M. Meertens and Jeffrey A. Joireman (1996). "How a structural solution to a real-world social dilemma failed: A field experiment on the first car-pool lane in Europe," *Social Psychology Quarterly* 59(4):364-374.

16. Chris Ann Dickerson, Ruth Thibodeau, Elliot Aronson and Dayna Miller (1992). "Using cognitive dissonance to encourage water conservation," *Journal of Applied Social Psychology* 22(11): 841-854.

individuals as more purposeful decision makers; they strive for balance in their beliefs. If presented with decisions or information that create dissonance, they use dissonance-reduction strategies to regain equilibrium, especially if the dissonance affects their self-esteem.

The theory was highly researched from its founding in 1957 through the late 1970s. Theoretical problems and conflicting findings lead to temporary replacement by similar "self" theories in the early 1980s, but cognitive dissonance regained its place as the umbrella theory for selective exposure to communication by the late 1980s. Research continues today as cognitive dissonance offers a wealth of insights about people's attitudes and their interaction with persuasive and factual messages.

Exercise:

Given enough incentive and opportunity, and minimum risk of detection, some people will steal, cheat, lie and behave in a variety of despicable ways and then make excuses about why their actions were either misinterpreted or beyond their control. To account for such behavior:

1. Offer a brief scenario of this kind of event that encompasses at least two cognitive dissonance principles, and underline the two principles. (See chapter sections titled "Founding the Theory" and "Dissonance and Self Esteem"; look at numbered lists.)

2. Some theorists say that cognitive dissonance cannot occur until a decision has been made; others say it can occur before a decision is made. Which statement is correct, and why. (See the chapter material on seat belts and buying a Mustang.)

3. Several of the studies mentioned in this unit involved experimental tactics that are ethically questionable.

    a) Identify one such study.

    b) Do you think the method used is justifiable? (Does the need for explaining behavior justify mistreating subjects?)

4. Returning to the issue of dishonest behavior, assume that an employer is losing 5% of profits to internal pilfering by employees. The employer doesn't mind an occasional ball point pen or notepad being taken home, but the situation is out of control with reams of paper, computer disks and even calculators missing. Which of the following strategies from cognitive dissonance theory should be tried:

    a. warn employees that the penalty for theft is being fired
    b. tell employees about new procedures to lock and account for supplies
    c. tell employees the extent of loss from pilfering, that it is threatening the company's future, and possibly their bonus
    d. tell employees how much confidence the firm has in them as capable and reliable individuals
    e. post signs that advise employees of the problem, but in a non-threatening manner ("Earnest Atwork" Defeats "Lefty Lightfingers")

5. Why did you choose the answer you did in question 4 above:

22
Attitudes and Attitude Change

Early study: Dorwin Cartwright (1949). "Some principles of mass persuasion: Selected findings of research on the sale of United States War Bonds," *Human Relations* 2(3):253-267.

Twenty years later: Major Steadman (1969). "How sexy illustrations affect brand recall," *Journal of Advertising Research* 9(1):15-19.

Another 20 years: John T. Cacioppo and Richard E. Petty (1989). "Effects of message repetition on argument processing, recall, and persuasion," *Basic and Applied Social Psychology* 10(1):3-12.

Some questions to ponder as you read this chapter:

1. Where do attitudes "come from"?

2. Do attitudes predict behavior?

3. Are attitudes related to "values"?

4. How susceptible are attitudes to change?

5. What strategies work in attitude change?

Attitude is probably the most studied and most frequently applied construct in social research. All disciplines that study human behavior use "attitudes" as an important variable in why people think and act as they do. The focus on attitudes has been central to social science since at least the 1930s, when Allport observed that, "No other term appears more frequently in experimental and theoretical literature."[1]

---

1. Gordon W. Allport (1935). "Attitudes," in Carl Allanmore Murchison, ed. *A Handbook of social psychology Vol. 2*. Worcester, MA: Clark University Press, pp. 798-844.

Attitudes are clearly powerful antecedents to human behavior, often determining *a priori* whether people accept or reject, believe or disbelieve, vote or not vote. **Attitudes** are defined as "an enduring system of positive or negative evaluations, emotional feelings, and pro and con action tendencies with respect to a social object."[2]

Attitudes range from positive to negative, from liking to disliking. Attitudes have implications for behavior, but the relationship is not clear. Sometimes an attitude is mitigated by other factors. For example, a person might object to an attitude object (dislike horror films) but tolerate it to avoid social rejection (friends like horror films and enjoy discussing them). Another example: A person might have a negative attitude toward education, but repress that attitude for purposes of employment.

Where do attitudes "come from"? Apparently, they are formed from an individual's **experiences**, **needs** and **desires**. An attitude is the expression of some things that preceded it, and perhaps some satisfactions that can be gained from it. Attitude gratification has been termed **value-expectancy theory**.[3] The idea is that a person's feeling about an attitude object might change if the person is subsequently persuaded that change brings personal benefits or penalties, as the case may be.

Attitudes do not always appear to make good sense. An individual sometimes will say, "I like the (Democratic or Republican) Party; my family has *always* been (Democratic or Republican)." The sentiment is sensible only if the political party best reflects the individual's interests. Political affiliation really should have little to do with family history. Similarly, a person might have a strong racial or ethnic feeling (pride or prejudice) without having a sensible explanation.

Another subtlety of attitudes is that sometimes they are firmly held but not well articulated. One's work ethic (attitude toward work), for example, represents a large set of experiences, assumptions and expectations that are not routinely and coherently articulated, but which profoundly affect the individual's job performance.

An attitude is a **construct**, a thing that is inferred from something else, a product of other learned connections or the interaction of previous cognitions. Researchers sometimes can accurately *infer* an attitude from statements or behaviors, but often respondents cannot articulate or do not wish to reveal their true feelings. This makes attitude measurement one of the most difficult (and interesting) aspects of studying human beings.

---

2. David Krech, Richard S. Crutchfield and Egerton L. Ballachey (1962). *Individual in society: A textbook of social psychology*. New York: McGraw-Hill.

3. Dominic A. Infante, Andrew S. Rancer and Deanna F. Womack (1996). *Building communication theory, 3d ed*. Prospect Heights, IL: Waveland, p. 167.

To measure attitudes, researchers rely on an index rather than a single item such as: "What is your attitude toward...?" A single-item measure usually is not adequate because attitudes most often are multi-dimensional. An **index** is a set of measures tapping multiple dimensions; for example, an index might include a broad series of questions or perhaps a combination of questions or behaviors.

Do you think that the U.S. judicial system is doing a good job? This is a question about which most people have an attitude, but the question is probably too encompassing to accurately assess people's attitude with a yes or no answer. Also, the question is not one about which most people have given a lot of thought. A better method of assessing attitudes about the U.S. judicial system is to break the topic into its component parts:

1) Are most U.S. judges qualified to hold their positions on the bench?
2) Do most judges apply the law properly and fairly?
3) Do you think that most juries reach the correct decision?
4) Are U.S. laws clear enough and precise enough to administer?
5) In most cases under U.S. law, does the punishment fit the crime?

These questions suggest that the issue includes dimensions such as competence, fairness, accuracy and comprehensibility, each of which should be accounted for in a measurement of attitudes toward the judicial system. The list of questions could continue several pages, and people who respond to these items could answer yes or no to each one with some sense of having accurately expressed their beliefs. By counting the number of yes answers, a researcher would determine if the person believes the U.S. judicial system is doing a good job or where each person should be placed on this attitude scale of agreement. Of course, measuring respondents' true attitude depends on how well the questions assess the U.S. judicial system.

Exercise:

Select **one** of these two issues and devise a set of fewer than 10 questions that you believe would accurately measure the underlying attitude:

1. Should young children ever be spanked?

2. Should the news media report the marital infidelities of public officials such as mayors, governors and presidents?

The literature on the subject of attitudes is vast, and the preceding was merely an introduction. The discussion will change now from the *nature* of attitudes to the *changing* of attitudes.

Attitude change

If you were the communicator who needed to identify and change an attitude, how would you proceed? Here are several attitude change models that reveal some of the intricacies of both the formation and change of attitudes. The first is McGuire's model of attitude change, which offers practical insights. He identified five "steps" in persuasion and four "communication factors."[4]   The five steps are:

1. **Attention**. Persuasion cannot begin until the listener's attention has been won. Advertisers have long been familiar with attention-getting techniques.

2. **Comprehension**. For communication to be effective, it must be understood.

3. **Yielding**. The listener must yield to the idea being presented. That is, if the listener rejects the information as useless or untrue, the persuasion will not succeed.

4. **Retention**. The listener must retain the communication long enough to act upon it. If the listener fails to retain it, persuasion likely will not succeed.

5. **Action**. The measure of success is whether the listener is motivated to action by the communication.

Subsequently, McGuire expanded the model to include:

a. **Exposure**. Attention cannot be gained if the individual is not exposed to the message.

b. **Interest**. Attention is more likely gained and retained if the message is of interest to the listener.

c. **Reinforcement**. If not reinforced, a message's impact can be lost over time.

d. **Consolidation**. If the attitude-behavior is rewarding, the new attitude will more likely be persistent over time.

McGuire suggested there were four "communication factors" that would also weigh heavily in any successful persuasion:

---

4. William J. McGuire (1969). "The nature of attitudes and attitude change" in Gardner Lindzey and Elliot Aronson, eds. *The handbook of social psychology Vol. 3, 2nd ed*. Reading, MA: Addison-Wesley, pp. 136-314. See Also: William J. McGuire (1989). "Theoretical foundations of campaigns," in Ronald E. Rice and Charles K. Atkin, eds. *Public communication campaigns, 2nd ed*. Newbury Park, CA: Sage Publications, pp. 43-65; William J. McGuire (1985). "Attitudes and attitude change," in Gardner Lindzey and Elliot Aronson, eds. *Handbook of social psychology Vol. 2, 3d ed*. New York: Random House, pp. 233-346.

1. **Source**. The persuader might get the listener's attention, but be rejected because of *perceived bias, personal characteristics* or perhaps *semantic noise* (some form of interference in interpreting the message the way it was intended). In other words, attention is necessary, but not alone sufficient to be persuasive.

2. **Message**. The message may interact with any of the steps of persuasion. For example, a message that gets the attention of the listener may be comprehensible but too complex to retain in sufficient detail for action.

3. **Channel**. Persuasion effectiveness might depend on how the message is transmitted. For example, a brochure might be best in one case, a film in another.

4. **Receiver**. Characteristics of the receiver, such as education, experience and personality, all have a bearing on successful communication.

McGuire subsequently added **context** to his source variables. This suggested that the context in which the persuasion was received could affect its reception.

Fishbein and Ajzen proposed a more direct approach to defining attitudes.[5] They said attitudes are a function of a person's beliefs (cognitions) about an attitude object, and those beliefs lead to *behavioral intentions* toward the object. Unless the intention is mitigated by other some factor, it should lead to overt behavior.

Notice that a behavioral intention and an action are different. For example, to change an attitude, the communicator must change the listener's beliefs about the object, such as convincing a skeptical buyer that an expensive car is safer. In this definition, the goal is to change a person's cognitions or beliefs about X. One method is to structure communication as McGuire suggested: by winning the listener's attention; enhancing understanding, yielding and recall; and urging action.

In the mid-1980s, Petty and Cacioppo offered their "elaboration likelihood model" (ELM) of persuasion.[6] The **ELM** deals with how an individual processes a message: sometimes by consciously evaluating it, sometimes unconsciously. In the ELM, the first test of a persuasive message is whether the listener is *motivated* to process it. The listener might find it relevant, might have no need for the information or might find it beyond the level of personal responsibility.[7]

---

5. Martin Fishbein and Icek Ajzen (1975). *Belief, attitude, intention and behavior: An introduction to theory and research.* Reading, MA: Addison-Wesley.

6. Richard E. Petty and John T. Cacioppo (1986). *Communication and persuasion: Central and peripheral routes to attitude change.* (New York: Springer-Verlag) 1986.

7. Curtis P. Haugtvedt and Richard E. Petty (1992). "Personality and persuasion: Need for cognition moderates the persistence and resistance of attitude changes," *Journal of Personality and Social Psychology 63*(2):308-319.

The second test is whether the individual has the *ability* to process the message. The message might be comprehensible or incomprehensible, or it might request something that the listener simply could not provide. On hearing the message, the listener either does or does not have a cognitive structure change. If yes, the new structure can lead to attitude change, relatively enduring; if no, the old attitude is retained or regained.

The Petty-Cacioppo model also suggests the importance of "peripheral cues," the non-message issues such as source credibility, number of arguments and channel factors, all of which can affect a persuasive message. And so, in the ELM, attitude change can occur along a "central route" (more or less directly from communicator to recipient, the conscious aspect) or along a "peripheral route" (an effect resulting from peripheral cues).[8] For example, when viewers watch a cold drink commercial, they might be influenced by the direct script message "only one calorie," or they might be influenced by the indirect visual message of trim youths playing volleyball on the beach. Although the ELM changes occur within individuals, the model certainly has implications for mass communication persuasion.[9]

Katz[10] pointed out that attitudes have **functions** for the individual. For example, an attitude object might have **utility**, providing some type of reward to the hearer. Or it might serve a function of **ego defense**. Some attitudes represent the expression of personal **values**, and some attitudes are formed from a need for **knowledge**, i.e., for cognitive consistency or clarity. Katz's functional model identified **arousal** and **change conditions** in which an attitude is susceptible to change.

Summary

"Attitude" is one of the most widely studied and applied terms in social research because attitudes are powerful in influencing behavior. Attitudes reflect liking or disliking, and they develop from a person's life experiences, needs and desires. Attitudes are not always logical or well articulated.

"Attitude" is a construct, inferred from statements or behavior. Multi-dimensional and complex, an attitude is usually measured as an index, a combination of measures. McGuire identified several "steps" in the persuasion process, and

---

8. Richard E. Petty, John T. Cacioppo and David Schumann (1983). "Central and peripheral routes to advertising effectiveness: The moderating role of involvement," *Journal of Consumer Research* 10(2):135-146.

9. Richard E. Petty and Joseph R. Priester (1994). "Mass media attitude change: Implications of the elaboration likelihood model of persuasion," in Jennings Bryant and Dolf Zillmann, eds. *Media effects: Advances in theory and research.* Hillsdale, NJ: Lawrence Erlbaum Associates, pp. 91-122.

10. Daniel Katz (1960). "The functional approach to the study of attitudes," *Public Opinion Quarterly* 24(2):163-204.

several source variables. Fishbein and Ajzen emphasized the role of cognition, belief and behavioral intention. Petty and Cacioppo developed the elaboration likelihood model (ELM), and Katz developed the functional approach.

Exercise:

Following are several statements that reflect an attitude toward the concept "higher education." Review each statement and indicate your level of agreement or disagreement, where SA = Strongly Agree, A = Agree, N = Neutral or Undecided, DA = Disagree, and SDA = Strongly Disagree.

	SA	A	N	DA	SDA
1. Income increases as education increases.	/	/	/	/	/
2. Educated persons feel more in control of their life.	/	/	/	/	/
3. A career in the professions is an important goal.	/	/	/	/	/
4. Education brings others' respect.	/	/	/	/	/
5. Learning is among the highest goals of life.	/	/	/	/	/
6. Education leads to greater self-respect.	/	/	/	/	/
7. Education opens doors that would be closed otherwise.	/	/	/	/	/
8. Everyone, whether consciously or not, wants more education.	/	/	/	/	/
9. Educated persons are better citizens.	/	/	/	/	/
10. Education is worth the expense to me.	/	/	/	/	/

Score your responses: SA=5, A=4, N=3, D=2, SD=1.
Add your scores for the 10 items and record the average: _____

(continued)

Now critique the exercise by answering each of these questions briefly:

1. The items in the questionnaire referred to issues of income, respect, citizenship and achievement. Are there some issues that should have been included but were not? Were the items sufficiently diverse to cover the dimensions of attitude?

2. Note that all the questions were posed in a way that was favorable to education. Did that have a biasing effect on the responses?

3. Did the response options give you a sufficient range of choices? If you felt a need to change the scales, how?

(continued)

4. Might the fact that you are enrolled in higher education have influenced your responses? To what extent? Would a non-college person score as high, on average, as a college person?

5. How much variation was there in your scores? A little or a lot? Explain.

6. Having responded to the items, do you feel that your responses accurately represented your **attitude** toward higher education?

Uses and Gratifications

Carolyn A. Lin
Cleveland State University

Early study: Herta Herzog (1940). "Professor Quiz: A gratification study," in Paul F. Lazarsfeld, ed. *Radio and the printed page*. New York: Duell, Sloan and Pearce, pp. 64-93.

Thirty years later: Elihu Katz, Michael Gurevitch and Hadassah Haas. (1973). "On the use of the mass media for important things," *American Sociological Review* 38(2):164-181.

Another 20 years: Deirdre D. Johnston (1995). "Adolescents' motivations for viewing graphic horror," *Human Communication Research* 21(4):522-552.

From among the following media, which would you miss most if you had to do without it, and why? Select **three**: your first choice to keep, and say why; your second choice to keep, and say why; and your third choice to keep, and say why:

____going to the movies

____watching TV

____watching your favorite cable TV channels

____reading the newspaper

____viewing video tapes

____computer on-line time (including email)

____reading magazines

____listening to music on audio tapes or compact discs

____reading books for pleasure

____listening to the radio

1) First choice to keep: _____ , and why:

2) Second choice to keep: _____ , and why:

3) Third choice to keep: _____ , and why:

*   *   *

The uses and gratifications perspective is one of a precious few theories that the communication discipline can truly call its own.[1] It examines media behaviors from the audience member's view, acknowledging that media users control their own decisions. Uses and gratifications has proven to be an **axiomatic theory** in that its principles are generally accepted, and it is readily applicable to a wide range of situations involving mediated communication.

In the abstract, the theory seeks to explain: 1) the psychological needs that help shape 2) why people use the media and that motivate people to 3) engage in media use behaviors to 4) derive gratifications to 5) fulfill those intrinsic needs, within the confines of a particular socio-cultural environment.[2] This perspective also recognizes that: 1) individuals differ along several psychological dimensions which, in turn, prompt them to make different choices about which media to patronize, and 2) even individuals exposed to the same media content will respond to it in different ways, depending on their characteristics.

---

1. Carolyn A. Lin (1996). "Looking back: The contribution of Blumler and Katz's 'Uses of Mass Communication' to communication research," *Journal of Broadcasting & Electronic Media* 40(4):574-581.

2. Jeffrey Jensen Arnett, Reed Larson and Daniel Offer (1995). "Beyond effects: Adolescents as active media users," *Journal of Youth and Adolescence* 24(5):511-518. See also: Alan M. Rubin (1983). "Television uses and gratifications: The interactions of viewing patterns and motivations," *Journal of Broadcasting* 27(1):37-51.

In placing so much emphasis on audience decision making, this theoretical approach fits into a category of **limited effects** theories that are not as much concerned with what *media do to audiences* as what the *audience member does with the media*. This reflects an **active audience**, in stark contrast to earlier views of audiences as almost completely "passive," homogeneous and readily manipulated by the media.

Uses and gratifications process

According to Katz, Blumler and Gurevitch,[3] uses and gratifications theory is founded on three basic tenets: 1) viewers are **goal directed** in their behavior, 2) they are **active media users**, and 3) they are **aware of their needs** and select media to gratify those needs. Based the work of scholars in the field, a model is offered here to illustrate the fundamental components, structure and functions of this theory.[4] The ensuing discussion defines each of the component functions in Figure 1 and their interrelationship with others in the paradigm.

Needs. Two basic psychological needs[5] are deficiency and non-deficiency needs. **Deficiency needs** derive from internal dissatisfaction, such as needs for love and security, and *rely mostly on other people* for need-fulfillment. The **non-deficiency needs** are considered **self-actualization needs** that can be fulfilled by sources independent from others and may help enhance one's self-development.

Media use needs are a type of self-actualization needs, and they are said to have social origins.[6] These involve such social factors as sociological characteristics (age, gender, race, income and other SES traits); social roles (full-time worker, friend, sibling, father); and social conditions (geographic mobility, car ownership, work schedules). Overall, five different self-actualization needs[7] are considered relevant to media uses and gratifications: 1) **cognitive** needs, such as the need to understand; 2) **affective** needs that strengthen aesthetic or emotional experience; 3) **integrative** needs that strengthen one's confidence, credibility or stability; 4) needs related to strengthening **contact** with family, friends and the world; and, 5) needs related to **escape** or **tension release**.

---

3. Elihu Katz, Jay G. Blumler and Michael Gurevitch (1974). "Utilization of mass communication by the individual," in Jay G. Blumler and Elihu Katz, eds. *The uses of mass communications: Current perspectives on gratifications research.* Beverly Hills, CA: Sage, p. 20.

4. This model is constructed based on the research model and findings from Carolyn A. Lin (1993). "Modeling the gratification-seeking process of television viewing," *Human Communication Research* 20(2):224-244.

5. Abraham H. Maslow (1970). *Motivation and personality, 2nd ed.* New York: Harper & Row.

6. Jay G. Blumler (1985). "The social character of media gratifications," in Karl Erik Rosengren, Lawrence A. Wenner and Philip Palmgreen, eds. *Media gratifications research: Current perspectives.* Beverly Hills, CA: Sage Publications, pp. 41-59.

7. Elihu Katz, Michael Gurevitch and Hadassah Haas (1973). See introductory study: "Thirty years later."

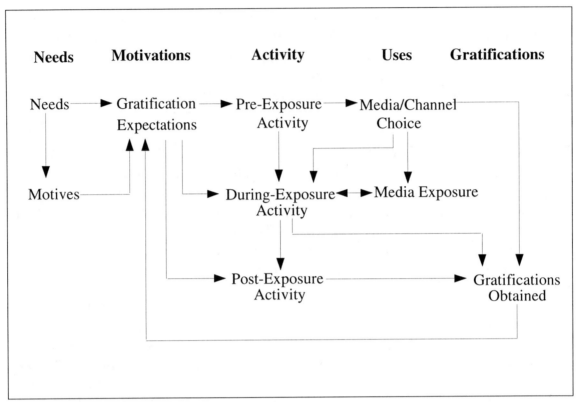

Figure 1. Uses and gratifications paradigm

Motives. This concept reflects the **desires** created by the types of needs that require further drive-reduction or fulfillment. As motives vary among individuals with different socio-demographic backgrounds, they can cover some or all of the following dimensions:[8]

1) **entertainment** — to seek fun, amusement or excitement;

2) **surveillance** — to keep up with what's going on in the world;

3) **information** — to learn about things that are interesting and useful;

4) **diversion** — to redirect one's attention to the "media reality";

5) **escape** — to forget about the problem at hand;

6) **social interaction** — to have something to do with or say to others;

7) **parasocial interaction** — to "talk back" to media personalities;

8) **identity** — to find people or ideologies with which to identify;

9) **pass time** — to relieve boredom and kill time; and,

10) **companionship** — to reduce the feeling of loneliness.

---

8. These items are adapted from Carolyn A. Lin (1993), *op. cit.*, and Alan M. Rubin (1983). *op. cit.*

Studies have identified motives associated with media use choices. For example, Livingstone found that escapism was the primary motive for watching soap operas, followed by realism, relationship with characters, critical responses, problem-solving, their role in the viewer's life, emotional experience and entertainment.[9] Music videos, however, are viewed by teenagers primarily for diversion, because they think the content is exciting and can help them improve their moods.[10]

Motivations. This notion describes the type of perceived incentives or rewards that can propel an individual to take action and engage in media use. Two dimensions of motivations for media use are: 1) a **cognitive** dimension, or the *thought* about the types of gratifications that one expects or seeks from initiating media use, and 2) an **affective** dimension or the *emotional* predisposition toward the types of gratifications that one expects or seeks from initiating such activity.

Past research did find support for a distinction between cognitive (such as surveillance and knowledge motives) and affective gratifications (including interpersonal utility, excitement and escape motives).[11] Other terms used to label this concept include: **gratification expectations** or **gratifications sought**.

Activity. This is the type of **cognitive**, **affective** and **behavioral process** involved in initiating and executing one's **media use activity**. The three phases of this process, involving audience pre-, during- and post-exposure activities, are thought to be influenced by the gratification expectations before exposure and to have an impact on the gratifications obtained after exposure.[12] They are:

Pre-exposure activity explains an individual's preparation process for media use activity. Some activities might include tuning into preselected channels, checking *TV Guide* or browsing channels to make choices for subsequent exposure. Audience content preference and affinity with a medium can help dictate the process and outcome of this particular activity phase.

9. Sonia M. Livingstone (1988). "Why people watch soap opera: An analysis of the explanations of British viewers," *European Journal of Communication* 3(1):55-80. See also: Herta Herzog (1944). "What do we really know about daytime serial listeners?" in Paul F. Lazarsfeld and Frank N. Stanton, eds. *Radio research 1942-1943*. New York: Arno Press, pp. 3-33.

10. Jane D. Brown, Kenneth Campbell and Lynn Fischer (1986). "American adolescents and music videos: Why do they watch?" *Gazette* 37(1-2):19-32.

11. Jean Dobos and John Dimmick (1988). "Factor analysis and gratification constructs," *Journal of Broadcasting & Electronic Media* 32(3):335-350.

12. Mark R. Levy and Sven Windhal (1984). "Audience activity and gratifications: A conceptual clarification and exploration," *Communication Research* 11(1): 51-78; Carolyn A. Lin (1990). "Audience activity and VCR use," in Julia Dobrow, ed. *Social and cultural aspects of VCR use*. Hillsdale, NJ: Lawrence Erlbaum Associates, pp. 75-92; Carolyn A. Lin (1993). *op. cit.*; Elizabeth M. Perse and Alan M. Rubin (1988). "Audience activity and satisfaction with favorite television soap opera," *Journalism Quarterly* 65(2):368-375.

During-exposure activity reflects the degree of audience involvement with the media content and the media themselves. Involvement is often defined by the existence of **concurrent activities** performed during actual media use.

Examples of concurrent activities include **distractive behaviors** such as thinking about something else, reading, eating, talking, doing chores or switching channels during commercials, changing to another program or watching two or more programs simultaneously.

Alternatively, concurrent activities could include during-viewing interactive behaviors such as discussing the program, parasocial interaction (such as making comments to the characters on television or "talking back" to the TV). Hence, the concurrent activities may influence the types of post-exposure activity audiences engage in and the degree of gratifications they may derive subsequent to exposure.

Post-exposure activity describes **short-term** and **long-term effects** toward the media exposure experience. Such actions may involve talking to someone about a tragic news story, feeling saddened by the news story or phoning in a donation to aid the needy family just after viewing the story; or they may have lasting effects on the audience's perception and attitude about this type of event. These activities may then be intimately linked to the gratifications the audience experiences after exposure.

A study of television news exposure identified the relevant audience activity as: 1) *intentionality*, or the extent to which news viewing is planned; 2) *selectivity*, or the degree to which viewing represents a purposive selection of content from known choices; and, 3) *involvement*, or the extent to which audiences pay attention to and think about media content.[13] These activities were empirically linked to motives or gratifications sought and attitudes.

Uses

This element deals with the specific **media/channel choice** or the specific *media type* (i.e., print or electronic) and *media channel* (i.e., *Newsweek* or *Time* or CNN) chosen for exposure as well as the duration of that *media exposure*. The media/channel choice is said to be a result of habitual or purposeful decisions by the audience during the pre-exposure activity period, such as being certain to schedule the evening's activity to watch a favorite police drama every week. The media/channel choice is also the impetus that helps drive the degree of media exposure and audience involvement with during-exposure activity, such as channel switching or even lack of distractive activity during viewing.

---

13. Alan M. Rubin and Elizabeth M. Perse (1987). "Audience activity and television news gratifications," *Communication Research* 14(1):58-84.

Gratifications

This component is the types and degrees — as well as the short- and long-term cognitive and affective aspects — of gratifications obtained from exposure that fulfill the original needs initiating the entire media use process. The degree to which an individual is satisfied with the **gratifications obtained** from the media use experience can, in turn, affect or reinforce future media use motives or **gratification expectations** (gratifications sought). For example, a person might enjoy a sitcom pilot (first episode) and decide to watch the show next week. But if subsequent episodes fail to deliver the same gratifications, the person will stop watching.

According to Katz, Gurevitch and Haas, television ranks highest or second highest among media in its perceived utility to gratify three-fourths of the needs measured. Television applied to the widest range of gratification functions.[14] Where television and film give pleasure, books cultivate the inner self and, along with newspapers, served the most specific purposes.

Other relevant theoretical developments

While many of the uses and gratifications studies established the validity of a goal-oriented and self-motivated, gratification-seeking audience, some studies discovered that such goals or motivations could be less clear-cut at times. Furthermore, the relations between gratification expectation (gratifications sought) and gratifications obtained vary from relatively weak to strong.[15] Additional theoretical elements were introduced to further explain the relations between expected and obtained gratifications. These theoretical additions are now presented:

Ritualistic vs. instrumental orientation. To explain why audience motivations could be less clearly goal-oriented, two motivational orientations were developed. **Ritualistic** describes audiences who often consume media content out of *habit* and have less well-defined gratification goals. **Instrumental** portrays audiences whose media consumption behavior is more *intentional*.[16] Ritualistically oriented television viewers tend to be motivated by diversion. They seek entertainment and relaxation, are less selective of media or channel choice and less involved with content during exposure. By contrast, the instrumentally oriented are more involved with program content. They interact with media characters and have post-viewing discussions.[17]

---

14. Katz, Gurevitch and Haas, *op cit.*

15. Philip Palmgreen, Lawrence A. Wenner and J.D. Rayburn II. (1980). "Relations between gratifications sought and obtained: A study of television news," *Communication Research* 7(2):161-192.

16. Alan M. Rubin (1984). "Ritualized and instrumental television viewing," *Journal of Communication* 34(3):67-77.

17. Alan M. Rubin and Elizabeth M. Perse (1987). *op. cit.* See also: Alan M. Rubin and Elizabeth M. Perse (1987). "Audience activity and soap opera involvement: A uses and effects investigation," *Human Communication Research* 14(2):246-268.

Expectancy-value model. This theory is rooted in social psychology. It posits that an individual's behavioral intentions are guided by the likelihood and value of its consequences.[18] Thus, **gratification expectations** associated with media or channel choice depend on how well that choice matches specific gratification(s) desired.[19] In other words, a person seeking international news for surveillance is likely to weigh the media or channel choices and select *The Christian Science Monitor* or *The New York Times* as international information sources.

Media dependency. This view presumes that audiences (social beings) show a certain degree of **dependency** toward the **media** or **media system**, a social system component, for **social-functional reasons** (e.g., to keep up with current events).[20] For example, people with high surveillance needs are more likely to choose print media; those with high entertainment needs are more likely to choose non-print.

One study reported that if audience members think a television news show will satisfy a gratification expectation, then they will depend more on that program for fulfilling future surveillance needs.[21] **Media dependency** on a media or channel choice (i.e., network TV news vs. "60 Minutes") is associated with specific audience gratifications obtained from past exposure to that specific media or channel choice.[22]

Uses and gratifications of new media

As the information revolution brings unprecedented choice among media options for entertainment and news or information, uses and gratifications theory has been applied to examine new media adoption intentions and decisions.

Using computer-mediated communication channels as an example, an early study of *electronic political bulletin boards* suggested that the need for **surveillance**, **personal identity** and **diversion** contributed equally to their use.[23] A decade later,

---

18. Martin Fishbein and Icek Ajzen (1975). *Belief, attitude, intention and behavior: An introduction to theory and research.* Reading, MA: Addison-Wesley.

19. Philip Palmgreen and J.D. Rayburn II (1982). "Gratifications sought and media exposure: An expectancy value model," *Communication Research* 9(4):561-580. See also: Austin S. Barbrow (1989). "An expectancy-value analysis of the student soap opera audience," *Communication Research* 16(2):155-178; Austin S. Babrow and David L. Swanson (1988). "Disentangling antecedents of audience exposure levels: Extending expectancy-value analyses of gratifications sought from television news," *Communication Monographs* 55(1):1-21.

20. Sandra J. Ball-Rokeach (1985). "The origins of individual media-system dependency: A sociological framework," *Communication Research* 12(4):485-510.

21. Philip Palmgreen, Lawrence A. Wenner and J.D. Rayburn II (1980). *op. cit.*

22. Lawrence A. Wenner (1982). "Gratifications sought and obtained in program dependency: A study of network evening news programs and '60 minutes'," *Communication Research* 9(4):539-560.

23. Gina M. Garramone, Allen C. Harris and Ronald Anderson (1986). "Uses of political computer bulletin boards," *Journal of Broadcasting & Electronic Media* 30(3):325-339.

the psychological motives for using electronic bulletin boards were **informational learning** and **socialization**.[24] Additional evidence showed that surveillance needs strongly predict adoption of news and information services via a *videotext system*.[25]

With regard to Internet use, an industry study found that on-line audiences seek gratifications in **escape, entertainment, interaction** and **surveillance**.[26] Jeffres and Atkin contend that need for communication is a predictor for Internet adoption intention.[27] Eighmey reported that both **entertainment** value and **personal identity** lead to commercial web site adoption.[28] Because **computer-mediated content** does *emulate*, extend and supplement traditional mediated content, a degree of parallelism in the uses and gratifications between the two could be expected. Early studies do indicate that audience motives for computer-mediated media use appear similar to those associated with traditional media use.

As the technology of mediated communication expands, digital two-way interactive TV is going to compete for audiences against computer-mediated media such as the Internet, PC-TV and TV-PC. These hybrids create new challenges for understanding the uses and gratifications associated with each, but they also offer an opportunity to further the application venues and scientific values of this particular theoretical perspective — a communication theory that we call our own.

Summary

Uses and gratifications examines media behavior from the audience member's view, acknowledging that media users control their own decisions. The theory explains psychological needs that shape why and how people use the media, and the gratifications they derive.

The theory's basic tenets are: 1) individuals have different needs that prompt different choices about which media to use, and 2) even those exposed to the same media content will respond to it differently.

---

24. Michael L. James, C. Edward Wotring and Edward J. Forrest (1995). "An exploratory study of the perceived benefits of electronic bulletin board use and their impact on other communication activities," *Journal of Broadcasting & Electronic Media* 39(1):30-50.
    25. Carolyn A. Lin (1994). "Exploring potential factors for home videotext adoption," in Jarice Hanson, ed. *Advances in telematics Vol. 2.*, pp. 111-121. Norwood, NJ: Ablex Publishing Corp.
    26. Thomas E. Miller (1996). "Segmenting the Internet," *American Demographics* 18(7):48-51. See also: Carolyn A. Lin (1997). "The relations between psychological gratification factors and Internet use." Paper presented to the Association for Education in Journalism and Mass Communication, Chicago.
    27. Leo Jeffres and David Atkin (1996). "Predicting use of technologies for communication and consumer needs," *Journal of Broadcasting & Electronic Media* 40(3):318-330.
    28. John Eighmey (1997). "Profiling user responses to commercial web sites," *Journal of Advertising Research* 37(3):59-66.

A uses and gratifications model is presented along with its component parts including: **needs**, **motives**, **motivations** and **activity**. The model examines **uses**, or the specific **media/channel choice** for *media exposure* and its duration. It also examines **gratifications**, including *gratification expectations* and *gratifications obtained*.

Theoretical refinements of the theory are the divisions of **ritualistic** vs. **instrumental orientation**, the **expectancy-value theory** and media **dependency theory**. Armed with these perspectives, the uses and gratifications theory is applied to recent studies on how audiences use new media.

Exercise:

Reflecting on your own television use experience, indicate what needs are gratified by the following program genres. Select your **five** favorite genres and write one paragraph for each genre to explain: 1) how your needs are gratified by that genre; 2) what needs the uses and gratifications theory would say that genre satisfies, according to the chapter's content; and, 3) if your needs mirror those "predicted" by uses and gratifications theory.

Morning Magazine Shows (e.g., "Today," "Good Morning America")

Daytime Celebrity Talk Shows (e.g., "Oprah Winfrey," "Regis and Kathy Lee")

Daytime Tabloid Talk Shows (e.g., "Jerry Springer," "Sally Jesse Raphael")

Daytime Soap Operas (e.g., "General Hospital," "All My Children")

Games Shows (e.g, "Wheel of Fortune," "Jeopardy")

Late Night Variety Talk Shows (e.g., "The Tonight Show," "David Letterman")

Local Television News

National Television Network News

News and Commentary Programs (e.g., "Cross Fire," "Face the Nation")

News Magazine Programs (e.g., "Primetime Live," "20/20")

Newsmaker Interview Programs (e.g., "Larry King Live," "Nightline")

Television Sports Programs (e.g., football, golf, wrestling)

Situation Comedies (e.g., "Friends," "The Drew Carey Show")

Television Dramas (e.g., "E.R.," "NYPD Blue")

Reality Shows (e.g., "911," "Cops")

Documentary Shows (e.g., history, geography, travel, science)

How-To Shows (e.g., "This Old House," "Frugal Gourmet")

McLuhan's Legacy

24

Postmortem critique: Daniel J. Czitrom (1982). *Media and the American mind: From Morse to McLuhan*. Chapel Hill: University of North Carolina Press, pp. 165-182.

Resurgent review: Gary Wolf (1996). "The wisdom of Saint Marshall, the holy fool," *Wired* (January), pp. 122-127, 182-186.

The following quotes are taken from Marshall McLuhan's work[1] to provide a flavor of his knack in turning phrases, tweaking thought and generally stimulating controversy about the impact of mass media on society's future. A challenging exercise is to select **four** of these five statements and: 1) define what McLuhan was saying in fewer than 100 words; 2) relate his statement to the human or mediated communication experience; and, 3) decide if the author was being serious:

1. "The past went that-a-way. When faced with a totally new situation, we tend always to attach ourselves to the objects, to the flavor of the most recent past. We look at the present through a rear-view mirror. We march backwards into the future. Suburbia lives imaginatively in Bonanza-land."

2. "The family circle has widened. The worldpool of information fathered by electric media — movies, Telstar, flight — far surpasses any possible influence mom and dad can now bring to bear. Character no longer is shaped by only two earnest, fumbling experts. Now all the world's a sage."

3. "The steady trend in advertising is to manifest the product as an integral part of large social purposes and processes. With very large budgets the commercial artists have tended to develop the ad into an icon, and icons are not specialist fragments of aspects but unified and compressed images of complex kind...[The] trend in ads, then, is away from the consumer picture of product to the producer image of process."

---

1. Marshall McLuhan (1964). *Understanding media: The extensions of man*. New York: McGraw-Hill. See also: Marshall McLuhan and Quentin Fiore (1967). *The medium is the massage*. New York: Bantam Books.

4. "The dominant organ of sensory and social orientation in pre-alphabet societies was the ear — "hearing was believing." The phonetic alphabet forced the magic world of the ear to yield to the neutral world of the eye. Man was given an eye for an ear...Printing, a ditto device...created the portable book, which men could read in privacy and in isolation from others. Man could now inspire — and conspire...The private, fixed point of view became possible and literacy conferred the power of detachment, non-involvement."

5. "All media work us over completely. They are so pervasive in their personal, political, economic, aesthetic, psychological, moral, ethical, and social consequences that they leave no part of us untouched, unaffected, unaltered. The medium is the massage."

Marshall McLuhan, 1911-1980, was to communication study as Margaret Mead was to anthropology, but he was far more controversial.[2] From the late 1950s until his death, he was the intellectual critic and prophet of the discipline, and so recognized for the last 15 years of his life.[3] For an academic to gain such renown is unusual enough, but McLuhan achieved his fame as a Canadian English teacher who studied philosophy, history, religion, art — almost every humanities field except communication. McLuhan's ideas far exceeded his persona: He was a contentious, non-charismatic lecturer whose outrageous ideas made him the hit of the talk show and speaking circuits. Arthur Schlesinger Jr. said of him in 1967:

"What then is McLuhanism? It is a chaotic combination of bland assertion, astute guesswork, fake analogy, dazzling insight, hopeless nonsense, shockmanship, showmanship, wisecracks and oracular mystification, all mingling cockily and indiscriminantly in an endless and random monologue. It also, in my judgment, contains a deeply serious argument."[4]

McLuhan's ideas were easily capable of keeping him at the center of attention even a generation after his death.[5] In fact, his pronouncements are enjoying a

---

2. Robert MacMillan (1992). "Marshall McLuhan at the mercy of his commentators," *Philosophy of the Social Science*s 22(4):475-491.

3. James W. Carey (1981). "McLuhan and Mumford: The roots of modern media analysis," *Journal of Communication* 3(3):162-178.

4. Arthur M. Schlesinger Jr. (1967). "The plugged-in generation," *The Washington Post*, (March 19), Book Review Section, pp. 1-2.

5. This truncated list shows that McLuhan is very much in vogue among a variety of disciplines: Robert D. McIlwraith (1994). "Marshall McLuhan and the psychology of television," *Canadian Psychology* 35(4):331-348; Arthur Kroker (1995). "Digital humanism: The processed world of Marshall McLuhan," *Canadian Journal of Political and Social Theory* 18(1-3):163-203; Gary Davidson (1996). "Real children and technology in the cosmic classroom," *Montessori Life* 8(1):27-31; Donna Weiss Ballard (1995). "The role of libraries in the global village," *Library Software Review* 14(3):154-160.

resurgence at the new millennium because so many of his predictions — which defied scientific inquiry — seem to be coming true.[6] Because there is so much to McLuhan (and so much of his writing is difficult to decipher), this chapter presents a limited selection of his ideas, perhaps enough for an appreciation of why McLuhan was and is an important contributor to the communication field.

First, McLuhan must be considered in the context of the time he theorized: the 1960s. Television was still in its youth in the late 1950s; still black-and-white; still dominated by "I Love Lucy"; and still approaching its household saturation level. Then, almost overnight it seemed, everyone had a color television set (probably two), and visionaries including McLuhan noticed that American lifestyles were changing. Instead of playing board games or helping their children with homework, instead of visiting friends or going bowling, people were deciding, "I think I'll stay home tonight and watch a little television." What they were not admitting is, "....just like I did last night and the night before." This was the McLuhan environment.

As the 1960s progressed, America's Vietnam war involvement escalated. All social critics of the time noted that young people, dubbed as the first television generation, were more defiant than preceding generations. Even after Vietnam, social unrest continued. It lasted through Woodstock, Watergate, the women's liberation movement, the drug counter-culture and even into the "me generation" prior to 1980. The ubiquitous mass media (especially television) were blamed for this explosion of liberalism, experimentation and rebellion. Regardless of the truth of such accusations, a new age was coming, and McLuhan was there at its dawn.

Ages of civilization

McLuhan divided human existence into three ages noted chiefly by their communication. The first was pre-literate or **tribal**, in which people lived together in villages and shared a common campfire. Communication consisted of story-telling: gestures or words for oral transmission of knowledge and human experiences. The communication medium was sight and sound; decision making was instant. Remote communication with other villages was impossible. A tribal society needs cooperation, a shared experience and shared rules, to exist. This age extends from the cave-dwelling era through the end of the Middle Ages, according to McLuhan.

The second phase of human existence came with movable type and the printing press: the **Gutenberg age** or age of literacy. With type, human existence changed dramatically for two reasons: 1) type brought sequential thought and 2) individualism. McLuhan differentiates between **linear**, sequential thinking brought

---

6. Lewis H. Lapham (1994). "Terms of endearment: O.J. Simpson case and Marshall McLuhan's theories," *Harper's Magazine*, (September), pp. 7-9.

about by the way alphabets, words and sentences are constructed, and the mosaic thought that preceded print. Stories told around a campfire, hieroglyphics or picture words, and even the artistic Asian characters that form word blocks constitute **mosaic** or holistic thought patterns. The receiver gets the message all at once.

But characters read left-to-right across a line of type form a consecutive pattern that led to Western logical thought (different from Eastern conceptualization or pre-Gutenberg reasoning). McLuhan said that mosaic thinking is discourse based on analogy while linear thinking leads to discourse based on sequential argument.

Sequential writing and thinking allow remote communication and empire building. Humans, who before were bound by interpersonal support communities, now became mobile and individualistic. They could strike out on their own carrying civilization in their books. They could begin the industrial age leading to nationalism.

McLuhan's third phase of civilization is the **electric age**. In it, communication and decision making are speeded by the telegraph and greatly increased by the two-way communication of telephone. Then the almost instantaneous media of radio and television burst on the scene bringing a return to non-sequential, mosaic communication. McLuhan also calls this age neo-tribal or the **Global Village**. As society enters this age, satellites send pictures of Olympic games and the victims of famine to viewers in every nation. The electric medium connects people and returns humanity to an oral and visual village of global interdependedness.

Media as extensions of senses

McLuhan defines a medium is anything that extends a human "sense." Light is a medium that allows us to see into the dark. Cars are media because they extend our legs and feet and allow us to travel farther. Clothing is a medium because it extends our skin; cities are a medium that accommodate larger groups.

Film and television extend our eyes and ears; radio extends our hearing; computers extend our central nervous system. Money is a medium replacing the primitive grasping and calculating that apes used to negotiate their mobility from tree limb to tree limb.

McLuhan said that a medium is a resource. It is a means of transferring messages, but it carries a message of its own. Technological media are natural resources or staples like wheat and coal. A society that relies on a few commodities such as radio and television pays a price of having those media flavor its culture. The price is extracted from the community's psyche. McLuhan said that the "'message' of any medium or technology is the change of scale or pace or pattern that it introduces into human affairs."

Hot and cool media

A **hot medium** is one that extends a single sense in high definition: it provides all the necessary data. A **cool medium** extends multiple senses in low definition, or with little information.[7] By these definitions, hot media include print, an extension of the eye; radio, an extension of hearing, in which all of the information is provided by the audio transmission; and photographs, which are high-definition depictions that extend our sense of sight. Conversely, a cartoon is a cool medium because it has low definition: it provides only a minimum of information from which the viewer tries to fill in the missing parts to make sense of the whole.

McLuhan said hot media are less receiver-involving. Impressionist painters depicted a scene or a person as if the viewer was looking through a window at the actual image. Then cubists and abstract artists painted images intended to be more receiver-involving. Passing these latter works in a museum, the viewer pauses to make sense of the image, to put the pieces together. Impressionism can be considered hot; abstract art is cool.

The hot vs. cool distinction is a continuum. For example, a movie shown in a theater is a hot medium. Although it extends the senses of sight and sound, and perhaps other bodily senses such as heart and pulse rates, tears or laughter, McLuhan considers film hot because it is a high-definition medium. Movies are like reading a novel: an individual experience with the medium providing all the data.

But television is considered a cool medium, one that "has nothing in common with film or photo." Instead of being the rendering of light on film, as is a movie, television is light on a screen composed of about three million dots flashing per second in electronic lines. The television viewer selects several dozen each instant to compose an image. The electronic dots render television a low-definition medium, one that requires viewer participation to make sense of the image.

"The medium is the message"

Perhaps the strongest statement in McLuhan's retinue, this is a theme that pervades all of his writing. He claims that not only are the ages of civilization determined by the prevailing medium, but that each medium has a power that far exceeds content. Actually, while McLuhan does use media content in examples to further his pronouncements, his single, overriding theme is that content should be ignored as critics evaluate the impact on society made by the advent of media.[8]

---

7. Raymond Gozzi Jr. (1992). "'Hot' and 'cool' media," *ETC: A Review of General Semantics* 49(2):227-230.

8. Jay Rosen (1990). "The messages of 'the medium is the message,'" *ETC: A Review of General Semantics* 47(1):45-51.

If his conception of media is taken literally, the implications of clothing as a medium that extends people's skin and the changes in society that clothing brought about might be considered. Also, there is probably little doubt that the railroad train brought changes in immigration, in settling vast continents, in shipping food and products: changes that far exceeded any single trip from New York to Los Angeles. The car brought a sense of freedom to people's lives and changed their daily routine in a variety of ways that make any single car or any single trip trivial (think about how you plan your day around traffic or parking).

But more to the point that must be taken literally, can you think of any single message — or even many messages — ever transmitted by television that has had more effect on the daily lives of human beings than the advent of television itself?

Explosion vs. implosion

"Explosion" indicates fragmentation, but it also suggests expansion or progress toward a stated point. With the coming of the Gutenberg age, society was fragmented by the print culture. Humans, who had existed in necessary, mutually supportive communities, were able to sustain themselves as individuals. People assumed specialized responsibilities that led to greater mobility, industrialization and the growth of complex societies as national entities.

Implosion is the blowing together of fragmented parts. With the coming of the electric age, the scattered peoples of the world are drawn together through the commonalty of instantaneous sights and sounds. The electronic communication media have caused the fragments to implode, recreating a global village.

Brain hemisphericity

Among McLuhan's many interests was cognitive psychology, particularly the research on brain **lateralization**. McLuhan followed the studies and knew that psychologists were finding evidence that the left side of the brain controls speaking, reading and math (the more logical processing functions), while the right side controls intuition, visual images and spatial relationships (the more creative functions). A psychologist's study showed that television viewing is related to right-brain processing with low involvement, while newspaper reading is related to left-brain processing with high involvement.[9] McLuhan wrote about these findings that fit his theory about hot and cool media.[10]

---

9. Herbert E. Krugman (1977). "Memory without recall, exposure without perception," *Journal of Advertising Research* 17(4):7-12.

10. Marshall McLuhan (1978). "The brain and the media: The 'western' hemisphere," *Journal of Communication* 28(4):54-60.

In the last twenty years, cognitive psychologists generally agree that the two brain functions are not separated. Most healthy people use both sides of the brain to process information. Still, McLuhan focused on the different processes and drew inferences about how cultures were changed by the prevailing media that influenced thought patterns. He speculated that races of people whose ancestors had not been as highly influenced by print as were Westerners' forebears would be more likely to process information from the right side of the brain, the holistic side.

Limited research on McLuhan's theories

Despite the criticism that McLuhan's theories cannot be tested empirically, some attempts were made to research aspects of his pronouncements and predictions. Here are some examples and their findings:

• A test of hot vs. cool media in which the same 20-minute film was shown to four randomly assigned student groups with one group each: watching it on television, seeing it as a film, listening to the audio only and just reading the script. Those who read the script or heard the audio were more persuaded by the message. Television was rated the coolest medium, but only in comparison to reading the script; film and television were rated equally cool. These conclusions contradict McLuhan's theory about hot vs. cool media and that the medium is the message.[11]

• Does radio offer a more creative environment for children than television? Groups of children watched the same story on television or listened to it as an audio recording. The story was stopped before the ending, and children wrote what would happen next. Those who only heard the story created more imaginative endings than those who saw it on television. Listeners used more action words, created new characters, and used more emotion or conversation in their endings. The researchers concluded that the medium affects the receiver, as McLuhan predicted, at least for audio vs. television.[12]

• Testing college students' interest in highly graphic morbid news events, three groups were exposed to six news stories, four of which covered morbid events. Each group was exposed to print only, photographs or to television treatment of the stories. No difference among media was found in arousing curiosity. The researchers concluded that the study did not support McLuhan's medium is the message idea.[13]

---

11. William P. Dommermuth (1974). "How does the medium affect the message?" *Journalism Quarterly* 51(3):441-447.
12. Patricia Greenfield, Dorathea Farrar and Jessica Beagles-Roos (1986). "Is the medium the message: An experimental comparison of the effects of radio and television on imagination," *Journal of Applied Developmental Psychology* 7(3):201-218.
13. Ellen M. Bennett, Jill Dianne Swenson and Jeff S. Wilkinson (1992). "Is the medium the message: An experimental test with morbid news," *Journalism Quarterly* 69(4):921-928.

• In a test of mosaic vs. linear thinking, 250 college students in an art appreciation class completed a mass media use survey and a test of right- vs. left-brain dominance. The students tried to identify images in abstract paintings. Those who relied on print media scored equally well in identifying the art images as those who relied on the visual media, indicating that media use is not related with mosaic thinking ability. However, right-brain students outscored the left-brain dominant in identifying the art images, as McLuhan might have predicted.[14]

McLuhan hot and cold

Marshall McLuhan was an enigma at the height of his popularity and remains so today. No one doubts the breadth of his intellect or his knack at borrowing examples from disciplines that were previously unrelated to communication studies. Even his critics, whose writing can be as hard to decipher as McLuhan's,[15] concede he was a gifted thinker who could twist a homily to his purpose, turn a clever phrase.

But his critics charge that McLuhan was far too exotic in his conjectures; that his substantiating examples were exceptions rather than the rule; that juxtaposing art, religion and architecture with communication theory was a forced marriage at best; and that his statements are vague, distorted and beyond proof. Certainly, the last of these criticisms seemed to be true. Although very few researchers tried to test his theories, little support was found for any of McLuhan's hypotheses.

McLuhan through the rearview mirror

Despite those who would deride McLuhan's theories, some of his ideas have not only stood the test of time, but time seems to have conferred more proof than the research. On his concept of a return to a global village, events lend credence to the idea of a shrinking world brought about through the electronic media.[16] The world

---

14. Gerald Stone (1995). "Testing the essence of McLuhan's ideas: Linear vs. Mosaic thought." Paper presented at the Association for Education in Journalism and Mass Communication, Washington, DC.

15. Some examples of complex but thought-provoking articles and books include: Glenn Willmott (1996). *McLuhan, or Modernism in Reverse.* Toronto: University of Toronto Press; Barry Brummett and Margaret Carlisle Duncan (1992). "Toward a discursive ontology of media," *Critical Studies in Mass Communication* 9(3):229-249; Michael S. Nilan (1993). "Speculations on the impact of global electronic networks on human cognition and human organization," *Internet Research* 3(3):47-56; Peter F. Morgan (1990). "McLuhan's use of the notion of play in his approach to ultimate reality and meaning," *Ultimate Reality and Meaning* 13(1):21-32; Marjorie Ferguson (1991). "Marshall McLuhan revisited: 1960s zeitgeist victim or pioneer postmodernist?" *Media, Culture and Society* 13(1):71-90; Michael Bross (1991). "McLuhan's theory of sensory functions: A critique and analysis," *Journal of Communication Inquiry* 16(1):91-107.

16. J. Herbert Altschull (1990). *From Milton to McLuhan: The ideas behind American journalism.* White Plains, NY: Longman, pp. 337-343.

unites in watching the Olympics. Previous United States dominance of the flow of information and entertainment has given way to international exchanges. Perhaps the most impressive example of a media-induced Global Village was the crumbling Berlin wall, attributed to the flow of information into the former Soviet Union, which itself was fractured by Glasnost's reduction in communication retraints. Using a broad historical framework, Stephens suggests that as a new medium the Internet may prove to be "as powerful and ultimately as rewarding as its predecessors."[17]

While the electronic media failed to solve many of the world's crises, they have led the way toward the implosion McLuhan predicted. Other 1980s theorists might have attributed a coming implosion to superior weaponry, economic instability, the United Nations, or the growth of international peace movements, but only McLuhan forecast the role mass media would play.

Summary

Although he is the single most recognized figure in the communication discipline, Marshall McLuhan remains an enigma nearly two generations after his height of notoriety in the late 1960s.

The chapter reviews his rise to public attention, presents some of his theories in a way that tries to capture the tone and scope of his pronouncements, and reviews some of the main precepts of his communication philosophy. Included are his ages of civilization, media as extensions of human senses, hot and cool media, explosion and implosion, and brain hemisphericity.

A review of some inconclusive research on McLuhan's theories is offered, along with an epilogue of how communication's evolution may be proving that McLuhan, if not an infallible prophet, was more than an interesting phrase-maker.

Exercises:

A. Read this article: Larry Press, "McLuhan meets the Net," *Communications of the ACM, 38,* (July 1995), pp. 15-20. (ACM is the Association for Computing Machinery.)

1) Press considers how Marshall McLuhan might have viewed the Internet as a communication medium. Taking quotes from McLuhan's *Understanding Media*, Press speculates that the Internet would cause McLuhan to reconsider his notion of a return to the global village. Write a one-page essay on why you either support or disagree with Press's assessment.

---

17. Mitchell Stephens (1998). "'Which communications revolution is it, anyway?'" *Journalism & Mass Communication Quarterly* 75(1):9-13.

2) Press discusses McLuhan's prediction that the education system would have to change to be compatible with the computer age. Write a one-page essay, with examples, on why you either support or disagree with Press's assessment of how education has not adapted to the computer age.

B. Using any source, including Marshall McLuhan's writings, answer these questions.

1. McLuhan was the guru of the television era, yet he slept through movies. He was also a college professor, but he is said to have taken little pride or interest in his teaching.[17] Did McLuhan like or dislike television as a medium? Explain:

2. Select which of these nouns best describes McLuhan's focus of attention: a) culture, b) media, c) history, d) environment or e) future. Write a brief statement of why you selected that noun:

3. Other than being chockfull of his newly coined platitudes, name a characteristic that makes a McLuhan book different from other books of the time:

_____

17. Gary Wolf (1996). See chapter's introductory "Resurgent review."

25

Knowledge Gap

Founding article: Phillip J. Tichenor, George A. Donohue and Clarice N. Olien (1970). "Mass media flow and differential growth in knowledge," *Public Opinion Quarterly* 34(2):159-170.

Recent article: Cecilie Gaziano, (1997). "Forecast 2000: Widening Knowledge Gaps," *Journalism & Mass Communication Quarterly* 74(2):237-264.

Before reading about the knowledge gap hypothesis, try answering these questions. Record your answers for possible discussion in class to see how your peers did as a group...no grades awarded for right or wrong answers.

1. Name the current vice president of
   the United States (first and last name): _____

2. How much does it cost to ride the bus in your city: _____

3. If you are a registered Democrat, can you vote for a
   Republican candidate in a general election (*circle one*)? yes   no

4. Name the mayor of your city (last name is okay): _____

5. Your friend has a sore throat, swollen glands and a fever. Which do you advise:
   a. wait 24 hours to see if it improves
   b. see a doctor now (costs $50; takes three hours)

6. If your income is $10,000, can you qualify for food stamps? yes   no

7. Is it safe for pregnant women to have one glass of wine a day? yes   no

8. What part of the body does calcium affect? _____

*   *   *

Some implications of these questions are: 1) Most people should be able to get at least half the questions right, but that might be optimistic; 2) Your class should score higher than a group of randomly selected people from the community because you are part of the educational elite; however, 3) Some questions deal with issues that don't concern you...should you be expected to know about these?

The knowledge gap hypothesis presumes that you *will* know more about these topics than people whose educational level is lower than yours, even if the topics don't directly concern your everyday life. Education gives you tremendous knowledge acquisition advantages, including how to use the mass media effectively.

In their 1970 article, Tichenor, Donohue and Olien tried to account for an effect social scientists noticed several decades earlier.[1] The population is divided into two distinct segments: a group of better-educated people who know more about most things, and those with low education who know less. Lower socio-economic status (SES) people, defined partly by educational level, have little or no knowledge about public affairs issues, are disconnected from news events and important new discoveries, and usually aren't concerned about their lack of knowledge.

Throughout most of the communication discipline's development, researchers were puzzled by the nearly consistent failure of public information campaigns. From presidential elections to new discoveries, messages simply did not get through unless the topics were extremely important (bombing of Pearl Harbor) and the audience was more educated. For topics such as elections, much of the audience merely voted along party lines.

The implications of such **limited effects** of communication messages are discouraging. If people ignore the message, they won't understand issues, and democracy assumes that *informed* citizens will choose truth in the marketplace of ideas. On a more pragmatic level, thousands of people died because the national seatbelt campaigns failed for more than 20 years.

Public issue messages have value beyond the self-interest of those sponsoring or disseminating them. Still, many of these campaigns are doomed to failure because of differences among the social classes based primarily on educational level. Some people gain knowledge; some do not. The fact was recognized in the 1940s and emphasized in a concentrated media campaign to inform citizens of Cincinnati about the United Nations. Even after six months of intense media coverage, very few people knew much about the U.N., but those with higher education knew more than the less educated.[2]

---

1. See "Founding article."
2. Shirley A. Star and Helen MacGill Hughes (1950). "Report on an educational campaign: The Cincinnati plan for the United Nations," *American Journal of Sociology* 55(4):389-400.

Public affairs issues

Studies of public issues by researchers in a variety of disciplines throughout the 1950s and 1960s found the same split in knowledge levels based on an individual's education. This difference led to the knowledge gap hypothesis, which said that as mass media information increases, higher socio-economic status segments of society will gain information faster than lower SES segments. Increases in information will increase the gap in knowledge between the higher and lower SES groups.

The national debt illustrates the knowledge gap hypothesis. Everyone has some knowledge about the national debt now, although a few years ago most people might not have been able to define the term. If a test were given then, few could correctly answer a series of multiple-choice questions such as why there is a debt, how large it is, the amount of interest paid, etc. However, even then, more educated people might have answered two questions while less educated people might have answered none. The knowledge gap score would have been 2.

According to the knowledge gap theory, most people gain knowledge as a topic becomes more heavily covered by the mass media, but the higher educated segment of the population will gain more knowledge. If a series of questions were asked today about the national debt, such as which political party is more intent on

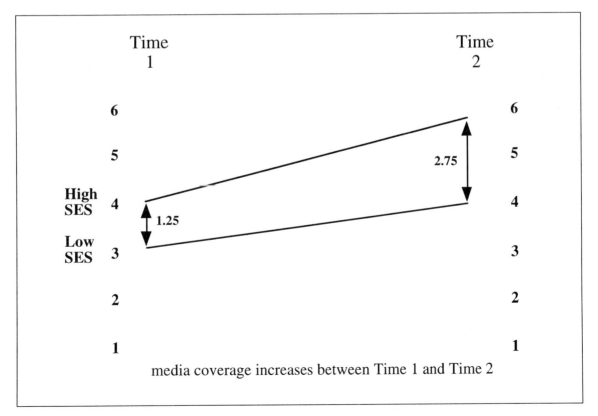

Figure 1. Widening knowledge gaps

reducing the debt, has the debt been reduced, or which presidential contender has debt as a key issue, the higher educated might be able to answer six of the questions while the lower educated might answer only two. Now the knowledge gap score has increased to 4. The hypothesis predicts that educated people not only know more, they learn increasingly more. The gap in knowledge widens.

Knowledge gap says nothing about individuals' innate intelligence. The theory merely recognizes that higher-educated people have several advantages: 1) a greater level of stored knowledge on a variety of topics; 2) better attention, comprehension, retention and general communication skills; 3) more reliance on the information-oriented print media rather than the entertainment-oriented non-print media; and, 4) greater numbers of relevant social contacts or friends who are likely to be knowledgeable about and discuss public affairs topics.[3]

Other advantages and some constraints have been reported during the nearly 30 years since the theory's origin. But as the national debt public affairs issue example suggests, the higher SES group is very likely to outscore the lower SES group, just as the knowledge gap theory predicts.

At this point, you should be piqued by a disturbing notion. If information is power, and if public affairs information is social power, then the theory suggests that society is being further divided by people's education level. In fact, that is the rather unsettling, long-term outcome knowledge gap implies. High and low SES groups can also be called **media rich** and **media poor**. The distinction has more to do with content use than with actual access. For instance, every family has a television, but watching sit-coms is not equivalent to watching the news. As the information media proliferate, the media rich will be society's power brokers and the media poor will be disadvantaged. The rift in society will widen just as the knowledge gap widens.

The basic knowledge gap hypothesis can be followed through nearly three decades of development because it is among the most narrowly defined programmatic communication research topics. **Programmatic** research is the kind that builds on itself, where one study's outcomes raise questions and other researchers take up the challenge to answer.[4] Communication has little programmatic research compared with most other disciplines, but knowledge gap is one of the best examples.

---

3. Herbert Gans (1969). "Culture and class in the study of poverty," in Daniel P. Moynihan, ed. *On understanding poverty: Perspectives from the social sciences.* New York: Basic Books. See also: Brenda Dervin and Bradley S. Greenberg (1972). "The communication environment of the urban poor," in F.Gerald Kline and Phillip J. Tichenor, eds. *Current perspectives in mass communication research.* Beverly Hills: Sage, pp. 195-233.

4. Shearon Lowery and Melvin L. DeFleur (1995). *Milestones in mass communication research: Media effects, 3rd ed.* White Plains, NY: Longman, p. 270.

Establishing the theory

The first decade of research on knowledge gap, that of the 1970s, saw a series of studies on environmental topics by the hypothesis' originators, who were in rural sociology and journalism.[5] They drew on diffusion studies about public knowledge of science topics, poll data, recall of technological topics in the news, and a comparison of towns with and without daily newspapers to establish the knowledge gap hypothesis. Only five years after proposing it, the founders offered a reconsideration including these points that might **reduce** the knowledge gap:[6]

1) the type of issue, especially an issue that really gets people's attention;

2) the size and type of community — small, rural, **homogenous** areas have lower gaps; cities with **pluralistic** subcultures have higher gaps;

3) how much and what type of media coverage a topic gets — cigarettes' link to cancer is constantly in the news (lower gaps); sexual harassment incidents get intense but inconsistent coverage (higher gaps); and,

4) an issue's level of conflict such as police brutality (lower gaps) vs. concerns about urban revitalization (higher gaps).

In certain cases, research showed that knowledge gaps did not increase and might even **reverse**, with lower SES groups knowing more about an issue than higher SES groups. A reverse might occur on the issue of safety in public housing complexes. Here lower SES are likely to know much more about the topic than higher SES.

Three other concepts were explored during the first decade.[7] The first is the idea of socio-economic **deficits**, or the view that SES groups at the poverty level lack a community organization structure and may be disadvantaged in basic communication skills (some research shows that low-SES children's sentence structure lacks cognitive growth). Deficits may occur through budget and technological disadvantages such as the cost of subscribing to a newspaper or access to computers.

---

5. Phillip J. Tichenor, George A. Donohue and Clarice N. Olien (1973). "Mass communication research: Evolution of a structural model," *Journalism Quarterly* 50(3):419-425. See also: Donohue, Tichenor and Olien (1973). "Mass media functions, knowledge and social control," *Journalism Quarterly* 50(4):652-659; Tichenor, Jane M. Rodenkirchen, Olien and Donohue (1973). "Community issues, conflict and public affairs knowledge," in Peter Clarke, ed. *New models for mass communication research.* Beverly Hills, CA: Sage; Donohue, Olien and Tichenor (1974). "Communities, pollution, and fight for survival," *Journal of Environmental Education* 6(1):29-37.

6. Donohue, Tichenor and Olien (1975). "Mass media and the knowledge gap: A hypothesis reconsidered," *Communication Research* 2(1):3-23.

7. James S. Ettema and F. Gerald Kline (1977). "Deficits, differences, and ceilings: Contingent conditions for understanding the knowledge gap," *Communication Research* 4(2):179-202.

The second concept is **differences**, which suggests that lower SES groups are equally capable in communicative skills but use them in a different way. Deficits imply that lower SES people will always be at a knowledge disadvantage; differences imply that interest can reduce knowledge gaps. For example, lower SES youngsters who don't have a home computer may be as proficient as their higher SES counterparts in using one at school. Likewise, lower SES adults may be highly motivated to learn about supervised activities available free to youngsters after school.

The third concept is **ceiling effects**. A ceiling means there is a finite amount of relevant information that might be provided on a general public interest topic, say five pieces of information about safety air bags in vehicles. When air bags were new, higher SES people might have known three facts about them while the lower SES might not know any. After extensive media attention, information might have reached ceiling levels because there's only so much to be learned about safety air bags. Knowledge gap predicts that the higher SES group will learn everything about the topic first (it hits the ceiling), then the lower SES group catches up. Today, both groups might be able to correctly answer all questions asked, eliminating the gap.

Interest, education and media

By the early 1980s, more than 60 studies were completed, and attention turned to other aspects that affect knowledge gaps.[8] Interest in a given topic became a primary research concern through the second decade.[9] Local topics usually get more interest than national topics, and international topics are of so little concern that wide knowledge gaps occur. Public affairs knowledge, the civics class textbook type, almost always yields knowledge gap differences between educational levels.

The education vs. interest theme winds through many studies; some link the two. For example, a college-educated person with a family history of diabetes is much more likely to seek preventative health information;[10] highly educated Jewish Americans are more likely than poorly educated Jewish Americans to follow news of Israel.[11] Finally, level of education is a strong predictor of interest in public affairs topics.

---

8. Cecilie Gaziano (1983). "The knowledge gap: An analytical review of media effects," *Communication Research* 10(4):447-486. See also: Olien, Donohue and Tichenor (1983). "Structure, communication and social power: Evolution of the knowledge gap hypothesis," in Ellen Wartella, D.Charles Whitney and Sven Windahl, eds. *Mass communication review yearbook Vol. 4.* Beverly Hills, CA: Sage, pp. 455-461.

9. B.K.L. Genova and Bradley S. Greenberg (1979). "Interests in news and the knowledge gap," *Public Opinion Quarterly* 43(1):79-91.

10. James S. Ettema, James W. Brown and Russell V. Luepker (1983). "Knowledge gap effects in a health information campaign," *Public Opinion Quarterly* 47(4):516-527.

11. Oscar H. Gandy Jr. and Mohamed El Waylly (1985). "The knowledge gap and foreign affairs: The Palestinian-Israeli conflict," *Journalism Quarterly* 62(4):777-783.

The type of media used may affect knowledge gaps. People who rely on the print media are likely to be more informed, partially because newspaper content is more thorough. Television is considered a knowledge-leveler. Lower SES people watch more than do higher SES people, but the higher SES group is more likely to watch newscasts. Still, everyone is exposed to a heavy dose of this medium, and it is difficult to avoid some knowledge gain about major news events.

The O.J. Simpson trial is a perfect example. Covered every evening on the national news, the sensational quality of the trial made it a staple on morning and afternoon talk shows; evening fare from "Entertainment Tonight" and "Court TV" to "20/20" and "Dateline NBC"; and a plethora of entertainment shows from sit-coms to the "Tonight Show." People couldn't avoid learning about the O.J. Simpson trial. With such events, the level of coverage climbs across all mass media as does the level of interpersonal communication, and the knowledge gap narrows.

During the decade, researchers tried to return to the essential implications of the theory: that public affairs knowledge is necessary for successful functioning in an increasingly complex world. In studies on neighborhood citizens groups[12] and water policy,[13] being involved increased knowledge levels, but education still prevailed. Higher SES people have more knowledge, but the lower SES can gain knowledge if they are motivated by leaders or superior information campaigns.

As the 1980s ended, knowledge about other public affairs issues such as housing, economic development, crime and quality of schools were studied in a variety of community settings with the same outcome: that interest, controversy and education affects knowledge level. But education and its association with print media use was the single consistent determinant of information gain.

Turn to television

As the theory matured in the 1990s, issues receiving attention included health, environment, and new technology as well as public affairs and politics. Many studies were based on communication campaigns designed to educate or persuade, and television received more attention. Studies focused on whether television, especially political ads, determines elections. People's general malaise toward politics and sense of powerlessness are blamed on television's campaign coverage and linked with low voter turnout. People say they get their news from television, yet television is thought to do a poor job of covering politics. Knowledge gap theory was linked with this conundrum.

---

12. Cecilie Gaziano (1984). "Neighborhood newspapers, citizen groups and public affairs knowledge gaps," *Journalism Quarterly* 61(3):556-566, 599.

13. Nicholas P. Lovrich Jr. and John C. Pierce (1984). "'Knowledge gap' phenomena: Effect of situation-specific and transsituational factors," *Communication Research* 11(3):415-434.

People who used newspapers to differentiate among candidates' positions on issues were more knowledgeable than those who read papers and also watched television news.[14] Television, then, didn't contribute to knowing about candidate stands and may even suppress learning. If true, television obstructs the political process because knowing candidate issues predicts whether a person will vote.

Even if television is the information source, higher SES individuals' greater information processing ability gives them a knowledge gain edge.[15] Recalling the gist of a topic is easier if it can be sorted, linked with previously stored information and rehearsed. This context approach to receiving and using new information is called **schemata**, and higher SES people are likely to have more stored knowledge and greater capacity to integrate new information.[16] While the lower SES learn more about complex issues from television than from newspapers, some evidence shows that both SES groups learn best from easily digested news presentations.[17] In a nutrition study, television built interest and knowledge gain for both SES groups.[18]

Television's role in the political process changed in the early 1990s. Candidates appeared on late-night programs, on talk shows such as "Larry King Live," and even on MTV. Politics on MTV did not improve campaign knowledge, but attention to the talk shows did.[19] The 1991 Persian Gulf War was a unique opportunity to test television knowledge gains. Network news and CNN provided greater knowledge to the lower SES group, but newspapers provided greater overall knowledge.[20] Again, SES was the chief predictor of knowledge about the Persian Gulf War.

14. Barry A. Hollander (1993). "Candidate issue discrimination and attention to the news," *Mass Comm Review* 20(1-2):76-85.

15. Beverly Eckhardt, Mary R. Wood and Robin Smith Jacobvitz (1991). "Verbal ability and prior knowledge: Contributions to adults' comprehension of television," *Communication Research* 18(5):636-649. See also: Gavriel Salomon (1984). "Television is 'easy' and print is 'tough:' The differential investment of mental effort in learning as a function of perceptions and attributions," *Journal of Educational Psychology* 76(4):647-658.

16. Robert H. Wicks (1995). "Remembering the news: Effects of medium and message discrepancy on news recall over time," *Journalism & Mass Communication Quarterly* 72(3):666-681. See also: Doris A. Graber (1988). *Processing the news: How people tame the information tide, 2nd ed.* New York: Longman; W. Russell Neuman, Marion R. Just and Ann N. Crigler (1992). *Common knowledge: News and the construction of political meaning.* Chicago: University of Chicago Press.

17. Jan Kleinnijenhuis (1991). "Newspaper complexity and the knowledge gap," *European Journal of Communication Vol. 6*(4):499-522. See also: Kenneth Abrahamsson (1982). "Knowledge gaps, bureaucracy, and citizen participation: Towards alternative communication models," *Communication* 7(1):75-102.

18. Fiona Chew and Sushma Palmer (1994). "Interest, the knowledge gap, and television programming," *Journal of Broadcasting & Electronic Media* 38(3):271-287.

19. Barry A. Hollander (1995). "The new news and the 1992 presidential campaign: Perceived vs. actual political knowledge," *Journalism & Mass Communication Quarterly* 72(4):786-798.

20. Zhongdang Pan, Ronald E. Ostman, Patricia Moy and Paula Reynolds (1994). "News media exposure and its learning effects during the Persian Gulf War," *Journalism Quarterly* 71(1):7-19.

These studies imply that television, including talk shows, is the medium of choice to reach the lower SES, but that campaigns should also use readable print media. Regardless of public affairs interest, knowledge gaps should be expected along socio-economic lines. For politics, prior knowledge, interest and education are such strong predictors that media use, especially television, hardly counts.[21]

A public affairs study in the U.S. found strong enough associations with knowledge levels to offer a model (see Figure 2).[22] Socio-economic status determines knowledge levels. SES acts on perceived utility of information (interest/motivation), which leads to differentiation in mass media use (television vs. newspapers), and results in knowledge gaps between the higher and lower SES groups. This is a return to the original knowledge gap hypothesis with the suggestion that communication efforts to reach the lower SES group must emphasize the utility of that information.

More varied topics

In the 1990s, knowledge gap studies turned to non-political topics. In a study of energy issues, lower SES residents in dwellings that waste more energy were expected to be more concerned and knowledgeable about the issue, but they weren't. Interpersonal discussions were expected to increase knowledge among this group, but did so in only one phase of the study.[23] This is another indication that those who might benefit most from media content on a topic are least likely to be reached by the information media.

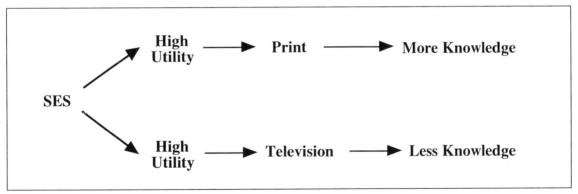

Figure 2. Knowledge gap model

21. Michael X. Delli Carpini, Scott Keeter and J. David Kennamer (1994). "Effects of the news media environment on citizen knowledge of state politics and government," *Journalism Quarterly* 71(2):443-456.

22. Douglas M. McLeod and Elizabeth M. Perse (1994). "Direct and indirect effects of socioeconomic status on public affairs knowledge," *Journalism Quarterly* 71(2):433-442.

23. Robert J. Griffin (1990). "Energy in the eighties: Education, communication, and the knowledge gap," *Journalism Quarterly* 67(3):554-566.

A two-year multi-media campaign to teach West African women how use oral rehydration solution to counteract diarrhea, an illness that kills hundreds of thousands of children, failed because of knowledge gaps.[24] The illness was so widespread that lower and higher SES families were affected equally. The campaign's initial stage was effective, but soon the lower SES women forgot the formula: the correct mix of sugar, salt and water for the solution, or they stopped using it. The very women who had more family diarrhea cases were most likely to forget how to make the formula. Radio, posters and interpersonal channels failed over time. Only a printed flyer with the formula maintained knowledge. In this campaign, knowledge and behavior had no initial gaps, but gaps appeared because higher SES women kept their knowledge gain.

In a campaign to reduce risk of diet-related cancer, high-risk people from all SES strata participated in a one-year home learning course.[25] This interested group learned more about diets to thwart cancer than did the general public, but educational levels within the group determined knowledge gain about dietary fat and fiber. Even among this highly motivated group, education predicted greater knowledge.

One recent study looked beyond socio-economic status to divisions within these broad groups, specifically whether minorities and females exhibit knowledge gaps of **disaffection**.[26] The term implies less trust in the media and the political system, which should be a turn-off that leads to lower knowledge levels. Instead, disaffection spurred the interest of more educated individuals at the same SES level. In a local school controversy, females and minorities with higher education also had higher levels of knowledge. Although exploratory, the study suggests that SES alone is too broad a categorization to explain people's attitude or issue knowledge.

Another non-political study dealt with increases in knowledge about AIDS following Magic Johnson's announcement that he tested positive for HIV.[27] Six months before the announcement, a knowledge gap was found between high and low SES groups on AIDS awareness. Ten days after the announcement, the higher SES group still possessed greater knowledge about the disease, but the lower SES group had gained in knowledge. A gap still existed, but it was narrowed by Magic Johnson's announcement and the subsequent media attention to the disease.

---

24. Leslie B. Snyder (1990). "Channel effectiveness over time and knowledge and behavior gaps," *Journalism Quarterly* 67(4):875-886.

25. K. Viswanath, Emily Kahn, John R. Finnegan Jr., James Hertog and John D. Potter (1993). "Motivation and the knowledge gap: Effects of a campaign to reduce diet-related cancer risk," *Communication Research* 20(4):546-563.

26. Eric S. Fredin, Teresa Haugen Monnett and Gerald M. Kosicki (1994). "Knowledge gaps, social locators, and media schemata: Gaps, reverse gaps, and gaps of disaffection," *Journalism Quarterly* 71(1):176-190.

27. Wayne Wanta and William R. Elliott (1995). "Did the 'Magic' work? Knowledge of HIV/AIDS and the knowledge gap hypothesis," *Journalism & Mass Communication Quarterly* 72(2):312-321.

Summary

After nearly 30 years of study, what can we say for sure about knowledge gap? The range of knowledge gap topics has been vast, from local issues to elections to health issues and international concerns. Given this variety of topics, conflicting outcomes should be expected, and the diversity of findings is great. Sill, there are themes that keep the theory from being hopelessly mired in the confluence of mixed approaches.

A fundamental thesis is that *knowledge gaps are likely to occur between the higher and lower socio-economic strata* of the population. The great preponderance of studies registers differences in knowledge based on **SES**, and **level of education** seems to remain the primary predictor of knowledge levels. Information campaigns that recognize the dichotomy in education and its attendant differences in **stored knowledge**, **interest** and **media use** will fare better than those that ignore this division.

Some campaigns, such as those aimed at national and international public affairs, must expect great difficulty in overcoming the inherent lack of interest by a large segment of the population. Getting messages through is not impossible, but success requires strategies that overcome the barriers. Other issues, such as health, the environment, controversies and major breaking news events have more likelihood of reaching the populace and narrowing gaps. Informing the public may require little advance planning in some situations, but campaigns that seek to ingrain real understanding are more difficult.

In a single-sentence: Educational differences result in knowledge gaps that widen or narrow depending on the **topic**, people's **interest**, and the **channels** of communication used. The preponderance of evidence supports the basic tenets of the original knowledge gap theory.

Exercise:

Even among your college-educated peers you have opportunities to test some of the knowledge gap theory precepts.

Here's an approach that controls for educational level. Each class member selects four students at random, two males and two females, possibly in a school cafeteria or similar leisure gathering place. Observe three cautions: 1) don't interview anyone you know; 2) make sure each is a junior or senior to better control educational level; and, 3) don't interview in a group setting — ask your subjects to walk with you to another table for a minute... otherwise you may spend half an hour in group discussion. Tell your subjects you're doing a class assignment, and ask them these questions:

1. From which media source would you say you get most of your information about public affairs issues, such as politics, the economy or health. Would you say television news or newspapers?

2. Let me ask you four questions about exercising:

   a. How do you feel after you exercise vigorously for 20-minutes? (those who exercise regularly should say "exhilarated," "invigorated" or some similar positive; those who don't should say "tired")

   b. What should a person do just before beginning a workout session to reduce the chance of injury?
   (*stretching or limbering up, either is correct*)

   c. People should drink a glass of water with a vigorous 20-minute workout session. Should they drink before or after the workout, or does it matter? (*after is the correct answer*)

   d. Regular, vigorous exercise reduces the risk of heart disease. How does exercise help the body reduce this risk?
   (*any of these is correct: strengthening the heart muscle, reducing fatty tissues in the arteries or clearing blood vessels*)

3. Do you exercise on a regular basis, at least 20 minutes three times a week? yes no

Thank your subjects. You may tell them the correct answers when you're done.

Now record the answers using the following table:

| | Information Source | | Number | Regular Exercise | |
	TV	Paper	Correct	Yes	No
female subjects					
male subjects					

Bring the results to the next class meeting, but consider the implications of your mini-study in light of your four-person sample and be ready to discuss the associated knowledge gap precepts from the chapter.

26

Agenda-Setting and Communication "Truths"

Founding article: Maxwell E. McCombs and Donald L. Shaw (1972). "The agenda-setting function of mass media," *Public Opinion Quarterly 36(2):176-187.*

Recent article: Michael J. Breen (1997). "A cook, a cardinal, his priests, and the press: Deviance as a trigger for intermedia agenda setting," *Journalism & Mass Communication Quarterly 74 (2):348-356.*

Rather than actually trying this challenging adventure, simply think about what might happen IF the class were to tackle this agenda-setting assignment. Think of agenda-setting as the mass media's inability to tell people *what* to think, but their stunning success at being able to tell people what to think *about*.[1]

Measure media agenda

First, find out which issues are most important today as determined by the amount of coverage they receive in the national news media.[2] This might seem like a massive undertaking that would include monitoring the network television news, radio, a variety of newspapers across the country and news magazines. Actually, a good approximation of the week's national news content can be made by counting the number of news stories on each topic carried in *Time, Newsweek* and *U.S. News & World Report* (see Content Analysis chapter).

---

1. Bernard C. Cohen (1963). *The press and foreign policy.* Princeton, NJ: Princeton University Press.

2. The transient nature of news means that some issues will crowd out others, so the salience of an issue is relative, even though it is measured in amount of coverage. Gladys Engel Lang and Kurt Lang (1981). "Watergate: An exploration of the agenda-building process," in G. Cleveland Wilhoit and Harold deBock, eds. *Mass communication review yearbook Vol. 2.* Beverly Hills, CA: Sage, pp. 447-468.

If the stories in the three weekly news magazines were counted for two months, or 10 issues each of the magazines, the list of national topics derived would mirror a list of topics taken from the much wider range of mass media.[3] In the United States, two items are likely to be on the list of six or seven important issues: 1) the economy and 2) crime. Other topics might be **issues** such as health or employment, or **events** such as wars, airline crashes, political scandals, etc.[4] Regardless of the issues, the first task is accomplished: a list of the media's most important issues. This list is called the **media agenda**, and it's the first step in agenda-setting research.

Measure public agenda

Task No. 2 is to determine the public agenda of important issues today. To assess public opinion about which national issues in the news are most important, a survey is needed. The essential question is: "What are the most important problems facing the United States today?" The survey might be of college students on a single campus, a community's general population or a national random sample survey. Obviously, the more generalizable the survey, the more likely it will tap public opinion and produce the most plausible list of issues the public perceives as most important. This list of half a dozen or so issues is the **public agenda**.

The public agenda cannot be expected to exactly mirror the media agenda. For example, crime might be the No. 5 issue on the media agenda, but it might be No. 3 on the public agenda. Why this happens is a topic of debate among communication researchers. Some suggest that the issues are mediated by public cognitions[5] such as, "The national economy is in bad shape, but my brother-in-law is unemployed, and that's worse." Others explain that news media coverage of an issue is couched in broad terms, often in a positive or negative context, and that the public perception of issues is subtle rather than just saying one issue is more important than another.[6] An example of this **priming** effect is, "I may not know where Bosnia is, but having our troops there is important to show the world that America cares about liberty."

The impact of interpersonal communication is another explanation of why the two agendas don't exactly match. People talk about issues, and their conversations

---

3. Gerald C. Stone and Maxwell E. McCombs (1981). "Tracing the time lag in agenda-setting," *Journalism Quarterly* 58(1):51-55.

4. The distinction between issues and events was made by Donald L. Shaw (1977). "The press agenda in a community setting," in Donald L. Shaw and Maxwell E. McCombs, eds. *The emergence of American political issues: The agenda-setting function of the press.* St. Paul, MN: West Publishing, pp. 19-31.

5. Lee B. Becker and Jack M. McLeod (1976). "Political consequences of agenda-setting," *Mass Comm Review* 3(2):8-15.

6. Shanto Iyengar and Donald R. Kinder (1987). *News that matters: Television and American opinion.* Chicago: University of Chicago Press.

can increase their perceived importance of an issue.[7] Other influences include the **need for orientation**, or a psychological attribute that relates to why certain people attend closely to the mass media,[8] the values people hold or their access to other communication channels. Regardless of why the two agendas aren't exact, most studies do find a high correlation between the media and public agenda: a close fit.

Measure cause and effect

The third task is to determine whether the media agenda influenced or caused the public agenda, which is what agenda-setting theory propounds. The alternative is that the public agenda causes the media agenda. If the latter proposition were correct, then the media would begin covering issues because people think they are important. Almost everyone who learns about the agenda-setting theory toys with this idea: That media, in their haste to capture larger audiences, respond to what interests the public by giving those topics greater coverage.

Of course, either or both of the agendas might be caused by some factor: They are similar agendas without being causative. One suggestion is that both are reacting to "real-world indicators," or actual events that the media and the public perceive at the same time but independently.[9] Another suggestion is a symbiotic relationship between the two agendas, that media personnel and public opinion gravitate to the same interest topics that merge over time. But whether the two agendas are independent or mutually interactive is a lesser debate.[10] Almost all agenda-setting researchers believe the two are related, and that one causes the other.

How might cause and effect be shown? The normal method is to see which comes first. If the public agenda is formed first, and the media agenda forms later, then the public is setting the media agenda. Several studies of the relationship dash this possibility. McCombs used cross-lagged analysis to show that the media's

---

7. Maxwell E. McCombs and David H. Weaver (1985). "Toward a merger of gratifications and agenda-setting research," in Karl Erik Rosengren, Lawrence A. Wenner and Philip Palmgreen, eds. *Media gratifications research: Current perspectives.* Beverly Hills, CA: Sage, pp. 95-108.

8. Jack M. McLeod, Lee B. Becker and James E. Byrnes (1974). "Another look at the agenda-setting function of the press," *Communication Research* 1(2):131-166.

9. Michael Bruce MacKuen (1981). "Social communication and the mass policy agenda," in Michael Bruce MacKuen and Steven Lane Coombs, eds. *More than news: Media power in public affairs.* Newbury Park, CA:Sage, pp. 19-144. See also: Karl Erik Rosengren (1983). "Communication research: One paradigm, or four?" *Journal of Communication* 33(3):185-207; Gary D. Gaddy and Enoh Tanjong (1986). "Earthquake coverage by the Western press," *Journal of Communication* 36(2):105-112; William C. Adams (1986). "Whose lives count: TV coverage of natural disasters," *Journal of Communication* 36(2):113-122.

10. Lutz Erbring, Edie N. Goldenberg and Arthur H. Miller (1980). "Front-page news and real-world cues: A new look at agenda-setting by the media," *American Journal of Political Science* 24(1):16-49.

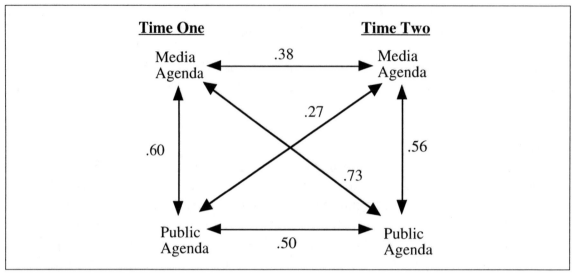

Figure 1: Cross-lagged analysis in agenda-setting

agenda sets the public agenda.[11] Cross-lagged analysis tests the strength of correlations between the two agendas at two points in time, checking associations in all directions. The Figure 1 example shows that all of the correlations are positive, as would be true in two measures of media and public agendas taken in the same six-month period. But the key figures, those in the "X," indicate that the association between the **media agenda at time one** and the **public agenda at time two** is far stronger (.73) than the association between the public agenda at time one and the media agenda at time two (.27). Thus, the media agenda precedes the public agenda.

If this evidence is not enough, consider intuition: How could an event such as a terrorist bombing or the discovery of a new cancer-fighting drug register on the public agenda unless the mass media placed it there? And if a true skeptic is still not persuaded, several researchers have studied the agenda-setting effect over time.[12] Their results were rather consistent in confirming that it takes from about one to four months for the media agenda to set the public agenda.

11. Maxwell E. McCombs (1977). "Newspapers versus television: Mass communication effects across time," in *The emergence of American political issues: The agenda-setting function of the press, op. cit.,* pp. 89-105.

12. James P. Winter and Chaim H. Eyal (1981). "Agenda setting for the civil rights issue," *Public Opinion Quarterly* 45(3):376-383. See also: Gerald C. Stone and Maxwell E. McCombs (1981). *op. cit.;* Chaim H. Eyal, James P. Winter and William F. DeGeorge (1981). "The concept of time frame in agenda-setting," in G. Cleveland Wilhoit and Harold de Bock, eds. *Mass communication review yearbook Vol.* 2. Beverly Hills, CA: Sage, pp. 212-218; Pamela J. Shoemaker, Wayne Wanta and Dawn Leggett (1989). "Drug coverage and public opinion, 1972-1986," in Pamela J. Shoemaker, ed. *Communication campaigns about drugs: Government, media, and the public.* Hillsdale, NJ: Lawrence Erlbaum; Michael B. Salwen (1986). "Time in agenda-setting: The accumulation of media coverage on audience issue salience." Paper presented at the International Communication Association, Chicago.

One of the problems in agenda-setting research is that not all news issues are created equal. The lightening-rod items, such as train wrecks and earthquakes, are **unobtrusive** because the public doesn't learn about these events until the media report them. Slow-boiling issues, such as inflation and abortion, are **obtrusive** because the public knows about them. Some research shows that the unobtrusive are brought to the public agenda by the media, but the obtrusive ones might go from building public concern to become a media coverage topic.[13] Still, for most news issues, it is generally conceded that the media set the public agenda.

Measure media effects

The final task, thus far a discouraging research mission, would be to assess the implications of agenda-setting. The overarching implication is that the media are extremely powerful if they can determine what the public deems is important by their decision of which issues to cover. Many studies have charted the substructure of issues. For example, the media agenda suggests which political candidates are viable by the amount of coverage given them, but voters also learn what the key issues are and candidates' stands on those issues. Voters may learn that crime is the key issue, and that Smith is the candidate who favors increasing the police force.

Rogers and Dearing made the connection between **public** agenda-setting, or the communication studies discussed here, and **policy** agenda-setting studies by political scientists.[14] The latter found many instances of legislators making policy decisions based on media coverage of issues.[15] Cohen reported that policymakers believe the media agenda is a better measure of the public agenda than are public opinion surveys.[16] This body of research attributes great influence to the mass

---

13. Harold Gene Zucker (1978). "The variable nature of news media influence," in Brent D. Ruben, ed. *Communication yearbook Vol. 2.* New Brunswick, NJ: Transaction Books, pp. 225-240. See also: Chaim Hirschmann Eyal (1979). *Time frame in agenda-setting research: A study of the conceptual and methodological factors affecting the time frame context of the agenda-setting process.* Unpublished doctoral dissertation, Syracuse University, Syracuse, NY; Roger W. Cobb and Charles D. Elder (1983). *Participation in American politics: The dynamics of agenda-building, 2nd ed.* Baltimore: Johns Hopkins University Press.

14. Everett M. Rogers and James W. Dearing (1988). "Agenda-setting research: Where has it been, where is it going?" in James A. Anderson, ed. *Communication Yearbook Vol. 11.* Newbury Park, CA: Sage, pp. 555-594.

15. Fay Lomax Cook, Tom R. Tyler, Edward G. Goetz, Margaret T. Gordon, David Protess, Donna R. Leff and Harvey L. Molotch (1983). "Media and agenda-setting: Effects on the public, interest group leaders, policy makers, and policy," *Public Opinion Quarterly* 47(1):16-35. See also: Martin Linsky (1986). *Impact: How the press affects federal policymaking.* New York: W.W. Norton; Donna R. Leff, David L. Protess and Stephen C. Brooks (1986). "Crusading journalism: Changing public attitudes and policy-making agendas," *Public Opinion Quarterly* 50(3):300-315.

16. Bernard C. Cohen (1973). *The public's impact on foreign policy.* Boston: Little, Brown & Co.

media's agenda, moreso even than the public agenda. Like Smith being seen as the police force candidate, there are even greater implications for national policy when "concern about Iran" reaches the top spot on the media's agenda.

"Truths" in communication research

The agenda-setting research provides an opportune departure to consider some "truths" obtained during the 60 or so years history of communication study. Sixty years is a very short existence for any academic discipline, and brevity alone may justify critics' lamentation that communication has provided few if any real "truths," and certainly no encompassing theories about how communication works.

Agenda-setting begins to resemble an encompassing theoretical perspective. The concept is about 30 years old with nearly 300 studies that focus directly on the topic,[17] including agenda-setting studies in a dozen different countries. Although there is no pretext that all of the research supports the concept as originally described, many of the studies suggest a number of "truths" worth noting:

1) The mass media are organizations whose product is information and entertainment. Those who operate the media are conditioned to seek out news and to disseminate it widely. This increases audiences and revenues. Reporters are adept at interacting with sources, many of whom are part of society's power elite (politicians, business and civic leaders). This exchange of information between sources and the media, and the process of disseminating it is called **gatekeeping**.

One type of information the media process is breaking-news stories, or events the public can only learn about through the mass media, such as oil spills or a treaty signed with another nation. Another type of information the media process is

---

17. Excellent reviews of the body of literature on agenda-settting are found in the following articles and books, including the "Recent article" at the beginning of the chapter: Everett Rogers and James W. Dearing (1988), *op. cit.*; David L. Protess and Maxwell E. McCombs (1991). *Agenda-setting: Readings on media, public opinion, and policymaking.* Hillsdale, NJ: Lawrence Erlbaum; Stephen D. Reese (1991). "Setting the media's agenda: A power balance perspective," *Communication Yearbook Vol. 14.* Newbury Park, CA: Sage, pp. 309-340; Maxwell E. McCombs, Edna Einsiedel and David H. Weaver (1991). *Contemporary public opinion: Issues and the news.* Hillsdale, NJ: Lawrence Erlbaum; Everette M. Rogers, James W. Dearing and Dorine Bregman (1993). "The anatomy of agenda-setting research," *Journal of Communication* 43(2):68-84; Maxwell E. McCombs and Donald L. Shaw (1993). "The evolution of agenda-setting research: Twenty-five years in the marketplace of ideas," *Journal of Communication* 43(2):58-67; and Hans-Bernd Brosius (1994). "Agenda-setting nach 25 jahren Forschungsaktivitat: Methodischer und theoreticher stillstand? *Publizistik* 39:269-288; James W. Dearing and Everett M. Rogers (1996). *Agenda-setting.* Thousand Oaks, CA: Sage; Wayne Wanta (1997). *The public and the national agenda: How people learn about important issues.* New York: Lawrence Erlbaum; Maxwell McCombs, Donald L. Shaw and David Weaver (1997). *Communication and democracy: Exploring the intellectual frontiers in agenda-setting theory.* New York: Lawrence Erlbaum.

continuing stories, or issues that build slowly and might be known by the public, such as problems in the state auto license bureau. Members of the public would recognize there is a problem if it takes a month to get new license plates. With breaking stories, the media locate new sources and rely on known sources for confirmation and official responses. With continuing stories, the media rely more on known sources among the public, many of whom share information with reporters on a continuing basis.[18] For example, a deputy in the state auto license bureau may tell a reporter about computer problems in the renewal division.

2) Information ebbs and flows among the media, but a few important issues remain high on the media agenda, the topics that continue to have news value and about which the public seems interested. Coverage of these issues increases, and members of the mass audience who attend to the news media most will know more about the issues, including more details. These individuals are the **opinion leaders**, each of whom is an early recognizer of information that is pertinent to that person. Opinion leaders have larger networks for interpersonal communication and may be among the first to tell others the information, a **two-step flow** precept.[19]

3) But opinion leaders may not be the first to provide information because the media serve this function directly in most instances. Audience attention to media messages will depend on people's interest in a topic and their use of the mass media, a **uses and gratifications** precept. With major issues, such as the top several media agenda issues, the flow of information will be so intense or so prolonged that most of the population will know about the issues, an **information diffusion** precept.

4) Once the information registers on the public agenda, people begin talking about the issues and merging media information with information gained from **interpersonal communication** sources.[20] Information from non-media sources

---

18. Hans-Bernd Brosius and Hans Mathias Kepplinger (1990). "The agenda-setting function of television news: Static and dynamic views," *Communication Research* 17(2):183-211. See also: Kim A. Smith (1987). "Newspaper coverage and public concern about community issues: A time-series analysis," *Journalism Monographs, No. 101*:1-32.

19. Gabriel Weimann (1994). *The influentials: People who influence people*. Albany: State University of New York Press. See also: Gabriel Weimann and Hans-Bernd Brosius (1994). "Is there a two-step flow of agenda-setting?" *International Journal of Public Opinion Research* 6(4):323-341; Hans-Bernd Brosius and Gabriel Weimann (1996). "Who sets the agenda: Agenda-setting as a two-step flow," *Communication Research* 23(5):561-580.

20. L. Erwin Atwood, Ardyth B. Sohn and Harold Sohn (1978). "Daily newspaper contributions to community discussion," *Journalism Quarterly* 52(3):570-576. See also: Lutz Erbring, Edie N. Goldenberg and Arthur H. Miller, *op. cit.*; Dominic L. Lasorsa and Wayne Wanta (1990). "Effects of personal, interpersonal and media experiences on issue saliences," *Journalism Quarterly* 67(4):804-813; Wayne Wanta and Yi-Chen Wu (1992). "Interpersonal communication and the agenda-setting process," *Journalism Quarterly* 69(4)847-855; David H. Weaver, Jian-Hua Zhu and Lars Willnat (1992). "The bridging function of interpersonal communication in agenda-setting," *Journalism Quarterly* 69(4):856-867.

may alter the public agenda and make it less like the media agenda, but it is more likely that discussion will help focus the public agenda and make it a closer match to the media agenda.

What happens then is less a certainty or "truth," as the term is being used here. Some studies suggest that the public, or the opinion leaders, provide **feedback** to the media. This may occur as audiences turn to other media sources when issues cease to hold their interest, by letters to the editor or by members of the power elite providing direct feedback to their reporter colleagues. Some suggest that the feedback becomes input that alters the media agenda and begins a new, circular process.

Summary

Agenda-setting is the concept that the media may be unable to persuade people what to think, but are quite adept at telling people what to think about. The issues that the media cover become the issues that the public believes are important, including the subtopics among those issues. This is a powerful-media theory.

Several steps are reviewed in the agenda-setting research process: 1) measure which issues are most important by the amount of coverage they receive in the news media, 2) measure the public agenda of important issues with a survey, 3) show that the media cause the public agenda, and 4) assess the agenda-setting implications.

The chapter turns from reviewing the agenda-setting process to using it as a broad-based communication theory that encompasses many perspectives. The discussion focuses on "truths" derived from 60 years of communication research from **gatekeeping** to opinion leadership in **two-step flow**, to **uses and gratifications**, **information diffusion**, **interpersonal communication** and **feedback**.

Exercises:

A. Other than the three weekly news magazines named in the first step to measure the media agenda, what source or sources might be used to assess the mass media agenda nationwide? Make a case for your suggestion in a one-page paper suitable for discussion in class or to be submitted for a grade. On a separate page, suggest what sources would be necessary to assess the media agenda in your town.

B. Shoot holes in the "truths" section of the chapter. Your teacher may ask you to: 1) argue the point that there are no real "truths" in the communication discipline, 2) focus on one of the "truths" given in the section and provide a convincing argument that the "truth" is false, or 3) write a one-page journal article synopsis in which the author(s) presents evidence that one of the "truths" may be false.

27

Principle of Relative Constancy

Founding ublication: Maxwell E. McCombs (1972). "Mass media in the marketplace," *Journalism Monographs 24.*

Resurgent review: Stephen Lacy and Ghee-Young Noh (1997). "Theory, economics, measurement, and the principle of relative constancy," *Journal of Media Economics 10*(3):3-16.

Complete the following inventory: your best guess of what a family of four with an annual income of $50,000 might spend **per month** on the these media. You may have to estimate for a year and then divide by 12:

1. Subscription to a local daily newspaper: _____
2. Two magazine subscriptions:_____
3. Cable or satellite television:_____
4. Faxes:_____
5. Cellular phone:_____
6. Going out to the movies twice a month:_____
7. Internet provider service:_____
8. Four videos:_____
9. Two music CDs:_____
10. Two audio cassette tapes: _____
11. Two paperback books:_____
Total the cost of these media:_____
Now multiply the monthly cost by 12 to get a yearly family expense: _____

Most of these media expenses are for "content." Some additional costs will be required for repair and new equipment. Estimate these possible equipment costs beginning on the next page, but some calculations will be required to annualize costs. For example, if a new color television set costs $300 and is replaced every five years, divide the $300 expense by five years ($\div 5$) to get the annual cost of $60.

<u>Annual</u>

12. Cost of a new color television set every five years: _____ (÷5) = _____

13. Cost of video cassette recorder-player every four years: _____ (÷4) = _____

14. Cost of buying a portable or home radio once a year: _____

15. Cost of buying/replacing car radio every three years: _____ (÷3) = _____

16. Cost of buying one audio tape player and headset every year: _____

17. Cost of buying a home CD player and associated
    music/stereo/speaker equipment every four years: _____ (÷4) = _____

18. Cost to repair/replace/upgrade cable or satellite tv equipment: _____

19. Cost of replacing fax machine every five years: _____ (÷5) = _____

20. Annual cost of cellular phone equipment repair/upgrade: _____

21. Cost of replacing home computer every five years: _____ (÷5) = _____

22. Three home computer software programs (new/upgrades/games): _____

Total these costs by adding all the annualized figures (far right column): _____

Add the two annualized totals for media (first 11 items plus second 11): _____

The last figure is the total estimated annual family expense for mass media. After deriving the media costs, complete the next few items in paragraph form:

1. If you think some "media" on the list should not be included (maybe they aren't comparable to others), justify their exclusion and recalculate to derive a new total:

        a. deleted media costs: _____   new total: _____

2. If some media are excluded from the list that you think should be included, justify their inclusion, and then recalculate the figures to derive a new total:

a. additional media costs: _____   new total:_____

3. Do you think that the total costs for family mass media that you derived or changed and justified are reasonable estimates:

*   *   *

We know we live in an age of mass media explosion. But the last few generations might have felt the same way with the advent of: radio and feature movies in the late 1920s; television and stereophonic music in the early 1950s; widespread cable television, video and audio tape cassettes in the late 1970s; and home computers, satellites and CDs in the late 1980s. Each of these advances greatly affected the time people devoted to the media. Given their impact, mass media developments greatly concern the media industries, the economy and society generally, and individuals. What might be predicted about the increase in mass media?

The media mix drew the industry's attention first. In 1959, Charles Scripps, then CEO of Scripps-Howard Newspapers, issued an economic study of media.[1] The newspaper industry was concerned about competition from television, which enjoyed huge success during the 1950s. The report noted that economic support for the mass media remained relatively constant. Expenditures on media varied with the economy's health, but the proportion of money spent on media stayed constant even though several media were added since about 1930. The report said, "mass communications have become a staple of consumption in our society much like food, clothing, and shelter. Its stability in times of economic stress indicates that consumers feel that mass communications is a necessity of life, although their selection of media may vary."[2]

---

1. Charles Scripps (1959). *Economic support of mass communications media: 1929-1957*. New York: Scripps-Howard Research.
2. *Ibid.*, p. 6.

Tenets of the principle

Scripps' observations became the basis for a landmark study by McCombs in 1972. Using the report's general findings, McCombs offered a theoretical framework he called the principle of relative constancy. Some of his predictions were:

1. The *proportion* of money, viewed as a part of the gross national product (GNP), spent on the mass media remains fairly constant over time. This is the **constancy** part of relative constancy. If the GNP is $10 trillion, the amount attributed to mass media will be about 3% or $300 billion. All expenses associated with mass media, from manufacturing television sets to the advertising dollars spent on magazines, will total about 3% of the economy. Likewise, if a certain portion of a family's income is spent on media, it will continue to spend about that same portion.

2. Because the economy varies from boom to depression, the GNP (and individual family income) also will vary. Sometimes the GNP will be $8 trillion; sometimes $12 trillion. Likewise family incomes (considered across the population) will vary. Sometimes families earn $40,000; sometimes $50,000. If the proportion spent on mass media remains constant, then the *actual dollars* spent on mass media will vary. This is the **relative** part of relative constancy. It suggests that some years $250 billion will be spent on media and other years the figure might be $350 billion. Likewise, a family making $40,000 might spend $1,200 on mass media, but if the family earns $50,000, then the dollars spent on mass media might be closer to $1,500.

Neither of these concepts is difficult to understand. GNP is composed of a variety of industries and products: cars, wheat, mortgages, hogs, gasoline, etc. The mass media are only one of many goods and services that comprise the figure, and they are subject to the dips and rises in the economy. Actually, mass media advertising is extremely sensitive to changes in the national economy. For instance, most manufacturers, services and retail stores spend a rather stable percentage of funds on advertising.[3] If the economy is booming and people are buying, ad expenditures may remain at 4% of sales but the actual dollars Sears spends on advertising may rise from $100 million to $200 million. In recessions, the percentage may stay at 4, but actual dollars spent may drop from $100 million to only $50 million. The individual or family expenditure is easy to understand. People who earn a big bonus might celebrate by buying a wide-screen stereo television; people who lose their job are likely to go to the movies less frequently.

3. Because the expenditures on mass media are relatively constant, new media must fight it out with existing media. Think of media expenditures as a pie.

---

3. For a discussion of concepts involved in budgeting advertising, see: John P. Jones, "Ad spending: Maintaining market share," pp. 38-42, and James C. Schroer, "Ad spending: Growing market share," pp. 44-48. *Harvard Business Review* (January-February, 1990).

When a new medium comes along, the pie doesn't automatically get bigger. New media must take their slice from existing media. This part of the theory is called **functional equivalence**. It predicts that any new medium will take its share from the existing media whose functions it most closely displaces. Displacement occurs when the new medium provides the same or greater gratifications at lower cost or with more convenience. For example, cable television cost more, but it offered commercial-free movies and an abundance of channels. Cable took its market share from existing broadcast television stations and networks. Audio tape cassettes replaced vinyl records; CDs replaced audio tape cassettes.

McCombs predicted that the principle of relative constancy and of functional equivalence would continue to apply to the introduction of new media. Examples of changes in the media mix through the 1970s fit so nicely with these predictions that the principle of relative constancy was accepted as axiomatic for more than a decade. McCombs and Eyal did a follow-up study in 1980 that compared spending on print media with new audio-visual media, and that used more sensitive consumer spending and income measures than overall GNP. Their findings showed that print media expenses remained constant, although the proportion of books and periodicals changed. Their findings reinforced the principle of relative constancy.[4]

Second thoughts

By the mid-1980s, several new media were on the scene. VCRs were the most dramatic new medium from an economic perspective because the cost of a home player-recorder dropped from a high of $1,200 in 1977 to about $900 in 1980 and then made the dip below $500 in about 1982.[5] At less than $500, VCRs became the new must-have gadget: the Christmas gift of choice. Additionally, VCRs were seen as **functional complements** to other media rather than functional competitors: VCRs opened a new market for movies; they allowed **time-shifting**, or taping from broadcast or cable television; and they stimulated interpersonal communication.[6]

Also at the start of the 1980s, cable television became an attractive product. Prior to that time, cable was a mom-and-pop operation that brought television signals to remote areas, or it was a commercial operation that wired apartment

4. Maxwell E. McCombs and Chaim H. Eyal (1980). "Spending on mass media," *Journal of Communication* 30(1):153-159.

5. Mark R. Levy (1980). "Home video recorders: A user survey," *Journal of Communication* 30(4):23-27.

6. Ghee-Young Noh and August E. Grant (1997). "Media functionality and the principle of relative constancy: An explanation of the VCR aberration," *Journal of Media Economics* 10(3):17-31. See also: Julia R. Dobrow (1990). *Social and cultural aspects of VCR use.* Hillsdale, NJ: Lawrence Erlbaum; John Dimmick and Alan B. Albarran (1994). "The role of gratification opportunities in determining media preference," *Mass Comm Review* 21(3-4):223-235.

buildings in metropolitan areas where television signals were obstructed by sky-scrapers. But by 1980, cable's array of channels guaranteed that the product would have high consumer interest. Larger companies bought out the smaller ones, and by 1985 half the U.S. homes were receiving and paying monthly fees for cable.

VCRs and cable arrived at nearly the same time, became so pervasive so quickly, and cost an average of perhaps $1,000 the first year (cost of the VCR at $450, cost of recording tape at $7, cost of renting pre-recorded movies at $5 each; cost of having cable brought to the house at $25, cost of renting switcher boxes and monthly cable fee at $25), and perhaps $500 annually after the first year.

Researchers recognized that wide adoption of these two media presented an opportunity to review the principle of relative constancy, and a series of studies focused on just such an investigation. They found conflicting evidence, but at this point a brief discussion of methodology is necessary.

Relative constancy is one of the few theoretical constructs that relates to mass media finances. While communication studies often use "soft" data like opinions, economics uses hard data like money. But economic data are usually gross figures gathered and grouped in awkward ways. For example, the Commerce Department's "media" data include sheet music, maps, and ticket sales to concerts and ball games; GNP is dominated by manufacturing and agriculture. Then there are the problems of adjusting for inflation, population growth and the decline in new media costs (the price of VCRs alluded to earlier). So while economic data may seem infallible, their validity is open to interpretation. There's no rule about which family income to use in measuring media spending decisions: gross income, adjusted gross, per-capita or disposable personal income.

Raising method and concept concerns about relative constancy, Wood said that past data don't preclude old and new media existing together: "new technologies will not be shut out of the market, nor will existing technologies be doomed...they will have to compete successfully for the consumer's time and money. This is the same constraint faced by the producers of every consumer good and service."[7] Wood speculated that media may follow luxury-item patterns like jewelry or furs.

Further exceptions to relative constancy said the principle lacks grounding in economic theory.[8] Among countervailing precepts are: **demand theory**, or people's demand for goods, such as the continued success of movies during the Great

---

7. William C. Wood (1986). "Consumer spending on the mass media: The principle of relative constancy reconsidered," *Journal of Communication* 36(2):39-51, see pp. 50-51.
8. Stephen Lacy and Ghee-Young Noh (1997). "Theory, economics, measurement, and the principle of relative constancy," *Journal of Media Economics* 10(3):3-16.

Depression; the **industrial organization (IO) model** indicating some media complement each other (television and VCRs) while others act as substitutes (cable and satellites); the **joint product** nature of media in which ads and entertainment exist together or in which the Internet combines aspects of many media; the idea of **windows,** or access opportunities, such as seeing a movie first at the theater, then on pay-per-view, as a video rental, on cable or finally on network television;[9] and **niche theory**, which predicts outcomes in a competitive and resource-limited market.[10]

A series of other studies either confirmed that consumer spending on the mass media remained relatively constant over the years or that it deviated greatly in the early 1980s because of VCRs and cable television.[11] And a retrospective study in 1997 cited five methodological problems with the principle of relative constancy.[12]

Predictions

If the development of relative constancy seems to have hit a snag or dwindled to nit-picking, consider the big picture. This theory tries to predict the success of emerging mass media and the new media's effect on existing media.

In the 170 years since the inception of the Penny Press, each generation saw a greater number of new media. The latter half of the 1980s brought computers, cellular phones and faxes; the 1990s brought CDs, satellites, digital, the Internet and high-definition television. Examples of the theory's validity abound since 1950.[13]

---

9. Bruce M. Owen and Steven S. Wildman (1992). *Video economics.* Cambridge, MA: Harvard University Press.

10. John Dimmick (1997). "The theory of the niche and spending on mass media: The case of the 'video revolution,'" *Journal of Media Economics* 10(3):33-43.

11. Relative constancy was supported with few exceptions by: Anita Werner (1986). "Mass media expenditures in Norway: The principle of relative constancy revisited," in Margaret L. McLaughlin, ed. *Communication Yearbook 9.* Beverly Hills, CA: Sage, pp. 251-260; Jinok Son and Maxwell E. McCombs (1993). "A look at the constancy principle under changing market conditions," *Journal of Media Economics* 6(2):23-36; Michael Dupagne (1994). "Testing the relative constancy of mass media expenditures in the United Kingdom," *Journal of Media Economics* 7(3):1-14. The theory was not supported in specific periods by: Maxwell E. McCombs and Jinok Son (1986). "Patterns of economic support for mass media during a decade of electronic innovation." Paper presented at the AEJMC, Atlanta; Hugh S. Fullerton (1988). "Technology collides with relative constancy: The pattern of adoption for a new medium," *Journal of Media Economics* 1(2):75-84; Jack Glascock (1993). "Effect of cable television on advertiser and consumer spending on mass media, 1978-1990," *Journalism Quarterly* 70(3):509-517; Ghee-Young Noh (1994). "New media departure in the principle of relative constancy: VCRs." Paper presented at the AEJMC, Atlanta; and William C. Wood and Sharon L. O'Hare (1991). "Paying for the video revolution: Consumer spending on the mass media," *Journal of Communication* 41(1):24-30.

12. Michael Dupagne (1997). "A theoretical and methodological critique of the principle of relative constancy," *Communication Theory* 7(1):53-76.

13. David Abrahamson (1998). "The visible hand: Money, markets, and media evolution," *Journalism & Mass Communication Quarterly* 75(1):14-18.

When television became established by the late 1950s, it almost put the film industry out of business. Just as relative constancy predicts, people turned to television because the new medium offered sound and pictures with the convenience of in-home entertainment at a reduced price. The new medium took its audience from the old medium whose properties it most closely reproduced. AM radio was demolished by FM's clearer sound; cable's variety hurt broadcast television. The functional equivalence precept of relative constancy seemed valid.

And yet, within 20 years, the movie industry was booming again after being helped by video cassette rentals and by television's relentless quest for content.[14] Magazines, which seemed doomed by television in 1960, were thriving again in the 1990s. The newspaper industry, worried about its future in the late 1950s, is changed but still very healthy today. These trends raise concerns about the constancy aspect of relative constancy.[15] They suggest a different future for emerging mass media.

If the constancy tenet is flawed (perhaps constancy is merely a legacy of early mass media development between 1920 and 1950), then assumptions about the advent of new mass media are flawed. We might actually predict that economic support and public acceptance of new mass media are limitless. Evidence for the "limitless" hypothesis is seen in some of the advertising studies. Families purchase a television set infrequently, but advertising spent on television and the other mass media seems to have no bounds.[16] This mass media-related part of the economy has been expanding exponentially for years, seemingly capable of underwriting all new media comers, wherever audiences turn, including the World Wide Web.

Though the jury is still out, the verdict on people's increased expenditures and use of the mass media since the rapid advent of new media technologies in the 1990s is leaning away from relative constancy. A 1997 study probed the economic consumption of media issue and found that the pie had expanded.[17] By far the largest new slice added was that for audiovisual media, which began growing in the early 1980s and showed no sign of abating. The study only estimated expenditures for computers and computer programs, and included just the earliest figures for Internet provider fees. The more traditional media, though seen as retrenching somewhat, were still faring well in the media mix of the 1990s.

---

14. The concept of new media introduction, growth to maturity, decline and alteration is presented in Donald L. Shaw (1991). *The rise and fall of American mass media: Roles of technology and leadership*. Bloomington: Indiana University Press.

15. David Pearce Demers (1994). "Relative constancy hypothesis, structural pluralism, and national advertising expenditures," *Journal of Media Economics* 7(4):31-48. See also: Michael Dupagne and R. Jeffery Green (1996). "Revisiting the principle of relative constancy: Consumer mass media expenditures in Belgium," *Communication Research* 23(5):612-635.

16. J.L. Renaud (1995). "Counting up growth," *Television Business International*, pp. 83-84.

17. Xabier Meilan-Pita and Haoming Denis Wu (1997). "The same old pie? The constancy hypothesis revisited." Paper presented at the AEJMC, Chicago.

Summary

Offered in 1959 as a report on whether the newspaper industry could survive television, relative constancy was stated in a testable principle by Maxwell McCombs in 1972. The first statement of the principle is that the **proportion** of money spent on the mass media remains fairly constant over time. The second statement of the principle is that the economy (and family income) varies from booms to depressions, so while the proportion spent on mass media stays constant, the **actual dollars** spent on mass media will vary.

The last statement of the principle is that new media added to the media mix must fight it out with existing media. This part of the principle is called **functional equivalence**, predicting that a new medium will take its share from the existing media whose functions it most closely displaces.

Although these principles are economic concepts, they make sense from our personal knowledge and experience about the mass media. Numerous examples are presented that seem to support the principles, at least through the 1970s. But with the advent of audiovisual media such as VCRs and cable, communication researchers noticed that past principles might be changing.

Since the early 1980s, researchers have debated whether the principle of relative constancy is still valid, and have wondered if past economic constraints will pertain to the flood of new media technologies.

Exercises:

A. The path of the chapter's presentation about new media technologies leads directly to the doorstep of the Internet.

1) Describe the Internet's properties that make it a mass medium (movies have sound and moving pictures; what does the Internet offer):

(continued)

2) Given the Internet's properties you have described, list in their order, with "a" as the first, the existing mass media that are likely to be most affected as Internet use becomes more widespread:

a. _____

b. _____

c. _____

d. _____

3) Write a short essay on whether the principle of relative constancy pertains to the Internet and defend your opinion using concepts presented in the chapter.

B. Several of the articles cited in this chapter offer cogent arguments about why the principle is flawed. To study the literature on this topic, find one or more of the references that actually list theoretical or methodological weaknesses in the principle of relative constancy as originally proposed in McCombs' 1972 monograph. Provide **five** such flaws as offered by later authors. Many of these can be found in:

Michael Dupagne (1997). "A theoretical and methodological critique of the principle of relative constancy," *Communication Theory* 7(1):53-76.

However, you may take only **three** from the Dupagne article. Use the chapter's footnotes to find two others. In your own words, state the flaw succinctly, explain it briefly, and provide the citation of the article from which you took the argument.

From Dupagne:

1.

(continued)

2.

3.

From other soures (cite your source):

4.

5.

28
Cultivation

Early article: George Gerbner and Larry Gross (1976). "The scary world of TV's heavy viewer," *Psychology Today* 9(11):41-45,89.

Recent article: Scott Stossel (1997). "The man who counts the killings," *The Atlantic Monthly*, (May), pp. 86-104.

As you read this chapter, consider the following questions:

1. Compared with your classmates, are you a person who spends a lot of time watching television, or a middling amount or less than average?

2. Are you a person who is highly concerned about issues of personal safety, or about average or not very concerned?

3. What is the risk that in any given week you will be victimized or involved in violence?

4. What percent of the workforce in your community are police officers?

5. In your view, can most people be trusted?

6. To what extent do you think your views about how things are in the real world are shaped by what you see in movies, newspapers or on television?

For about as long as mass media have existed, people have been concerned about the media's power to shape what others think and how they behave. What people think, of course, is called "public opinion," and public opinion can be very powerful. Because of that, until the early 1700s, American printers were required to secure the government's permission before offering information for public distribution, and when they got permission they were expected to watch their words.

For example, James Franklin, Benjamin's brother, was jailed in 1722 for saying the governor of his province was too slow in turning away coastal pirates.[1] The truth of his information was not a defense since the principle operant at that time was "the greater the truth, the greater the libel." Franklin's criticism is mild by today's standards, but the point is that governments have long been concerned about public opinion and the media's power to influence the masses.

In the almost 275 years since the Franklin episode, the focus of public concern about the effects of media broadened from politics to culture. Many people came to believe that the media have a greater impact on the public well-being and behavior than would be desired. Increasingly, especially from the 1920s forward, academic research reflected that concern.

Do media affect our thinking and behavior, and if so, how? Given that so many people (260 million in the U.S., many millions elsewhere) spend so much of their time (several hours daily) consuming mass media, could some sort of effect **not** exist? Can you imagine watching television six hours a day, year-in, year-out, *without* being influenced in some way? And if some effect does occur, could it be reflected in behavior?

Do consumers learn only the socially desirable ideas such as knowledge of foreign cultures, science, technology and health? What about the socially undesirable content, such as murder, other types of violence, theft, promiscuity and insensitivity? These concerns apply to movies and some print media as well as television, but television draws the brunt of public attention and concern.

The media-culture connection got its first great push from the Payne Fund studies in the 1920s and 1930s, an investigation of the impact of movies on young people. Then, like now, people were concerned about the increase in violence among the young. The Payne Fund studies reported that the movies disrupted viewers' sleep, challenged and eroded moral values, over-stimulated emotions, changed attitudes for both good and ill, and provided compelling but troublesome models for behavior.[2] Sound familiar? Also important in that time period were studies of propaganda, the inflammatory and patriotic communication of combatants in the First World War. The research reflected great concern about the power of information to mobilize the population and to fortify opposition to aggression.

In the 1950s, public concern was focused on comic books. Often called "funny books," not all were funny. They presented not only fanciful and humorous

---

1. Frank Luther Mott (1962). *American journalism: A history: 1690 to 1960, 3rd ed.* New York: The MacMillan Company, p. 20.
2. Stanley J. Baran and Dennis K. Davis (1995). *Mass communication theory: Foundations, ferment and future.* Belmont, CA: Wadsworth Publishing, p. 186.

characters, but increasingly violent and vengeful ones, and children consumed the books with enthusiasm. It was not uncommon for a youngster to own a great stack of comic books, and to trade them among friends. Schramm estimated in 1958 that up to 70% of children had begun to read comic books by age 9.[3] The popular concern was the same then and now: Were the children learning dreadful things through their exposure to comics, and were the comics changing children's behavior?

In the 1960s, the struggle for control of media content broadened to include the television advertisement of cigarettes and alcohol. Congress eventually banned tobacco ads from broadcasting, and television producers voluntarily adopted a practice of keeping alcohol use by actors off-screen. (Consumption might be implied, but not shown.) Later, the pressure point moved to issues of obscenity/pornography, and more recently to issues such as indecent material on the Internet.

The cultural impact of media was articulated in the 1960s by Melvin DeFleur in his *Theories of Mass Communication* under the heading of "cultural norms theory."[4] He proposed that one way the mass media could influence behavior was through the development or manipulation of **cultural norms**:

> "....the mass media, through selective presentations and the emphasis of certain themes, create impressions among their audiences that common cultural norms concerning the emphasized topics are structured or defined in some specific way. Since individual behavior is usually guided by cultural norms...the media would then serve indirectly to influence conduct."[5]

Subsequently, the National Commission on the Causes and Prevention of Violence, 1967-68, and the Surgeon General's Scientific Advisory Committee on Television and Social Behavior, 1972, pushed the issue to the forefront of public awareness.[6] These reports and hearings examined the possible connection between what is seen in mass media and what is seen in citizens' behavior.

During that period, George Gerbner, who consulted with both the National Commission and the Surgeon General's report, initiated his study of television violence.[7] The work produced a controversial **violence index**, an annual measure

---

3. Wilbur Schramm (1960). *Mass communications*. Urbana: University of Illinois Press, p. 457.
4. Melvin L. DeFleur and Sandra J. Ball-Rokeach (1989). *Theories of mass communication, 5th ed.* New York: Longman, p. 129.
5. *Ibid.*
6. Dominic A. Infante, Andrew S. Rancer and Deanna F. Womack (1996). *Building communication theory, 3rd ed.* Prospect Heights, IL: Waveland Press, p. 383.
7. George Gerbner, Michael Morgan and Nancy Signorielli (1994). "Growing up with television: The cultivation perspective," in *Media effects: Advances in theory and research*, Jennings Bryant and Dolf Zillmann, eds. Hillsdale, NJ: Lawrence Erlbaum Associates, pp. 17-41.

of the violence being presented on network television.[8] The index was controversial because of Gerbner's definition of violence. For example, is it reasonable to call an act "violent" when Roadrunner drops one his countless bombs on Wiley Coyote? Is it "violence" when one of the Three Stooges swings a mop into the face of another? And is a verbal threat "violence?" Counting incidents of violence is fraught with problems, and Gerbner's Violence Index depended entirely on his definitions. Broadcasters claimed that the Violence Index was inflated.

In later research, Gerbner defined violence as "the overt expression of physical force (with or without a weapon, against self or others) compelling action against one's will on pain of being hurt and/or killed or threatened to be so victimized as part of the plot." He said idle threats, verbal abuse or gestures without credible violent consequences would not be coded as violence, but "accidental" and "natural" violence would be.[9]

In the early 1970s, he and his University of Pennsylvania colleagues found acts of violence in 80% of programs.[10] Gerbner believed the frequent portrayal of violence would lead viewers to **overestimate** the actual incidence of violence in the real world. He began to think of this as a **cultivating** influence of mass media in that the mass media would "cultivate" a mistaken image or impression in the public mind. For example, Gerbner asked viewers to respond to questions such as these: 1) What is the risk that in any given week you will be victimized or involved in violence? 2) In your view, can people be trusted? and 3) What percentage of all males who have jobs work in law enforcement and crime detection? Is it 1% or 5%? (1% is the correct answer; 5% is the television answer.)

Gerbner hypothesized that persons who could be categorized as heavy viewers of television, and therefore who watched countless programs that included acts of violence, would overestimate crime and deceit. In other words, heavy viewers would tend to be "cultivated" to believe the world is like it is shown on television.

Here is the logic. In the first question about the risk of being involved in violence in any given week, suppose the correct statistical answer as indicated by police records is 3%. If a greater number of people chose 5% or higher, Gerbner would conclude that the choice represented cultivation toward the media reality, which is different from life. Is that a justifiable conclusion? The method seems

---

8. George Gerbner and Larry Gross (1976). "Living with television: The violence profile," *Journal of Communication* 26(2):173-199.

9. George Gerbner, Larry Gross, Michael Morgan and Nancy Signorielli (1980). "The 'mainstreaming' of America: Violence profile No. 11," *Journal of Communication* 30(3):10-29.

10. George Gerbner, Larry Gross, Michael Morgan, Nancy Signorielli and Marilyn Jackson-Beeck (1979). "The demonstration of power: Violence profile No. 10," *Journal of Communication* 29(3):177-196.

straightforward enough, but in fact not all studies support the concept. Variables other than television use might explain an overestimate. Living in a crime-ridden area could lead to an estimate higher than the average for the wider community.

But if Gerbner's hypothesis is correct, then heavy viewers would be cultivated toward television's portrayal of reality. Because prime-time series emphasize action-drama, those who are cultivated by television programming are likely to have what Gerbner called a scary or **mean world** view: They view life as being more frightening and dangerous than it really is. If heavy television viewing actually does affect people's worldview in this way, *such media effects are powerful indeed.*

Cultivation is an intriguing concept that can be readily applied to behaviors other than crime. For example, if family interaction is ridiculed on television, might viewers come to assume that family tension is normal? If sexual promiscuity is presented as entertainment, might it lead viewers to overestimate the extent to which individuals are promiscuous?

Over the past 25 years, "cultivation" has spawned many research articles. In the 1970s-1980s, some of the assessments of the idea were sharply critical. One of the arguments was that Gerbner's data could be explained readily by factors other than cultivation, factors such as income/education and neighborhood circumstances.[11] Others concluded cultivation might exist, but only to a small extent.[12]

Gerbner and his associates countered that cultivation was real and that it was of two types, mainstreaming and resonance.[13] They said mainstreaming could be thought of as "a relative commonalty of outlooks that television tends to cultivate." (Before television, popular images were perhaps not so uniform because no single medium had sufficient coverage.)

Resonance suggests that the power of television to influence popular imagery increases when what is seen *fits the life circumstances of the viewer.* In other words, if what is seen on the screen "resonates" with the viewer — seems consistent with experience — it is more likely incorporated into the person's notion of "reality."[14]

---

11. Paul Hirsch (1980). "The 'scary world' of the nonviewer and other anomalies: A reanalysis of Gerbner et al.'s findings on cultivation analysis, Part I," *Communication Research 7* (4): 403-456.

12. Michael Hughes (1980). "The fruits of cultivation analysis: A reexamination of some effects of television watching," *Public Opinion Quarterly* 44(3):287-302.

13. George Gerbner, Larry Gross, Michael Morgan and Nancy Signorielli (1980), *op. cit.*

14. Robert P. Hawkins and Sharon Pingree (1982). "Television's influence on social reality," in David Pearl, Lorraine Bouthilet and Joyce B. Lazar, eds. *Television and behavior: Ten years of scientific progress and implications for the eighties Vol. 2, Technical Reviews.* Washington, DC: U.S. Government Printing Office, pp. 224-247.

Here are some other recent studies involving cultivation or related notions:

• Oliver and Armstrong studied enjoyment of reality-based and fictional crime tv shows.[15] The cultivation hypothesis suggests that individuals who watch a lot of crime shows are more likely to take on the tv-based "reality" of crime and victimization (to think that crime and violence is greater). The authors proposed that while cultivation researchers investigate what tv can do to individuals' beliefs, they should also investigate the role of viewers' attitudes in selecting and enjoying such programs (see Uses and Gratifications chapter).

Oliver and Armstrong concluded that reality-based programs were most enjoyed by viewers who evidenced higher levels of authoritarianism, reported greater punitiveness about crime and reported higher levels of racial prejudice. What does this mean for cultivation research? For one thing, cultivationists might want to control for such attitude measures to learn their impact on the cultivation effect. For another, it shows that the cultivation effect might be deeper than simply the number of hours of viewing.

• Potter and Chang pointed out that any cultivation test must have at least two measures, cultivation and exposure to television.[16] The cultivation measure usually is an estimate of the meanness or violence found in a respondent's world. Exposure to television is measured as the number of hours "on an average day" or the number of evenings per week in which tv is viewed "at least one hour." Other measures include the diary method and check-list, and ordinal response options (always, a lot, once in a while). As these measures do not all produce the same estimate of viewing, Potter and Chang investigated whether one measurement of tv viewing produced stronger correlations with the cultivation "violence" measure.

The researchers concluded that the *least* successful measure of tv exposure was "total viewing," e.g., a measure of viewing "on an average day," and the *best* measure was a "proportional" measure, for example the exposure to programs relevant to the cultivation idea. In other words, proportional viewing among program types "is a better predictor of cultivation than is total viewing."

• Potter investigated the development of a "television reality" among adolescents. The concept "reality" is a linchpin of cultivation theory, with television helping to construct reality for the viewer, or at least some viewers. Presumably, young people are more vulnerable to a television-imposed reality than older people.

---

15. Mary Beth Oliver and G. Blake Armstrong (1995). "Predictors of viewing and enjoyment of reality-based and fictional crime shows," *Journalism & Mass Communication Quarterly* 72(3):559-570.

16. James W. Potter and Ik Chgin Chang (1990). "Television exposure measures and the cultivation hypothesis," *Journal of Broadcasting & Electronic Media* 34(3):313-333.

In a five-year panel study, Potter found that the youngest respondents were inclined to see television as a "magic window," but that their reliance subsequently turned to a "utility" function and then an "identity" function. He concluded that youngsters' views of television reality are complex and dynamic.[17]

What is the status of cultivation research today? The jury is still out, so to speak, as some researchers support the concept and others question its existence.[18] But the reader is invited to reflect again on an earlier point: Can people watch *so much* television without learning *something*? And if they learn something, what do they learn? Is it positive and constructive, what might be called pro-social learning,[19] or anti-social or both?

Cultivation theory seems plausible, but the research has not consistently or perhaps even preponderantly supported it. How could this be? Are the research methods faulty? Is the research question too broad? And as a result of uncertainties, will cultivation theory go the way of some other theories that held intuitive appeal but lacked empirical support?

Stay tuned!

Summary

Since the earliest days of print media, radio and television, people have been concerned about the ability of these media to affect behavior. In the 1920s, the concern was about how youthful behavior might be affected by the burgeoning movie industry. In the 1950s, the concern was for comic books. In the 1960s, the concern broadened to include television. Pornography and crime were of particular concern. More recently, the focus of concern is television and movie violence.

DeFleur wrote of the ability of mass media to define **cultural norms**. Gerbner said the mass media **cultivate** a perception of reality that mirrors what is seen in the media. He subsequently refined the idea to suggest a **mainstreaming** effect (commonalty of outlooks) and a **resonance** effect (the impact is greater when the media images fit the life circumstances of the viewer).

Voluminous research on cultivation, several of which are presented in the chapter, has produced a mixed bag of results, but research on the topic continues.

17. James W. Potter (1992). "How do adolescents' perceptions of television reality change over time?" *Journalism Quarterly 69*(2):392-405.

18. Barrie Gunter (1994). "The question of media violence," in Jennings Bryant and Dolf Zillmann, eds. *Media effects: Advances in theory and research, op. cit.*, pp. 163-211.

19. Alexis S. Tan (1985). *Mass communication theories and research, 2nd ed.* New York: John Wiley & Sons, p. 299.

Exercises:

A. Have you heard of a social problem (such as the rate of crime in your community) today that was different years ago? For example, have you heard that in the 1940s and 1950s many people felt secure enough in their homes to not lock their doors at night? But what about the facts: how does the crime rate today compare with the rates of an earlier time in your home town or state?

Here is another question: Do you think the frequency of television-crime-as-entertainment has increased in the past two-to-three decades? And is it the case today that the crime rate is not so bad as people think it is? If that is so, are people getting a wrong impression that crime is rampant?

In a **two**-page essay, address those questions. Include a critique of cultivation theory. Try to support or condemn it. What social problem/life condition of today, other than crime, might illustrate the cultivation theory? Consider interviewing senior citizens about how they see the changing perception of crime.

B. Use your library's search mechanisms to find and read at least one journal article by George Gerbner, and another written by Hirsch or Hughes (see footnotes). Write a synopsis of Gerbner's research method and findings, including an evaluation of the piece, and a synopsis of one of the other authors' critiques of Gerbner's method.

C. Following is a brief questionnaire for you to fill out. Your instructor might wish to tabulate responses of all who participate in order to describe or illustrate individuals' responses to issues of personal safety in your town.

Cultivation Survey Instrument
Please answer the following questions. Do not discuss your responses with your classmates; your responses should be your own.

1. Please give your estimate of how much time per day you
spend watching television, on average, to the nearest half-hour: _____

2. When you watch television, do you have a preference for a particular kind of program? Select your single **top choice** from the following list:

a. sit-com	d. talk-show	g. game show
b. movies	e. sports	h. news/weather
c. action-drama	f. soaps	i. other
		j. no preference

If you said "other," please explain: _____

3. Do you watch television mostly (if at all) in the:
   a. mornings (6 a.m. to noon)
   b. afternoons (noon to 6 p.m.)
   c. evenings (6 p.m. to 11:30)
   d. late nights (11:30 to 6 a.m.)

4. Please indicate your gender: _____ male _____ female

5. Do you agree with the statement, "Most people can be trusted"? (*check one blank*)

/_____/_____/_____/_____/_____/
   strongly   agree   undecided   disagree   strongly
   agree   disagree

6. What is your chance of being the victim of criminal violence in any given year?

/_____/_____/_____/_____/_____/
   highly   unlikely   somewhat   likely   very
   unlikely   unlikely   unlikely

7. If you walk alone near your home, what is your chance of being a crime victim?

/_____/_____/_____/_____/_____/
   highly   unlikely   somewhat   likely   very
   unlikely   unlikely   unlikely

8. How safe are children in the community of your residence?

/_____/_____/_____/_____/_____/
   extremely   very   somewhat   not very   extremely
   safe   safe   safe   safe   unsafe

9. Would walking alone in your town's downtown section after dark concern you?

/_____/_____/_____/_____/_____/
   extremely   very   somewhat   not very   not at all
   concerned   concerned   concerned   concerned   concerned

At the instructor's discretion, the responses of the class will be tabulated and discussed. What do you anticipate others will have said about their concern for crime and personal safety? Will their views be correlated with the amount of time they spend watching television? Be prepared to discuss.

29

Spiral of Silence

Founding article: Elisabeth Noelle-Neumann (1974). "The spiral of silence: A theory of public opinion," *Journal of Communication* 24(2):43-51.

Recent article: Carroll J. Glynn, Andrew F. Hayes and James Shanahan (1997). "Perceived support for ones opinions and willingness to speak out: A meta-analysis of survey studies on the 'spiral of silence,'" *Public Opinion Quarterly* 61(3):452-463.

As you read this unit consider the following:

1. If you were in a van with acquaintances, and a startling political statement came on the radio, are you likely to be the first in the group to comment on it? If not, why not?

2. Given the same scenario, would your decision to comment depend on the circumstances? For example, would it depend on your degree of familiarity with the others in the van? Can you think of other circumstances that might matter?

3. Do you generally assess the attitude of people around you before venturing an opinion, so as to avoid saying something that might isolate you from others?

One of the most profound expressions of mass media power is public opinion, a shifting consensus about what is and ought to be. What was public opinion yesterday might not be so today. Shifts in public opinion come with the introduction of new or revised information, and in these days of electronic technology they come swiftly. The speed of opinion change is vastly different from the days when information was largely disseminated by the press and by word-of-mouth. Today, public opinion in some cases can develop almost instantly. Public opinion is an important area of research in several disciplines, including communication theory.

In 1974, the German pollster Elisabeth Noelle-Neumann introduced her "spiral of silence" as an attempt to explain in part how public opinion is formed (see chapter's Founding article). Her thinking about the spiral probably was colored by her social and political experience in Germany before World War Two. As she formulated the theory, she was aware that the German people had in the 1930s-1940s adopted and supported wrong political positions that subsequently led to national defeat, humiliation and ruin. She must have wondered: How did it all happen? American researchers have wondered the same thing.

Christopher Simpson of American University critiqued the "spiral of silence" in the context of Noelle-Neumann's social and political background.[1] He asked: "To what extent did the social and political events of Noelle-Neumann's early life, particularly her association with Josef Goebbels' Ministry for Popular Enlightenment and Propaganda, shape her later articulation of the 'spiral of silence'?"

Simpson concluded that the ideas she nurtured before and during WW II continued to shape her thinking and her work as the pre-eminent public opinion pollster in Germany, and that her *Schweigespirale* (spiral theory) reveals more about her and her times than it does about the formation of public opinion. In other words, the theory is more a manifestation of her personal and political histor than it is a universal phenomenon (See Social Construction chapter). However, the spiral of silence has enough persuasiveness about it to retain the interest of the research community, and numerous researchers have supported it, at least in some degree.[2]

Spiral of silence theory

Noelle-Neumann proposed that when a new idea is broached among strangers, individuals react in characteristic ways. She said they make a quick assessment to see whether their own private thinking might be supported by the others around them. This quick check was said to be quasi-statistical (people assess or mentally "count" their level of support in the group). She was expressing the point that

---

1. Christopher Simpson (1996). "Elisabeth Noelle-Neumann's 'spiral of silence' and the historical context of communication theory," *Journal of Communication* 46(3):149-173.

2. Elsa Louise Mohn (1983). "Testing the spiral of silence theory of public opinion." Paper presented at the annual meeting of the Midwestern Association for Public Opinion Research, Chicago. See also: Diana C. Mutz (1989). "The influence of perceptions of media influence: Third person effects and the public expression of opinions," *International Journal of Public Opinion Research* 1(1):3-23; Michael B. Salwen, Carolyn Lin and Frances R. Matera (1994). "Willingness to discuss 'official English': A test of three communities," *Journalism Quarterly* 71(2):282-90; Hiroshi Tokinoya (1989). "Testing the spiral of silence theory in East Asia," *KEIO Communication Review* 10:35-49; Terry Wedel (1994). *The spiral of silence in popular culture: Applying a public opinion theory to radio station popularity*. Unpublished thesis, California State University, Fullerton; Carroll J. Glynn (1989). "Perceptions of others' opinions as a component of public opinion," *Social Science Research* 18(1):53-69.

everybody has this **quasi-statistical organ** or sense about whether their opinion is acceptable to the group. For example, if standing in a group of young professional women, a person might calculate the likely support level before commenting that verbal sexual harassment should be protected as a freedom of speech issue.

If the "calculation" indicates support for an opinion, people will be more likely to speak up; without support, they will be more likely to remain silent. If some people remain silent, the ones who do speak up would then seem to have even greater support on their side, and so they could be bolder. The combined **boldness of one side and the silence of the other creates the spiral of silence**.

Noelle-Neumann reasoned that people's reluctance to take an unpopular position is based on **fear of isolation**. She said: "To the individual, not isolating himself is more important than his non-judgement. This appears to be a condition of life in human society; if it were otherwise, sufficient integration could not be achieved." (see Founding article). She added it is not only fear of isolation but **doubt about one's capacity for judgment** that makes the individual vulnerable, and she pointed out that social groups can punish members who do not conform to group standards with ostracism. She extrapolated from individuals' willingness to speak out in their social groups to a community's or an entire nation's willingness to speak out if the populace perceives their view is a minority position.

In fact, the viewpoint may be one that *is* shared by the majority, but people's refusal to speak out may cause the position to dwindle to that of a minority position. Noelle-Neumann expounded on these aspects of the theory in book form.[3] She called the effect **pluralistic ignorance**, the result that a large group of people may erroneously believe that the direction and strength of public opinion on an issue is exactly opposite what it really is.[4]

What is the overwhelming view that the public holds about abortion? Abortion rights supporters often remain in the background. Current law supports their position, so they are content to remain quiet unless an incident triggers them to speak out. But those who are against abortion have been vocal in their opposition. Almost every community in America has one or more billboards that are either "pro-life" or dramatically anti-abortion. Churches generally agree that abortion is taking the life of an unborn, but living person. Anti-abortion commercials are common on television, sponsored by a variety of national church and civic groups. Pickets have lined sidewalks at abortion clinics for years, and the media frequently report about

---

3. Elisabeth Noelle-Neumann (1993). *The spiral of silence: Public opinion, our social skin, 2nd ed.* Chicago: The University of Chicago Press.
4. Hubert J. O'Gorman and Stephen L. Garry (1976). "Pluralistic ignorance: A replication and extension," *Public Opinion Quarterly* 40(4):449-458.

bombing incidents and protesters who chain themselves to abortion clinic fences. Legislatures in dozens of states pass anti-abortion laws every year, and there seems to be overwhelming support for a constitutional amendment outlawing abortion.

An observer, perhaps a visitor from Bulgaria, might assume that Americans are strongly anti-abortion. Yet if public opinion polls in the United States are correct, Americans favor the current legal decisions on abortion rights by a majority of at least 65%. This two-thirds majority view has remained stable for at least 30 years, but those who agree with it may perceive themselves to be in the minority. Few people would be comfortable making a strong pro-abortion statement in unfamiliar surroundings (perhaps not even in this class).

According to the spiral of silence theory, the campaigns waged against *Roe vs. Wade* (the Supreme Court case that legalized abortion in 1973), should have had an effect on public opinion. The more vocal and more visible anti-abortion group should have eroded attitudes by making those who favored abortion perceive they were in the minority. Believing that their views were minority views, pro-abortion individuals should have changed their opinion. This is what the spiral of silence predicts, but polls seem to refute the spiral of silence effect. Similar social issues may include owning handguns, the right to place indecent material on the Internet, affirmative action policies and a host of other issues where one side mobilizes an information campaign that is designed to sway public opinion. Spiral of silence predicts that the *perception* of a dominant viewpoint will result in actual dominance by that viewpoint.

A study done in Orange County California presents the spiral of silence idea as applied to liberal vs. conservative political opinion.[5] Orange County was a conservative stronghold with 55% of voters being Republican and only 35% being Democrat when the surveys were done in 1988-89. Three random telephone surveys asked Orange County voters their party affiliation and then sought their willingness to discuss their views with a reporter. This study reported no support for the spiral of silence theory. Democrats were as willing as Republicans to speak out despite their known minority opinion.

While several researchers have supported her theory, others have identified its weaknesses.[6] Glynn and McLeod said the idea was open to criticism from both theoretical and methodological grounds, and that Noelle-Neumann's concepts

---

5. Cheryl Katz and Mark Bladassare (1992). "Using the 'L-word' in public: A test of the spiral of silence in conservative Orange County, California," *Public Opinion Quarterly* 56(2):232-235.

6. D. Garth Taylor (1982). "Pluralistic ignorance and the spiral of silence: A formal analysis," *Public Opinion Quarterly* 46(3):311-335. See also: J. David Kennamer (1990). "Self-serving biases in perceiving the opinions of others: Implications for the spiral of silence," *Communication Research* 17(3):393-404; Yassin Ahmed Lashin (1984). *Testing the spiral of silence hypothesis: Toward an integrated theory of public opinion*. Unpublished dissertation, University of Illinois at Urbana-Champaign.

were not always clearly explained.[7] Using data from U.S. elections, they found only partial support for the theory. They added, however, that the idea held important implications and urged working out the theory's definitional entanglements.

The 1991 Gulf War presented another opportunity to test the hypothesis. Was U.S. support for the war really a consensus view, or did media coverage contribute to a spiral of silence that dampened opposition to the war? In a survey that asked about people's opinions, what they thought others believed, their information sources, demographics and political predispositions, respondents were clearly less supportive of the war than the popular support depicted by the media. Those who watched television and perceived that the public supported the war, were more likely to support the war themselves. This study supports the spiral of silence and suggests that people are swayed by bandwagon effects rather than fearing social isolation.[8]

Research on the spiral of silence has not approached the frequency and depth of such topics as cultivation and agenda setting, but the idea has intrigued researchers internationally for a quarter-century.[9] Glynn, Hayes and Shanahan (see chapter opening Recent article) tried to make sense of the accumulating data by conducting what is called a meta-analysis of spiral-theory articles. **Meta-analysis** is a process by which the researchers reduce diverse studies to a so-called common metric, such as a correlation coefficient, to decide whether the literature as a whole suggests a significant effect,[10] in this case a spiral of silence effect.

Based on 17 published articles and conference papers that involved some 9,500 respondents, Glynn et al. concluded there was a "very small but statistically significant relationship between the degree to which a person believes others hold similar opinions and the willingness to express those opinions." Correlations ranged from -.10 to 0 to +.25, but most were very small. Nineteen correlations were positive and three negative.

Despite the statistical significance, Glynn et al. concluded there was "little evidence" to support the claim that willingness to express opinions is influenced by perceived support for those opinions. They said the failure of research to support

7. Carroll J. Glynn and Jack McLeod (1984). "Public opinion du jour: An examination of the spiral of silence," *Public Opinion Quarterly* 48(4):731-740.

8. William P. Eveland Jr., Douglas M. McLeod and Nancy Signorielli (1995). "Actual and perceived U.S. public opinion: The spiral of silence during the Persian Gulf War," *International Journal of Public Opinion Research* 7(2):91-109.

9. Charles T. Salmon and F. Gerald Kline (1985). "The spiral of silence ten years later: An examination and evaluation," in Keith R. Sanders, Lynda Lee Kaid and Dan Nimmo, eds. *Political Communication Yearbook 1984*. Carbondale, IL: Southern Illinois University Press, pp. 3-30.

10. John E. Hunter, Frank L. Schmidt and Gregg B. Jackson (1982). *Meta-analysis: Cumulating research findings across studies*. Beverly Hills, CA: Sage.

the spiral might be due in part to faulty measures, and they suggested that future research should concentrate on *observation* of willingness to speak out rather than on *hypothetical* (questionnaire-based) measures.

Summary

The spiral of silence theory was presented by Noelle-Neumann in 1974. The research has been criticized for ambiguity and for methodological weaknesses, but the idea has persisted.

Among precepts of the theory are that before speaking out people employ a **quasi-statistical organ** or sense about whether their opinion is acceptable to the group. If they perceive support, people will be more likely to speak up; without support, they remain silent. If some people remain silent, those who speak up seem to have even greater support on their side and can speak more boldly. The combined **boldness of one side and the silence of the other creates the spiral of silence**.

People are wary of speaking out because they **fear of isolation** and they may **doubt their capacity for judgment**. The effect of not speaking out is **pluralistic ignorance**, or a large group of people erroneously believing that the direction and strength of public opinion on an issue is exactly opposite what it really is.

Evidence of the spiral effect is usually in trace (very small) amounts. A meta-analysis of 17 research articles on the topic revealed a small but significant effect. The meta-analysts suggested that direct observation of the effect might be better than a hypothetical measure.

Exercises:

A. Identify and record below a topic that involves controversy and importance. It can be proximal or distant, but preferably one that is "emerging," not one for which nearly everyone has already fixed an opinion. The topic could be something seen recently in the news.

Topic:

Assuming the topic you chose can be put in an agree/disagree context, give your best estimate of the percent of students in your class (and school) who feel as you do on the issue:

Percent of class who agree: _____   Percent of school who agree: _____

Is your own position on the *majority* side or on the *minority* side (*circle one*)?

majority   minority

Now imagine the following: You are in a group of 10 of your classmates, people known only casually to you, and the talk is generally light until a controversial issue is broached. How likely are you, after estimating the level of support for your position, to speak your mind on the issue?

/_____/_____/_____/_____/
extremely   somewhat   somewhat   extremely
likely   likely   <u>un</u>likely   <u>un</u>likely

If you spoke up, only to find your position was not widely shared, would you feel isolated?

Write your comments below about the usefulness or legitimacy of the spiral of silence concept:

B. If a person is **unwilling** to speak up, could it be because of something *positive*, rather than something *negative* (fear of isolation, ostracism)? For example, could it be because the speaker simply does not want to offend a listener, as tact sometimes requires? Or, if a person does speak up, could it be due to that person's own psychological makeup (outspoken; insensitive) more than a social construction? As you imagine yourself in such situations, what variables or conditions might contribute to how a discussion might develop? Write a maximum **one**-page essay on this topic.

C. Focus on *this class* and answer what you believe will be the *majority* class opinion for each topic. Your answers may be part of an in-class discussion.

1. The work load required in this class is: too much   reasonable

2. Foreign cars are: better than American   worse than American

3. The president should be a: Democrat   Republican

4. Sexual harassment in the workplace is: overstated   understated

5. Today's movies are too violent: yes   no

6. Most welfare recipients are: African American   white

7. Burning the American flag should be a crime: yes   no

8. The FBI should keep a file on all U.S. neo-Nazis: yes   no

9. A second rape conviction should
    require a penalty of mandatory castration: agree   disagree

10. Assisted suicide should be a felony: agree   disagree

30

Third-Person Effect

Stephen A. Banning
Texas A&M University

Founding article: W. Phillips Davison (1983). "The third-person effect in communication," *Public Opinion Quarterly* 47(1):1-15.

Recent article: Vincent Price, Li-Ning Huang and David Tewksbury (1997). "Third-person effects of news coverage: Orientations toward media," *Journalism & Mass Communications Quarterly* 74(3):525-540.

Before beginning this chapter on the third-person effect hypothesis, spend a few moments answering these six questions that foreshadow the chapter's content:

1. Who do you think would be more likely to be influenced by advertisements in general, *you* or *other people in this country*? (Circle one number on the continuum below; "0" indicates equal influence.)

     ME   -5 -4 -3 -2 -1 0 1 2 3 4 5   OTHERS

2. Who do you think would be more likely to be influenced by a tabloid newspaper article such as the *National Enquirer*, *you* or *other people in this country*?

     ME   -5 -4 -3 -2 -1 0 1 2 3 4 5   OTHERS

3. Who do you think would be more likely to be influenced by negative political advertisements in general, *you* or *other people in this country*?

     ME   -5 -4 -3 -2 -1 0 1 2 3 4 5   OTHERS

4. Who do you think would be more likely to be influenced by a violent movie, *you* or *other people in this country*?

      ME   -5 -4 -3 -2 -1   0   1   2   3   4   5   OTHERS

5. Who do you think would be more likely to be influenced by a public service announcement, *you* or *other people in this country*?

      ME   -5 -4 -3 -2 -1   0   1   2   3   4   5   OTHERS

6. Who do you think would be more likely to be influenced by a talk radio commentator, *you* or *other people in this country*?

      ME   -5 -4 -3 -2 -1   0   1   2   3   4   5   OTHERS

Now add all the negative scores together and subtract their total from the total of positive scores. Your total score may be negative, so include the sign.

Score: _____

The questions you answered may show whether you see yourself as less vulnerable to media messages than others. Any question in which you circled zero indicates that there was no effect for that particular question. If everyone saw themselves as being just as vulnerable to media effects as everyone else, most people would circle zero on these questions and the average of all six scores would tend to be zero. However, research indicates a tendency for people to believe others are *more* affected by media messages. In the set of six questions above, this latter tendency known as the third-person effect would show up in scores with a positive number.

The scales used in this series of questions (-5 through zero to plus 5) might seem peculiar. For example, each question is really asking two questions: 1) who is more influenced, me or others; and, 2) to what extent? Also, the scale numbers are not labeled: What value is a person indicating when giving a -3 or a 2 response? Still, the scale used here is the one that many third-person effect researchers used. (See Media Use Inventory chapter, questions No. 8 and 9.)

Exercise 1:

If the class completed the Media Use Inventory questionnaire, calculate your score on questions 8 and 9 using a method similar to that described above for the six opening questions in this chapter. Compare your score on the two Media Use Inventory questions to the score you got for the six questions in this unit. Be prepared to discuss the outcome and implications in class.

The **third-person effect** is: 1) the tendency of people to believe message effects are greater on others than on themselves and 2) that this tendency is an overestimation (it's not true). The third-person effect is thought to be an ego-related phenomenon in that people see themselves in a better position to judge the effects of the media. There may be a tendency to believe that others are gullible, and that others are more likely to believe what they see and hear from the media.

If your score on the six questions were averaged with all the others in class, and that average is a positive number, then the entire class will have shown a third-person effect. This is what the hypothesis says will happen. A score with a negative sign would indicate a reverse third-person effect, which will be discussed later. It is possible that individuals and/or the entire class did not show a third-person effect. This happens occasionally, and researchers are trying to find out why.

Consider the implications of the third-person effect. If people generally tend to think that others are more influenced by media messages than they are, such a view could affect the entire society. But how? For example, how might the stock market be influenced by media reports of a slight dip? How might voter turnout in an election be influenced by media reports that one candidate is a front-runner? Of the many ways the tendency might impact society, decide if those influences are good or bad. If the impacts seem to have negative effects on society, your thinking is similar to those who research this tendency.

The research into this tendency is too recent to be very extensive. In a 1983 article in *Public Opinion Quarterly*,[1] Davison coined the term the third-person effect for the tendency, because, he said, people see others or *third-persons* as more affected by media messages then they see themselves to be. Davison also claimed that the amount of a message's effect attributed to others was an overestimation.

Davison used an illustration of a U.S.-held island in the South Pacific during World War II in which the Japanese dropped leaflets intended for African-American soldiers, encouraging them to desert their troops. Davison notes that the leaflets did not appear to affect the African-American soldiers, who knew propaganda when they saw it. However, the message did effect the white commander, who overestimated the leaflets' impact and pulled African-Americans off the Island.[2]

---

1. W. Phillips Davison (1983). "The third-person effect in communication," *Public Opinion Quarterly* 47(1):1-15.
   2. *Ibid.*, pp. 1, 2.

Davison claimed that this simple tendency could have **great effects** on society in many areas, including censorship, propaganda and consumer behavior.[3]

Since 1983 many researchers have shared Davison's concern for the potentially harmful impact of the third-person effect on freedom of speech.[4] One concern is libel damage awards. Juries in libel cases often must estimate the damage caused by a message: essentially to assess the effect of a message on third-persons.[5] If the effect is present, the jury will tend to overestimate the impact of the libel on others. This could result in a pattern of overcompensating the amount of damages awarded.[6]

Another implication of the third-person effect is on election coverage. Mutz noted: "Despite the more restrained conclusions of academic researchers, campaign managers perceive media coverage to be highly influential in persuading voters." Mutz added that even if the media content does not influence the public, it has a great impact on elections because people think the media content influences the public.[7]

The third-person effect could also be partly responsible for what Washington, D.C., critics call the beltway mentality. The **beltway mentality** concept suggests that politicians inside the District of Columbia beltway are removed from the real world and often miscalculate public opinion as a result.

If it is true that people tend to overestimate the impact of the media on others, the third-person effect may result in poor decision making and poor public policy. Platform speeches, legislation and election-year issues may be particularly susceptible to the third-person effect. Because of this threat to representative leadership, the third-person effect is a threat to the concept of a democratic government itself.

---

3. *Op. cit.*, p. 14.

4. Michael B. Salwen (1997). "Perceptions of media power and fairness in campaign '96: The third-person effect and support for press restrictions." Paper presented at the Association for Education in Journalism and Mass Communication (AEJMC), Chicago. See also: Diana C. Mutz (1989). "The influence of perceptions of media influence: Third-person effects and the public expression of opinions," *International Journal of Public Opinion Research* 1(1):3-23; Changhyun Lee and Seungchan Yang (1996). "Third-person perception and support for censorship of sexually explicit visual content: A Korean case." Paper presented at AEJMC, Anaheim, CA; Mark A. Paxton (1995). *The third-person effect and attitudes toward freedom of expression.* Unpublished dissertation, University of Tennessee-Knoxville.

5. Albert Gunther (1991). "What we think others think: Cause and consequence in the third-person effect," *Communication Research* 18(3):355-372.

6. Laurie Mason (1995). "Newspaper as repeater: An experiment on defamation and the third-person effect," *Journalism & Mass Communication Quarterly* 72(3):610-620.

7. Diana C. Mutz, *op. cit.*, p. 4. For more on election impacts and the third-person effect, see also: Yu-Wei Hu (1996). "Testing a theoretical model on the third-person effect: Perceived impacts of election polls." Paper presented at AEJMC, Anaheim, CA; Yu-Wei Hu and Yi-Chen Wu (1997). "The third-person effect of election news: The synthesis of contingent factors in a causal model." Paper presented at AEJMC, Chicago.

Research findings

While the research is too scant to call the third-person effect a theory, it has gained enough support to be considered a strong hypothesis. Specific information on the third-person effect has been difficult to uncover. While knowing that the third-person effect seems to exist can alert people to its potential dangers, lack of knowledge about what causes the effect prevents controlling it. Researchers do have ideas about what drives the third-person effect in certain studies. The problem has been finding all of the aspects that work together to create the third-person effect.

One way to think of the third-person effect research process is as a "who-done-it" investigation. Imagine a scene from a Sherlock Holmes story in which the famous detective is trying to track down the cause of several mysterious murders. The detective's first task is to look for evidence that the deaths were in fact murders, and that there is an actual criminal to investigate. The next task is to try to find the identity of the criminal. Finally, with a good description of the perpetrator in hand, the detective finds and arrests the culprit, rendering society safe again.

Using the detective analogy, research into the third-person effect is between the second and third stage. Researchers are quite sure that the third-person effect exists, accomplishing task No. 1. The current priority is to describe it in more detail, and attempt to discover how to control it. When researchers achieve task No. 3, they will be able to assess its dangers and recommend how best to limit its harmful effects.

In the second stage of investigation, several studies identified factors that seem to increase or decrease the level of the third-person effect. First is the research on the message *receiver* , followed by research on *the message itself*. Mutz looked at the third-person effect in relation to message importance: Is the effect greater for messages perceived as important? Results indicated that greater **issue salience**, or perceived importance, creates a greater third-person effect. People who thought a message was important were more likely to display a greater third-person effect.[8]

Perloff did a similar study focusing on **ego-involvement** in relation to the third-person effect.[9] This study indicated that people with a strong political *partisan*

---

8. Mutz, *op. cit.*, pp. 3-23. For other studies on issue salience and the third-person effect see also: H. Allen White (1995). "Issue involvement and argument strength as mediating factors in the third-person effect." Paper presented at AEJMC, Washington, DC; Frances R. Matera and Michael B. Salwen (1997). "Issue salience and the third-person effect: Perceptions of illegal immigration in a Southwestern region." Paper presented at AEJMC, Chicago.

9. Richard M. Perloff (1989). "Ego-involvement and the third-person effect of televised news coverage," *Communication Research* 16(2):236-262. In regard to self concept and the third-person effect, see also: Li-Ning Huang (1995). "The role of the self in the third-person effect: A view from cognitive and motivational perspectives." Paper presented at AEJMC, Washington, DC; David Prabu and Melissa A. Johnson (1997). "The role of self in third-person effect: Perceived influence of media on women's body image factors." Paper presented at AEJMC, Chicago.

position tended to have a higher third-person effect in regard to political messages, while people with a neutral political position had less of a third-person effect.

Lasorsa did a study in 1989 that looked at **perceived expertise** as a possible independent variable of the third-person effect. Perceived expertise is similar to Mutz's issue salience and Perloff's ego-involvement. Lasorsa noted that while there was much concern that a television mini-series would have major impact on public opinion, it didn't. The study also indicated that those who believed they were experts on the subject were more likely to exhibit a third-person effect.[10]

Another study on ego-involvement was based on the idea that **partisanship**, liking or disliking a political candidate, impacts the third-person effect. Specifically, Cohen and Davis sought to determine if a person's feelings toward a political candidate would influence the third-person effect among people who perceived themselves as experts. The study results indicated that when an individual supported a candidate, the individual was more likely to believe others would be more affected by negative political advertisements about the candidate.[11] In other words, die-hard Republicans or Democrats are more likely to experience a third-person effect when they hear negative media messages about their candidate for president.

Other message receiver aspects were researched by Tiedge et al. The results indicated that the third-person effect seems to depend on the message receiver's **education level** and **age**. Those with higher education or who were older had more of a third-person effect, seeing themselves as less influenced by media messages.[12]

Other researchers have examined the messages themselves. Gunther explored the third-person effect on libel trials. He hypothesized that **source credibility** would affect the level of the third-person effect. More specifically, he sought to determine if more credible media message sources (*The New York Times* vs. the *National Enquirer*) increased the third-person effect. Subjects who read an article attributed to the *NYT*, believed the article would affect others to a greater extent than was indicated by the subjects who had read the article attributed to the *Enquirer*. The greater credibility of the *NYT* created a greater third-person effect.[13]

---

10. Dominic L. Lasorsa (1989). "Real and perceived effects of 'Amerika,'" *Journalism Quarterly* 66(2):373-378, 529. For more studies on television and the third-person effect, see also: Guy E. Lometti, Linda L. Ashby and Wendy Welch (1994). "The nature of the public's objections to television programs: An examination of third-person effects." Paper presented at AEJMC, Atlanta.

11. Jeremy Cohen and Robert G. Davis (1991). "Third-person effects and the differential impact in negative political advertising," *Journalism Quarterly* 68(4):680-688.

12. James T. Tiedge, Arthur Silverblatt, Michael J. Havice and Richard Rosenfeld (1991). "Discrepancy between perceived first-person and perceived third-person mass media effects," *Journalism Quarterly* 68(1-2):141-153.

13. Albert Gunther (1991), *op. cit.*

Gunther and Thorson looked at **emotional intensity** of message content in relation to the third-person effect. The study indicated that the higher an advertisement's emotional intensity, the greater the reverse third-person effect elicited. A **reverse** third-person effect means people perceive themselves to be more affected by a message than others. Non-emotional messages elicited a third-person effect.

The Gunther and Thorson study also looked at **message type** to see if type determined a greater third-person effect. The researchers compared commercial ads with public service announcements (PSAs) and found a third-person effect for the ads but not for the PSAs. Gunther and Thorson indicate the positive nature of PSAs in general reduced the subjects' need to claim others were more influenced than they, themselves, were. The researchers suggested the positive or negative nature of the message influences the third-person effect.[14] People may see being influenced by PSAs as positive, and being influenced by commercials as improper.

Society sometimes looks at those who are easily influenced as weak and not in control. Perhaps people subconsciously regard the possibility of being personally affected by a message for a product with a stigma because people do not want to feel gullible, weak or easily influenced.

Using the DARE program as a hypothetical example, young people involved in such a program might not report that the program affected them. Young people might deny being influenced because there may be a societal peer stigma attached to being persuaded by a police officer. If a greater third-person effect were created by the message stigma, young people in a DARE program might not report being affected even if the program had influenced them. This line of reasoning suggests that the third-person effect may result in inaccurate program evaluations.

Related concepts

As the third-person effect hypothesis has been investigated, researchers have found that it seems to be related to several other communication concepts. Three of these concepts are differential impact, pluralistic ignorance and the spiral of silence.

The differential impact hypothesis is broader than the third-person effect hypothesis. The third-person effect hypothesis states that people will see others as affected by a media message to a greater extent than they themselves would be

---

14. Albert Gunther and Esther Thorson (1992). "Perceived persuasive effects of product commercials and public service announcements: Third-person effects in new domains," *Communication Research* 19(5):574-596. See also: Ekaterina Ognianova, Robert Meeds, Esther Thorson and James Coyle (1996). "Political adwatches and the third-person effect." Paper presented at AEJMC, Anaheim, CA; Hernando Rojas, Dhavan V. Shah and Ronald J. Fabar (1995). "For the good of others: Censorship and the third-person effect." Paper presented at AEJMC, Washington, DC.

affected, and that this is an overestimation of reality. The **differential impact** hypothesis merely states that people see others as being affected by a media message *differently* than they believe they themselves would be affected.[15]

Pluralistic ignorance occurs when people believe others are more different from themselves than is actually the case. The concept of pluralistic ignorance existed before the third-person effect,[16] and the third-person effect can be seen as a specific variety of pluralistic ignorance in that the third-person effect is the result of people believing others are different from themselves regarding a reaction to a media message.

The spiral of silence hypothesis is also seen as being related to the third-person effect. The **spiral of silence** hypothesis suggests that people are less likely to voice support for opinions they perceive as less popular, causing the perceived unpopular opinions to get less and less support (see Spiral of Silence chapter).[17]

This overview of related concepts reveals an important aspect of the third-person effect hypothesis. While the third-person effect hypothesis indicates that media messages can ultimately have great effects on society, the effects are *not* seen as the direct result of a persuasive message alone. In other words, instead of receiving a message and reacting to it as some traditional communication models have suggested, the third-person effect suggests people receive a message and the persuasion is based partly on how much people believe other people are affected by the message.[18] In simpler terms, researchers believe subconscious *peer pressure* may be an important factor in how people process a message.

---

15. Tom R. Tyler and Fay Lomax Cook (1984). "The mass media and judgments of risk: Distinguishing impact on personal and societal level judgments," *Journal of Personality and Social Psychology* 47(4):693-708.

16. Hubert O'Gorman and Sedman L. Garry (1976). "Pluralistic ignorance: A replication and extension," *Public Opinion Quarterly* 40:449-458. See also: L. Erwin Atwood (1994). "Illusions of media power: The third-person effect," *Journalism Quarterly* 71(2):269-281; Tamara K. Baldwin (1991). *Response to an earthquake prediction in Southeast Missouri: A study in pluralistic ignorance.* Unpublished dissertation, Southern Illinois University at Carbondale; Insook Kim (1996). *The impact of communication behaviors and the third-person effect on pluralistic ignorance about environmental issues in South Korea before and after environmental campaigns.* Unpublished dissertation, Southern Illinois University at Carbondale.

17. Elizabeth Noelle-Neumann (1974). "The spiral of silence: A theory of public opinion," *Journal of Communication* 24(2):43-51. See also: Lars Willnat (1994). "Testing the interaction of the third-person effect and spiral of silence in a political pressure cooker: The case of Hong Kong." Paper presented at AEJMC, Atlanta.

18. Richard Perloff (1989). "Ego-involvement and the third-person effect of televised news coverage," *Communication Research* 16(2):236-262.

Summary

The third-person effect hypothesis is a relative newcomer to the field of mass communications theory. However, it has stirred interest because of its potential to result in great effects on individuals and society as a whole.

Davison described the third-person effect as a tendency by people to assume media messages affect others more than themselves. Researchers are currently studying the third-person effect hypothesis in relation to many areas, including the electoral process, freedom of speech and advertising.

Some researchers believe the third-person effect may be caused by the ego. This is supported by research which indicates that the more personal expertise people have in a particular area, the more likely they are to show a third-person effect.

A number of factors seem to increase the third-person effect. These include issue salience, perceived expertise, specialized knowledge, source credibility, age and education level.

Exercises:

Write a short essay answer to each of the exercise questions that follow using the information contained in the chapter or from additional sources.

A. Funding for many programs at the state and federal level are based on formative and summative evaluations that ask program administrators to estimate the impact of the program. How might the third-person effect have a negative influence on these evaluations and how might these kinds of evaluations achieve a more accurate assessment?

B. Past presidents have used polls to avoid relying on their own gut reactions. Can you think of any other ways the leader of a country could avoid miscalculating public opinion based on the third-person effect?

31
Framing and Priming Effects

Lyombe Eko
University of Maine

Media framing article: Stephen D. Reese and Bob Buckalew (1995). "The militarism of local television: The routine framing of the Persian Gulf War," *Critical Studies in Mass Communication* 12(1):40-59.

Audience framing article: Joel J. Davis (1995). "The effects of message framing on response to environmental communications," *Journalism & Mass Communication Quarterly* 72(2):285-299.

When movies became a mass medium early in the 20th century, politicians, religious leaders and social workers wondered what influence moving pictures had on audiences. Researchers also took an early interest in the issue. This chapter deals with two theoretical perspectives — framing and priming — that attempt to explain the effects of the presentation of mediated reality on audiences. Framing has its origins in sociology and psychology, while priming is grounded in cognitive psychology. Both perspectives hold that the mass media have powerful, if transient, effects on audiences.

Exercise:
One of the major scientific events of 1997 was the landing of NASA's space rover, Sojourner, on Mars. The spacecraft performed several unprecedented technological feats. One of the most exciting was that as soon as it landed on Mars, it started beaming video images and still pictures back to earth. Those images can be seen by surfing the Internet. Go to the National Aeronautic and Space Administration (NASA) web page, or the web page of the Smithsonian Institute, which also has these images from Mars. The World Wide Web addresses are:

NASA — http://wwwmpf.jpl.nasa.gov/ops/fpress-img.html
Smithsonian Institute — http://www.nasm.edu/galleries/gal209/gal209.html

You may wish to take some notes on your *general impressions* of what these sites contain to be prepared for an in-class exercise.

*   *   *

Framing is a widely used sociological and psychological **construct**, a concept that is invented or adopted to describe an abstract phenomenon that can be observed and measured. **Framing** refers to the activities of the mass media as they select, emphasize and present some aspects of "reality" to audiences, while ignoring others. **Frames** can also be thought of as general principles around which information is structured, defined, labeled and categorized. They are like mental pegs on which information, usually expressing a point of view, is hung.

Gregory Bateson is credited for using the frames concept to describe human communication.[1] A psychiatrist who studied schizophrenics' communication patterns, Bateson advanced the idea that context "frames" speech. He said that schizophrenics' behavior is explained by their inability or unwillingness to understand conventional framing messages: They **misframe** or take messages out of context, fail to discriminate fantasy from reality and interpret metaphors literally. Bateson likened "frames" to picture frames which tell people that the wallpaper design outside the frame is not part of the picture. Bateson's perspective places communication messages in the context of cues. For example, the tone of voice in which a message is given frames the message and helps people understand it.

Media framing process

Sociologist Erving Goffman wrote the archetypal book on framing.[2] He described it as the process of observing and making sense of events. To Goffman, framing was "the organization of experience." He claimed that because of different perspectives or frames of reference, one person's view of an on-going event is likely to differ from that of another person. For example, when interpreting an event, a reporter employs frameworks or **schemata** of interpretation — categories that exist in the mind — that enable the reporter to locate, perceive, identify and label that event or occurrence. Goffman concluded that all observers actively project their **values** and **perspectives**, or frames of reference, onto the world around them.

---

1. Gregory Bateson (1972). *Steps to an ecology of mind.* New York: Ballantine Books. See also: David Lipset (1980). *Gregory Bateson: The legacy of a scientist.* Englewood Cliffs, NJ: Prentice-Hall.
2. Erving Goffman (1974). *Frame analysis: An essay on the organization of experience.* Cambridge, MA: Harvard University Press.

In a ground-breaking study of media construction of reality, sociologist Gaye Tuchman observed how the news was put together in a television station, a daily newspaper and at a city hall press room in New York. She also analyzed the activities of reporters who covered women's issues. She found that news is a **window on the world**, and through its frame, audiences learn about themselves and others. She concluded that because people actively construct reality by interpreting and imposing meanings on events, "news is perpetually defining and redefining, constituting and reconstituting social phenomena."[3]

As the framing perspective became common in communication research, it also became difficult to define with any precision. Robert Entman's explanation of the framing concept is probably the most succinct. He said that framing is to: 1) select certain aspects of a perceived reality, 2) highlight them and 3) communicate them in a way that promotes 4) a particular version of a problem, 5) interprets its causes, 6) passes moral judgment and 7) prescribes a remedy for the problem described.[4] According to this perspective, news gathering is framing.

Over the years, researchers have concluded that when communicators print or broadcast news, they use news frames. These are abstract or concrete cues, frameworks or organizing principles that *help audiences categorize, label, interpret and evaluate information*. News frames can be the **themes** or **styles** that are used to make the news **appeal** to viewers, and directly or indirectly **influence their judgments** of the issues. In short, **news frames** are organizational structures used by the mass media to present specific perspectives or points of view. A news frame can also be described as the "take, spin or angle" of a news story.

Here is a concrete example of news frames. Several states have initiatives to legalize doctor-assisted suicides. Anyone who reads an article on this issue will notice that certain expressions, adjectives, metaphors and even cartoons are used to "frame" or place the issue in certain contexts or perspectives. When periodicals describe the issue as "doctor-assisted suicide," they frame it as a medical and legal issue. Supporters of the initiative who are quoted in the mass media, usually frame the controversy as "the right to die" issue. It is obvious that those who frame the issue in these terms see it not as a moral issue but as a matter of personal preference.

One of the most significant studies of media framing was carried out by Pippa Norris, who analyzed framing of the Cold War by the American news media.[5] She

---

3. Gaye Tuchman (1978). *Making news: A study in the construction of reality.* New York: Free Press, p.184.

4. Robert M. Entman (1993). "Framing: Toward clarification of a fractured paradigm," *Journal of Communication* 43(4):51-58.

5. Pippa Norris (1995). "The restless searchlight: Network news framing of the post-Cold War world," *Political Communication* 12(4):357-370.

found that, in keeping with Entman's definition of framing, the Cold War frame highlighted certain events as international problems, identified their sources, offered judgments about the parties involved in the problem and recommended particular policy solutions. She concluded that the Cold War frame's main theme was that *virtually all international events were interpreted in terms of a Superpower rivalry* with some countries labeled allies and others "enemies" or "adversaries." This changed after the Cold War to media frames of global economic cooperation and competition.

Sometimes news frames evolve from ideas and expressions in mediated **popular culture**. The mass media give such expressions new meanings and by frequent use they pass into the general public's vocabulary. An example is the Reagan Administration's 1980s Strategic Defense Initiative (SDI). This was a space-based system intended to neutralize Soviet nuclear missiles aimed at the United States. The mass media parodied SDI as "Star Wars," a reference to the special effects and electronic gimmickry of the popular movie whose characters and themes were part of U.S. popular culture.

SDI became known by the public as "Reagan's 'star wars' defense program." It also was the symbol around which anti-nuclear activists rallied to denounce the Reagan Administration's perceived unrealistic militaristic ambitions. This media framing was so effective that SDI was reduced to an object of ridicule, an unrealistic pipe dream out of Hollywood, like Ronald Reagan himself and perhaps his ideas.

Framing effects and trends

Researchers usually find that news framing does indeed have an impact on audiences, the most significant of which is the *frame of mind created in audiences*.[6] Murray Edelman advanced the idea that audience interpretation of news events depends the way the issues are framed. Edelman wrote, "Far from being stable, the social world is...a kaleidoscope of potential realities, any of which can be readily evoked by altering the ways in which observations are framed and categorized."[7]

If news frames are the organizing structures, and if people use them to process the news and retain items that are consistent with their previous knowledge or interests, then these certainly are effects. Research has shown that news frames have an impact on news interpretation.[8]

---

6. Kenneth J. Dunegan (1993). "Framing, cognitive modes, and image theory: Toward an understanding of a glass half full," *Journal of Applied Psychology* 78(3):491-503.

7. Murray Edelman (1993). "Contestable categories and public opinion," *Political Communication* 10(3):231-242.

8. See for example: Susanna Hornig (1992). "Framing risk: Audience and reader factors," *Journalism Quarterly* 69(3):679-690.

After determining that news frames do indeed affect audiences, researchers went one step further to study the psychological effects of framing. This involves analyzing the impact of news frames on the mental processes of audiences. A recent and significant study of the effects of news story frames on the thoughts of audiences was carried out by Price, Tewksbury and Powers.[9] Four groups of students read a fictitious news story about possible reduction of funding for their university in an experiment designed to determine the specific thoughts activated by each news frame. Each group read a version of the story with a different journalistic frame: conflict, human interest or personal consequences. Students were then asked to list their thoughts, which differed depending on the story frames. The researchers concluded that by activating certain concepts at the expense of others, news frames directly influence what enters the minds of audiences.

Although much of the previous research looked at only one side of the coin by studying either media frames or audience frames, the trend in methodology is to investigate both media and audience effects in a single study on a specific topic.[10] In fact, the two sides of the coin formed separate theoretical areas: framing vs. priming.

Priming effects

> **Early priming study**: Percy H. Tannenbaum (1953). "The effect of headlines on the interpretation of news stories," *Journalism Quarterly* 30(2):189-197.

> **Recent priming study**: Matthew Mendelsohn (1996). "The Media and intepersonal communications: The priming of issues, leaders, and party identification," *The Journal of Politics* 58(1):112-125.

Framing stresses media selection and presentation, while **priming** emphasizes mental processing of the information supplied by the mass media. Priming is grounded in cognitive psychology, the study of how people think. As such, it is

---

9. Vincent Price, David Tewksbury and Elizabeth Powers (1997). "Switching trains of thought: The impact of news frames on readers' cognitive responses," *Communication Research* 24(5):481-506.

10. See for example: Iyengar Shanto and Adam Simon (1993). "News coverage of the Gulf Crisis and public opinion: A study of agenda-setting, priming, and framing," *Communication Research* 20(3):365-383; Eunkyung Park and Gerald M. Kosicki (1995). "Presidential support during the Iran-Contra affair: People's reasoning process and media influence," *Communication Research* 22(2):207-236.

concerned mainly with information-processing in the brain or mind. The classic study in the field was Jean Piaget's 1928 work on communication between children that recognized the need for an overlap in experience between a speaker and a listener. Piaget wrote, "....when the explainer and his listener have had, at the time of the experiment, common preoccupations and ideas, then each word of the explainer is understood, because it fits into a schema already existing and well defined within the listener's mind."[11] The words spoken by one child *excite* related processing structures that already exist in the mind of the other child.

Priming asks: Do the mass media activate or trigger ideas in the minds of audiences? If so, can these ideas be translated into pro-social or anti-social acts? Consider these events: On July 12, 1991, "Boyz N the Hood" opened to sporadic audience violence in cities across the United States. The movie, which dealt with life in a gang-controlled, drug-ridden neighborhood in Los Angeles, triggered violence among audience members. By the time the carnage was over, two movie goers were dead and 30 injured. Twenty-one theaters promptly dropped "Boyz N the Hood," and those that kept showing it provided extra security for movie goers. Though the film grossed more than $100 million worldwide and earned director John Singleton an Academy Award nomination, the film raised fears that audience violence would negatively affect the movies of young, African-American directors.[12]

The violence that erupted as a result of "Boyz N the Hood" can be explained by priming effects. Priming is based on the biological theory that the human brain is a network of interconnected neurons or cells that process information. Thus, every time a person is exposed to a sound or image, information travels through a network of brain cells and activates similar or related images that were stored in the mind from previous experiences. The result of this activation is the so-called **priming effect**. Viewed from this perspective, all images and messages that people are exposed to on the Internet, or through the more traditional media, have the *potential to trigger other images that exist in their memory from previous experiences.*

According to **cognitive psychologists**, who study the nature of human intelligence and what takes place as the brain manipulates information, the human brain is an information-processing network in which in-coming messages prime or activate pre-existing similar or related ideas. The brain can be compared to the Internet, the worldwide network of computer networks. By clicking on Internet links, web pages can be activated to find desired information stored in networked servers. Mass media messages activate pre-existing or similar ideas in the mind in the same way, and this is priming. Priming is generally a **stimulus-response** perspective because the new media messages are said to stimulate, prime or trigger

11. Jean Piaget (1959). *The language and thought of the child, 3rd ed.* New York: Humanities Press, p. 133.
12. John Leland (1991). "A bad omen for black movies?" *Newsweek,* (July 29), *118*(5):48-49.

the thought processes of listeners and viewers. Thus, when audiences see striking images on television or on the Internet, these images prime or activate other images or concepts that are similar or related in meaning to the images seen. For example, viewing a horror movie induces or opens viewers' mental structures and brings to the fore previously learned experiences such as fear or excitement.

The violence during the screening of "Boyz N the Hood" did not happen because audience members decided to imitate the senseless violence they saw in the movie. From a priming effects perspective, the film activated images, ideas and experiences of violence already existing in the minds of some audience members. The film was merely the stimulus that led to severe priming effects: violence.

Neuropsychologists have directly studied priming processes and effects in laboratory situations. Schweinberger studied priming effects by showing experimental subjects a picture of former Soviet leader Mikhail Gorbachev, and then showing them the faces of Boris Yeltsin and Arnold Schwarznegger. Brain wave activity of the subjects was measured with an electroencephalograph (EEG), and their response time was recorded. The image of Gorbachev's face activated or primed measurable mental processes that helped subjects associate Gorbachev with Russian President Boris Yeltsin. Subjects recognized Yeltsin's name and identified him as a Russian politician after being primed by Gorbachev's image.[13]

In the 1970s and 1980s, priming effects studies focused on how mediated violence affects human mental structures and processes. Leonard Berkowitz summarized the priming effects studies of media violence.[14] He found that ideas activated by the mass media temporarily evoke other related thoughts in the audience. These activated or primed thoughts can lead to conduct similar to that portrayed by the mass media. When a person views a violent movie, aggressive ideas suggested by the movie can activate related thoughts, recollections and even specific actions. Berkowitz concluded that depictions of violence in the mass media increase the chances that people in the audience will act aggressively because of the priming effects. For example, movies portraying sexual violence against women increased male viewers' beliefs that the portrayed behavior was acceptable.

The alternative is also a possibility: Positive thoughts and ideas activated by the mass media can lead to pro-social activities. Priming effects can therefore be both negative and positive. However, priming effects are only temporary. Ideas and states of mind activated by media messages decline as time passes.

---

13. Stefan R. Schweinberger (1996). "How Gorbachev primed Yeltsin: Analyses of associative priming in person recognition by means of reaction times and event-related brain potentials," *Journal of Experimental Psychology: Learning, Memory, and Cognition* 22(6):1383-1407.

14. Leonard Berkowitz (1984). "Some effects of thoughts on anti- and prosocial influences of media events: A cognitive-neoassociation analysis," *Psychological Bulletin* 95(3):410-427.

News priming effects

The priming effects concept was applied to television news coverage of the U.S. president by Shanto Iyengar and Donald Kinder. Drawing on cognitive psychology's information-processing approach, they asserted that television news' selective coverage of events and issues activates mental processes in its viewers and *triggers only ideas related to the issues in the news.* The researchers described priming effects from the media's selective coverage of issues: "By calling attention to some matters while ignoring others, television news influences the standards by which governments, presidents, policies, and candidates for public office are judged."[15]

Thus, if television news stresses an issue such as the country's economic situation, viewers become preoccupied with the economy and then judge the president by his success in improving the economic situation. To test this hypothesis, Iyengar and Kinder had participants watch newscasts that emphasized specific issues, and then asked them to rate the president's performance. Viewers who had been shown news stories about a particular issue gave more weight to that issue in their overall evaluation of the president. The researchers concluded that news powerfully shapes the standards viewers use to evaluate the president.

Iyengar and Kinder state that priming effects occur because when people are faced with an issue, they use mental shortcuts rather than complicated analyses. One such mental shortcut is to rely on the information that is most current and most accessible in their minds. Thus, when people are asked to judge a president, they use only the information that comes to mind at the time of the assessment. Because most people get their information from television, the more television primes a specific issue, or pays attention to it, the more frequently the issue will be accessed by viewers and incorporated in their overall judgment of the president.

Trends in priming effects research

Using Iyengar and Kinder's priming model, Pan and Kosicki studied what effects the media emphasis on the Gulf War vs. emphasis on the U.S. economy had on voters' evaluations of President George Bush's job performance.[16] The study treated the mass media as a priming agent. The researchers found that between 1990 and 1991, Bush's overall rating was very high. His public approval ratings increased significantly with his handling of the Gulf War and foreign affairs. However, after the war, the media focus shifted to the economic recession. Voters accorded significant weight to the economy, and Bush's overall job performance rating plummeted.

---

15. Shanto Iyengar and Donald R. Kinder (1987). *News that matters: Television and American opinion.* Chicago: The University of Chicago Press.

16. Zhongdang Pan and Gerald M. Kosicki (1997). "Priming and media impact on the evaluations of the president's performance," *Communication Research* 24(1):3-30.

The Pan and Kosicki study also showed that priming effects are temporary and depend on the circumstances that bring issues to the minds of the public. Furthermore, the effects of mass media saturation coverage of an issue fade away as the issue recedes into the background, and other dominant issues come to the fore.

Kepplinger and Daschmann reported that in news processing, human cognitive or mental structures are shaped by past media consumption.[17] As a result, new media messages are like amplifiers that make possible or even magnify general media effects. This model holds that viewers interpret media messages in terms of their perception of reality, which is in turn shaped by their previous media use.

Power, Murphy and Coover found that stereotypes, which Walter Lippmann described in 1922 as being very partial and inadequate portrayals of the world,[18] can be primed. The researchers exposed a group of students to stereotypic and counter-stereotypic portrayals of an unknown African-American male in a newsletter. They found that the portrayal can sway an individual's subsequent interpretations and judgments of actual controversial media events involving African-American males. The researchers also found that students who had been exposed to a stereotypic portrayal of females in a passage, were least likely to believe the women involved in the William Kennedy Smith rape trial and the Clarence Thomas confirmation hearing.[19]

Discussion

Framing is a sociological concept that has psychological consequences. The type of information that is selected and the framework within which it is presented affect how people evaluate issues. Priming is primarily an internal, cognitive process that may have an observable or measurable behavioral component.

Recent studies show that there is a trend toward convergence of framing and priming effects research. Some researchers test both perspectives in the same study and use them as mirror images of the same media effects. The position expressed here is that a look at their origins shows that the concepts are sufficiently different in emphasis to warrant being studied separately. From a research perspective, each concept can stand on its own two feet, so to speak.

---

17. Hans Mathias Kepplinger and Gregor Daschmann (1997). "Today's news — tomorrow's context: A dynamic model of news processing," *Journal of Broadcasting & Electronic Media* 41(4):548-565.

18. Walter Lippmann (1922). *Public opinion*. New York: Harcourt, Brace & Co.

19. J. Gerard Power, Sheila T. Murphy and Gail Coover (1996). "Priming prejudice: How stereotypes and counter-stereotypes influence attribution of responsibility and credibility among ingroup and outgroups." *Human Communication Research* 23(1):36-58.

Summary

The hypothesis that the mass media have immediate and direct effects on audiences has been the driving force behind a lot of mass communication research. This chapter deals with two theoretical perspectives — framing and priming effects — that have their origin in sociology, psychiatry and cognitive psychology.

Framing refers to the activities of the mass media as they select, emphasize and present some aspects of "reality" to audiences, while ignoring others. News frames are general principles around which information is structured, defined, labeled and categorized. News frames can be themes, metaphors, frames of reference or even cartoons. The main thing about frames is that they *organize information and usually express values either directly or indirectly*. A news frame can also be described as the "take, spin or angle" of a news story.

The chapter reviews several major studies of framing and presents an overview of what researchers have learned about this process, with special emphasis on news framing. The studies reviewed and the insights provided extend from the mid-1970s to the mid-1990s.

Priming has its origins in cognitive psychology. From a mass communication perspective, **priming effects** are the consequences of media messages activating information processing networks in the mind, and triggering similar or related ideas which may or may not lead to specific action. Again, the chapter reviews relevant research studies and their findings from the 1970s through the mid-1990s.

Research on framing and priming shows that both perspectives attribute powerful, if transient, effects by the mass media on audiences.

Exercises:

A. Write short responses of less than half a page to each of the following three questions. Base answers on the chapter's presentation of framing and priming:

1. The mass media are accused of helping to destroy the social and moral fabric of society by disseminating excessive amounts of sex and violence. Is this accusation justified in light of the framing and priming effects perspectives?

2. The priming effects perspective holds that the mass media can prime or activate both anti-social and pro-social ideas and behavior on the part of audiences. How can pro-social behavior be encouraged and anti-social behavior be discouraged by the mass media?

3. Why do you think the mass media frame issues the way Tuchman said they do?

B. By reading newspapers and magazines, listening to the radio, watching television and surfing the Internet, try to identify the frames or contexts in which the following entities and persons are described. Remember that frames can be moral, ethical, religious, ethnic, economic, medical, stereotypical, metaphorical and so on. They can also be cartoons and pictures. Each issue or person's media framing should be kept to a few sentences. Be prepared to discuss your findings in class and to submit your work for a grade.

1. Big business:

2. Heroin chic in advertising:

3. Islam:

4. The tobacco industry:

(continued)

5. Bill Gates:

6. Nuclear power:

7. Underground militia groups:

8. Ethnic cleansing:

C. Abortion is an emotionally charged political issue in the United States. With advances in medical technology, abortions can be performed when a woman's pregnancy is more than 12 weeks, without much danger to the health of the woman. Read news magazines, listen to the radio or watch television news about this issue. Note how it is framed. Depending on their political and religious beliefs, some reporters refer to the controversial late-stage abortion procedure as "partial-birth abortion," while others refer to it either as "abortion" or "late-term abortion." Try to determine how periodicals and broadcasts frame the issue. Then answer this question in a **one**-page essay: How would you frame the issue?

D. Every time people use mass media, they may experience negative or positive priming effects without realizing it. In the following grid, try to assess your first occurrence of a priming effect. For example, if you read a magazine article on famine in an African nation, you might write "nothing unusual" or "children are always the victims" or "third-world dictatorships." This exercise tests your awareness of how the mass media you use prime or activate certain ideas or thoughts in your mind.

Before the next class meeting, view one national television network newscast, one local television newscast, listen to one radio newscast, listen to recorded music, look at one newspaper, and look at the current edition of *Time* magazine. Stop when you experience what you believe is a priming effect and identify the stimulus story and your stored thoughts.

	Prime or Stimulus Story	Subject Matter from Memory
Network TV		
Local TV		
Radio News		
Music		
Newspaper		
Time magazine		

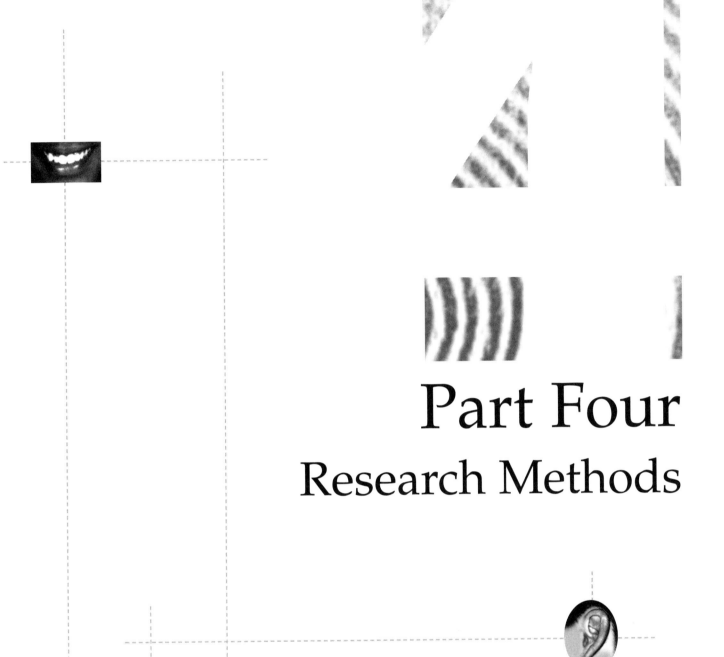

Part Four
Research Methods

32
Reliability, Validity and Sampling

Reliability article: Christopher L. Heavey, Brandon M. Larson, Daniel C. Zumtobel and Andrew Christensen (1996). "The Communication Patterns Questionnaire: The reliability and validity of a constructive communication subscale," *Journal of Marriage and the Family* 58(3):796-800.

Validity article: Kathleen Hall Jamieson and Joseph N. Cappella (1996). "Bridging the disciplinary divide: Political science and communication," *Political Science & Politics* 29(1):13-17.

Sampling article: Robert Abelman (1996). "Can we generalize from Generation X? Not!" *Journal of Broacasting & Electronic Media* 40(3):441-446.

Reliability and validity are researchers' tools to determine if the measurement instruments they use are accurate within an acceptable range of error. Researchers in the social sciences appropriately expend a lot of effort to demonstrate that their measurements are credible. Samples are portions of the population being studied, and in many studies the sample's quality determines the credibility of the research, especially whether findings from one study can be generalized to the population.

Reliability

Reliability refers to *consistency* and *stability* in measures. Measures that are not reliable are not useful for theory or decision making because their outcomes are not dependable. **Consistency** suggests *reproducibility*. It addresses the question, "Does the measure produce the same outcome in other comparable samples?" **Stability** refers to whether the same outcome can be obtained by any qualified researcher. A reliable instrument should produce the same result in repeated measures regardless of who administers it.

In the natural sciences, reliability is less a problem. For example, the biologist counting white cells in repeated smears of blood can be confident about getting the same result each time. But the social scientist cannot be so confident. A certain amount of error is expected, and some of it just can't be accounted for. For example, did the respondent tell the truth? Did the respondent comprehend fully?

In communication, a discipline that depends on measuring human attitudes and behaviors, researchers rarely attempt true replications. Even those studies that use the same procedures and measuring instruments (questionnaires or experimental manipulations) often report different outcomes than the original research. When dealing with people's behaviors, measurement reliability can be a real problem.

Measurement always includes error, either random or non-random.[1] **Random errors** are those related to sampling, coding, environmental conditions and anything else beyond the researcher's control. They are inevitable, and totally non-systematic. But the *random* errors are less troublesome in social science than are the *non-random* errors, for the latter suggest systematic bias, a flaw fatal to validity.

Non-random errors send an outcome consistently in one wrong direction or another. An example is a fixed rifle with an improperly gauged sight that consistently fires one foot to the right of a target, or a personality scale that excessively attributes certain qualities to individuals. Non-random errors result in invalidity, which is to say the instrument did not measure what it was intended to measure.[2]

Reliability does not guarantee validity. A measuring instrument *must be reliable if it is also valid,* but reliability by itself is not sufficient to assure validity. For example, an instrument (like the fixed rifle) could be highly reliable, obtaining the same wrong result time after time, and therefore invalid. Still, there are several methods to test reliability. Some require that the data be **parametric** or scores that have decimal values. (Reliability for content analysis is treated separately.)

1. **Test/re-test.** In this method, measurements are taken at two different times and the scores correlated. Weaknesses include: people's scores on the first measure can influence their scores on the second; the impracticality of getting two measures from the same sample; or something happened between the two measures that affected the outcome.[3]

1. Fred N. Kerlinger (1986). *Foundations of behavioral research, 3rd. ed.* Fort Worth, TX: Holt, Rinehart and Winston.

2. Edward G. Carmines and Richard A. Zeller (1979). *Reliability and validity assessment, 5th ed.* Beverly Hills: Sage Publications.

3. Mario F. Teisl, Kevin J. Boyle, Daniel W. McCollum and Stephen D. Reiling (1995). "Test-retest reliability of contingent valuation with independent sample pretest and posttest control groups," *American Journal of Agricultural Economics* 77(3):613-619.

2. **Alternative forms**. In this method there are two versions of an instrument. If they are reliable the results of the two should be similar.

3. **Split halves**. Here the test is divided into two parts and compared. Because the reliability calculated in this way is for only half of the instrument, a statistical adjustment must be made.[4]

4. **Internal consistency**. This is a measure of the intercorrelation of items in the instrument. The most popular measure of the type is known as Cronbach's Alpha,[5] based on the consistency or variance of scores. If the variance is small, the consistency of the items in the scale is high, hence a high Alpha.

Validity

As suggested, internal validity addresses the question, "Did the instrument measure what it was intended to measure?" In other words, a measured outcome by itself is not sufficient; it must be valid. For example, if a researcher claimed to have demonstrated a "cultivation" effect of television viewing, was it more likely accounted for by the respondents' environment? If so, the research outcome was invalid.

Using the "fixed rifle" example, validity is something like moving the target one foot to the right and concluding that because the shots now hit the bull's eye, the rifle is accurate. The new measurement might be correct (hitting the bull's eye), but the rifle is still not sighted properly; it won't hit the next target. There are several types of validity:

1. **Criterion based**. This is the validity referred to most commonly. It uses an *external criterion to corroborate the goodness of the instrument*. For example, successfully driving a car might validate the driver's license written test. Success in college classes might validate the SAT/ACT.

Criterion validity can be either concurrent or predictive, although the two are related. **Concurrent validity**, for example, would be a verbal report on the likelihood of voting two days before an election followed by whether the person actually voted. **Predictive validity** would be a college junior's estimate of first-year annual salary validated by the person's annual salary the first year after graduation. Criterion validity is not always possible to establish because *intention* is not always followed by *behavior*. Also, the more abstract the variable, the less like the criterion

---

4. Edward G. Carmines and Richard A. Zeller, *op. cit.*, p. 41. The correction is called the Spearman-Brown prophecy formula. The result is a coefficient that can vary from 0 to 1.0.

5. Lee J. Cronbach (1951). "Coefficient alpha and the internal structure of tests." *Psychometrika* 16(3):297-334.

variable. In some cases, there are simply no criterion variables. For example, what criterion might validate a person's attitude toward capital punishment for terrorists?

Another type of criterion validity is sometimes called face validity or logical validity. **Face validity** means the measure has the *appearance* of validity.[6] For example, if the researcher measured "interest in collegiate athletics," the presence of season tickets would tend to validate the measure.

2. **Content validity** refers to how well a measure reflects its particular content. For example, a test of interest in news should really reflect interest in news, not interest in the lives Hollywood celebrities. The researcher must understand the dimensions of the topic, create items to measure them and assure the reliability of the items. Another example: An instructor lectures on a topic, then prepares an objective test, examining each item for relevance and asking a colleague to also evaluate the items. This would be a test of the content validity of the instrument.[7]

3. **Construct validity** is used in the absence of an external criterion. *Constructs* are ideas formed from sets of concepts. For example, combining three questions on the likelihood of being victimized with one question asking how many locks are on a person's door forms a construct to represent fear in a "cultivation" study. Validity then is the correlation of the two. Another example might be a teenager's number of trips to the mall per week and "number of close friends" as measures of sociability. Yet another example is a scale that measures people's anxiety about their body size.[8]

If the validity overview seems complex and abstract, it is. These three categorizations of validity are only one approach to testing validity, which is a process that should continue throughout a research design. Brinberg and McGrath call it "a concept designating an ideal state...validity is like integrity, character, or quality, to be assessed relative to purposes and circumstances."[9] Hence, a researcher must be constantly on the vigil to ensure that validity is part of the research design, methodology, analysis and the interpretation of findings.

Reliability in content analysis

This section reviews *reliability* in content analysis, not content analysis itself (see Content Analysis chapter). The method is described by Holsti, by Krippendorff

6. Earl R. Babbie (1989). *The practice of social research, 5th ed.* Belmont, CA: Wadsworth, p. 393.

7. Fred N. Kerlinger (1986), *op. cit.*, p. 417.

8. Trent A. Petrie, Nancy Diehl, Rebecca L. Rogers and Courtney L. Johnson (1996). "The Social Physique Anxiety Scale: Reliability and construct validity," *Journal of Sport & Exercise Psychology* 18(4):420-425.

9. David Brinberg and Joseph E. McGrath (1985). *Validity and the research process.* Beverly Hills, CA: Sage, p. 13.

and others,[10] and is widely used in communication research. Content analysis is defined as the systematic, objective, quantitative analysis of the manifest content of communication.[11] **Systematic** means without overlooking items; **objective** means without bias; and **manifest** means relying on what is there, not what one might imagine is there.

The analyst decides what to count, defines it and assigns each occurrence to a category. Categories are exclusive (a unit can be placed in only one category) and exhaustive (every unit must be assigned to some category). Clearly, a content analysis' value depends on the merit of the definitions used. Reliability in content analysis then is largely a measure of the goodness of the category definitions. If two or more persons analyzing the text report the same occurrences, the analysis is reliable. The agreement between coders can be reported as a percentage; two coders agreeing on 8 of 10 occurrences indicates 80% reliability.

The percentage reliability coefficient is a staple of the field, but since some agreement between coders could be due to chance (with only three categories, two coders could agree sometimes merely by chance) it tends to overestimate reliability. To account for this, Scott offered a correction called "Pi." The formula is:

$$Pi = \frac{(Po - Pe)}{(1 - Pe)}$$

where Po = percentage agreement, and Pe = percentage agreement expected on the basis of chance. To calculate Pe, merely square and sum the percentage responses for each response option.[12] The formula will produce a reliability coefficient that is more conservative (lower) than the simple percentage (see Exercise B for further details).

Scott's Pi applies in the case of two coders, but often the coding involves more than two. In that case, a more sophisticated variation of the formula must be used.

---

10. Ole R. Holsti (1969). *Content analysis for the social sciences and humanities.* Reading, MA: Addison-Wesley Publishing Co. See also: Klaus Krippendorff (1971). "Reliability of recording instructions: Multivariate agreement for nominal data," *Behavioral Science* 16(3):222-235.

11. Bernard R. Berelson (1952). *Content analysis in communications research.* New York: Free Press, p. 18.

12. William A. Scott (1955). "Reliability of content analysis: The case of nominal scale coding," *Public Opinion Quarterly* 19(3):321-325. See also: Brian R. Patterson, Nicholas C. Neupauer, Patricia A. Burant, Steven C. Koehn and April T. Reed (1996). "A preliminary examination of conversation analytic techniques: Rates of inter-transcriber reliability," *Western Journal of Communications* 60(1):76-91.

Sampling

A sample is any sub-set of a population. A **population** could be as large as every registered voter in the United States or as small as all the citizens in a rural community of 5,000. Samples can be either random or non-random.

Random samples give every element of a population an **equal** chance to be selected. They are called **probability** samples, and they include the simple random sample (lottery type), systematic random sample (use of a **roster**, directory or other sample frame), and random-digit telephone dialing. Random sampling allows researchers to **infer** that a sample reflects a much larger population.

While randomness is the ideal of probability sampling, it is seldom perfectly achievable because some people don't want to be sampled, and others are not accessible for some reason: They are relocating, in ill health, on vacation, their telephone was disconnected, etc. Being unable to reach a person selected for the sample introduces an element of uncertainty to the outcome of a probability survey.

Still, if researchers were to let the difficulties of sampling stymie them, survey research would come to a screeching halt. Fortunately, experience has shown that if a sample is large enough, and fairly close to random, minor flaws can be overlooked. How nearly random must the sample be to be considered adequate? There is no formula, but if a survey outcome is to be inferred to a population, then the random sample must have all the integrity that planning and execution can give it.

Non-random samples include street-corner surveys, telephone call-ins, newspaper-inserts, mall intercepts and focus groups. These are non-random because representation of all elements in the population cannot be assured. They are called **non-probability** samples. Using a non-random sample **prevents inference** to the larger population from which it was drawn.

If a researcher stood on a corner and interviewed *every* person who passed, would the survey be random? No, as not every person would be available at that particular corner. Some are employed elsewhere, some never pass that corner, some are house-bound and so-on. So, even if 1,000 people were interviewed at the corner, their responses could not be safely generalized to a city-wide population.

Similarly, telephone call-ins and newspaper inserts have poor **external validity**, or generalizability to the population, even when their respondents number in six or seven figures. Respondents to such polls are self-selected, which often means they have a special interest that sets them apart. Some could respond many times, unduly biasing the outcome of the poll. Regardless of how large a non-random sample may be, sample size does not by itself overcome problems of external validity.

Making inferences from samples

Even in the best published surveys, the pollsters don't interview everyone in America. Instead, they interview a small subset of the population, which they claim represents the whole population. Their samples usually number from 400 to 1,500. Their inference is an act of faith, because they cannot know the feelings of those they don't question. But their faith is based on experience and the logic of math.

Here's how the inference works. Say a city has a population of 150,000, and it is *known* from the U.S. Census that the average age of the population is 38.3 years. Nevertheless, the researcher puts the name and age of every person on a slip of paper and places them in a bin. After mixing them well, the researcher pulls out a *sample* of 200, and calculates the average age. Say the average age of the sample was 37.6, not the same as the true average, but close. Then the names are put back in the bin, and the process is repeated. If this is done over and over and over, the researcher can expect most of the sample averages to be very close to the population average of 38.3, but any one sample might be off a bit, higher or lower. Still, on average, the sample should approximate the population.

But if the "true" population average is not known, how is it possible to know if the sample is accurately reflecting the population? Mathematicians have found that if *random* samples of 200 or so were drawn repeatedly (infinitely) from a population, most would cluster closely around the true mean of the population. This is called the **sampling distribution**, and it is represented by the so-called **bell-shaped curve**.

The mathematicians have calculated that the mean of 68% of random samples will fall within plus or minus 1 **standard deviation** (an estimate of variation) of the center of the normal curve, 95% will fall within 2 standard deviations and 99% within 3. Using the knowledge that underlies the normal curve, it's possible to estimate not only the error level associated with a sample size, but also the confidence one can have in believing it!

As can be seen, the credibility of the survey depends on the nature of the sample. If it is to any extent **biased**, or non-random, inference from a sample to a population is not possible. That is why street-corner surveys, telephone call-in surveys and newspaper-insert surveys, to name a few, have greater entertainment value than representative value.

And so, with the logic of random sampling, a sample of 400 people could be used to reflect a city's population of 150,000 or more. Even though 400 is a very small number, a small sample can represent a very large population. Contrary to what might be expected, the size of the sample is **not** related to the size of the population. A sample of 400 could reflect the population of 20,000 or 10,000,000, at least in theory.

On the other hand, sample size *is* important in this regard: Every sample has an **error margin**, an estimate of how much it might differ from the "true" population score, if that score were known. The smaller the sample, the larger the error margin. To reduce the error margin by half, four times the sample size is needed. That is important because the cost of the survey will increase with each additional respondent. For example, a sample of 400 has an error margin of about 5%, while a sample of 1,600 has an error margin of about 2.5%.

For any survey, the sample is an **estimate** of the population, and the true population score could be a little higher or lower than that of the sample. Polling companies typically use samples of 1,000 to 2,000 for national surveys. It's not uncommon to see political polls that are accurate within 1%-to-2% of the final vote.

Through trial and error and through careful planning, the national firms have developed sampling frames that closely reflect the population. At the same time, there have been some spectacular failures. In the 1994 presidential election, for example, a few of the hundreds of surveys that were reported were significantly inaccurate, sometimes by 8%-to-15%. That is important to know, because some voters use the polls to decide whether to vote, or for whom.

Probably the most spectacular failure of the opinion polls occurred in connection with the 1932 election of Franklin D. Roosevelt. A very popular national magazine called *Literary Digest* conducted its usual mail-in opinion poll, the same as it had done successfully in several previous elections. With more than a million responses, the *Digest* reported that Alf Landon would defeat Roosevelt by a large margin. Of course, Roosevelt won by a large margin, and the error was a severe embarrassment to the *Digest*, which shut down within a year.

The *Chicago Tribune* suffered a similar major embarrassment in the 1948 election of Harry S. Truman vs. Thomas Dewey when the paper wrongly ran a banner headline that read "Dewey Wins." The newspaper wanted to be timely with the election results, and based the headline on opinion polls taken several days prior to the election. The *Tribune's* error was in letting its survey data get old. Today, editors and researchers know that there is a lot of last-minute shuffling of political opinion, and so their polling continues right up to the closing of the polls. The *Tribune* did not go out of business.

Summary

Researchers use reliability and validity to determine if their measurement instruments are accurate within an acceptable range of error. Social scientists appropriately expend considerable effort to demonstrate the credibility of their measurements.

Reliability refers to consistency and stability in measures. *Consistency* suggests reproducibility or whether the measure produces the same outcome in other comparable samples. *Stability* is whether the same outcome can be obtained by any qualified researcher. Reliable instruments should produce the same result in repeated measures. Measurement always includes **error**, either random or non-random. **Random errors** are beyond the researcher's control. **Non-random** errors send an outcome consistently in the wrong direction and result in invalidity.

Reliability in **parametric** data is shown through: 1) test-retest, 2) alternate forms, 3) split-halves, and 4) internal consistency. **Validity**, or "Did the instrument measure what it was intended to measure?" takes several forms including: 1) criterion-based, 2) content, and 3) construct. The chapter presents methods to test reliability in **content analysis**, a frequently used communication research strategy.

Sampling is the process that allows an **inference** from a small sub-set of a population to the population as a whole. Samples can represent probability or non-probability. **Non-probability** sampling has low or no external validity. These are the street-corner sample, telephone call-ins, newspaper inserts, mall intercepts, convenience samples and the like. **Probability** samples are the lottery type, the systematic random sample and random-digit dialing.

The sampling process and the logic of making inferences from a sample are discussed as are principles of random **sample selection**, **sampling distribution**, **sampling error**, **bias** and **sample size**. Careful samples can have high accuracy. Notable failures were due to sampling techniques used, not to sampling as a process.

Exercises:

A. Prepare a brief test, say 5-10 items, on a topic that you are studying in this class. Write the test questions you think your teacher should write for that material. Ask a small number of classmates (5-10) to take your "test." Next, table the responses to study the reliability of the items ("1" is a right answer; "0" is a wrong answer):

	Test Items								
	1	2	3	4	5	6	7	8	etc.
Test Taker									
1	1	1	0	1	1	1	0	1	1
2	1	0	1	1	1	1	1	1	0
3	1	1	0	1	1	1	0	1	1

etc.

Analysis. The *rows* show the success of the individual in answering the set of questions. The *columns* show how well a test item served its purpose. If every person got every item correct, the test might have been too easy. Note that this technique can be used to assess the reliability of any test instrument.

B. Conduct a simple content analysis of a newspaper. Examine 20 stories in a recent edition and categorize each as being either "good news," "bad news" or "neutral/indeterminate." To do this systematically, number the first article by marking a "1" on it in red, the same for article 2, etc. Make a record of your decisions, which will look like a vertical list 1-20 with " good," "bad" or "neutral/indeterminate" by each. Next, another student categorizes the stories using the same marked newspaper.

With the two "coding" sheets, count the disagreements, and divide by the total number of agreement opportunities (20). This will give you a percentage "reliability" score. Next, compute Pi. Remember, to calculate the Pe of the formula, square the percentage agreement *in each of the three response options*. Subtract Pe from Po, and divide by 1 minus Pe. Scott's Pi will give you a more modest estimate of reliability, but one in which you can be more confident.

C. Sample variation. Here is an illustration of how samples can vary. Ask 10 class-mates their age in months; for example, the age of Student A, 19 years and 6 months, would be $19 \times 12 + 6 = 234$ months. Take the average of the 10. Repeat the procedure with another 10 students. Is the average of the first 10 the same as the second 10? The difference is "sample error." Sample error declines as sample size increases, so with enough samples, the averages would cluster at a single point, the center of a curve.

Another way to illustrate the point is with a table of random numbers. In a TON, any number is as likely as another other. Find any two-digit number and with that as a starting point, work downward recording 20 numbers. Calculate the average. Then, find a new starting point and repeat the process 5 times.

D. Sample size. When the need for a sample survey arises, the first question always is, "How big a sample do I need?" In general, the smaller the sample, the larger the error level, so it is prudent to go for a larger sample; but as sample size increases, so does cost. At some point the researcher has to compromise. Sample size depends on: 1) the level of *confidence* needed in the outcome, 2) the level of *error* you can live with, and 3) the relative *ambiguity* of the issue as represented by the percentage of responses. The three elements make up a formula:

Sample size = Confidence-squared divided by Error-squared times Percentage. ($C^2 / E^2 \times \%$)

The three elements of the formula are:

Confidence. The concept is based on the sampling distribution. For simplicity, consider that 95% confidence in a sample has a factor of 2 (or more precisely 1.96). Confidence at the level of 99.7% has a factor of 3.

Error. If the survey topic is important to health or wealth, researchers will want to minimize error level, but in many social research situations, an error level of 5% can be tolerated. The error level can be set at any number, but usually it is 5%.

Percentage. The formula for calculating sample size includes an estimate of the percentage split in responses. Conservatively, the researcher proposes that the responses will split 50%-50%. This produces a slightly larger sample than would, say, an estimated split of 70%-30%, as is demonstrated in the examples. In the formula for sample size, multiply the percentage (e.g., 50) by its other part (50).

If the Confidence factor is $2^2 = 4$, and error is $5^2 = 25$, divide 4 by 25 = .16; multiply .16 times (50x50 = 2500) = .16 x 2500 = 400. Thus, a sample of 400 will yield about 95% confidence and a 5% error margin in representing a very large population. Try it for yourself with the following numbers:

1. Confidence=2; error=2.5%, %= 50x50, sample size = _____

2. Confidence=3; error=5%, %=50x50, sample size = _____

E. Error level. Any random sample can be like or unlike the population it represents; that's the nature of a random process. Most often a random sample will be very much like its population. The error level estimates the outer limits of variation of a sample from the population. The error level can be calculated for any random sample. It is the square root of the percentage of responses divided by the sample size and multipled by 2 to reach the 95% confidence level.

If the outcome of a survey is totally uncertain, multiply 50% x 50% (50x50=2500) and divide by the sample size, say 400; 2500/400=6.25. Take the square root of 6.25 = 2.5 and multiply by 2 to reach 95% confidence. This says a sample of 400 should be no more than 5% plus or minus the true population score, if it were known. An error level can be calculated for any sample. Try it for yourself with these numbers:

1. Percentage=50x50; sample=300; take $\sqrt{}$; multiply by 2; error = _____

2. Percentage=50x50; sample=800; take $\sqrt{}$; multiply by 2; error = _____

33
Survey Research

Questionnaire construction: Michael W. Traugott and Paul J. Lavrakas (1996). "How are questionnaires put together?" in *The voter's guide to election polls*. Chatham, NJ: Chatham House Publishers, pp. 96-122.

Response rate: Don A. Dillman, Michael D. Sinclair and Jon R. Clark (1993). "Effects of questionnaire length, respondent-friendly design, and a difficult question on response rates for occupant-addressed census mail surveys," *Public Opinion Quarterly 57*(3): 289-304.

Questions to ponder as you read:

1. Have you ever been asked to participate in a survey that was conducted by a professional polling organization? Did you participate? How much of your time did it require? Would you do it again?

2. If you were asked to respond to a telephone survey or a mail survey that would require, say, 40 minutes of your time, would you participate?

3. Aside from the length of the survey, what kinds of things would encourage or discourage your participation in a survey? Interest in the topic? An inducement, such as a report of the outcome, or a token, such as $1 or $5?

4. If telephone polling is too frequent, or if marketers disguise sales messages as interviews, does it threaten the continued viability of survey research?

Survey research has four particularly important aspects, each requiring training and skill: 1) sampling, 2) questionnaire design, 3) administration, and 4) data analysis. Sampling is discussed in the previous chapter. This chapter focuses on questionnaire design and administration. The assumption is that a researcher has already determined that survey research is the procedure of choice. For example, if the information needed can be secured in another manner (perhaps it already exists in document form, such as a census report or Standard Rate and Data Service; or perhaps a similar survey already has been done, such as those by the Gallup or Michigan social studies research organizations), don't spend the time and resources trying to do a new survey.

Interviewing methods

Very early in a survey research project, the researcher must decide whether to conduct the survey by **phone, mail** or **in-person**. Each method has its strengths and limitations.

Telephone.
Strengths:
1. Data are gathered quickly, often overnight.
2. Cost is moderate.
3. Calls can cover a wide geographic area.
4. External validity can be assured.
5. Telephone data can be immediately input for processing.

Limitations:
1. Questions require simplicity.
2. Delicate topics are inadvisable.
3. Response options should be few and clear.
4. Interviewers can influence responses.
5. Interview time should be brief, 6-10 minutes.

Mail.
Strengths:
1. A longer, more complex questionnaire can be used.
2. Mail can cover a wide area.
3. Cost is comparable to or less than that of a telephone survey.
4. Detailed response options and detailed responses are possible.
5. Delicate topics can be addressed in private, issues of ethics notwithstanding.

Limitations:
1. Responses are slow, sometimes many weeks.
2. Researcher loses control over who answers (never quite know who filled out the form).
3. Respondents are somewhat self-selected (similar to No. 2).
4. Response rate is low, often 35%-45% or below.
5. Ambiguities (misinterpretations) cannot be corrected.

In-Person, In-home.
Strengths:
1. Questionnaires can be longer and more complex.
2. Great control of external validity.
3. Improved accuracy of responses.
4. Opportunity for follow-up questions.
5. Opportunity to clarify questions, build rapport.

Limitations.
1. Very expensive.
2. Very slow accumulation of data.
3. Possible danger to interviewers being on the street.
4. Liability for unexpected incidents in the home.
5. Slow input of data.
6. Requires special care in sample construction.

Which of the methods is most cost effective?

Telephone. If the telephone interview takes 10 minutes, an interviewer can complete no more than 6 calls per hour. Calls should be made from 6-9 p.m. Sunday through Friday. Late evening calls, daytime calls and Saturday and Sunday calls can hurt the response rate.

If the researcher needs to complete about 400 interviews in *one* evening (the usual number for 5% error and 95% confidence) 20 interviewers each working about 4 hours will be needed, which is a considerable logistical challenge. In a national survey, using a WATTS line, interviewers can begin calling at 6 p.m. in the Eastern time zone and still call to the Pacific time zone six hours later, when the time there is only 9 p.m. At $7 per hour, plus an hour of training, the cost in wages will be $700, not including telephone charges, supervisory costs, computer costs and so-on.

Note that when 400 completions are needed, several times that many telephone numbers (perhaps 2,000) should be available to account for disconnected numbers, business numbers, answering machines, individuals not at home to receive the call and refusals to cooperate. All of these factors slow the survey completion rate.[1] Professional interviewers, those who are experienced and have excellent telephone skills, make more than $10 per hour and can complete surveys approaching 80% of the answering households. But novices may achieve only 60% completion from answering households, raising costs and validity concerns.

---

1. James H. Frey (1989). *Survey research by telephone, 2nd ed.* Newbury Park, CA: Sage, p. 177.

Mail. In mail surveys as well, far more questionnaires must be sent than are likely to be returned. The return rate for mail surveys can be less than 30%, but the researcher should take all possible steps to achieve a better return because the lower the return rate the greater the uncertainty about the sample's external validity.[2]

Costs for mail surveys can be substantial, equaling or in some cases exceeding telephone surveys. Costs include stamps, printing, questionnaire design, data input and supervision. First-class stamps for 1,000 letters in 1998 cost $320, but usually the cost is not limited to one stamp per respondent. For example, a questionnaire and a return envelop could require two stamps plus the cost of a pre-mailing announcement and one or more follow-ups. Clearly, the mail survey is not necessarily a low-cost medium, although it is convenient for many research needs.

In-person, In-home. Because in-home interviews require travel time, appointments and usually long interviews, their costs will be several times greater than the other two methods. An in-home or in-office interviewer is unlikely to complete even one interview per hour, partly because the questionnaires tend to be longer and more involved, but also because of travel time and interruptions. Other costs will include insurance for interviewers and liability for accidents. Further, in-person interviewing requires more training than other methods.[3]

Questionnaire design

Questionnaires can be as plain as 8.5 x 11-inch bond paper or as fancy as a slick, four-color process can make them. In general, the questionnaire should look professional and command attention and respect. It should be pleasing to look at, not a jumble of type crammed onto a page. It should invite easy reading and participation.

Any questionnaire should be preceded by a letter or an introduction explaining the general purpose of the survey and addressing issues such as compulsory compliance, confidentiality and anonymity. The respondent should be advised of any reward or inducement for completing the survey, such as "contributing to knowledge of how X works," or a copy of the outcome on request.

Note that the use of **human subjects** for any research conducted in or for an academic institution must have institutional review board (IRB) approval. Usually, IRB approval is slower and requires more documentation if the research can be

---

2. Neil Atherton Day, David R. Dunt and Susan Day (1995). "Maximizing response to surveys in health program evaluation at minimum cost using multiple methods: Mail, telephone, and visit," *Evaluation Review* 19(4):436-450.

3. James H. Frey and Sabine Mertens Oishi (1995). *How to conduct interviews by telephone and in person.* Thousand Oaks, CA: Sage.

perceived as psychologically or physically threatening for any participant. Even in the case of a harmless telephone interview, an IRB might require this kind of introduction:

> Hello, I'm _____ calling from X University, and I'm doing a mass media survey. May I speak with the person at this residence who is 18 or older and who had the most recent birthday — is that you or someone else?
> (IF SAME PERSON:) As I was saying...
> (IF DIFFERENT PERSON:) Hello, my name is _____ and...
> I'm an X University student doing a class assignment on people's views about the mass media. This survey has been reviewed and approved by the University's Human Subjects Committee. Your residence was selected randomly, and your answers will be completely anonymous. Can you spare 10 minutes to help me complete my class assignment?
> (IF YES:) Let's begin now with the first question:

The second paragraph contains all of the ethical requirements, as approved by an IRB: 1) interviewer's name, 2) sponsoring institution, 3) general topic of survey for **informed consent** purposes — the respondent knows enough about what will follow to make an informed judgment about whether to participate, 4) IRB approval, 5) how the subject was selected — often people are suspicious about receiving calls from people they don't know, 6) confidentiality, and 7) length of the survey. Additionally, the IRB requires a verification statement at the end of call:

> Thanks for your help. Any questions you may have about this survey's legitimacy can be verified by calling (608) 453-4543. Good night.

Once past the IRB requirements, there are many nuances in the construction of a questionnaire. Excellent texts and walk-through guides exist,[4] but even after tapping into this accumulated knowledge, a researcher learns these lessons partly by experience...by making errors along the way. Still, here are a few things to watch for:

---

4. Michael Wilson (1996). "Asking questions," in Roger Sapsford and Victor Jupp, eds. *Data collection and analysis.* Thousand Oaks, CA: Sage, pp. 94-120. See also: Paul B. Sheatsley (1983). "Questionnaire construction and item writing," in Peter H. Rossi, James D. Wright and Andy B. Anderson, eds. *Handbook of survey research.* New York: Academic Press, pp. 195-230; Jean M. Converse and Stanley Presser (1986). *Survey questions: Handcrafting the standardized questionnaire.* Beverly Hills, CA: Sage Publications.

1. Open with interesting but not-too-demanding questions, lest the respondent be quickly discouraged.

2. In most cases, like-items should be grouped in one portion of the instrument.

3. When numerous items have the same response options, arrange them in the manner of a **check list** so that unnecessary repetitions of response options do not clutter the page.

> example:
>
>   1   2   3   4   5
>
> item 1 xyxyxyxyxyxyxxyxyxyxyx   /___/___/___/___/___/
>
> item 2 yxyxyxyxyxyxyxyxyxyxyx   /___/___/___/___/___/

4. Arrange the content of the questionnaire in a manner that **flows logically** from topic to topic. For example, in a questionnaire about organizational communication, all the items dealing with co-workers should be grouped, then all the items about management, then all the items about the corporate structure.

5. Use **transitions**. After completing the section on co-workers, say or write, "Now, think about your recent conversations with supervisors or your department head," and move into that section of questionnaire.

6. Use **simple language**. Regardless of how clear the instructions or statements may seem, people will misinterpret. After writing each item, become a respondent, anticipating all the ways an item might be interpreted. Ask several friends to read the statement and respond.

7. Response options should offer approximately **equal intervals**, and be **mutually exclusive**: intervals must not overlap. For example, do not use "1 to 5 years" or "5 to 20 years" because the intervals are unequal, and a "5-year" person could be in either group.

8. Offer a **neutral/no opinion option** for each question.

9. Avoid **leading questions** such as, "Do you read a lot?"; **double-barreled** questions such as, "Do you like dogs and cats?"; and **prestige** questions such as, "About how many magazines do you read each month?"

10. Put **demographics** at the end.

11. Estimate the time required to complete the instrument, and in general, **keep it short**.

12. Conduct a **pretest**. Actually try out the questionnaire on several respondents who are intended to complete the finished instrument, to learn whether people in the sample see problems the researcher might have missed.

Mail questionnaire format

When money is not an issue, select high quality paper, use tasteful colors, plentiful graphics and professional-quality printing. The more competence the instrument seems to reflect, the more respect it will receive from respondents. However, in the likely event that money is an issue, and if the project will be done in-house (not sending the form out to a printer), here is a simple, efficient format.

Select a good bond paper, 8.5 x 14 (legal size). Turn it long-way and fold at the middle in the form of a four-page booklet. Many copiers will feed legal-size paper this way, and the larger copiess will even print 11 x 17 (which allows four pages 8.5 x 11). Use the front and back of each page. On the front, put the title of the survey, accompanied by a visual or a graphic (it could be computer clip art), and the name of the sponsoring individual or institution. On the inside cover page, write a brief introduction of the survey and its purpose. Suggest a one-week or so deadline for return of the instrument. Convince the respondent that completing the form is worth doing.

After the introduction, move to page three. Begin the questions, arranged in the most orderly, symmetrical and attractive way that can be managed. If the survey is long, additional pages might be added, but keep in mind that the finished instrument should be kept as short as possible. Simple graphic components, such as horizontal divider lines or shadow boxes, help make the form attractive if used judiciously.

One of the significant problems of the mailed instrument is loss of control over who will fill it out. For example, a questionnaire to a corporate chief executive officer most likely will be completed by someone else. This may be beyond the control of the researcher. However, some evidence indicates that mail surveys may be as effective at reaching the intended respondent as the other two types of surveys.[5]

---

5. John M. Bushery, et al. (1993). "The schools and staffing survey: How reinterview measures data quality." ERIC: National Center for Education Statistics.

Telephone questionnaire format

Telephone questionnaires also require a brief introduction to the respondent, usually something along these lines:

> Hello, my name is _____, and I am calling on behalf of the _____ . We are asking people in this area how they feel about _____. I would appreciate it if you could take just a few minutes of your time to answer a few questions. First, do you have a current email account..., etc.

One point to make about the technique is that permission to continue the interview is **implied**, not overtly stated. This is a little delicate, for the preferred method would be to ask plainly, "May I ask you a few questions?" But it is risky to await the approval of the respondent because "No!" comes very easily. In fact, the usual practice is to pause for only a second and then continue. The respondent can terminate the conversation at any point by hanging up.

Telephone interviewers must be carefully trained to avoid inflection, word changes and other cues that might send a response in an inaccurate direction. The intent is for all respondents to answer the same questions. Training typically is a group affair in which interviewers are told of all proper procedures and practices. Even professional interviewers must be trained prior to beginning a new survey, and supervised throughout.[6]

The telephone questionnaire, if not on screen, can be on plain 8.5 x 11 paper. So as not to confuse the interviewers, attention should be paid to neatness in layout. Put instructions (such as filter and contingency directions) in upper case/boldface to distinguish from the items that will be read to respondents.

Measurement

One of the most popular measuring devices is the Likert scale developed by Rensis Likert some 50 years ago. It typically offers five response options: strongly agree, agree, undecided, disagree and strongly disagree.

Another device is called the thermometer scale. It is a graphic device that looks like a thermometer, but its intervals are used to measure a person's "warmth" or "coolness" toward an object. For example, if a respondent's attitude toward police dramas is warmish, that person might mark an 80 or perhaps 86 on the scale.

---

6. Paul J. Lavrakas (1993). *Telephone survey methods: Sampling, selection, and supervision, 2nd ed.* Newbury Park, CA: Sage.

Measures are often "forced choice," meaning that the respondent must chose one of two or three options, not finer gradations and not open-ended. For example, the options might be yes, no and undecided. The problem with this measure is that it might not very accurately fit the respondent's "true" feeling about the object. Researchers avoid open-ended (long-hand, write-in) responses because they are difficult to quantify.

Rank-order measures can be useful. For example, respondents could be asked to list five issues in the news, then to put the number 1 by the issue most important to them, 2 for the next, etc. In general, the more sophisticated the measure, the more possibilities for analysis. Advanced survey research students will want to investigate "magnitude estimation scaling" and the "semantic differential."

Believability

Despite the extensive use of survey research for the better part of the 20th century, social scientists still debate its validity. Considering all of the readily acknowledged faults in sampling methods and questionnaire construction, all of the subtleties of question wording and voice inflection, can people's answers really be believed? For example, those who denounce survey research point to all of its methodological flaws and then add that respondents often: 1) don't have a firm opinion about a topic, yet they will answer questions; 2) misinterpret questions and get "coached" by the interviewer; and, 3) have difficulty articulating an opinion when they do have one.

Critics of survey research usually are fundamentally opposed to quantitative research and believe that an array of numerical responses cannot possibly convey people's true attitudes and opinions. These critics are joined by social scientists who champion quantitative research but recognize the many pitfalls that interfere with adequate and accurate measurement.[7] Is there an answer to the conundrum: Can surveys really be believed?

If the methodological difficulties are considered in advance — if researchers are careful to follow the guidelines established during three generations of survey research — the outcomes can be believed. People who agree to respond to surveys generally do take them seriously. They provide answers to the best of their ability. They tell the truth.

---

7. Daniel Yankelovich (1991). *Coming to public judgment: Making democracy work in a complex world*. Syracuse, NY: Syracuse University Press, pp. 24-37. See also: John Brehm (1993). *The phantom respondents: Opinion surveys and political representation*, Ann Arbor: University of Michigan Press, p. 181; Peter V. Miller (1995). "The industry of public opinion," in Theodore L. Glasser and Charles T. Salmon, eds. *Public opinion and the communication of consent*, New York: The Guilford Press, pp. 121-122.

Summary

Of the four important aspects of survey research — sampling, questionnaire design, administration and data analysis — this chapter focuses on **questionnaire design** and **administration**. The sponsor of the research must decide whether to conduct a **telephone, mail** or **in-person** survey. Strengths and limitations, and the costs of each method are compared.

Most questionnaires should include a brief introduction with a justification for the effort required and an appeal for anonymous, confidential participation. The introduction also should include ethical considerations related to using **human subjects** and **informed consent**.

Twelve guidelines for questionnaire preparation are presented, including **grouping similar topics**, arranging items in a **logical order**, using **transitions**, the variety of **questions** and measurement **scales** to use, **simplicity**, **brevity** and **pre-testing** the instrument. A low-cost, in-house questionnaire is described.

Specific format suggestions for mail questionnaires and telephone interviews are presented along with the types of measurements found in most surveys. The chapter ends with a discussion of whether questionnaire respondents can be believed.

Exercises:

A. Review the "Media Use Inventory" presented in an earlier chapter of this text, and use it to prepare an attractive instrument in the manner suggested under this chapter's heading "Mail questionnaire format."

Using legal-size bond paper, fold into a booklet form; put the questionnaire title and a graphic on the cover; put an introductory letter or paragraph on the inside page, and begin the questionnaire on the next page. Emphasize a concern for appearance and readability. (If setting the text in the right position on the page is a problem, as it will be for some PC users, cutting and pasting to achieve the desired effect will be sufficient.)

B. Select a topic in the news and prepare a questionnaire to measure public awareness and concern for the issue. For example, suppose there is a political scandal in Washington, D.C. Create a questionnaire to measure your respondents' *interest* in the issue and *knowledge* of it. Try to write at least 10 substantive questions in addition to several demographic items. Use a variety of response options; for example, write some items as yes/no/; agree/disagree; thermometer scale; rank order; etc.

34
Experiments

Early study: C. Arnold Anderson (1928-29). "An experimental study of 'social facilitation' as affected by 'intelligence,'" *American Journal of Sociology 34*(1-6):864-881.

Recent study: Stephen R. Flora and Richard E. Logan (1996). "Using computerized psychology examinations: An experimental analysis," *Psychology Reports 79*(1):235-241.

Business applications: Rita Koselka (1996). "The new mantra: MVT." (multivariable testing for product qualty control; example about movie theater profits) *Forbes*, (March 11), *157*(5):114-118.

This exercise may be assigned for submission at the start of your next class (you're allowed to read the chapter before doing the exercise).

Near the end of the term, students in many college classes do a teacher/class evaluation. Some teachers believe that these evaluations are invalid: They can't really measure the level of learning that takes place, or the ratings may depend on a variety of factors including how well the instructor tells a joke. Other teachers believe that students can effectively assess the class learning environment. Assume you are one of the former, a teacher who has doubts about the validity of these end-of-semester evaluations.

To prove your point, you devise an experiment based on the hypothesis that grades affect the evaluation. This term you teach two separate sections of the same class. You decide that in one section, the week before the evaluations, you'll give a difficult test. You'll hand back a set of low grades from the test, tell students they need to study harder for the final, and then let the class do the evaluations after you leave the room. In the other section, you'll give an easy test, hand back a set of high grades, tell students they seem well prepared for the final, and then let the class do the evaluations.

1. What outcome would support your hypothesis that the class/teacher evaluations are not a valid assessment of the semester's learning experience in the class?

2. Does the experiment, as described, effectively **mask** the purpose of the experiment? Explain why.

3. Does this experiment breach **ethical** standards of research? Explain:

4. Is there a **control group** in this experiment?

(continued)

5. List and briefly explain **five** possible **intervening variables** that might account for the differences in class/teacher evaluation outcomes that have nothing to do with the experimental treatment:

a)

b)

c)

d)

e)

6. Assume that the easy-test class gives significantly higher evaluations than the tough-test class. From your perspective, as the teacher who doubts the validity of the class/teacher evaluations, does this experiment provide evidence that the evaluations are not a valid assessment of the semester's learning experience?

* * *

The experimental method is rooted in the human experience. Carl Sagan attributed its initial use to the development of thinking as hunter-gatherer clans learned to track prey, but more formally to ancient Greece.[1] As a distinct research tactic, the procedure was described in rules for medical experiments in the 11th century and used by Sir Francis Bacon in 1627 to determine which concoctions wheat seeds should be steeped in to speed germination and yield hearty growth (cow urine was better than wine).[2] Experimental design was perfected across a variety of natural and social science disciplines, with communication being a recent devotee.

While surveys are said to be the principal data-gathering technique in communication today,[3] the distinction may actually belong to experiments. Commercial firms engage in **proprietary** research using experimental design to test product messages and their effects. When Madison Avenue advertising agencies in Manhattan develop commercials, couriers take the video tape to the north shores of New Jersey where a thriving experimental testing industry grew to meet the demand. Test results are kept and analyzed by the sponsoring firms.

Experiments are used to test a specific hypothesis under controlled conditions. They are the primary instrument in the researcher's arsenal to establish a case for cause-and-effect. A well designed experiment allows researchers to conclude that people prefer message A to message B, or that a new commercial will be an effective sales tool: The message will increase product sales.

Such a powerful research instrument can be difficult to wield, and it is true that experiments require careful planning and execution to deliver the clear-cut answers researchers seek. To demonstrate of steps in the experimental steps, here's how a new 30-second commercial for "Evian," a bottled water, might be tested.

Experimental procedures

1. Select a setting. Experiments are popularly depicted as being done by white-jacketed researchers in a laboratory with wires from machines connected to mice scampering through a maze. In the lab, scientists have maximum control over the experimental conditions. They can keep the lighting and room temperature constant, place the maze in a fixed position and start each mouse on the same spot.

---

1. Carl Sagan (1996). *The demon-haunted world: Science as a candle in the dark.* New York: Random House, pp. 312-317; 309-310).

2. William G. Cochran (1997). "Early development of techniques in comparative experimentation," in Raymond O. Collier Jr. and Thomas J. Hummel, eds. *Experimental design and interpretation.* Berkeley, CA: McCutchan Publishing, p. 5.

3. Susanna Hornig Priest (1996). *Doing media research: An introduction.* Thousand Oaks, CA: Sage, pp. 37-48. See also: Michael Singletary (1994). *Mass communication research: contemporary methods and applications.* New York: Longman, p. 10.

With human subjects, a laboratory setting is usually a meeting room, theater-type auditorium, or a viewing room with television monitors or projection screens. Again, this kind of lab offers maximum control over the setting. All subjects go through the experiment under exactly the same conditions. The obvious disadvantage is that the setting is contrived, and people might behave differently in a lab than they would as they go about their normal daily routine.

Researchers know they will get measurable "outcomes" in a lab experiment because subjects will receive a large dose of the experimental variable. They will be asked to view and pay attention to the Evian commercial being tested. After it is shown, the lab subjects will be given a questionnaire that measures their impressions of the commercial or the product. Subjects will be able to complete the questionnaire because they just watched the commercial, and the researcher will be able to measure effects from the experimental treatment of viewing the commercial.

In the course of daily television viewing, most people will not see the commercial or remember it. If survey subjects were given the same questionnaire two weeks after the Evian commercial began airing, most would not be able to answer specific questions about the commercial. The survey is likely to produce minimum measurement because most of the questions will be left blank. For some research topics, a **natural setting**, out in the real world of daily living, is the only way to assess effects. The lab is a **contrived setting** but necessary for controlling conditions extraneous to the experimental variable.

2. Sample subjects. Unlike survey research, experimental design is not intended to be generalizable to a larger population. Because the subjects are not selected by a random sampling of the general public, their responses cannot be expected to equal those of the general public. Finding that 70% of the experimental sample liked the Evian commercial tells nothing about the actual percentage of television viewers who might like it. Still, researchers use experiments to test how variables affect behavior and attitudes, and they assume that if the experimental subjects like the commercial, so will the public.

Samples for experiments are either volunteers, such as sophomores in a communication class who participate for extra credit, or paid subjects who answer a newspaper ad. Obviously such subjects do not represent the general population, though they may possess some prescribed trait. For instance, if the product were toupees, and 95% of toupee purchasers were older men, the ad for experimental subjects might call for males over age 50 or balding males. Subjects for women's perfume commercials might be restricted to women in a given age or income group.

The Evian commercial testing might not require any special subject characteristics, or it might require that applicants for the experiment be people who have purchased bottled water in the past six months. The sample should be composed of people who are potential purchasers of the product, but within that limit the group should be diverse.

While samples for surveys are relatively large (400 to 1,200 people), experimental samples are small, usually about 15-30 in a group. The reason for small samples is that in experimental design **external validity** is not the main issue. The concern is whether the manipulation (the commercial) is effective: Whether Group A's responses are significantly different from Group B's responses as a result of seeing the commercial. If people in the Evian experiment say they like the commercial, the researcher has every reason to suspect that another sample of 25 people will like it, too...within the normal latitude of chance. However, experiments often are repeated to be on the safe side. The researcher might run another 25 through the same experiment to be sure the results are similar. If the researcher's job depends on being right, the experiment might be run several more times, or in half a dozen other cities if the commercial is to be aired nationally.

One other aspect of experimental samples should be noted. Most experimental designs require two or more groups (as discussed in the next section), and it is necessary to apportion the subjects among those groups in a manner that distributes their characteristics equally. One method is to divide the groups by **randomizing** the subjects, such as giving a pre-numbered card to people as they enter the assembly room, then determining which group they will be in by drawing lots.

Another method is **matching,** or purposely forming the groups based on distributing important characteristics equally among the groups. Gender, race or age can be parceled easily, but matching usually requires that subjects complete a questionnaire to determine more essential variables for the study such as subjects' past purchases of Evian. Matching by using a questionnaire runs the risk of telling subjects too much about the experiment, so in most cases randomizing is the more efficient and preferred method to equalize groups.

3. Experimental designs. Depending on the experiment's purpose, a variety of groups is necessary to accomplish the goal of controlling variables. Researchers use these notations[4] to describe experimental designs: R = randomize, O = observation or measurement, X = treatment or presenting the experimental manipulation. They are listed left-to-right, so the following string: R O_1 X O_2 means to randomize, then take a first measurement (observation 1), then administer the experimental variable, then take a measurement at time two (observation 2).

---

4. Donald Campbell and Julian Stanley (1970). *Experimental and quasi-experimental designs for research.* Chicago: Rand McNally.

A simple experiment called a **single-shot study** is described by the notation:

Experimental group   X   O

bring in the experimental group, show a commercial, measure the effects by a questionnaire. Although simple, this design might suffice for determining whether subjects liked the commercial. But two intervening or confounding variables could be influencing this outcome. No baseline has been measured, so the researcher has no idea about the subjects' impression of the product before they saw the commercial. What if many of these subjects' were Evian devotees prior to seeing the commercial, and the commercial lowered their initial enthusiasm for the product? They might still give the commercial good ratings even though they thought it was a weak endorsement of one of their favorite products. The other confounding variable is called the Hawthorne effect, in which subjects are prone to give positive ratings to any experimental treatment to please the researcher.[5]

Accounting for these effects is done with **control** groups, or groups that are not given the experimental variable, and the experimental design is more advanced:

$$\begin{array}{lllll} \text{Group 1} & R & O_1 & X & O_2 \\ \text{Group 2} & R & O_1 & & O_2 \end{array}$$

This is called a **pretest-posttest control group** design. Here two groups are used, with the subjects for each group selected by randomization. Group 1 is the experimental group, receiving a measurement that includes subject's use and opinion of Evian before seeing a commercial (the experimental treatment), then getting another measurement after the treatment that measures opinion of the product. Group 2 is the control group; there is no X, the group gets no experimental treatment. Instead Group 2 gets the same prior measurement about use and opinion of Evian, then the group is treated to a video of waterfalls accompanied by Mozart's music, and afterwards completes the measure of opinion toward the product.

Both groups are expected to score equally on the pretest, establishing the baseline, but Group 1 should score significantly higher than Group 2 on the post-test if the Evian commercial was effective. Group 2's post-test score provides a control for any Hawthorne influences of the experimental situation because this group's post-test score cannot be attributed to the commercial. This design also controls

---

5. Joan Gay Snodgrass, Gail Levy-Berger and Martin Haydon (1985). *Human experimental psychology*. New York: Oxford University Press, pp. 272-274. See also: Donald Granberg and Soren Holmberg (1992). "The Hawthorne effect in election studies: The impact of survey participation on voting," *British Journal of Political Science* 22(2):240-247; Gary D. Gottfredson (1996). "The Hawthorne misunderstanding (and how to get the Hawthorne effect in action research)," *Journal of Research in Crime and Delinquency* 33(1):28-48.

confounding events that may occur in experiments between time one and time two. Yet a another potentially confounding variable should be considered: **sensitization**, or effects that can be attributed to similarities between the pretest and post-test.

Sensitization is a real problem in any experimental situation. Researchers try not to let subjects know the purpose of the experiment because if they discern the study's intent, that might influence their responses on the post-test. The most common method of hiding intent is to **mask** the real purpose of the study. In the Evian example, masking might be accomplished by showing three commercials: one for a popular carbonated soft drink, one for Evian, and one for a fruit juice drink. Masking involves a predetermined effort to trick the subjects to some extent, and any deceit raises ethical concerns. But, if the deception is not harmful or embarrassing, and if subjects are told about the experimental methods in a debriefing session, minor subterfuge is considered necessary to achieve the study's intent.

Still, in the Evian example, sensitization is likely to result from any pretest that mentions bottled water or the product itself. Researchers can estimate sensitization from Group 2's post-test in the previous design, but here is a better design:

Group 1	R	X	$O2$
Group 2	R		O_2

This is called the **posttest-only control group** design. It utilizes the concept that randomization will equalize the two groups: Any score that would be measured if a pretest had been administered to the two groups would be equal. Not administering the pretest eliminates sensitization. Because Group 2 is measured only at time two, its score can be considered the actual baseline because this is Group 2's first measure.

A final experimental design is supposed to control all confounding variables:

Group 1	R	O_1	X	O_2
Group 2	R	O_1		O_2
Group 1	R		X	O_2
Group 2	R			O_2

This is called the **Solomon Four-Group** design, a much more sophisticated procedure but a classic experimental tactic. Despite its ability to provide complete control, it is not used frequently in communication research or in other social science experiments because of the additional costs and the exponential difficulty in analyzing the outcomes.[6]

_____

6. For more explanation about these designs see: Mildren L. Patten (1997). *Understanding research methods: An overview of the essentials.* Los Angeles: Pyrczak Publishing, pp. 5, 13, 79-88.

4. Do a pilot study. As should be evident from the description, experiments are fraught with potential procedural disasters. A **pilot study**, or mini run-through of the experiment using two or three people who are similar to the actual subjects, can demonstrate whether the procedures will work. The equipment can be tested, the questionnaires or measuring instruments can be analyzed to be sure subjects will understand the form, and any deficiencies noted in the pilot test can be rectified.

Experiments require time and a lot of forethought. They are relatively expensive to do. And because their purpose is to test hypotheses, there is no room for making errors that might allow extraneous variables to interfere with the direct relationship between the experimental and outcome variables.

More experimental considerations

The Evian experiment example is a rather simple, one-shot design: Show subjects the commercial, ask them to assess it. But what happens if the advertising agency develops three different commercials and wants to select the most effective one to air? This kind of experiment might require several treatment and control groups simply to eliminate effects that might be attributed to the order in which subjects are shown the three commercials.

Some experiments require measuring effects over time. For instance, a school system might develop an eight-week *television series* designed to teach adult learners basic reading skills. Those administering the program would want a prior measure of reading skills and another measure after the series to assess reading information gain. A control group of adult non-readers, who will not view the series, should be used to be sure there is no intervening influence during the eight weeks, such as a local library offering basic reading groups. Further, the reading skill increases from the television series should be compared with another experimental group of adult learners who study basic reading in *evening classes*. Finally, a second outcome measure might be scheduled for three weeks after the television series to determine if the reading gains remained. Scheduling post-tests several weeks after an experiment to assess lasting effects is a normal experimental procedure.

In the case of advertising, as with many other experimental situations, the dependent variable measured in the lab may be only an attitude change: Are subjects more favorable toward the commercial or the product? The true test of effects is: Will subjects purchase the product? Such natural-setting outcomes are sought in a variety of social science and communication experiments because researchers know the limitations of measuring human behavior in the contrived setting of a lab. An experiment that is carried out in a natural environment is called a **field test**. While difficult to design and chancy to control, field tests yield some of the most innovative and convincing findings about people's actual behavior.

Summary

Experiments are a powerful research procedure designed to test cause-and-effect in a clearly defined hypothesis using strict controls. The four major elements in an experiment are: 1) the setting, 2) the sample subjects, 3) the experimental design, and 4) a pilot test.

Because controlling intervening variables is essential in this research procedure, designing an effective experiment is a complicated task. Experiments can be designed to research a wide variety of topics both in the lab and in natural settings. Depending on its purpose, a variety of controls may be needed, but the experiment is still a potent method of charting human behavior.

Exercises:

A. You are the research head of Gannett, a media conglomerate that is testing a new billboard for a chemical treatment product to be used by Midwest corn farmers this summer. Billboards rent for $3,000 a month, and the chemical firm will rent 1,000 billboards from May through July. The creative people designed two billboards. One shows the product in its blue 55-gallon drum with the slogan: Blue Bomb Blasts Bugs. The second uses the same graphic with the slogan: Stronger, Longer Performer. The experimental test is, "Which billboard is more effective in selling the product?" Here are some decisions to make:

1. What **type of subjects** will you use as your experimental sample to choose the right slogan:

2. If you pay 60 subjects $200 each, and fly them to a Chicago airport hotel, **what procedure** will you use to divide them into groups to view the two billboards:

3. If you use a pretest before showing the groups the billboards, will you need to use a **control group**:   Yes   or   No   (*circle one*)

4. Provide one question that should be on your **pretest**:

5. Provide one question that should be on your **post-test**:

6. The experiment's results show that subjects gave favorable ratings to both slogans, but the ratings were nearly equal. What recommendation would you give the client about its 1,000 billboard advertising campaign?

B. This is the hypothesis: Music interferes with students' concentration. To test the hypothesis experimentally, a group of students will be brought into a room and given a story to read while music is played in the room. When the students complete the reading assignment, they will be given a series of questions testing their recall about the story to see if the music interfered with their concentration. A control group of similar students will go through the same process, but no music will be played while they read the story. If the hypothesis is supported, the control group's recall scores should be significantly higher than those of the experimental group.

List three intervening variables — other than demographics — that might interfere with the direct cause-and-effect relationship between playing music and ability to recall details from the story. For instance, all conditions of the room, such as lighting and temperature, should be the same for both groups.

1.

2.

3.

35

Content Analysis

Article 1: David P. Phillips (1978). "Airplane accident fatalities increase just after newspaper stories about murder and suicide," *Science 201*(4357):748-750.

Article 2: Michael L. Klassen, Suzanne M. Wauer and Sheila Cassel (1990/1991). "Increase in health and weight loss claims in food advertising in the eighties," *Journal of Advertising Research 30*(6):32-37.

Article 3: James B. Weaver III (1991). "Are 'slasher' horror films sexually violent? A content analysis," *Journal of Broadcasting & Electronic Media 35*(3):385-392.

Article 4: Edward E. Adams and John V. Bodle (1995). "Research presented at conventions: How well are women doing?" *Journalism & Mass Communication Educator 50*(2):14-22.

How important is content analysis to communication research study? The answer can be taken from a content analysis — actually just a perusal — of the articles that appeared in a major communication journal in the mid-1990s. Forty percent of the articles were based on content analysis.[1] The reason is apparent from the classic Berelson definition of content analysis: "a research technique for the objective, systematic and quantitative description of the manifest content of communication."[2] The "manifest content communication" is anything spoken (and recorded), written,

---

1. Several scholarly studies of content analysis articles in communication journals have been done. See: Daniel Riffe and Alan Freitag (1997). "A content analysis of content analyses: Twenty-five years of Journalism Quarterly," *Journalism & Mass Communication Quarterly 74*(4):873-882.

2. Bernard Berelson (1952). *Content analysis in communication research.* Glencoe,IL: Free Press, p. 18. See also: Michael H. Walizer and Paul L. Wienir (1978). *Research methods and analysis: Searching for relationships.* New York: Harper & Row; Klaus Krippendorff (1980). *Content analysis: An introduction to its methodology.* Beverly Hills, CA: Sage Publications; Fred N. Kerlinger (1986). *Foundations of behavioral research, 3rd ed.* New York: Holt, Rinehart & Winston.

published, broadcast, presented as a graphic or on film, or digitized. In short, it's what communicators do: They produce and send messages that leave a trail. Once a trail exists, it's possible to analyze that trail.

Uses of content analysis

What benefit accrues from analyzing the content of communication? Many have been suggested.[3] The first is to **describe the content** itself. For example, the issues presented and how they are presented is useful to know. A study of newspaper content might show that 30% of page-one stories are local news; 20%, national; another 20%, international; 15%, state; and the other 15%, county news. Evaluating this classification, an editor might might decide to hire more reporters to increase local news coverage. Much can be learned about what is being communicated by counting and classifying the manifest content. Mere description of what appears probably ranks as the most frequent type of content analysis study.

Often, however, a researcher is trying to do more than merely describe. Usually the researcher is wondering if some observation is correct. This is the prelude to stating an hypothesis, and **hypothesis testing** is the second reason for content analysis. Perhaps the observation is that there seem to be a lot of antacid products, health foods, prescription drugs and vitamin supplements advertised on the network evening news. Does this suggest that network news caters to an over-40 audience? A content analysis of the ads could at least support or refute whether most of the ads are for these products. Actually, every effective content analysis requires a clearly stated hypothesis. Otherwise the counting could go on forever.

Documenting trends is another reason for doing content analysis. Here, the researcher tries to determine changes over time. Are movies really more violent today? A content analysis of films from the 1990s might be compared with films produced in the 1960s and with those from the 1930s. Regardless of the categorization ("violence" is a slippery conceptual topic), it should be possible to determine if the movie industry serves up appreciably more violent fare today than it did in the past.

Relating media content to the real world is another content anlaysis purpose. The objective is to compare what appears in communication messages with a known statistic of reality. For example, about 80% of U.S. businesses have fewer than 10 employees. Yet the published reports on communication in organizations may be entirely on firms of 10,000-plus employees. Students who study communication in organizations might get the impression that only large corporations need advice.

---

3. Klaus Krippendorff (1980), *op. cit.* See also: Roger D. Wimmer and Joseph R. Dominick (1997). *Mass media research: An introduction, 5th ed.* Belmont, CA: Wadsworth; Daniel Riffe, Stephen Lacy and Frederick G. Fico (1998). *Analyzing media messages: Using quantitative content analysis in research.* Mahwah, NJ: Lawrence Erlbaum.

Part of the comparison of media content to the real world is the comparison of groups as depicted in the media to the group's status in the real world. Many studies of women, racial minorities, job categories, etc., have been done. For example, if African Americans are not included in mainstream mass media, such as being main characters in novels, prior to 1960, or if they are depicted in a demeaning manner, such a finding has implications about both the *media content* and the *society*.

Lastly, a growing research interest area is content analysis and text analysis[4] that attempts to **assess the motives of the messenger** (see Framing and Priming chapter). Here the message is analyzed to discover the intent of those who created and disseminated it.

If this seems like a lapse from reality, remember that virtually all communication is purposeful. Analyzing the content of the message should infer the messenger's intent. For example, Congress has accused the Public Broadcasting System of being elitist and radically liberal. If a content analysis of the PBS programs showed that 75% did contain socialistic or counter-culture themes, a case might be made that PBS's programmers do have a leftist political agenda.

These five categories are only a few of many approaches suggested for doing content analysis research,[5] which owes its popularity to these advantages: 1) it's inexpensive, 2) material is usually accessible, 3) it's unobtrusive — CA studies don't influence people's responses, as can occur in surveys and other research methods, 4) it yields quantifiable data, and 5) it deals with either current or past events.[6] These advantages far outweigh the disadvantages, although content analysis is not without its detractors.[7]

---

4. Carl W. Roberts (1997). *Text analysis for the social sciences: Methods for drawing statistical inferences from texts and transcripts*. New York: Lawrence Erlbaum. See also: Robert E. Scholes (1985). *Textual power: Literary theory and the teaching of English*. New Haven, CT: Yale University Press.

5. Irving L. Janis (1965). "The problem of validating content analysis," in Harold D. Lasswell, Nathan Leites and Associates, eds. *Language of politics*. Cambridge, MA: MIT Press, pp. 55-82. See also: Ole R. Holsti (1969). *Content analysis for the social sciences and humanities*. Reading, MA: Addison-Wesley; Robert Plant Armstrong (1959). "Content analysis in folkloristics," in Ithiel de Sola Pool, ed. *Trends in content analysis*. Urbana: University of Illinois Press, pp. 151-170.

6. Arthur Asa Berger (1982). *Media analysis techniques*. Beverly Hills, CA: Sage Publications, p. 107.

7. Content analysis has become the focus of a social science research methods debate that drives to the heart of interpreting reality. Several articles that encompass these concerns appeared in *American Behavioral Scientist Vol. 33*. See also: William A. Evans (1990). "The interpretive turn in media research: Innovation, iteration, or illusion?" *Critical Studies in Mass Communication 7*(2):147-168; Thelma McCormack, ed., (1982). "Content analysis: The social history of a method," in *Studies in Communications Vol. 2*. Greenwich, CT: JAI Press; Eric Woodrum (1984). "'Mainstreaming' content analysis in social science: Methodological advantages, obstacles, and solutions," *Social Science Research 13*(1):1-19; Sari Thomas (1994). "Artifactual study in the analysis of culture: A defense of content analysis in a postmodern age," *Communication Research 21*(6):683-697.

Steps through a CA study

This is an actual content analysis done 20 years ago for the Los Angeles *Herald Examiner*. An African-American welfare mother was in her front lawn brandishing a kitchen knife to keep a city worker from turning off her utilities. The Los Angeles Police Department called in a SWAT team, which circled the yard and then opened fire on the woman (possibly by mistake). Her death resulted in riots and accusations that the LAPD used unnecesary force because the woman was a minority.

Step 1. **Stating the hypothesis.** Did the LAPD overreact in racial situations, as community leaders claimed? More specifically, do white LAPD officers have a greater tendency to use lethal force against minority suspects? The newspaper wanted to know, so it secured several years of news releases issued by the LAPD's public information officer following investigations of police officers firing a weapon (an inquiry is required after every police weapon firing).

Step 2. The reports are rather dry and technical: "At 2:27 a.m. Tuesday, March 23, Detective R. Vincent Jones, 38, a white married male assigned to Narcotics Division 5, who is an 11-year veteran with a junior college degree, fired three shots from his service revolver at a fleeing robbery suspect at 15th and Madison. Shot once in the shoulder was...." The reports are the basis of media stories on the outcomes of hearings, but the media stories rarely include the detail or data consistency of the reports. The reports can be considered excellent sources of content[8] because they include all relevant data on every case in which an LAPD officer fired a weapon, the criterion for the **population of incidents the study sought to investigate**.

Step 3. **Selecting a sample.** Much has been written about selecting samples for content analysis because most studies include far more content than can possibly be counted. For example, if a study sought to determine how television depicts people in the age categories of under-30, 30 to 60, and over age 60, thousands of depictions would occur each week. To reduce the number of depictions to a manageable size, the study would have to be limited to depictions on prime-time sit-coms with a further limit to main characters, defined as those with speaking parts.

But television sit-coms come and go, and their characters vary even during one season. To control for changing shows and roles, and to make the case that the study does represent age depictions during a single year, some sampling would be required. It would be possible to select one week of fall-season shows and another week in the spring, but two specific weeks might not accurately reflect the entire range of shows during the year. A better method is to randomly select a Monday from the fall and spring, then select a Tuesday, etc., until a **composite** week of shows

---

8. Eugene J. Webb, Donald T. Campbell, Richard D. Schwartz and Lee Sechrest (1971). *Unobtrusive measures: Nonreactive research in the social sciences.* Chicago: Rand McNally, pp. 29-32.

builds a sample of 45 hours of prime-time viewing (three hours per night for ABC, NBC and CBS, over five weeknights). The 45 hours of fare sampled this way might support a case that the sample represents the range of depictions for the year.

However, the LAPD police shootings content analysis was unusual because it did not require sampling. There were fewer than 500 reports of shooting incidents for the period under study, and while this amount was unwieldy, it was not impossible. A **census** was used rather than a sample.

Step 4. The **unit of analysis selected** in the LAPD shooting study was the entire report. Again, this is somewhat unusual in a content analysis. For example, in the depictions of characters' age in television sit-coms, the unit of analysis was reduced from every character depicted on screen to only characters with speaking roles. However, this definition might include waiters, delivery people, neighbors and a wide range of other minor characters...far too many to analyze, and beyond the scope of the study (depictions of the central-plot characters). A better unit of analysis might be only those characters listed on the credits that introduce the show.

The important aspect of selecting a unit of analysis is that the unit chosen must reflect the study's purpose. Each police shooting report captures an incident of a police officer firing a weapon.

Step 5. **Construct quantifiable categories to be analyzed**. In the television sit-com study, the categories would be the three age ranges of under 30, 30 to 60, and over age 60. The police shooting study was considerably more complicated. Because the purpose was to determine if white police officers were more likely to use lethal force against minorities, a variety of categories had to be accounted for. Many of these would serve as control variables for later analysis. Figure 1 shows the coding form that includes the categories and the quantification system.

This may not be the most extensive coding form in the history of content analysis, but it stretches the limits of comprehensiveness. Using each report as the basis for completing one (or more) of these coding forms, the coders were given a separate sheet of instructions with codes.

Step 6. The coders used the initial forms and sheet of instructions, then reported problems, and the coding form and instructions were changed to increase clarity. This process included **training the coders and conducting a pilot study on the actual material** to be coded to determine if changes were needed. In such a complicated coding form, several were required. But after the pilot study, coders had little difficulty using the forms. An **intercoder reliability** test was done to ensure that the instructions were clear and that two or more coders could complete the forms with high reliability (see Reliability, Validity and Sampling chapter).

Looking at the categories, the essential items of information can be seen as well as some of the control variables needed in the study. Some considerations were:

1) It was necessary to code each incident of shooting as a whole: the officers involved, the situation and the suspects.

2) Perhaps some "divisions" or sections of the city would have more shootings than others; residential areas might have fewer incidents than in center city, and most incidents might occur in parts of the city that had more bars and nightclubs.

LAPD Police Shooting Coding Form   **Number** ☐☐☐

Police Officer:

Age ☐☐   Race ☐
Years on force ☐☐
Rank ☐
Assignment ☐
Division ☐☐
Duty Status ☐
Number shots fired ☐
Type of weapon ☐
Injured ☐
Condition ☐

Suspect:

Age ☐☐   Race ☐
Shots fired ☐
Type weapon ☐
Critical shot ☐
Secondary shots ☐
Condition ☐
Alcohol/drugs ☐

Situation:

Year ☐   Month ☐☐
Day of month ☐☐
Day of week ☐
Time of day ☐☐
Division ☐☐
Who shot first ☐
Number officers who fired ☐
Number suspects who fired ☐
All officers at scene ☐
All suspects at scene ☐
Initial crime/incident ☐
How officers got there ☐
Which person shot ☐
Bystander/hostage shot ☐

Additional Information:

Officer education   ☐
Officer marital status ☐
Disposition of policy ruling ☐
Dispatch accuracy ☐

This is a second or third form on the same shooting incident   ☐
          (1) yes, police
          (2) yes, suspect
          (3) both
          (4) no

Figure 1. Coding form for police shootings content analysis study

3) The kind of assignment an officer had might affect the study because patrol officers might have more opportunities to fire their weapon than those working vice or prostitution; narcotics officers might have higher incidents of using their weapons.

4) A suspect's condition was considered important because a critical shot (the most damaging shot) might have been in the leg or it might have been in the head or trunk of the body, indicating the officer was "shooting to kill." Each of these had a code number on the instruction sheet. For example, the critical shot was coded (1) for a head or trunk shot and (2) for a shot to a limb. Likewise the condition of the suspect was coded (1) dead, (2) critical condition, (3) serious condition, (4) stable condition, and (5) released from the hospital.

5) Aspects of the situation were important, such as whether the incident occurred at night, how many suspects were at the scene, whether the suspects or the officers fired first, the kind of incident the police dispatcher sent the officer to investigate (a drunk-and-disorderly vs. a robbery in progress), etc.

6) Aspects of the suspect seemed important, such as whether the suspect was drunk or on drugs, did the suspect have a weapon and what type, whether the suspect was shot once or more than once.

7) The additional information also seemed necessary. For example, an officer called to investigate a light on in a jewelry store might find a robbery in progress. And the outcome ruling of the weapon firing investigation was important, although the officers were almost always exonerated.

The extent of coding required by the form in Figure 1 seems overwhelming, but most of the data were easily taken from the police reports and placed into the correct category on the form. Items like the year, day of the week, type of weapon fired, suspect's race, etc., were merely transcribed from the reports to the form.

Only about 10% of the reports involved multiple officers or suspects. These second or third forms on the same incident required extra coder time and thought, but coding in content analysis usually goes very quickly once coders get into the pattern. Even a seemingly intricate content analysis coding task can be completed quickly.

Step 7. **Analysis of data**. If the study is prepared with skill, all aspects of the research are designed to provide answers to the hypotheses or research questions. In content analysis studies, this is almost always achieved through computer analysis. The analytical investigation provides the numbers and percentages for each category, or the **frequencies**, and the tests of hypotheses that guided the study's research design.

Content analysis findings

The LAPD police shooting study produced a rich lode of data and a variety of interesting outcomes. First, the hypothesis was not supported. Police officers, regardless of race, were not using excessive force against minority suspects. Of course, it is possible that the study did not dig deeply enough into this aspect to accurately measure it (a more sophisticated analysis might have supported the hypothesis), but the study certainly coded every item in the reports that might have had a bearing on the hypothesis. What the study found was that officers were likely to fire their weapons if they thought the suspect was armed. The coded item under "Suspect" dealing with "type of weapon" included a variety of possible weapons from belt buckles that might have looked like knives to pieces of pipe that might have injured an officer. If the officer felt threatened by a suspect's "weapon," the officer was likely to shoot.

Most of the officer weapon firings did not result in death or serious injury to suspects. In most of the reports, nobody was injured by gunfire. Also, there was no association between firing a weapon and the type of assignment the officer had or what district the officer was in. Most of the weapon firings were single shots, probably in the air and probably designed to stop a fleeing suspect.

The study did find a high correlation between the day of the month and the likelihood of firing a weapon. Further data analysis showed that the firing occurred at night on weekends near the end of the month. The researchers could not explain this finding and asked police about it. The police laughed and said "full-moon madness." Apparently it is a well-known fact among law enforcement and emergency room personnel that more crime takes place during the full moon, and consequently more police action occurs then. This finding added **face validity** to the study. It provided a real-life indicator that the data were a true reflection of police activity.

Among other outcomes were the kind of findings that the LAPD could have used to better "police" their officer ranks and to offer training as indicated:

1) Officers who fired their weapons were likely to be either relatively new on the force or relatively far along in their careers. Young officers and older officers were more likely to be involved in incidents of firing a weapon.

2) Officers with more education were less likely to fire their weapons.

3) Officers who were middle-aged and divorced were significantly more likely to fire their weapons than officers who were married.

4) Even among fewer than 500 reported weapon firing incidents it was evident that an officer who had fired a weapon once was more likely to be involved

in additional weapon-firing incidents. This outcome was not related to the kind of assignment the officer had, the officer's district or any other variable in the study.

The researchers suggested that other variables might account for the significant recurring weapon firing finding: that the officer was trigger-happy, an alcoholic, unable to control stress, having family problems or just needed additional training. Whether the LAPD used this information to improve the force is not known.

Some content analysis cautions

Even experienced researchers go awry in content analysis studies by making a variety of careless errors. Here are some traps to avoid:

1) State hypotheses in terms that can be measured quantitatively. If the study focuses on horror films, provide enough definition of what constitutes a horror film. Remember that others judging the study may have their own ideas, so it is best to rely on previous definitions or be prepared to defend original definitions.

2) Look for logical populations of incidents, or content, that offer common-sense evidence to support hypotheses. If the research deals with trends in popular music, "incidents" probably should be the music itself rather than articles in *Billboard* magazine or CD reviews in the local newspaper.

3) Sampling is usually done in a multi-stage design from the widest range of content to subsets of that range. However, try to ensure that the material actually analyzed or counted still *represents* the widest range of content. Forethought will be required to ensure that the final sample is neither too sparse nor overwhelming.

4) Physically gathering the material can be the most troublesome part of the study. Issues of a publication will be unavailable, pages will be smeared, audio recordings will be static-ridden. Collecting the sample of video or digital material will require special equipment, special skills and far more time than ever anticipated.

5) The **researcher should avoid doing the coding**. A consumer or critic of research should always be skeptical of findings from a content analysis study in which anyone who knew the hypothesis participated in the coding. The reason is that borderline cases (often there are many) tend to be recorded in ways that support the hypothesis.

For example, the critical piece of information in the LAPD study is the suspect's race. Perhaps the police report said the "fleeing culprit was believed to be Hispanic." Those who don't know the hypothesis are likely to code suspect's race as (0) blank; those who know the hypothesis might code this (2) minority.

6) Research consumers or critics should be skeptical of intercoder reliability reports. If 10 decisions are made, and coders have complete agreement about nine of the 10 decisions, the intercoder reliability reported will be at least 90%, a convincingly high level. If nine decisions on the LAPD form are just recording the year, day, etc., these should be perfunctory: 100% agreement. But these aren't the key aspects of the study. Race, who shot first, critical shot, etc., are the key aspects. A content analysis study should report agreement levels on each of the key categories.

Summary

Content analysis is one of the most frequently used research methods in communication research because it involves the objective, systematic and quantitative description of the manifest content of communication.

The five most frequent uses of content analysis include: 1) **describing** the content itself, 2) **testing** hypotheses, 3) documenting **trends**, 4) relating media content to the **real world**, and 5) assessing the messenger's **motives**.

An example of a content analysis project dealing with the LAPD's reports of officers firing their weapons is used to explain the seven steps of doing a content analysis project: 1) stating the **hypothesis**, 2) deciding the **population of incidents** the study will investigate, 3) selecting a **sample**, 4) selecting the **unit of analysis**, 5) constructing **quantifiable categories** to be analyzed, 6) **training coders** and conducting a **pilot study** on the actual material, and 7) **analyzing the data**.

The chapter closes with some cautions about doing content analysis studies and evaluating them. Several of these suggestions relate to major problems researchers encounter in designing and carrying out content analysis projects.

Exercise:

Using concisely constructed paragraphs that contain enough information to explain the concept, answer the following questions:

1. The hypothesis is: Children under age 8 are exposed to significant amounts of "alien" fantasy. What "population of incidents" might you study?

2. The hypothesis is: Corporations are not serious about hiring minorities. What "population of incidents" might you study?

3. The hypothesis is: When U.S. presidents are in trouble on domestic issues, they focus attention on international issues. What "population of incidents" might you study?

4. Describe a method for sampling popular major U.S. magazines (those with more than one million circulation and monthly publication) to determine the average number of full-page ads.

5. Describe a method for sampling the studies presented at academic conferences to determine if the number of female authors has increased during the past 10 years.

36
Qualitative Research

Sandra Bowman Damico
Emory University

Mid-1980s article: Edward F. Pajak and Joseph J. Blase (1984). "Teachers in bars: From professional to personal self," *Sociology of Education* 57(3): 164-173.

Recent article: Roberta Maso-Fleischman (1997). "Archetypal research for adver-tising: A Spanish-language example," *Journal of Advertising Research* 37(5):81-84.

Qualitative research is the generic term for a variety of types of research that have been growing in popularity and perceived usefulness during the past decade. Some of the more popular approaches include: ethnography, field studies, naturalistic studies, interpretive research, life histories and case studies.

Although lumped under the qualitative research heading, many of these approaches must meet specific criteria. For instance, an **ethnography**[1] is designed to *describe the culture of a group* and is the type of study completed by anthropologists such as Margaret Mead.

The purpose of **qualitative research** is to develop understanding, provide detailed description, discover truths about events or generate hypotheses that can be tested using other methods. Unlike other forms of social science, qualitative research *does not pose a hypothesis to be tested*. Rather the researcher starts with a question about a social event or phenomenon. This does not mean, however, that there aren't clear guidelines about how to go about designing and conducting a qualitative study. This chapter presents the types of research questions appropriate

---

1. Norman K. Denzin (1996). *Interpretive ethnography: Ethnographic practices for the 21st century.* Thousand Oaks, CA: Sage Publications. See also: Ken Erickson and Donald Stull (1997). *Doing team ethnography.* Thousand Oaks, CA: Sage Publications.

for qualitative study, provides an overview of qualitative data collection methods, and shows how the data collected can be used to make meaning of social situations.[2] Along the way, examples of real studies are shown with the suggestion to try them out. Qualitative research can be fun!

Regardless of label, all forms of qualitative research share common characteristics. First they are used to understand and *explain social phenomena in their natural setting*. This means that behavior, situation or setting are not manipulated as in experimental studies where "subjects" are randomly assigned to treatments.

The chapter on Content Analysis described a study of the Los Angeles Police Department. The hypothesis being tested in that study was, "Are white LAPD officers more likely to use lethal force against minority than non-minority suspects?" This hypothesis was rejected, but the researcher did discover that officers who fired weapons were likely to be either relatively new to the force or far along in their careers. The more education officers had, the less likely they were to fire a weapon. These data are interesting, and may be contrary to what was anticipated.

The findings from the LAPD study prompt another question: Why are officers at the beginning and near the end of their careers more likely to use weapons? Answering this kind of question requires a qualitative study. A qualitative study is used to answer *how* or *why* questions. Note that a frequent use of qualitative research is to understand **patterns discovered using other research approaches**. The first exercise at the end of this chapter is to design a qualitative study to answer the follow-up research question posed from the LAPD study.

Design issues in qualitative research

Before describing several different methods of collecting qualitative data, it is appropriate to grapple with some design issues, especially since they vary from those encountered in other types of research. This section discusses sampling, reliability and validity, and gaining entrée, or access, to a research site or population.

---

2. Sage Publications offers more than 20 recent titles in qualitative research methodology including: John W. Creswell (1997). *Qualitative inquiry and research design: Choosing among five traditions*; Gretchen B. Rossman and Sharon F. Rallis (1998). *Learning in the field: An introduction to qualitative research*; Richard E. Boyatzis (1998). *Transforming qualitative information: Thematic analysis and code development*; Valerie J. Janesick (1998). *"Stretching" exercises for qualitative researchers*; Janice M. Morse (1997). *Completing a qualitative project: Details and dialogue*; Norman K. Denzin and Yvonna S. Lincoln (1998): *The landscape of qualitative research: Theories and issues, Strategies of qualitative inquiry* and *Collecting and interpreting qualitative materials*; Thomas A. Schwandt (1997). *Qualitative inquiry*; Karen Golden-Biddle and Karen D. Locke (1997). *Composing qualitative research*; Gale Miller and Robert Dingwall (1997). *Context & method in qualitative research*. See also: W. James Potter (1996). *An analysis of thinking and research about qualitative methods*. Mahwah, NJ: Lawrence Erlbaum.

Sampling. Quantitative studies use random sampling to ensure that results can be generalized to a larger population. But it is usually impossible to use random sampling in a qualitative study. One reason for this is that the researcher may not know who is included in a larger population; the population may not have well defined boundaries. To illustrate this difference, a quantitative study might randomly select voters in a metropolitan area to ascertain their views on major issues facing the community. Results may be reported on the evening news with the caveat that they are accurate within ±3%. On the other hand, a qualitative researcher wanting to study critical-care nurses' interactions with patients who have been coded as "do not resuscitate," would have difficulty determining the sample from which to randomly select.

But the qualitative researcher still has to make sampling decisions. As in any type of research, sampling is a crucial step after having developed a hypothesis or research question. Qualitative researchers use what is called **purposeful sampling**. Criteria are first developed to guide the selection of a site or people to be studied to answer the research question. A few of the sampling strategies used in qualitative studies are: typical case, unique case, convenience sample, snowball/chain or network, and ends of a continuum (i.e., most effective vs. least effective).

Exercise 1:

Each of the sampling strategies is described along with an example of its use. After reading them, write a paragraph that describes another situation in which each of the strategies might be the preferred sampling choice. The entire paper should be less than **three** double-spaced pages.

Typical Case. This sampling strategy is used to study an average person, situation, event, institution, etc., such as the social patterns that develop during high school football games in mid-sized Midwestern states. The research question is that students attend the games for the activity occurring in the stands rather than on the field. Select a "typical" high school in the Midwest geographical region.

Unique Case. Researchers often want to study a unique event, activity or individual. Several different social science fields, including anthropology, sociology and communication, study community response to catastrophes. If an earthquake hits Southern California, the researcher wouldn't sit in the office and say, "I think I'll wait until another earthquake hits and then randomly select which one to study." The researcher would be on the first plane out. A researcher who studies how major events crystallize a nation's sense of community might have wanted to study Great Britains' reaction to Princess Diana's death. Such unique cases don't lend themselves to random selection. They are opportunities not to be missed.

Convenience Sample. This selection process is exactly what it sounds. A researcher wants to study something and has access to an example of "the case." How do students in wheelchairs navigate campus? Perhaps the researcher has a good friend in a wheelchair who consents to being followed for a week. The researcher traverses the campus and records all the things the friend does, people encountered and problems in navigation that arise.

Or, a researcher might be interested in how university students use space. Students are always congregating in an area outside the student union, and the researcher wants to know if the types of students who gather there vary during the course of a day. The researcher notes who is there first thing in the morning, at mid-morning, noon, mid-afternoon and late afternoon. In this instance, the location rather than the individual was selected for convenience.

Snowball/Network Sampling. There may be times when it is difficult to know who to include in a sample. One strategy is to include one member and then ask that person for a referral to someone similar. A researcher might be interested in why one person in dual-career couples gives up a good job and moves with the spouse to a new location. In beginning the research, the first problem would be locating couples that meet this definition. However, if the researcher knows one qualifying couple, that first interview might identify another couple who had a similar experience, and so forth. This is snowball sampling; each respondent potentially increases the sample size.

Network Sampling. Similar to the snowball tactic, this procedure might be used to study gifted eighth graders. Identifying one qualifying eighth grader, with permission, the researcher accompanies the student during the school day. The researcher includes any activities between the student and all friends, gifted or not, in the study's sample. What develops is the friendship network of gifted students.

Ends of the Continuum. Contrasts can sometimes reveal more about a social phenomenon than including all examples. Suppose the researcher is trying to determine causes of high achievement levels among minority students at one school. If another school, with a similar student population, had very low achievement levels, including these two schools (both ends of the achievement effectiveness continuum) might show key differences in organization, policies, curriculum, etc. The differences would highlight what contributes to the achievement rates.

Reliability and validity. Researchers *always* focus on reliability and validity (see Reliability, Validity and Sampling chapter), the component parts that assess the accuracy and believability of a study's measurement procedures. Quantitative studies examine the appropriateness of the sample, the types of instruments used to collect data and how the data were analyzed.

A similar process occurs in qualitative studies, but the component parts differ. A qualitative study provides detailed information about: 1) the sample, 2) the data collection strategy, 3) how the data were actually collected, 4) how the data were analyzed, and 5) conditions established to control for researcher bias.

Qualitative researchers frequently talk about **validity being more important** to their studies than **reliability**. Qualitative researchers' evidence of validity is through detailed description of the research process from the criteria for sample selection through every aspect of data collection, including thoughts and changes that occurred during the study. Those who will evaluate the study's validity can follow closely the research trail. If the description and details provided aren't believable, reliability really doesn't matter.

Entrée or access. Before beginning a qualitative study, researchers often must negotiate entrée. Those who control access are called "gatekeepers," and they can refuse to give permission to conduct the study. The head of a television station may deny permission to study the camera crew; a high school principal may decide that teachers or students can't be interviewed during the school day. For permission to conduct a study, provide a typed, general description of the study's requirements. Be prepared to answer the gatekeeper's questions and provide something in return for access. Generally, a summary of the findings should be offered. Check with local officials if clearance is needed from a Human Subjects Committee.

There are, however, many research sites that don't require approval. Public locations fall into this category. Teenagers can be studied in a video arcade, adults can be studied shopping in grocery stores, students can be studied as they eat lunch under the trees on campus. Wonderful studies exist of the nonverbal behavior of couples eating in restaurants. The researcher never intruded upon those studied.

Exercise 2:

What other places can you think of to study where you wouldn't need permission of someone in authority? Bring a list of three places not included in this chapter to class for possible in-class group discussion.

1.

2.

3.

Types of data collection in qualitative studies

There are three major categories into which all qualitative data collection tends to fall (not including collection of artifacts, diaries, journals, etc.): observation, interviewing and visual data (photographs or video tape). Many studies combine two or more of the methods.

Observation. This form of data collection requires that the researcher use notebook and pen to accurately record what is going on. Because more is going on in all social situations than an individual can record, the research question should focus attention. For example, in observing/recording interactions between male-female pairs, there is no need to record male-male interactions. This sounds easy, but some rules must be followed: This is research, not a journal of personal musings.

Observation notes **must be devoid of evaluative judgments**. In describing a little boy eating an ice cream cone, avoid writing that he is dirty. Instead, describe the way the ice cream dripped down his arm, that his shirttail wasn't completely tucked in, and that one shoelace was untied. Leave the summary of these descriptions — dirty — to the reader. Using full description rather than summary judgment terms takes practice, but when writing observations, pretend not know what is happening. Record only what you see with your eyes. Anthropologists call this "making the familiar strange," and it takes work.

While observing, normally it is possible to record only brief notes, so it is essential to type out a full description from the notes as soon after the observation as possible. Complete this phase of the research process before making another observation to avoid sorting errors. When detailing observations, some thoughts, comments or summary beliefs about what was seen may have developed. These may be important later, so write them as a "Memo to Myself." One other caution: Avoid spending too much time observing on any single occasion because the amount of detail becomes overwhelming.

Observing is not always straightforward. Roles can vary from a complete **outsider** (subjects don't know they are being researched) through **participant-observer** (the researcher participates in the activity to some extent), to complete **participant** (subjects don't know they are being studied, and the observation takes on a secondary role). Each role places different pressures on the researcher.

Observation over time will reveal patterns of behavior that the researcher may have been unaware of, even in familiar settings. A researcher was interested in the dynamics that occurred during staff meetings at a counseling center. After half a dozen of these observations (participant-observer), the researcher discovered a game of "one-upmanship" was occurring between two of the counselors. Their behavior was seriously disrupting the goals of the staff meeting.

Exercise 3:

Observing can be lots of fun. Try it in any public place. Sit in McDonald's or some other fast-food restaurant and observe what people do. See what happens in the aisle of a magazine counter or at a bookstore. Try breakfast at a truck stop or the blue-plate special at the city cafe. Select a location, either one that is familiar or one that is novel, and spend half an hour observing. Write a **two**-page essay that includes a brief description of the site, why you chose it and at least one "surprising" observation. Concentrated focusing will reveal a lot.

Interviews. Use this research strategy to find out what someone else believes or thinks, to tap into another's mental world. Although surveys are often used to measure beliefs, they are only as good as the questions a researcher asks. The questions may not have been the right ones to aid understanding. Surveys with close-ended questions may obscure the complexity of the topic under investigation.

Interviews are complex communication events that should be thought of as "guided conversations." First, this means that the researcher should carefully plan the interview topics and the order in which they should be introduced. Second, the researcher must keep the interview on topic and progressing. This is guiding. Finally, the interviewee should do most of the talking. A researcher who talks 40% or 50% the time, as in a regular conversation, is not conducting research.

The researcher has to actively listen to the interviewee while monitoring his or her own behavior to avoid giving nonverbal cues in response to the interviewee's statements. Without being conscious of doing so, interviewees will talk longer and elaborate more on their responses when they pick up nonverbal cues that they are giving answers the researcher wants.

There are several different types of interviews. The one that is appropriate for a study will depend on the research question and sample. A study of an institution or corporation may involve observation complemented by on-going, informal interviews with those who work there. This type of interview is used to clarify what is observed or overheard. Questions would probably be developed spontaneously based on the situation.

Probably the most frequent form of interview in research studies is the semi-structured, open-ended interview. Here the researcher has developed several general questions and some accompanying probes. All those interviewed will be asked the same open-ended questions, but follow up questions and the depth of responses to some questions may vary from individual to individual. Remember, the objective is to learn what the interviewees think, feel or believe, so interviews will vary somewhat from one individual to another.

Another form of interview is a group interview, generally called a **focus group**. This can be an excellent way to gather information quickly from several people. Groups offer another advantage. What one individual says may trigger a response from someone else, a response the person may not have thought of if interviewed singly. Focus groups are among the most popular communication research strategies chiefly because of this interplay among individuals. For example, a company advertising a hair-care product might learn more about people's use of the product or their hair-care needs in a focus group than any other way. One group member says, "You know, I'd rather spend less time on my hair," and another replies: "Me too. When I was younger, it was a pleasure. Now it's a chore." If others agree — and if further research validates the view — instead of a commercial showing a person luxuriating in the shower, hair rich with shampoo bubbles, the ad might emphasize speed and efficiency: no second application with this product.

But focus group interviews require great skill and caution to ensure that one or two individuals don't monopolize the conversation. Those who feel they have lower social status may also fail to voice their opinions. The main research drawback of focus groups is the validity problem: **findings cannot be generalized**. In the hair-care product example, no company would risk a $5 million run of commercials without far more sophisticated research than focus group comments. These are only a few of the cautions associated with focus groups, around which an entire industry and body of knowledge has grown during the past fifteen years.[3] Focus group leaders are highly trained interviewers who earn lucrative fees for their services, making this a new communication career field.

One last caution about qualitative research interview questions is that they must be **genuinely open-ended**. Avoid asking questions that can be answered with one or two words. The objective is to encourage the interviewee to talk. Instead of asking students if they like this school (a "yes" or "no" question), ask them what they like most about the school and what they like least. As they talk, probe for examples. Don't assume you know what someone means; ask for clarification.

An interview should never begin with a factual question. If respondents don't know the answer, they may feel "dumb," and this will color the rest of their answers. Always begin an interview with a question about experience, behavior, opinion, feeling or sensory experience (what is seen, heard, touched, etc.). Save knowledge and demographic questions until later in the interview.

---

3. Sage Publications of Thousand Oaks, CA, offers a series entitled "The Focus Group Kit." Among titles are: David L. Morgan (1997). *The focus group guidebook* and *Planning focus groups* and *Focus groups as qualitative research*; Richard A. Krueger (1997). *Developing questions for focus groups* and *Moderating focus groups*; Richard A. Krueger and Jean A. King (1997). *Analyzing and reporting focus group results*; Thomas L. Greenbaum (1997). *The handbook for focus group research.*

Visual Data. Photography and video tape are the two main sources of visual data used in qualitative studies. For years anthropologists relied on photography to document their research settings. They, and other social scientists, soon realized that visual data could be valuable in other ways. For example, researchers use photographs to accompany interviews. This can be a valuable approach if interviewees are not very verbal. Seeing pictures of activities or events may help people talk about what is happening and how they feel about the events.

Subjects may also be given a camera and asked to take pictures in response to some direction. Robert Ziller, a social psychologist, spent years studying people's perceptual worlds through the photographs they produced.[4] In one study he gave university males cameras and asked them to take a series of six photographs that described "woman" and six that described "man." Ziller gave the same assignment to female students. The contrasts between the photographs of males and females is startling. Males' pictures tended to define "woman" as a sex object. One such photograph was of a poster of a shapely female in a wet t-shirt. A representative photograph of "woman" taken by a female included two females on a walkway deep in conversation. Friendship was an overriding theme in female's photographs.

Use can also be made of published collections of photographs. Sharon Knight used three books of published photographs in a study of high-achieving graduate student females of alcoholic parents.[5] Her study participants got a packet of post-its, three books of photographs and a time limit. Subjects identified three pictures that described what their life was like as a child and three that were the antithesis of their childhood. The selected photographs were a rich data source in themselves, but Knight later used the selected pictures as an interview probe with her subjects.

Video tape seems an ideal medium for research. It works well for certain types of research questions, but it captures an overpowering amount of data about individuals' internal/perceptual worlds. Video tape helps in studying interactions among a group. In this instance, the tape can be replayed repeatedly. A communications graduate student who wanted to study individuals' use of power and influence in groups gave participants a role to play in a high-conflict business setting. Video taping the experience and using replays, it was easy to see those who asserted themselves and how others responded. Others have studied movies to examine the roles of women, teachers and minorities as portrayed in popular films.

4. Robert C. Ziller (1990). *Photographing the self: Methods for observing personal orientations.* Newbury Park, CA: Sage Publications. See also: Sandra Bowman Damico (1985). "The two worlds of school: Differences in the photographs of black and white adolescents," *Urban Review* 17(3):210-222.

5. Sharon Knight (1990). *Academic attainers in the context of their family and schooling experiences: The perceptions of doctoral students who are daughters of alcoholics.* Unpublished dissertation, University of Florida, Gainesville.

Exercise 4:

The use of photography or video tape is limited only by the researcher's imagination. Today, disposable cameras and one-day film development allow completion of a project within a week and for under $20. Ask a friend to take a set of photographs that describe who that person is. Or, take a set of photographs yourself and ask others what they mean. Your teacher may suggest another approach for this project. Regardless of the assignment given, you will be surprised by the amount of data you can quickly accumulate.

Analyzing qualitative data

After collecting qualitative data, it is time to do the analysis to answer a research question. Qualitative data analysis is similar in some respects to content analysis. Develop a set of codes and then apply them to the data. But this form of analysis differs from content analysis in important ways. First, the codes "grow" out of the data rather than being **pre-set**. Take some time to read through the observations, interviews or review photographs. Jot down patterns or themes that seem to be important. Based on these patterns, develop an initial set of codes.

The second major difference between content analysis and qualitative analysis is how the codes are used. Qualitative research is less concerned with **frequency** of particular occurrences. Instead, look for patterns and themes that help clarify what is being studied. Lack of frequency data means that no statistical analysis is required. Here is one example from the author's past qualitative research studies:

A state education department wanted to know if students viewed rules and policies differently depending on whether they attended a high school with a graduation rate above the state average or one below the state average.[6] This was an interview study of "average" students. One of the findings was a difference in student perceptions of fairness of rules. Students attending the above-state average graduation rate school thought that their school's rules were fair and consistently enforced. Those attending the low graduation-rate school believed that what happened to a student caught breaking a rule depended on who the student was. In other words, something very different happened to the captain of the football team than to an average student. Such a finding could not easily be captured by a survey.

Although the qualitative researcher doesn't have "numbers," the researcher still has data. In place of statistical tables, vignettes from the observation record,

---

6. Sandra B. Damico and Jeffrey Roth (1993). "'A different kind of responsibility': Social and academic engagement of general-track high school students," in Robert Donmoyer and Raylene Kos, eds. *At-risk students: Portraits, policies, programs and practices.* Albany, NY: State University of New York Press, pp. 229-245.

quotes from interviews or photographs are used. These help the reader understand what type of data was coded. Those evaluating the research can decide if they agree with the conclusions. In the process, these data also support the validity of the study: Did what the researcher said happened really happen?

As the chapter demonstrates, a variety of qualitative approaches can be used to help researchers understand their environment. Remember that these are "real" research techniques, and that studies must be carefully designed after developing a research question. Some experience using the techniques will convince communication researchers that qualitative approaches are valuable additions to their arsenal of tactics and rather interesting, enjoyable methods.

Summary

Although the method doesn't test hypotheses, **qualitative research** is designed to *develop understanding*, provide *detailed description*, *discover truths* and *generate hypotheses* that can be tested using other methods. Researchers start with a question about a social event or phenomenon and use clear guidelines to design and conduct a qualitative study. Topics appropriate to qualitative research are discussed.

All forms of qualitative research share common characteristics: They are used to understand and *explain social phenomena in their natural setting*; to answer *how* or *why* questions; and to understand **patterns found by other research approaches**. Some special qualitative design issues are: **sampling, reliability and validity**, and **gaining entrée**, or access, to a research site or population. Sampling strategies used in qualitative studies are: *typical case, unique case, convenience sample, snowball* / chain or *network*, and *ends of a continuum* (i.e., most effective vs. least effective).

The three major categories into which all qualitative data collection tends to fall are: **observation, interviewing** and **visual data** (photographs or video tape). The chapter reviews these data collection types, with special attention to interviewing through **focus groups**, and provides examples and cautions about each method.

Through the chapter's examples, a case is made that qualitative approaches are valuable additions to the communication researcher's arsenal of tactics and are rather interesting, enjoyable methods.

Exercises:

A. Design a qualitative research study that will answer the follow-up question from the LAPD study (see Content Analysis chapter): "Why are officers at the beginning and near the end of their careers more likely to use weapons?" The study design should address the chapter's points about qualitative research:

1. General scope of design:

2. Sampling plan:

3. Entrée or access:

4. Data collection (if interviews are involved, provide two key questions to include, and phrase them properly):

5. Data analysis:

Name Index

•*Key: (n=footnote; names in text and footnote on the same page use text listing only)*

Subject Index